19.99

The British General Election of 2001

**Books are to be returne
the last date b**

Other books in this series

The British General Election of 2001

David Butler
Fellow of Nuffield College, Oxford

Dennis Kavanagh
Professor of Politics, University of Liverpool

palgrave

First published 2002 by
PALGRAVE
Houndmills, Basingstoke, Hampshire RG21 6XS and
175 Fifth Avenue, New York, N.Y. 10010
Companies and representatives throughout the world

PALGRAVE is the new global academic imprint of
St Martin's Press LLC Scholarly and Reference Division and
Palgrave Publishers Ltd (formerly Macmillan Press Ltd).

ISBN 0–333–74032–7 hardback
ISBN 0–333–74033–5 hardback

This book is printed on paper suitable for recycling and made from fully managed and sustained forest sources.

A catalogue record for this book is available from the British Library.

Library of Congress Cataloging-in-Publication Data applied for.

10   9   8   7   6   5   4   3   2   1
11   10   09   08   07   06   05   04   03   02

Printed and bound in Great Britain by
Antony Rowe Ltd, Chippenham, Wiltshire

To BD

Contents

List of Tables

List of Illustrations

Figures

Party advertisements

Conservative

Labour

Liberal Democrat

Newspaper headlines

Cartoons

List of Plates

1. Tony Blair and David Blunkett are greeted by schoolchildren as they arrive at St Olave's school in South London, where Tony Blair announces the election date, 8 May 2001 [FT Pictures, photograph by David Ahmed]

2. Tony Blair and Gordon Brown at a press conference at Millbank at the start of Labour's election campaign, 10 May 2001 [FT Pictures, photograph by Malcolm Watson]

3. John Prescott punches a protester, 16 May 2001 [United Television News]

4. Peter Hyman, Douglas Alexander, Philip Gould, and Margaret McDonagh in Millbank [Peter Hyman]

5. William Hague launches the Conservative manifesto, 10 May 2001 [Conservative Party]

6. Michael Portillo launches Tax poster, 15 May 2001 [Conservative Party]

7. William Hague with Michael Ancram in the background [FT Pictures, photograph by David Ahmed]

8. Francis Maude gives a press conference on the threat from Brussels to fuel prices, 14 May 2001 [Conservative Party]

9. Andrew Lansley and Liam Fox launch 'Labour's failure to deliver' poster, 2 May 2001 [Conservative Party]

10. Charles Kennedy with members of his shadow cabinet (Menzies Campbell, Dr Jenny Tonge, Colin Breed, Don Foster, Alan Beith, Malcolm Bruce), 8 May 2001 [FT Pictures, photograph by Johnny Eggitt]

11. Paddy Ashdown and Charles Kennedy after the announcement of the leadership election result [*Liberal Democrat News*]

12. Lord (Chris) Rennard [*Liberal Democrat News*]

13. John Swinney launches 'Standing for Scotland', the SNP theme for the Westminster elections, 22 January 2001 [photo by courtesy of the SNP]

14. Ieuan Wyn Jones [Martin Delyth/Plaid Cymru]

Preface

This is the sixteenth in a series of British general election studies sponsored by Nuffield College since 1945. David Butler has been involved since the beginning, Dennis Kavanagh from 1974. We would like to record that the 2001 election, dismissed by so many as a bore with a no change result, filled us with as much interest as any contest in this long calendar. With the help of many insiders and many observers, we followed the latest evolution of campaigning techniques as, in changed circumstances, each of the participants sought to exploit the new thinking about strategy and the new methods of communication which made the 2001 contest so different from those of a generation earlier.

In the pages that follow we describe the single-minded way in which Labour sought to exploit the strong position the party had achieved – after a full term and seemingly assured of another landslide. In Chapter 3 we also cover the muted but continuing debate at the upper echelons of the Conservative Party about how it should cope with the legacy of Thatcherism, the move by Labour to the centre ground and the lessons of its 1997 defeat. Should it follow a 'core vote' or a 'reach out' electoral strategy in trying to recover the ground lost since 1992? These discussions reverberated throughout the Parliament and beyond the 2001 defeat. The Liberal Democrats were in a welcome but exposed position as they pondered how to build on their record haul of seats in 1997. Chapters 8 and 9 explore the extent to which the election relinquished some of its traditional priority in the broadsheets and on the air. Chapter 11 points to the new – but not fully realised – campaigning possibilities opened by e-mail and the internet.

The conduct and result of the 2001 election raised broader questions about citizenship in the twenty-first century. The bias of the electoral system against the Conservative Party reached the point where, for the Conservatives to win a clear majority of seats, they would need to be at least 11 per cent ahead of Labour in votes (discussed in Appendix 2). The election again suggests the arrival of a greater degree of entrenchment for incumbent MPs. But the failure of advanced techniques of modern electioneering to engage a large portion of the electorate and the dramatic fall in turnout also prompts concern. On the other hand they may confirm the claim of one Labour moderniser that the age of representative democracy is passing away. If so, what will take its place?

We have also to express our gratitude to our colleagues in Nuffield College and the University of Liverpool for all the support they have given. We also have to thank the Leverhulme Foundation for again being so generous in financing our operations and for imposing so little in the way of bureaucratic restraints. Our friends in each of the political parties, among the pollsters and in the media know how much we owe to them – but they might not thank us for naming them.

We owe particular debts to all the contributors whose names appear in the table of contents, not least for meeting our demanding deadlines. Among the many who have provided helpful comments on our repeated drafts we should particularly thank Hugh Berrington, Adrian Blau, Vernon Bogdanor, Peter Bradshaw, Nicky Ellis, David McKie and Anthony Teasdale. Martin Range and Dominic Crossley did valuable research work for us. Helen Kavanagh heroically endured her father's handwriting and dictation as the text emerged. Chris Ballinger did much more than could be expected of any research assistant, as well as producing a chapter of his own.

Lastly we must once again thank our long-suffering wives for bearing up with our electoral enthusiasms.

David Butler
Nuffield College, Oxford

Dennis Kavanagh
University of Liverpool

August 2001

1
The Political Scene, 1997–2001

The general election of 1997 had opened a new era in British politics. The election of 2001 ensured its continuance. But any account of the detail of these two campaigns, with all their carefully planned strategies to confirm or switch voter loyalties, has to be set in the context of an increasingly globalised world where the technologies of production and communication are being revolutionised. Britain, a significant democracy, but only one of many, confined to a small island off the coast of Europe, voted on its future in terms of which party would control the local instruments of government. But its future was actually being determined far more by the condition of the United States' economy, the cost of Middle East oil, the movements in world trade, the decisions of the European Union and by the international march of innovation.

By midnight on 1 May 1997 it was plain that New Labour had won a massive victory. By dawn as many of the party as could get there were at the Festival Hall celebrating a clear majority of 179 seats. The 18 years of Conservative rule were over. Since 1832 no government had lasted so long – but, when the end came, it was on a swing far larger than any since 1945. A wave of euphoria swept the left – and the centre. Even the Conservatives, who had been resigned to defeat, accepted the situation gracefully. Labour's campaign theme 'Things can only get better' struck a national chord. The Blair government took office against a background of expectation so high that disappointment was inevitable. The public anticipated change; yet Labour had won partly by offering reassurance that change would not be too marked.

The new government immediately set about diminishing the power it had won. Within days it handed over control of interest rates to the Monetary Policy Committee of the Bank of England and launched

Scotland and Wales on the road to devolution, with rival centres of authority in Edinburgh and Cardiff. Moreover, for the representative bodies in Europe, in Scotland, in Wales, and in London, it introduced electoral systems that could not help the Labour Party. It also toyed with a voting system for Westminster that would inevitably reduce its majority.

The 1997 government inherited a sound economy. Gordon Brown was the first Labour Chancellor of the Exchequer who did not from the outset confront problems of overseas debt, or inflation, or industrial unrest – or all three. In the past such difficulties had encouraged Conservative warnings that Labour was not 'fit to govern'. Nonetheless, Gordon Brown made a great virtue of prudence. He accepted the Conservatives' spending plans for the next two years and he stood firm against back-bench demands for immediate outlays on social welfare. The government was fortunate in the policies left by the Conservatives and in the continued success of the United States' economy, although the strength of the pound created growing difficulties for manfacturers of exports. Inflation stayed below 3 per cent. GDP grew annually by about 2.5 per cent over the next four years. Opposition prophecies of doom were refuted regularly by the monthly economic statistics. Unemployment fell from 1.9 million in 1997 to under 1 million in 2001.

Gordon Brown was able to boast of his achievement in paying off a sizable proportion of the national debt, helped by buoyant tax revenues and by £22bn from the sale of digital channels in 2000. £34bn of government borrowing was paid off and debt servicing fell from 44 per cent to 32 per cent of government expenditure between 1997 and 2001.

A generation earlier the British were regularly depressed by international league tables showing how the country was falling back in productivity and economic management. But in the late 1990s such comparisons on GDP and growth became much more favourable. However new European contrasts began to be invoked: on health care, crime and transport, with Britain often coming near the bottom. Ministers and the public were being educated that not enough public or private money was being spent on them to deliver high-quality services or to maintain crumbling infrastructures.

Labour's first term was surprisingly free of crises. Not until the final 12 months – with first the fuel blockade and later the foot and mouth outbreak – was the government seriously forced on the defensive. Meanwhile its internal disputes were largely kept behind closed doors, despite gossipy articles and, later on, the books of inside-dopesters.

Tony Blair and his colleagues entered office without previous ministerial experience – only one had ever served in a Cabinet. But the transition was smooth, largely thanks to preparatory work by Sir Robin Butler, the Cabinet Secretary, and by Jonathan Powell, Tony Blair's Chief of Staff. The Prime Minister quickly established a personal dominance. He brought in a new style of government and new arts in handling the media. Alastair Campbell, the Number 10 Press Secretary, and Charlie Whelan, briefly Gordon Brown's spokesman, were vigorous in timing and planting stories and in cajoling or threatening the press. In 1998 Tony Blair was awarded a 'Freelance of the Year' accolade because over 200 articles with his by-line had appeared in the past year. It was noted that announcements were, more and more, made in his name rather than in the name of the government. The skills of the media machine were especially evident after the death of Princess Diana on 31 August 1997. This tragedy evoked a remarkable outpouring of national emotion, and Downing Street played a visible role in guiding the public relations of the Royal Family.

However, after the initial honeymoon, resentments developed. 'Spin doctor' was used increasingly as a headline cliché and 'all spin and no substance' became an Opposition mantra. Journalists seemed sometimes to devote more attention to the messengers than to the message. Moreover, the government had to face an increasingly hostile press. *The Times*, the *Daily Telegraph*, and the *Daily Mail*, as well as the nominally pro-Labour *Sun*, were fiercely Eurosceptic, and they gave ministers a rough ride.

It was a very stable Cabinet. Not since 1924–29 had reshuffles left the top offices so untouched. The Prime Minister, the Lord Chancellor, the Chancellor of the Exchequer, the Foreign Secretary, and the Home Secretary all stayed put. Harriet Harman soon fell from Social Security. Frank Dobson later left Health to run for Mayor of London and George Robertson moved from Defence to head NATO. Personal catastrophes befell Peter Mandelson (twice) and Ron Davies, but there were no other heavyweight casualties. However no new stars arose in the firmament; the recruits to the Cabinet (Alistair Darling, Stephen Byers, Alan Milburn, Andrew Smith, Geoff Hoon, and John Reid) were seen as 'safe hands' rather than high flyers.

Gordon Brown established a unique dominance as Chancellor, not only by his initial insistence on prudence in spending but by his active and detailed intervention in social policy. He used the first year's 'windfall' taxes on utilities to finance a 'Welfare to Work' programme with special emphasis on youth unemployment; he also fashioned a tax policy that was covertly egalitarian. A notional minimum wage was introduced in April 1999 and, despite much criticism from business, produced few adverse effects. These measures, together with a tax and benefits policy that was discreetly redistributive to the working poor, and the introduction in his 1999 Budget of a 10 per cent bottom rate of income tax and continuing falls in unemployment, did bring about redistribution to the benefit of the poorest in society. Nonetheless, the gap between rich and poor actually increased with the growth in salaries and bonuses for top earners in commerce and industry.

However, the public spending standstill for the first two years meant that it took a long time to achieve any visible improvements in the core public services. In 2001 the government talked increasingly about growing investment (a euphemism for tax and spend, as one insider admitted) and about the need for patience with regard to 'delivery'. But polls showed a steady increase in the numbers disillusioned with the government's performance on health and education and their resentment of spin. Administrative reorganisation in the NHS and new testing to raise school standards won little acclaim. The Institute of Fiscal Studies calculated that between 1997 and 2001 real growth in public spending went up by 1.4 per cent, (much less than under John Major) but the tax receipts increased by 4 per cent.

Labour spent much of the Parliament struggling to keep the five pledges it had listed in the 1997 manifesto:

1. Cut class sizes to under 30 for 5–7 year olds
2. Introduce fast punishment for young offenders, halving the time between arrest and sentence
3. Cut NHS waiting lists by 100,000
4. Remove 250,000 under 25s from benefit
5. No rise in income tax rates; VAT on heating cut to 5 per cent

The last two promises were easily met. But the first three caused longer-term embarrassment. Two of them were partially taken out of Westminster control by devolution to Scotland and Northern Ireland. The NHS came under great strain during epidemics in the first three winters and waiting lists rose rather than fell. It was widely alleged that pressure to cut the lists distorted medical priorities. The Conservatives' internal maket for the NHS was dismantled but there was continuing unrest among doctors and nurses and complaints from patients multiplied. Tony Blair's election eve cry, '24 hours to save the NHS', sounded increasingly hollow as the years passed by.

At the outset of his government Blair told his staff that he wanted to make progress on Northern Ireland, to improve relations with the European Union, to make significant strides in education and welfare and to secure better relations with business. But turning around the public services would be a long-term task. Blair realised that he had been naïve in promising that 1999 would be 'the year of delivery'. It is notable how 'delivery' became a key term in the Blair years. Often it was used as a stick to beat the government. Blair ensured that Labour occupied the centre ground and supported policies not because of their ideological correctness but because they would work.

David Blunkett proved an energetic Secretary of State for Education. He tried to reform the examination system and literacy and numeracy standards did improve. Infant schools' class sizes in the end fell, but even that seemed only to highlight the failure to improve the situation in secondary schools. And the government faced much unpopularity for imposing fees on university students and ending maintenance grants, at a time when it was trying to increase the numbers entering higher education. Jack Straw at the Home Office tried to be tough on crime but he was not able to meet the pledge on young offenders who still had to wait more than the promised time before facing the courts.

Labour did not face an impressive Opposition. John Major resigned the day after his party's defeat. After a six-way, six-week campaign, the 165 Conservative MPs handed the leadership to the 36-year-old William Hague. Kenneth Clarke was the choice of the public and the constituencies but the MPs, largely influenced by his pro-European views, preferred his younger, more Eurosceptic, rival.

William Hague felt the need for a fresh start: the Conservatives knew they had made mistakes, and so he decided to 'apologise and move on'. The front bench was gradually stripped of all the survivors from John Major's Cabinet. New faces came and, in some cases, went. In the key portfolios, Francis Maude, Ann Widdecombe and Michael Portillo (after he returned at the November 1999 Kensington and Chelsea by-election) failed to impress the House. It often seemed that William Hague was sturdily leading a one-man band. He usually fared well in his weekly jousts with Tony Blair at Prime Minister's Questions. To some extent he overcame the early images of the cartoonists who pictured him as a helpless bald foetus. But the Conservatives were seen as divided because their heavyweights, Michael Heseltine and Kenneth Clarke, so patently disagreed with the party line over Europe. In the frustrating task of opposition, the party also found itself portrayed as negative and opportunistic, jumping on every passing bandwagon.

The 1997 general election had substantially increased the proportion of Conservative MPs who were hostile to the euro and even to Europe. Mr Hague rapidly developed a Eurosceptic stance; his pledge not to enter into Economic and Monetary Union (EMU) in the current Parliament or the next was endorsed by the Shadow Cabinet in October 1997 and then by the membership in the country. William Hague himself invented the slogan 'In Europe, not run by Europe', which was the key to the party's campaign in the 1999 elections to the European Parliament (even though it was later criticised for epitomising a hostile and negative attitude towards everything European). The Conservatives sniped continuously against the Blair government's 'surrenders' to Europe after every summit, and they were buoyed up by increasingly Eurosceptic findings in the opinion polls (by 2001 only 20 per cent of the public were for accepting the single currency and only 50 per cent for staying in the European Union at all).

Tony Blair's aspiration to place Britain 'at the heart of Europe' was hardly more successful than John Major's. The British Presidency of the EU (January–June 1998) left no strong mark. Tony Blair was hamstrung by the UK's reluctance to join the 11 countries which, following the Maastricht treaty, had agreed to join the EMU from its start in January 1999. Brown laid down five rather imprecise conditions that would have to be met before the government could recommend a 'yes' vote in the referendum promised before entry. Joining the euro would have to: (1) be good for Britain; (2) be good for employment; (3) be good for the City of London; (4) offer sustained convergence; and (5) guarantee adequate EU flexibility to cope with change.

The stance of 'prepare and decide' was claimed as an advance on John Major's 'wait and see'. Impatient businessmen, like euro-enthusiasts in all parties, became increasingly critical of the government's failure to take a more active role in educating the country to accept the euro. Gordon Brown used the first spending review in July 1997 as well as the public service agreements between the Treasury and individual departments to influence the politics of the rest of Whitehall. His authority in Whitehall was such that some talked of him sharing a dual premiership with Tony Blair – to the indignation of aides at Number 10.

The glittering launch of an all-party Britain in Europe campaign on 14 October 1999, with strong business back-up, came to very little. Polls showed a two-to-one majority intending to vote 'no' if a referendum were held on the new currency and this, coupled with the unremitting hostility of the *Sun*, as well as the whole of the Conservative press, induced continued caution in the government, though it was widely rumoured that Mr Brown was much more sceptical than Mr Blair.

The ongoing crisis over beef and BSE proved a difficult inheritance. Efforts to lift the ban on the export of British beef, imposed by the European Union in 1996, kept busy Jack Cunningham and then Nick

Brown, successive Ministers of Agriculture. The European Union lifted the ban from 1 August 1999 but the French continued to embargo UK exports. The beef ban was only one of the blows to British agriculture as farmers' incomes dipped catastrophically.

A series of minor scandals had dogged the Major government and some reverberated well beyond the election and helped in the general decline in the reputation of politicians. Jonathan Aitken, the former Chief Secretary to the Treasury, was sent to prison for perjury. Neil Hamilton, another ex-minister, was censured by the Standards Committee and spectacularly failed to clear his name in a protracted libel action. Lord Archer, the Conservative Party's original choice for Mayor of London, fell into disgrace and was charged with perjury – and later convicted. The Belize business background of the Conservatives' wealthy Treasurer, Michael Ashcroft, caused dispute, even though he was eventually awarded a peerage (itself the subject of hesitation by the Political Honours Scrutiny Committee).

These echoes from the past may have meant that Labour suffered less from its own lapses. An early scandal came in November 1997: one week after the motor-racing tycoon and donor of £1 million to the Labour Party, Bernie Ecclestone, had visited Tony Blair, it was announced that the new rules against tobacco advertising would be abated for four years for motor racing. Following a media outburst, the Labour Party returned the £1 million to Mr Ecclestone and Lord Neill's Committee on Standards In Public Life was asked to look into party funding. But large gifts from multi-millionaires continued to offer problems for the parties and their images.

In December 1998 it emerged that Peter Mandelson, who had recently joined the Cabinet as Secretary for Trade and Industry, was beholden to Geoffrey Robinson, the millionaire Paymaster-General, for an undisclosed £373,000 loan to buy a house. It took only two days for both ministers to be forced to resign. Peter Mandelson returned to the Cabinet after nine months – but in January 2001 he was again forced to resign for his apparent lack of candour. It was alleged that, after the Hinduja brothers had agreed to sponsor the Faith Zone in the Millennium Dome, Mandelson had sought to help one of them towards acquiring a British passport. It later seemed that Tony Blair was over-hasty in letting Mr Mandelson go, especially as Keith Vaz, the Minister for Europe and a friend of the Hindujas, appeared to have more to explain on this and other matters. Conservatives, remembering the accusations of 'sleaze' in 1994–97, complained that so little mud had stuck to Labour after all its promises to be 'whiter than white'.

Table 1.1   Economic and political indicators, 1997–2001

	(1) Real personal disposable income (1995=100)	(2) Weekly earnings (1995=100)	(3) Retail Prices (13 Jan 1987=100)	(4) Year on Year inflation	(5) Unem- Ploymen (UK) (%)	(6) Days lost in strikes (000s)	(7) Gross domestic product (1990=100)	(8) Balance of Payments (£m)
1997 1	104.5	106.4	154.4	2.9	5.9	75	110.3	2496
2	106.5	107.0	156.9	2.6	5.5	97	111.6	1695
3	106.5	108.6	157.1	2.8	5.1	18	113.6	2296
4	106.7	110.0	158.1	2.8	4.8	42	115.2	136
1998 1	106.7	111.5	158.4	2.6	4.6	68	117.0	–470
2	105.6	113.1	160.9	2.9	4.5	90	118.7	–86
3	105.8	114.4	161.1	2.5	4.4	89	120.3	1875
4	107.2	115.3	162.1	2.5	4.4	35	121.2	–1399
1999 1	107.4	116.6	162.4	2.5	4.3	70	125.5	–4671
2	110.9	118.3	164.6	2.3	4.2	71	123.6	–1741
3	109.6	119.8	164.6	2.2	4.1	40	125.9	–2822
4	111.8	121.4	165.6	2.2	3.9	61	128.1	–648
2000 1	112.7	123.2	165.8	2.1	3.8	35	128.1	–3466
2	112.5	124.6	168.1	2.1	3.7	31	130.5	–4963
3	112.6	124.6	168.1	2.1	3.5	243	132.0	–4046
4	115.5	126.7	169.1	2.1	2.4	188	133.2	–3696
2001 1	114.2	125.4	168.9	1.9	2.3	131	134.7	–180

Sources: 1–5, 8, 12–13 *Economic Trends*; 9–11 *Financial Statistics*; 6 *Employment Gazette*; 14–15 MORI

Other scandals hit the Cabinet. Robin Cook abruptly parted from his wife in August 1997 after a newspaper revealed a sustained extra-marital affair (he subsequently married the lady concerned). In October 1998 Ron Davies, the Secretary of State for Wales who had done so much to promote devolution, was caught in a 'moment of madness' on Clapham Common and resigned immediately. However three other openly gay politicians served without difficulty in the Blair Cabinet.

The new arrangements for standards in public life led to mild embarrassments to MPs of all parties who had not fully reported outside earnings or interests. However fewer MPs looked outside for emoluments; the number reporting employment as a consultant fell by two-thirds between 1996 and 2000. But it cannot be said that the public reputation of politicians was enhanced during the Parliament.

The government showed increasing confidence in their management of the economy and the Conservatives had to backtrack on their earlier opposition. Michael Portillo on taking over as Shadow Chancellor early in 2000 switched to accept the minimum wage and the independence of the Bank of England. In June he also abandoned a rash Conservative promise to lower tax as a percentage of national income.

(9) FTSE 100 Share index (1 Jan 1984 = 1000)	(10) US$ to £	(11) Sterling Exchange Rate Index (1990=100)	(12) Interest Rates (%)	(13) House Prices (1987 = 100)	(14) MORI 'State of the Economy Poll': Net Optimists	(15) MORI Polls (Voting Intention) Con Lab LD
4298	1.63	96.9	6.0	151.2	+1	30 52 12
4554	1.64	99.6	6.3	152.6	+20	28 50 15
4933	1.63	102.5	6.9	153.4	+8	25 57 14
5026	1.66	103.1	7.2	154.3	+3	25 57 15
5587	1.65	105.4	7.3	154.5	+2	28 53 14
5919	1.65	105.3	7.3	156.4	−6	27 55 14
5572	1.65	104.4	7.5	156.4	−28	27 54 14
5452	1.68	100.6	6.8	157.3	−36	27 53 14
5587	1.63	101.1	6.7	157.5	−15	27 54 14
5919	1.61	104.1	5.2	159.2	−4	27 53 13
5572	1.6	103.8	5.1	159	−1	27 51 16
5452	1.63	105.9	5.4	159.8	−1	27 55 13
6052	1.61	108.4	5.9	159.8	−5	29 51 15
6403	1.53	107.7	6.0	161.7	−13	31 49 14
6250	1.48	106.4	6.0	161.4	−11	32 46 13
6426	1.45	107.6	6.0	162.3	−8	33 46 17
6003	1.46	104.5	5.8	161.9	−13	31 50 14

Although Gordon Brown cut the basic rate of income tax, the Conservatives made much of 45 'stealth taxes'; the share of national income taken by the government grew from 35 per cent to 37 per cent through rising indirect levies. The most notable of these was the escalating 'green levy', the 5 per cent above inflation annual increase in petrol duty, brought in by the previous government to encourage a switch from cars to public transport. Although the increases were discontinued in the 2000 Budget, the rise in crude oil prices meant that petrol taxes yielded more and more.

Northern Ireland, for 30 years a nightmare to every British government, took up a great deal of time in Downing Street. Mo Mowlam, the Secretary of State, working with the Irish Taoiseach and the American mediator, former Senator George Mitchell, successfully negotiated in April 1998 the Good Friday Agreement for a power-sharing administration at Stormont. The deal was endorsed by a 71 per cent 'Yes' vote in a Northern Ireland referendum the following month (with just over 50 per cent of Unionists on the majority side). On 25 June an Assembly was elected and on 1 July David Trimble (Ulster Unionist) assumed office as First Minister, with Seamus Mallon (SDLP) as his Deputy. Sinn Fein took two ministerial posts.

Table 1.2   Chronology of Events, 1997–2000

1997

1 May	Labour wins General Election (Lab 419, Con 165, LibDem 46).
2 May	Blair becomes PM and announces Cabinet
6 May	Chancellor announces Bank of England monetary policy committee to set interest rates.
14 May	Queen's Speech: 26 Bills promised.
16–17 Jun.	Amsterdam EU Summit.
19 Jun.	Hague defeats Clarke, 92 to 70, to win Con Leadership.
26 Jun.	Aitken libel claim against *Guardian* collapses.
30 Jun.	Hong Kong returned to China.
2 Jul.	Labour's first Budget gives £3bn to education from 'windfall tax' on utilities but confirms Conservative spending limits.
2 Jul.	Parliamentary Commissioner finds five Con MPs guilty of accepting money from M. Fayed.
10 Jul.	100,000 pro-hunt campaigners in Hyde Park demonstration.
17 Jul.	Government endorses PR for 1999 European Elections.
23 Jul.	Dearing Report leads to £1,000 p.a. university tuition fees from Oct. 98.
31 Jul.	Cons win Uxbridge by-election with increased majority.
31 Aug.	Princess Diana killed in car crash.
11 Sep.	Referendum shows 74.3% 'Yes' for Scottish Parliament.
18 Sep.	Referendum shows 50.3% 'Yes' for Welsh Assembly.
29 Sep.	Mandelson fails to be elected to Lab NEC.
30 Sep.	Blair first speech to Lab Conference as PM.
7 Oct.	In Con referendum, 80% endorse Hague and his party re-organisation.
10 Oct.	Hague's first speech to Con Party Conference as leader.
27 Oct.	Chancellor announces UK will not join euro until economic conditions are right.
10 Nov.	Labour returns £1m gift to Formula 1 Chief Executive, Bernie Ecclestone.
20 Nov.	In Winchester by-election LibDems transform majority of 2 to 21,536.
10 Dec.	47 Lab MPs vote against government on lone parent's benefit.

1998

1 Jan.	UK takes over EU Presidency.
1 Mar.	200,000 join 'Countryside March' in London.
13 Mar.	Bill to outlaw hunting fails for lack of parliamentary time.

10 Apr.	'Good Friday Agreement' signed in Belfast.
7 May	Conservatives make advances in local elections.
	Referendum endorses London Mayoral elections – 72% Yes.
22 May	Referendums in Ireland endorse 'Good Friday Agreement'. NI 71% Yes; Eire 94% Yes.
1 Jun.	Con Shadow Cabinet reshuffle. Lilley becomes Deputy Leader.
21 Jun.	Peter Temple Morris MP asks for Labour Whip.
9 Jul.	Margaret McDonough becomes Gen Sec of Labour Party.
27 Jul.	In Cabinet reshuffle Margaret Beckett is switched to lead Commons, Lady Jay to lead Lords, Mandelson to Trade, and Darling to Social Security. Ld Richard, Harriet Harman and Frank Field are sacked.
3 Oct.	84% in Con referendum support Hague's policy of retaining sterling.
	Con promise year on year tax reduction.
13 Oct.	Ld Neill's Report on party finance is published.
14 Oct.	Blair joins with Heseltine and Clarke in launching 'Britain in Europe' campaign.
17 Oct.	Ex-President of Chile, Gen. Augusto Pinochet, arrested at London Clinic.
27 Oct.	Davies, S. of S. for Wales, resigns after 'moment of madness' on Clapham Common.
29 Oct.	Ld Jenkins' Report on Electoral Systems published.
18 Nov.	Lords defeat European Elections Bill for the fifth time in manoeuvre against Lords Reform.
12 Nov.	Commons approve Amsterdam treaty. Con vote against on 3-line whip.
2 Dec.	Hague dismisses Vt Cranborne as Shadow Leader of Lords for conniving with Lab over Lords reform.
23 Dec.	Mandelson and Robinson resign office over private loan.

1999

1 Jan.	Euro is introduced in 11 EU countries.
13 Jan.	European Parliamentary Elections Act passes under Parliament Acts.
19 Jan.	Aitken is found guilty of perjury.
20 Feb.	Alun Michael, S. of S. for Wales, narrowly beats Rhodri Morgan to be Welsh Labour Leader.
24 Feb.	Macpherson report on the Lawrence case published.
9 Mar.	Brown's third Budget announces new 10% starting rate of tax; basic rate cut to 22% from April 2000.

Table 1.2   Chronology of Events, 1997–2000 *continued*

15 Mar.	EU Commission resigns over scandal but stays on as caretaker administration.
24 Mar.	Kosovo air strikes begin.
1 May	Amsterdam Treaty becomes law across EU.
6 May	Elections to Scottish Parliament and Welsh Assembly fail to produce clear majorities.
	Cons advance in local elections.
13 May	Lab and LibDem agree on Scottish coalition with Donald Dewar as First Minister.
	Lab decide to rule as minority government in Wales.
10 Jun.	European elections send 36 Con, 29 Lab and 10 LibDem to Strasbourg; 3 UKIP, 2 Green, 3 SNP and 2 PC are elected. Turnout is only 24%.
12 Jun.	British troops enter Kosovo.
15 Jun.	Con Shadow Cabinet reshuffle. Lilley is sacked. Widdecombe moved to shadow Home Office and Maples to Foreign Affairs.
18 Jun.	Anti-capitalism riots in City of London.
28 Jul.	Murphy succeeds Michael as S. of S. for Wales.
1 Aug.	EU lifts ban on export of British beef. France & Germany continue ban.
9 Aug.	Kennedy succeeds Ashdown as LibDem Leader.
9 Sep.	Patten Report on reform of Royal Ulster Constabulary published.
11 Oct.	In Cabinet reshuffle Mandelson returns as NI Sec; Mowlam succeeds Cunningham as Cabinet 'enforcer'; Milburn succeeds Dobson at Health and Hoon succeeds Robertson at Defence.
26 Oct.	Right of hereditary peers to sit in Parliament ended (except for 92 elected hereditaries).
3 Nov.	52 Lab MPs vote against government over invalidity benefit.
20 Nov.	Ld Archer stands down as Con candidate for London Mayor.
29 Nov.	NI Executive established under Trimble as First Minister.
30 Nov.	Portillo returns as MP in Kensington & Chelsea by-election.
18 Dec.	Shaun Woodward MP crosses from Con to Lab.
21 Dec.	Scottish Parliament defies UK policy on student fees.

2000

1 Jan.	Opening of Millennium Dome.
20 Jan.	Ld Wakeham's report on Reform of Lords published.
30 Jan.	Kilfoyle resigns from government to become 'critical friend'.

1 Feb.	Shadow Cabinet reshuffle. Portillo becomes Shadow Chancellor. Redwood and Maples sacked.
9 Feb.	Michael resigns as Welsh First Secretary and is succeeded by Morgan.
11 Feb.	Mandelson suspends NI Executive and restores direct rule from London.
20 Feb.	Dobson selected 51%–49% over Livingstone as Lab candidate for London Mayor.
3 Mar.	Ex-President Pinochet of Chile welcomed home in Santiago.
25 Mar.	Trimble re-endorsed as UU leader.
27 Apr.	Sell-off of third-generation mobile 'phone networks raises £22.5bn for the Treasury.
1 May	Anti-capitalism riots in central London.
4 May	Livingstone elected as London Mayor.
	LibDems win Romsey by-election. Cons advance in local elections.
9 May	45 Lab MPs defy government over privatising air traffic control.
20 May	Leo Blair born.
27 May	Trimble wins endorsement as UU leader.
29 May	NI Executive resumes office following IRA promise to put arms 'beyond use'.
7 Jun.	Blair heckled during speech to Women's Institute.
28 Jun.	Ld Wakeham warns press not to intrude on Prince William's Gap year.
11 Aug.	Portillo withdraws pledge of year on year tax reduction.
8 Sep.	Blockade of fuel depots causes crisis and Labour poll slump.
2 Oct.	Human Rights Act 1998 comes into effect, incorporating ECHR into English law.
4 Oct.	Widdecombe announces Con zero-tolerance drugs policy (withdrawn 17 Nov 2000).
12 Oct.	Worst flooding in 40 years.
23 Oct.	Michael Martin elected as Commons Speaker.
3 Nov.	Hatfield train crash leads to massive disruption.
29 Nov.	Passage of Political Parties Elections and Referendums Act.
30 Nov.	Freedom of Information Act becomes law under Parliament Acts. Homosexual age of consent lowered to 16 by Parliament Acts procedure.
9–11 Dec.	Nice EU Summit.
15 Dec.	Gore concedes Presidential victory to Bush.

A bomb at Omagh on 15 August, which killed 29 people, was a reminder that the breakaway 'Real IRA' was still committed to violence whatever the position of the Provisional IRA. The release of prisoners was followed by ugly feuds between Unionist paramilitaries in North Belfast. Attempts to implement reforms in the Royal Ulster Constabulary were frustrated on all sides. Nonetheless the devolved Executive did work in a fashion until February 2000, when the Unionists, infuriated by delays in IRA decommissioning of arms, forced Peter Mandelson, who had taken over from Mo Mowlam, to suspend the Executive. The latter resumed office on 29 May but delays in surrendering weapons by Sinn Fein and divisions amongst Unionists left the province in a very uncertain state as the general election approached.

Throughout the Northern Ireland troubles a bi-partisan approach was on the whole maintained at Westminster, although the Conservatives made critical noises about any concession to Dublin or Sinn Féin, notably over the early release of prisoners and over the legislation in 2000 to allow Irish citizens to sit on UK-elected bodies.

One charge heard increasingly was that Tony Blair was a 'control freak'. It had been voiced even before he took office but it came to the fore in November 1998 when the party machine, aided by trade union bloc votes, prevented Rhodri Morgan from succeeding Ron Davies as party leader in Wales. It was echoed more stridently during Mr Blair's belated efforts to prevent Ken Livingstone becoming Labour's candidate for Mayor of London. After some confusion Ken Livingstone was allowed to stand for nomination against the preferred Frank Dobson, but when, again on trade union votes, the latter narrowly won the nomination, Ken Livingstone left the party to stand, triumphantly, as an independent.

Another own goal of the same type came when Dennis Canavan, a left-wing MP, was denied nomination in the Scottish Parliament elections. He stood as an Independent and won handsomely. These episodes made it easy to accuse Labour of being unwilling to relinquish the central control that it had given away by devolution.

For 45 years every government has suffered by-election defeats and adverse opinion polls. But New Labour lost no Westminster seats and, apart from the blip in September 2000, stayed comfortably ahead in the polls. Yet this was not translated into success in 'second-order' elections. The party suffered a totally unexpected set-back in the Euro elections of June 1999 when, on a record low turnout (24 per cent), it secured only

Prescott and Blair try to stop Ken Livingstone becoming the Labour candidate for London Mayor.

Garland, *Daily Telegraph*, 12 November 1998

29 seats to the Conservatives' 36 and the Liberal Democrats' 10, with 3 for the UK Independence Party and 2 for the Greens.

Labour also lost quite heavily in the May local elections of 1998, 1999 and 2000. Yet, at the end of the Parliament, the Conservatives had a majority in only 10 of the 34 shire counties. They controlled no authorities in Scotland or Wales. In April 2001, 96 of the 380 local authorities in England were in their hands – almost all of them in dormitory towns or rural areas.

Labour lost some ground in the 1999 Scottish and Welsh devolution elections, doing particularly badly in Wales, although in each it ended up as the largest party. It had to form coalition executives with the Liberal Democrats (although in Wales they tried minority government for a spell). The new electoral system proved a boon for the Conservatives and the smaller parties, particularly the Nationalists.

Tony Blair's government, buoyed up by the polls, suffered far less internal trouble than previous Labour administrations. Rumours of tensions between the leaders – or their sidekicks – were occasionally reported in analyses and biographies, but the rifts between Blair and Brown or Prescott and Mandelson did not seem to interfere with the processes of government, although ministers could have done without the indiscreet

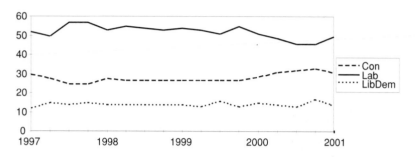

Figure 1.1   Opinion poll trends, 1997–2001

Source: MORI

briefings in which the tribes of advisers sometimes indulged. In Parliament the huge Labour majority meant that there were no major anxieties even when 50 or so MPs rebelled over payments to lone mothers or privatisation of air traffic control. Revised procedures and a relatively contented rank-and-file saved the government from the old-style upsets that the annual conferences used to inflict on the leadership. But the resignation from office of the Liverpool loyalist Peter Kilfoyle in January 2000 was significant: he explained that the new Millennium was bringing fresh challenges, across the political spectrum and particularly 'within the Labour heartlands', with which he could not engage 'within the constraints of office'. For the rest of the Parliament, there were government protestations that the Labour Party was concerned to foster its grass-roots core support and to reach out to rural Britain.

The Liberal Democrats, despite securing 46 MPs (twice the number any third party had ever reached since 1931), made little impact in Parliament. But they had one major breakthrough when, in a May 2000 by-election, they won the safe Conservative seat of Romsey. They also held on quite well in local council elections, most notably in winning control of Liverpool in 1998 and of Sheffield in 1999.

In 1999 Paddy Ashdown stepped down after ten years as leader of the Liberal Democrats. His understanding with Tony Blair had yielded proportional representation for European elections and seats on a Cabinet committee on constitutional problems, but his dreams of a fuller *rapprochement* or even a coalition had come to nothing, in the face of Labour's overwhelming majority and the overt hostility of many of its senior members. The party voted for Charles Kennedy over Simon Hughes as Paddy Ashdown's successor – but the change was more of style than substance. Mr Kennedy won full support for his positioning of the party on the one hand as critical of Labour's failure to do more on the social and educational front, while on the other hand plainly accepting Mr Blair's policies as, in almost all respects, preferable to those of Mr Hague.

Labour claimed to be a reforming government. But it was only in the constitutional field that major legislation was passed. It was not just on devolution: the composition of the House of Lords was transformed and the electoral system was subject to far-reaching review. Meanwhile the government had asked a Royal Commission headed by a Conservative, Lord Wakeham, to suggest a permanent solution to House of Lords reform. Its Report (Cm 4534), published in January 2000, recommended a largely nominated House but with a substantial elected element. Although the Report was accepted by the government, it was widely criticised and most observers believed that the interim arrangements could well prove permanent.

The Labour manifesto pledge to end the right of hereditary peers to sit in the House of Lords was partially realised with the House of Lords Act passed in November 1999. This left a chamber mainly of Life Peers but with 92 hereditaries elected by other hereditaries in their own party and non-party groups as well as Bishops and Law Lords. Effectively, the Bill echoed a private deal between Viscount Cranborne, the Conservative leader in the Lords, and Downing Street. William Hague dismissed Robert Cranborne for negotiating the arrangement behind his back, but the Conservatives accepted the new situation. The government found it no easier to get legislation through the revised House than the previous one. The old House had repeatedly voted down the closed-list electoral system for the Euro elections, which was only passed under the provisions of the Parliament Act. But the new House proved even more obdurate than the old. It voted against the repeal of Section 28 of the 1988 Local Government Act, which had banned local authorities from promoting homosexuality or teaching the acceptability of homosexuality in maintained schools. In all the government suffered 108 defeats in the Upper House.

The electoral system came under scrutiny and not only through the new systems introduced with devolution. The Jenkins Commission, which reported in October 1998, recommended a complicated semi-proportional system for Westminster, but it was plain that the government was too disunited on the subject to call the referendum promised in the 1997 manifesto.

However, also in October 1998, the Neill Committee on Standards in Public Life produced a report on party fund-raising and election expenditure which was largely implemented in the Political Parties, Elections and Referendums Act 2000. This set up a statutory Electoral Commission to register party names, to oversee the public reporting of donations and campaign expenditure and to report generally on the conduct of elections and make proposals for reform. Central election-year outlays by the parties were to be limited to £20m (or £14.5m in an abbreviated 2001). It also allowed for the February 1998 judgment of the European Court of Human Rights in the *Bowman* case; henceforth outside bodies or 'third parties' could spend limited amounts on propaganda during election campaigns. The Act also provided for a rolling register and much easier postal voting.

The Local Governnment Act 2000 opened up far-reaching changes, offering local government authorities the option, subject to a referendum, of changing to a cabinet system or a directly elected mayor, thus abandoning the committee system which had prevailed since the Municipal Corporations Act of 1835 and further enshrining the use of referendums in British governmental practice.

The Human Rights Act 1998, which came into force on 2 October 2000, empowered citizens to seek remedy against public authorities in domestic courts under the European Convention on Human Rights without having to go to Strasbourg. This offered the prospect of more work for lawyers in an increasingly litigious world.

Two racial issues echoed throughout the Parliament. The alleged flood of asylum seekers and illegal immigrants placed increasing strains on the social services in south-east England, and the government endured much criticism as it sought measures to deal with the consequent problems in a humane but efficient way. There was also controversy over the follow-up to the murder of Stephen Lawrence, a young black man, in 1993. The public inquiry set up under Sir William Macpherson by Home Secretary Jack Straw reported in February 1999 that the Lawrence case had been seriously mishandled by the Metropolitan Police partly because of a culture of 'institutional racism' (Cm 4262). This allegedly had serious consequences for police morale and recruitment. When William Hague dwelt upon this theme in a speech in December 2000, he was attacked as racist, and he rather hastily endorsed the Macpherson Report.

The Labour Party's commitment to a ban on hunting with hounds led to protracted tensions. After a Private Member's Bill in the 1997–98 session was stalled, the subject was referred to a committee under Lord Burns. This offered a compromise that fell short of an absolute ban. But the initial bill had provoked a spectacular demonstration in Hyde Park in March 1998 under a Countryside Alliance banner. The suggestion that

Labour was an urban and anti-countryside party played a large part in the fuel blockade of September 2000 and had later echoes in reaction to the handling of the outbreak of foot and mouth disease.

During 2000 concern over transport rose as a major public issue. Headlines were made by two railway crashes outside Paddington in September 1997 and October 1999 and still more by one at Hatfield in November 2000. The last of these, caused by a broken rail, revealed endemic weaknesses in track maintenance by Railtrack. The ensuing speed restrictions caused chaotic delays throughout the network for several months, although the blame fell more on the fragmented structures left by the Conservative privatisation programme than on the Labour government. The distress that followed the Hatfield crash was exacerbated by months of exceptional rainfall, which caused widespread flooding and greatly added to the woes of the farmers. The nationwide rail troubles were echoed in the continuing rows between the government and Ken Livingstone over the part-privatisation of the London Underground.

The long-planned celebrations of the Millennium proved to be a muted success, largely because the centrepiece, the Millennium Dome at Greenwich, drew only half the expected number of visitors and provoked headlines about mismanagement and waste of money and tackiness, with Peter Mandelson and then Lord Falconer being made particular scapegoats. Yet the end of the century was marked by the transformation of communications with an extraordinary increase in the use of mobile phones and the internet.

Apart from the continuing problems of European Union politics, foreign affairs seldom obtruded on the political scene. But in 1999 Tony Blair boldly took the lead against the Serbian attempt to drive ethnic Albanians from Kosovo. Britain joined in a selective bombing campaign which, after an alarming three months, forced President Milosevic to withdraw his forces. Britain then contributed the largest contingent of land forces to police the peace. The Kosovo war absorbed much of the Prime Minister's energies but it seemed to leave little imprint on British politics.

In the summer of 2000 things began to go wrong for the government. In June Tony Blair was slow-handclapped when he addressed a Women's Institute Conference as he was thought to be using this normally well-behaved group for political purposes. In September rising oil prices provoked a sudden and shattering crisis. Farmers and lorry drivers blockaded petrol depots and, after panic-buying, the pumps ran dry. Public sympathy was largely with the protesters and the government's standing in the polls plummeted abruptly. In late September polls briefly put the Conservatives ahead – for the first time since 1992. After some reassurances the blockade was called off and a threatened repeat in 60 days came to nothing. Labour recovered its poll ratings but it had been badly shaken. The Conservatives were greatly heartened by the evidence of public volatility which offered the possibility that the tide could again suddenly turn their way. Yet in spite of Labour's troubles, by the end of the year the Conservatives were again trailing in the opinion polls by some 20 points. The by-election result in the safe Conservative seat of Romsey in May 2000 had been a reminder of how weak their position was. On a 57 per cent turnout tactical voting by Labour supporters gave the Liberal Democrats a comfortable victory.

The next chapters chronicle the way the parties reacted to the 1997 result and prepared for 2001. Broadly, Labour took over the middle ground and the Conservatives moved to the right. But the picture was confused because, despite all the talk of modernisation, Labour seemed to be trying to match the Conservative hard line on law and order while the Conservatives accepted almost all of Labour's spending plans on health and education. Labour had hardly matched the high public expectations of 1 May 1997.[1] There was nothing comparable to the achievements of the Attlee government of 1945, or Thatcher's of 1983, both following landslide victories. But the pound was flourishing and Labour could claim that it had laid the foundations for future achievements. However, the clearest goal evident in Blairite policy was to win a second term.

1 For assessments of Labour's record see A. Seldon *The Blair Effect* (2001) and P. Toynbee and D. Walker *Did Things Get Better?* (2001).

2
Labour in Power

Labour enjoyed a remarkable dominance throughout the 1997 Parliament. There had been no post-war Parliament in which the government was so continuously assumed to be certain of re-election. It was the first full Parliament since 1900 when the governing party held every seat it defended in a by-election. In no other full Parliament had the government been ahead of the opposition in the opinion polls every month but one: the September 2000 drop in Labour's popularity was remarkable for being so shallow and so short. Tony Blair was determined to compile a record in government that would ensure re-election and to achieve an historic full second term. Running the economy well, demonstrating competence and ending the long-running debate about Labour's fitness to govern were important means to this end.

Since 1970, office with an assured parliamentary majority had been a rare luxury for Labour; in January 2001 it was still possible to hear one of Blair's closest advisers mistakenly referring to Labour's 'Shadow Cabinet'. A Number 10 aide said 'Ours is a four-year campaign. It started on 1 May 1997.' Before taking office, nearly all the 1997 Cabinet had only experienced political life on the opposition benches. The combination of incumbency and confidence about re-election presented a new mix of opportunities and threats for Blair's team.

The professionalism of Labour's 1997 election campaign was widely noted, not least by Conservatives. It might be suggested that, given the intense dislike of the Conservative government and the widespread wish for change after 18 years, Labour did not have much to beat; but it had set new standards in agenda-setting, rapid rebuttal, disciplined adherence to a 'message', and identifying and contacting target voters. Conservatives in Smith Square were certainly impressed, as they sought to learn lessons from the defeat. Once in government could the Labour Party maintain its momentum? Its leading political figures were now involved in running departments and had their own reputations to defend. Some forward-looking advisers held informal meetings in Number 10 about the problem of incumbency, worrying that a large parliamentary majority, an unpopular opposition and a benign economic climate would not be enough to make a government sure of re-election. Voters, particularly among the working class, had high expectations and were fickle and ungrateful; the media were cynical; there would be problems in implementing reform. If the Conservatives could sort themselves out life could become hazardous. Some of the key campaign strategists found the shift to government difficult. One said: 'Opposition campaigning is sailing a boat with a stiff breeze. Incumbency is like sailing a boat with no wind at all. In government, holding the relationships together is much harder. There is less time, less sense of shared endeavour.'

The Blair administration, more than any of its predecessors, tried to conduct itself as a campaigning government. Partly this derived from the long experience of opposition, partly from the lessons of Bill Clinton's election victories and partly from the perceived successes of the 1994–97 period in opposition. Tony Blair desperately wanted to lead the first Labour government to achieve two successive full terms. Aides in the early months sometimes quoted President Clinton's advice to Blair – not to repeat his own initial error of forgetting the need to communicate and campaign while in office. In an attempt to coordinate and centralise communications from the centre, Blair created a powerful Number 10 Press Office under Alastair Campbell. Later a Strategic Communications Unit and a Research and Information Unit, under Bill Bush, a recruit from the BBC, were established. Many of the extra staff brought into Number 10 had communication skills. Moreover, many of Blair's appointees had worked with him before. In Whitehall, press officers and other officials were strongly reminded by Campbell of the need to be vigorous and pro-active in presenting the government case, emphasising that good communications were not an add-on but a core part of good policy. All this soon gave rise to mutterings among senior civil servants, and complaints from the media about excessive spin.

The Conservative Party's unpopularity was a continuing asset to the Labour administration; indeed, it had been so since John Major's government left the ERM in humiliating circumstances in September 1992. As noted, Labour enjoyed record leads in the polls for a government. Its only brief reverse in the opinion polls came three-and-a-half years into its term of office. By then it was being blamed for failures to improve public services, notably in transport and health, and for the rise in violent crime, as well as for the steep increase in petrol prices. Yet many voters still blamed the Conservatives for the failings of public services and appeared willing to believe that Labour would do a better job in the future.

In 1997, New Labour could claim that it was neither old Labour nor Conservative. Blair's aides calculated confidently that the absence of a credible Conservative threat meant that in 2001 Labour would have to run against itself. 'This is much harder for us. We could smash them (the Conservatives), but to run on our record against our earlier claims and against popular expectations is more difficult. Last time it was a referendum on the Conservatives. This time it will be a referendum on us.' Popular expectations of what the party would do had been high in 1997, and were increased by the huge parliamentary majority.

Labour had forged a new coalition of supporters in the 1997 election. It had succeeded in becoming a more national party, geographically and socially, making inroads in the South East and among the middle class and former Conservative voters. A third of Labour's 1997 support was drawn from people who had not voted for the party in 1992, and many of them had been motivated by a wish to get rid of an unpopular Conservative government. How could Tony Blair keep these so-called Middle England supporters in his big tent in 2001, without the incentive of an unpopular Conservative government to mobilise them? Blair's popularity with voters ran well ahead of his party's. Because he so clearly disavowed tribal politics and was eager to retain the support of the converts he had won over in 1997, some party traditionalists felt neglected. He seemed to prefer the company of businessmen and celebrities to trade union leaders and he was keen to leave NEC meetings early.

Voter apathy in the party's heartlands was a concern for some Labour strategists, who thought that it might dent, though not deny, Labour an overall majority. Turnout levels in local, European, and by-elections slumped during the Parliament, particularly in solid Labour areas and among core supporters. On the other hand, Labour actually increased its support among the middle class and in the South East. These trends only confirmed electoral behaviour in the 1997 general election. According to the study, *The Rise of New Labour* (Heath et al., 2001) voters detected a sharp decline between 1987 and 1997 in Labour's concern for trade unions, the working class and the unemployed. On the other hand, they thought that Labour had become sympathetic to the interests of big business and the middle class.[1] These were exactly the sorts of change in the party's image that Labour modernisers were trying to achieve. In the 1997 election, it was among the trade unionists, working-class council tenants and the unemployed that turnout fell most sharply. The authors interpreted the decline in enthusiasm among the party's traditional supporters as a reaction to New Labour's '... move towards the centre, its distancing from the trade unions, and its active courting of the middle classes'. There was, however, no denying the significant electoral gains that came from the trade-off between core and non-core support.

There was debate at different levels in the party about how to balance the appeal to Middle England with that to Labour heartlands. Middle England was thought to favour a more right-wing agenda, including the avoidance of tax increases and maintaining good relations with business and keeping the readers of the *Daily Mail* on side, while Labour's heartland voters favoured more spending on public services and more redistribution to the less well-off. Some commentators regarded Blair and Peter Mandelson as spokesmen for the former, Gordon Brown for the latter. But the reality was more complex. It was Blair who pledged to end child poverty in 20 years, and Brown who did not increase income tax rates. And the middle class as much as the working class favoured spending on public services over tax cuts.

The public spending squeeze in the first two years, with its pressure on public services, angered many activists, and some complained that too much of Westminster's attention was frittered on issues such as repealing Section 28, constitutional reforms, and on ending foxhunting. In 1997 Labour supporters had been intent not just on getting rid of John Major's government but on a speedy increase in spending on health and education. They were impatient at the lack of tangible improvements in key public services. In the Commons, Malcolm Chisholm resigned from the government over the cut to lone parent benefits in 1997. When Peter Kilfoyle, a junior defence minister and MP for Liverpool Walton, resigned from the government in January 2000, he complained that MPs like himself and Labour's traditional working-class supporters were being taken for granted.

Labour traditionalists and a number of cabinet ministers (including John Prescott, Gordon Brown, Jack Straw and Margaret Beckett) acquiesced in rather than supported the 'Blair project' of forging closer relations between Labour and the Liberal Democrats. They appreciated the benefits of anti-Conservative tactical voting in constituencies, they accepted a joint Cabinet Committee and cooperation in some local authorities and in Scotland and Wales, but they drew the line at a reform of the electoral system which would cost Labour seats or a Westminster coalition which would mean a sacrifice of ministerial posts. Peter Mandelson's second resignation from the Cabinet in January 2001 removed one of the few senior supporters of the project.

All incumbents have to strike a balance between defending their record and offering a positive vision for the future. Gordon Brown believed that most people voted prospectively not retrospectively; he was keen to show how his prudent economic management was generating a financial surplus that could be used to improve public services. He and Tony Blair wanted Labour to be the party of change and reform at the next general election.

The party also had to work out its line of attack against the Conservative Party. Over the first two years some New Labour mantras had emerged in House of Commons debates, media interviews and Question Time in the House of Commons. Most notable were 'economic stability versus Tory boom and bust' or 'Tory tax cuts versus investment in public services'. In his conference speech in October 1999, Blair attacked the 'forces of conservatism' who resisted modernisation and this was echoed in many subsequent attacks, notably against the Eurosceptic press in November 2000. Alistair Darling commented during a political cabinet discussion in January 2001 that in the 1983 election the Conservatives had successfully portrayed Labour as 'both useless and dangerous'. Labour should now return the compliment. Charges that William Hague was opportunistic, jumped on bandwagons, took extreme positions and was a weak leader, took hold among target voters. But Labour also tried to discredit Conservative plans for tax reductions; this could only be done, ministers argued, at the cost of cutting planned investment in public services. Ministers wanted to show that William Hague and his party did not constitute a serious alternative prime minister and government. In opposition, Blair had used Old Labour imagery to impress voters with his success in changing the party. Now he regularly used selective reminders of the last Conservative government (tax increases, boom and bust, cuts, privatisation) as the yardstick for comparison with his new administration.

Before 1997, Blair and Brown had been determined to protect Labour from the tax and spend charge that the Conservatives had successfully made against them in the past. They pledged that a Labour government would not increase marginal rates of income tax for the lifetime of the next Parliament. This constraint did not, however, prevent Gordon Brown from raising considerable amounts from indirect taxes as well as from the tax receipts coming from the increased numbers at work. At first, ministers justified these increases on the grounds of sorting out the public finances. Conservative critics accused Brown of building a war chest so that he could introduce a popular pre-election budget. In July 2000 Gordon Brown announced the results of his second comprehensive spending review that promised an extra £63 billion of accumulated spending on the public services over the following three years.

There was, perhaps, no greater change in public attitudes towards the parties than on assessments of their relative economic competence. For most of the 50 years until 1997, the Conservatives had been seen as the best party to manage the economy. In 1997, in spite of Black Wednesday, some polls still showed Labour behind the Conservatives as the best party to run the economy. By November 2000, Labour's private polls showed that it led the Conservatives by 18 points on economic management. Labour had long been preferred on public services, but it had now broadened its battleground to include economic management. The strong economy could be used as the springboard for improving public services. Delivering the second was impossible without the first.

For much of the electorate the terms of the political economy debate had shifted. Tax was now inseparable from the quality of (or investment in) public services. Although both major parties sought to walk the tightrope between extra spending on the core public services and a concern for taxpayers, there was a change of emphasis. The Conservatives were more sympathetic to tax cuts, Labour to increased public spending (or 'investment', as Brown always called it). Labour was convinced by its research that the public would back its line. The public mood had changed from the 1980s when Labour was often on the defensive about its plans for increased public spending ('Where's the money coming from?'). In the new climate after 1997 Conservative tax cutters were on the defensive ('Where will the cuts in services come?'). Whereas in 1997 Blair and Brown had accepted the Tory plans of no more income tax rises and no more spending for the first two years of government, in 2001 Hague and Portillo were matching the bulk of Labour's promised extra spending in health, education, and law and order up to 2003.

Over time, the energetic communications operation conducted from Number 10 produced a hostile reaction in much of the media and the public, who grew increasingly cynical over the many policy initiatives and statements which were launched and then relaunched, at the notorious double and treble counting of funding for services, and at the alleged leaning on the media. The claims were at odds with the public's frequently grim experiences with the NHS, trains and crime. The media were fascinated with the 'spin' by government spokesmen and were determined to unmask the spin doctors. Alastair Campbell, Peter Mandelson, Charlie Whelan (the press spokesman for Gordon Brown), and other special advisers became media stories (see Chapter 1). Few were more assiduous in reporting this activity than the BBC's Nick Jones. Andrew Rawnsley's (2000) much-publicised *Servants of the People* recorded how Labour ministers' spin doctors sometimes seemed to be fighting against each other as much as against the Opposition.

Number 10, in spite of its own vigorous efforts at agenda-setting, expressed concern that sections of the press were breeding popular cynicism. Tony Blair, notwithstanding claims to the contrary, was himself not exempt from pandering to the media. In one leaked memo, dated 29 April 2000, he asked his aides to provide him with 'headline grabbing initiatives' on touchstone issues that would change public perceptions of the government. He wanted proposals that are 'tough, with immediate bite, and send a message'. He added: 'I should be personally associated with as much of this as possible.' Asked about the public mood in June 2000 in the wake of Blair's disastrous Women's Institute speech (see p. 19), one frustrated adviser replied: 'Read the bloody *Daily Mail*.' Newspapers like the *Daily Mail* and the *Daily Telegraph* appeared to have their own anti-government agenda and on some issues this influenced the readers. Ministers complained that they could not respond to the public mood, without allowing the media to set the agenda for them. Alastair Campbell established a short-lived monitoring unit, headed by the Labour MP Gerald Kaufman, to rebut the flood of anti-Labour stories in the *Daily Mail*. Blair confronted the media in his 'forces of conservatism' speech in October 1999 and in his attack on the Eurosceptic press in November 2000. He complained bitterly about the frenzy in targeting Peter Mandelson in the events leading to his two resignations and about the pressure on Keith Vaz to resign in early 2001. But Blair and Campbell also went to great trouble to court the *Sun*, often giving it scoops ahead of the loyal *Mirror*, including the date of the general election.

Blair and Campbell sought new ways to communicate directly with the voters. Articles with Blair's by-line were planted in national newspapers; he held regular meetings with regional press editors and specialist magazines; and he had many question-and-answer sessions with voters and party supporters. Philip Gould, drawing on suggestions from Clinton advisers, urged Blair to concentrate less on trying to influence the daily headlines, leaving the government's achievements to speak for themselves. As part of this strategy, Campbell scaled down formal (but not informal) briefings for the Lobby.

The BBC and ITV first raised the prospect of a television debate between the party leaders. At a Press Gallery lunch in November 2000 Alastair Campbell suggested in reply to a question that this might help to stimulate greater interest in politics. This quickly became a story when the opposition parties announced their acceptance in principle. Four of the five key actors in launching the debate (two party leaders and the two television networks) had accepted. But it had not been cleared with Blair, and most aides were strongly opposed to the idea. They were surprised that with such a big party and leader advantage in the opinion polls the idea was ever entertained. 'What's in it for us?' said one. They were aware of the Gore–Bush debates in the United States, which showed that the underdog (Bush) could benefit if he met or surpassed modest expectations. 'We will enthusiastically support the idea until the moment we can extricate ourselves with dignity', said one adviser. On 17 January 2001 a Labour spokesman announced that Blair would not participate in any debates.

Policy thinking for the future was driven largely from Number 10. The position was very different from that in the 1970s when Labour prime ministers had to battle with the NEC to exclude left-wing ideas from the manifesto. The head of the Number 10 Policy Unit, David Miliband, and Ed Richards, another Policy Unit member, had responsibility for drafting the manifesto. Because Policy Unit members were caught up in short-term political concerns Richards had been recruited in 1999 to concentrate on the second-term agenda. A first draft of the manifesto was circulated to key figures in early December 2000. In many areas the significant thinking was reflected in published long-term (ten-year) plans for transport, health, crime and education, and in the comprehensive spending review, or major ministerial speeches, such as Blair's reflections on the EU in Warsaw in November 2000. One aide concerned with the development of the final document privately suggested that the manifesto itself would not be so important. 'It will be the icing on the cake. The important ideas have already been revealed. Other ideas will not be spelt out in the manifesto, because they are not costed. But they will be significant in the second term.' He had in mind radical reforms in the public services, including a greater role for the private sector in the delivery of services. The potentially sensitive passages on the voting system for Westminster elections, as well as on foxhunting, taxation, and the euro were left to Blair and Brown.

New policy thinking was encouraged by think-tanks sympathetic to the centre-left. The IPPR, Demos, the John Smith Institute (close to Gordon Brown) and the Foreign Policy Centre all floated ideas. They were not, however, influential on the manifesto. The Fabian Society suggested a series of second-term reforms in the *New Statesman*, and in late 2000 issued a comprehensive report from its Commission on Taxation and Citizenship. Its proposals for raising the top marginal rate of income tax from 40 per cent to 50 per cent and hypothecating some taxes to spend on core public services fell on stony ground. Nor did the trade unions or the various party committees have much impact on the manifesto. The

Policy Unit and departmental ministers were more influential. Tony Blair and Bill Clinton held seminars to promote a Third Way, an approach supposed to combine the best aspects of the First Way (social democracy) and the Second Way (the market). Blair described it as combining policies for economic dynamism with social justice and social cohesion. Some on the left showed an interest and the idea of marrying fairness and enterprise, according to the surveys, was popular. But others criticised the concept for being vague and a euphemism for 'pick and mix' political pragmatism.[2]

Tony Blair wanted a more constructive relationship with the EU than John Major. Exercising significant influence in the EU seemed impossible without membership of the single currency. But Blair was also aware of the public hostility and press scepticism toward the euro. He and Brown wanted to stall speculation about whether and when Labour would call a referendum on the issue. Having set firm conditions for a positive decision in October 1997, Brown saw himself as the judge and jury of when the decision on British entry to the single European currency would be taken. Peter Mandelson was a much stronger supporter of the project and wanted ministers to make a positive case for it, well in advance of a referendum. But Brown and Blair agreed that, because of the unpopularity of the euro (as many as 70 per cent opposed entry), they did not want the issue debated before or during the general election. Although the intellectual position of the party for a 2001 election was a real concern for Tony Blair, party management and campaign preparation were also important.

The agency BMP, which had handled Labour's advertising in 1997, did not seek the account for 2001. In April 2000 the US-owned TWBA was appointed over competition from Saatchi and Saatchi and JWT. Its remit was to prepare the party's posters, television broadcasts, leaflets and 'events' before and during the election campaign. The agency had not worked for a political party before, although it had handled advertising for Women Against Rape. Trevor Beattie, the creative director, noted in the industry for the Wonderbra campaign, had helped on the party's 'Freedom and Fairness' campaign in 1986. His team liaised regularly with the pollster Philip Gould, the new MP Douglas Alexander and Peter Hyman, a member of the Policy Unit, who collectively agreed the political brief for the agency. The first fruits of the campaign were seen in the November poster campaign 'If you voted for change in 1997, thank you', with a reference to such positives as lower inflation, more nurses and more teachers. The decision to give credit to Labour voters was stimulated to some extent by the public perception that the party, and Blair especially, were becoming arrogant and out of touch. The general election posters were approved by Blair in January 2001. They included the especially memorable poster of Hague with Thatcher's hair (see page 109).

Within a few weeks of the 1997 election, the party headquarters on the first floor of Millbank Tower was much depleted. This was not an unusual post-election situation. People appointed on one-year contracts left and other talented staff moved to Whitehall as special advisers. The Excalibur rebuttal computer was run down and the Millbank operation was conducted on a reduced budget. The departure of the main political figures from the building to work in government allowed remaining staff more freedom, although they were soon heavily involved in the Scottish and Welsh referendums, to be followed by the Scottish and Welsh elections and the European elections.

In October 1998 Margaret McDonagh was promoted from Election Coordinator to succeed Tom Sawyer as General Secretary of the Labour Party. This appointment had long been expected but was not uncontentious. Unlike her predecessors, who had often been elderly trade unionists, she was young and had worked as a party organiser, running the key seats campaign in 1997. She also had been involved in New Labour campaigns since 1992 and continued to canvass her local constituency at weekends. Margaret McDonagh had a reputation for getting things done as well as a reputation for abrasiveness. Millbank was considered as guilty as Number 10 when the media aired charges of control freakery over discipline and candidate selection.

Matthew Taylor, Head of Policy, soon moved to head the IPPR think-tank. He calculated that such a position would give him more opportunity to proselytise on behalf of progressive politics than one in Millbank or even in Number 10. He was replaced by Nick Peccorelli. In summer 2000 more staff moved from Number 10 to Millbank, both to prepare for the election campaign and to improve liaison between the two centres. Lance Price, Campbell's deputy in Number 10, became Director of Communications at Millbank, assisted by Steve Bates. Pat McFadden, Deputy Chief of Staff in the Number 10 Private Office, moved to become political coordinator between Number 10 and the party machine.

As in 1997, the party established a number of task forces to cover the key campaigning tasks. One on field operations was led by David Evans and one on policy by Nick Peccorelli, both Assistant General Secretaries; Greg Cook continued to monitor polls; Spencer Livermore, a special adviser at the Treasury, moved to Millbank to take charge of an 'attack' (and rebuttal) operation. Centralised canvassing of target voters in 146 priority seats, largely those gained in 1997, was conducted from a telephone bank in North Shields. By March 2001, party organisers claimed to have contacted over 1 million voters by phone.

Party membership, which had passed the 400,000 figure by the end of 1997, declined to 311,000 by December 2000 and by mid-2001, was down to little more than 260,000. Falling party membership has been a long-standing problem for British political parties, and the era of mass membership parties has passed. Recent reforms had empowered individual members, so that they could select the party leader, candidates for Parliament and constituency representatives for the NEC. But a mixture of 'old Labour' sentiment, as well as resentment at the explicit interventions of Number 10 and Millbank in candidate selection, may have helped to disillusion many activists. Certainly, when members had the opportunity, they often rebuffed the centre and Tony Blair. In spite of heavy Number 10 lobbying, Frank Dobson only narrowly beat Ken Livingstone in the contest to choose the party's candidate for the London mayoral election. But in the actual election in May 2000 Dobson was easily defeated by Livingstone, running as an Independent.

In Number 10 Sally Morgan, Blair's Political Secretary, maintained links with Millbank and the party. Her office contained four staff who were responsible for contacts with the Unions, the PLP, ethnic minority voters, and Scotland and Wales. Party management in the devolved Scottish and Welsh systems proved a major embarrassment. The election of Number 10's candidate, Alun Michael, over Rhodri Morgan as Leader of the Welsh Party was ascribed to an electoral college system with a trade union block vote and was widely discredited as a 'fix'. In Scotland the closed list system of PR for selecting top-up candidates for elections to the Scottish Parliament in May 1999 was used to exclude or give an unfavourable listing to candidates (usually left-wing) deemed 'unreliable'. When Dennis Canavan, the veteran left-wing Labour MP for Falkirk West, was not even selected as a possible candidate, he stood as an independent in retaliation – and won by the largest majority of any MSP. Evidently devolution stopped when it came to the Labour Party. To be regarded as Millbank's or 'Tony's candidate' was not an advantage. The party saw its share of the vote tumble in the London 2000, and Scottish and Welsh 1999 elections. After these experiences the NEC agreed to reconsider the closed list system.

The left declined as a force in the 1997 Parliament. Many former left-wingers had moderated their views to accommodate Blair's New Labour ideas. Tony Benn and Denis Skinner, on the back benches, were relics of an earlier period, and marginal figures in the party. Ken Livingstone was expelled after standing against Frank Dobson in the London mayoral election. Labour MPs rebelled on welfare reform and air traffic control, but proved much less troublesome than they had been under previous Labour governments. The Labour MPs first entering Parliament in 1997 proved to be more loyal than new Labour MPs of earlier generations. The large majority in the Commons allowed the party managers to release Labour MPs in marginal seats from parliamentary duties to spend more time in their constituencies. Although the whips had a relatively easy time, they regularly reminded MPs of the damage that indiscipline had caused to previous Labour governments and even to John Major's. In turn, MPs complained about the lack of discipline shown in ministers' cooperation with authors whose books reported bitter divisions and backbiting at the top.

The National Executive Committee had been a diminishing force in the party since the late 1980s. By the time Neil Kinnock resigned as leader in 1992, it was no longer the stronghold of the left, providing a rival to the parliamentary leadership as it had in the 1970s and early 1980s. Under the new *Partnership in Power* arrangements, which were approved by Conference in 1997, MPs were excluded from standing in the NEC's constituency and trade union sections (they now had their own section), and the women's section was abolished. Although this hurt the dissidents, the left-wing Grassroots Alliance won four of the six constituency seats in the 1998 election for the NEC in which the favoured Peter Mandelson was rejected. The NEC now met every two months instead of monthly.

Conference also ceased to be the adversarial forum of the 1970s and 1980s, becoming increasingly stage-managed for the benefit of television. Its direct influence on policy was reduced, as policy was to be developed by a two-year rolling programme of reports from policy committees. A small Joint Policy Committee, chaired by Blair, decided policy. But Conference could still embarrass the leadership. At Brighton in 2000 the government was defeated when Conference (thanks to the unions) voted to re-establish the link between increases in average earnings and pensions. Party members and MPs were angry at Gordon Brown's 75p annual uprating to the old age pension (a consequence of the low inflation rate) that came into effect in April 2000.

The new arrangements for the NEC and annual conference also involved a reduction in trade union influence in the party. As a result of changes to the party constitution the unions lost their majority on the reconstructed NEC, and had to settle for 30 of 175 seats on the new National Policy Forum. But union leaders were delighted with the government's incorporation of the EU's Social Chapter, and with the

Employment Relations Act 1999 which provided that the unions would gain recognition when, on at least a 40 per cent turnout, a majority voted for it in a ballot. The minimum wage was also introduced and generously uprated in 2001. Not all unions, however, were convinced that the link with Labour was a benefit. At its 1998 annual conference the RMT railway union was only seven votes short of passing a motion to disaffiliate from the Labour Party.

New spending limits imposed under the Political Parties, Elections and Referendums Act 2000 meant that the election campaign would cost no more than in 1997 (see Chapter 1). But large donations from wealthy businessmen were still sought and presented their political problems. Lord Hamlyn, the publisher, Christopher Ondaatje, the author, and Lord Sainsbury of Turville, a government minister, each contributed £2 million. There was controversy when it was revealed that the Lord Chancellor, Lord Irvine, had held a fund-raising dinner for Labour-supporting lawyers. Critics complained that this was inappropriate for the chief law officer of the state who had the power of making key judicial appointments.

Shortly after the 1997 general election Philip Gould joined forces with James Carville and Stan Greenberg, who had taken polls for Clinton in 1992, to form a new agency GCGNOP. This began occasional tracking polls for Labour in September 1997 and monthly from February 2000. During 2000 Gould conducted an average of two focus groups a week. Following the much-publicised leaks of Gould's memos to Tony Blair, focus groups were taken over by the party's advertising agency TBWA in June 2000, and Gould did not resume them until the election was called. In Millbank, Greg Cook was the party's polling coordinator and closely involved in the design of the questionnaires. He initiated and finessed polls in Scotland and Wales, and developed constituency profiles that were used in the key seats campaign. Gould made regular reports about the state of public opinion to Blair and occasional presentations to the Cabinet. Until the dip in support in early autumn 2000, the private (and public) polls told a uniformly favourable story. On the tracking questions of handling the economy, public services, pensions, living standards, taxes, leadership, economic competence, trust and sense of direction, Labour was comfortably ahead of the Conservatives. These issues and themes emerged as the party's battleground. The polls also showed that the party's support among the middle class and in Middle England held up, indeed more so than among the working class and in Labour heartlands.

Gould did not always convey good news. In summer 1999 he reported a sense of disappointment about the NHS and crime. There was also declining trust in Blair and the government; this was due to a perception of sleaze and spin, of evasions, misleading information, and unjustified boasting. The gloomiest findings came in October 2000, following the September petrol blockade. No government had seen its support tumble so fast since regular polling had started in the late 1940s. It appeared that the Conservative messages on tax cuts, toughness on crime, and Euroscepticism were gaining ground. On the tracker issues and themes (except for leadership, the NHS and education) Labour leads were significantly down. And, for all the strength of the economy, many target voters felt pessimistic over their own economic circumstances. They claimed to be hard-pressed, they did not feel that they had become better off since 1997 and did not expect to do so in the near future. Blair and the government were seen as arrogant and out of touch ('emotionally disconnected from the people') and a growing number saw the Conservatives as 'standing up for people like us'. But by December much of the dissatisfaction had dissipated and Labour's remarkably large leads on voting intentions and on the issues had been restored. The widespread support for the petrol blockade showed how volatile public opinion was, and how it could be inflamed when it held the government responsible for something like rising petrol prices.

In a presentation to the Cabinet on 30 January 2001, Gould reported that Labour led on all the key attributes which it had been tracking. It polled 45 per cent or higher as the party likely to do the best job giving pensioners a better deal, improving the NHS and health care, boosting standards in schools, keeping inflation under control, managing the economy, standing up for 'people like me', keeping taxes at the right level, and offering policies to take Britain into the future. Relatively less favourable issues for the party were: improving people's trust in government, cutting crime, taking the right approach to asylum seekers, and taking the right approach to Europe. But Labour still led the Conservatives even on these latter issues. Gould pointed to the forces working for Labour:

- growing sense of economic stability
- strengthening signs of improved public services, particularly education
- awareness of increasing investment, in schools and hospitals
- increasing sense of government endeavour, 'on my side'

The forces working against were:

- disillusionment – 'all are as bad as each other'
- scepticism – 'figures are manipulated, can't believe what they say'

- perceptions of slow public service delivery (although taxes are higher)
- absence of an effective opposition makes election a referendum on Labour's record

Yet as Chapter 1 showed (p. 15), the electoral strategy was not a success on all fronts. Although Labour was regularly supported by about 50 per cent of voters in the opinion polls (with the Conservatives around 30 per cent), the results of 'second order' elections told a different story. The actual numbers of votes cast in Scotland and Wales in local elections, and in Euro elections, showed that Labour and the opposition parties were more evenly matched. Labour fought a low-key campaign in the European elections, relying largely on the government's record in national politics. In the 17 by-elections during the Parliament, Labour's share of the vote was 13 per cent down on its share in the same seats in the 1997 general election. The Conservative share increased by 1 per cent (to 27 per cent), while the Liberals rose 8 per cent (to 22 per cent). In the European parliamentary elections the Conservatives defied the polls and defeated Labour, but on a turnout of only 24 per cent. Ivor Crewe noted the Blair government's electoral conundrum, that it had done remarkably well *in* the polls but, by-elections aside, remarkably badly *at* the polls (Crewe, 2001, p. 92).

As far as possible Labour wanted to replicate the 1997 campaign structure, with the same people in broadly similar positions. Once more Gordon Brown would head the Campaign Strategy Committee and Peter Mandelson the Campaign Planning Committee. Brown's small strategy team met at 8 a.m. in Number 11 during 2000. But by early 2001 it had drawn up a draft grid of what the party would do on each election day and prepared a war book and key messages for party leaders (largely devised by Peter Hyman). Brown also convened a group each morning in the Treasury to set an agenda for the media. Mandelson's planning group met weekly at Millbank. The deputy leader on both teams was the 34-year-old MP for Paisley, Douglas Alexander, who had worked closely with Brown on the 1999 Scottish Parliament election campaign.

From early 2000 Blair began to include campaign preparations as a regular item in his schedule. The key campaign members would again be Brown, Campbell, Gould and Mandelson, and they provided the essential continuity from 1997. An additional figure was Douglas Alexander. In September a separate campaign meeting was arranged for 9.45 each Monday, to follow Blair's 9 a.m. office meeting with his civil service and political advisers. Blair also planned weekly Thursday morning meetings just with Brown and Mandelson, but these did not prove fruitful and Blair moved to holding larger meetings of key campaign figures fortnightly. He also met task force leaders weekly at Millbank.

Some leading party figures were concerned that Blair was prepared to hand the key campaign posts to Brown and Mandelson. These two men were often not on speaking terms. Their poor personal relations had been a strain during the 1997 campaign and later events had not brought them any closer. The hostility dated back to Peter Mandelson's decision in 1994 to back Blair in the election for party leader, when Gordon Brown thought Mandelson was committed to him. The details of these troubles had been recounted in great detail in newspaper-serialised biographies of the two men. 'The fundamentals are fine. We just need to get the personal relations right', said one frustrated aide. When Mandelson resigned from the Cabinet and from his campaign post in January 2001, Alexander effectively replaced him and John Prescott acted as an honorific chair.

The outcome was a rather labyrinthine structure. Sally Dobson had the title of general election coordinator in Millbank, Pat McFadden that of political coordinator (between Millbank and Number 10) and Douglas Alexander that of campaign coordinator. In addition there was a so-called 'Group of Six' which met twice a week in Alastair Campbell's office to try and coordinate the work of the various groups. This consisted of Campbell, Gould, Alexander, Ed Miliband (a special adviser to Brown), David Miliband and Peter Hyman (the last two being members of the Number 10 Policy Unit).

Gordon Brown was determined to base Labour's claim to a second term of office on his management of the economy. Unemployment fell steadily and by February 2001 was at its lowest level for 25 years; inflation hovered around 2 per cent and interest rates were at their lowest for many years. For the first time ever over a sustained period a Labour government was trusted to run the economy more competently than the Conservative Party. On the eve of the election Brown reflected: 'In 1997, the Conservatives were on the defensive because of their record, and the voters worried over our past. Now, we have reassured voters about our record and we have to create momentum by creating confidence for the future.' Al Gore had paid the price for not making enough of the Clinton economic record in the recent presidential election; Brown would not make the same mistake. As Chapter 5 shows he intended to use his final budget of the Parliament as a launch pad for the election campaign.

Notes

1. *The Rise of New Labour* (Heath et al., 2001) p. 126.
2. *The Third Way and its Enemies* (Giddens, 2000)

3
Conservatives

Tony Blair's reinvention of his party as New Labour in the years after he took over in 1994 was played out before a largely admiring public and media. William Hague faced a similar challenge in 1997 but his public was less sympathetic. He tried to create a new image for the Conservative Party, out of office for the first time in 18 years, and he did much to change its leadership and organisation. His efforts failed, however, to excite the popular approval that Blair had won. But there was another contrast. Blair had shone in comparison with Major's discredited and divided administration. Hague had to compete with a popular prime minister and a Labour government that enjoyed much goodwill.

During the four years of William Hague's leadership, the Conservative Party had to deal with a decline that was more complex and deep-seated than many in the party realised. Like John Major, William Hague had to come to terms with the legacy of Thatcherism – was that approach still applicable in changed circumstances? He also had to cope with Labour's successful move to the political centre and his party's loss of command on so many issues. Finally, he had to assess the reasons that led to the loss of so many supporters in 1997. Could these be regained and, if so, how? Should the party challenge Labour on the centre ground or should it seek clear blue water between the parties by moving to the right? The dilemma was neatly illustrated in late 1997 at a breakfast meeting of leading Conservative politicians. An opinion pollster asked if anybody present could anticipate what Labour's message might be in a 2001 general election. Receiving no answer, he suggested, 'Give us four more years to finish our work.' He then asked how the Conservatives might counter that message. He did not receive a reply.

In the enforced absence of Michael Portillo, five candidates stood for the party leadership in succession to John Major. William Hague seemed to offer the best chance of a clean break with the past. He was by far the youngest, and the other four candidates had been long-established ministers under Major and, in some cases, under Margaret Thatcher. Initially, William Hague had only toyed with standing for the leadership, and for a time supported the claims of Michael Howard. When he was persuaded that Howard would not win, he decided to enter the race. Like John Major in 1990, he appealed to the centre-right of the party: he was seen as the best hope of restoring unity with his euro line of not entering 'for the foreseeable future', and because of his low profile he had few enemies. He finally triumphed over Ken Clarke on the third ballot, after Clarke had arranged an implausible alliance with John Redwood who had been eliminated in the second ballot.

Throughout the contest Clarke was ahead in the opinion polls and enjoyed the support of the party grass roots, or at least those consulted by constituency chairmen. Over the next four years, as Hague failed to break through a wall of public scepticism and even hostility, some looked back to the contest and wondered 'what if?' Most of Clarke's supporters concluded that he could not have led such a Eurosceptic party effectively.

Table 3.1   Conservative party leadership election 1997

1st Ballot (10 June)		*2nd Ballot (17 June)*		*3rd Ballot (19 June)*	
K. Clarke	49	K. Clarke	64	W. Hague	92
W. Hague	41	W. Hague	62	K. Clarke	70
J. Redwood	27	J. Redwood	38		
P. Lilley	24				
M. Howard	23				

William Hague was educated at a state school and Oxford University, and then by McKinsey, the management consultants. He seemed an ideal modern Conservative. He had achieved national prominence, when, as a 16-year-old, he addressed the Conservative Conference at Blackpool in 1977 (something that did not help his image 20 years later). He had been appointed to John Major's Cabinet as Secretary of State for Wales at the age of 34. Now, aged 36, he was the youngest Tory leader since William Pitt.[1]

The crushing 1997 defeat provided Hague with an opportunity to make radical changes. Because many of Mrs Thatcher's achievements were now common ground between the parties, some Conservatives claimed that the party had to find a way of moving on, as Blair had done for Labour. But there were difficulties about distancing himself too openly from the

Someone didn't do his homework.

WHO THINKS THE TORY MANIFESTO SUMS ADD UP? JUST WILLIAM. Labour
www.labour.org.uk

Conservative record of the previous 18 years; after all, many of his colleagues were associated with it. One significant decision Hague made after the party's 1997 conference was to abandon the 'wait and see' line of John Major about Britain's approach to the single currency: he ruled out entering at least for the present Parliament and the next one. Although this gave the Europhiles an excuse to stay on, it clearly defined the Conservatives as the Eurosceptic party.

Hague came into an unenviable inheritance. For many Conservative politicians life after May 1997 was a painful change. They were deprived of ministerial cars, red boxes, media attention, and the routines and pleasures of ministerial life. Only 11 MPs had previous experience on the Opposition benches. More seriously, as the polls showed, the party had been marooned with the support of some 30 per cent of voters for nearly five years. It had lost all of its MPs in Scotland and Wales, as well as half of its English MPs; it had little presence in local government or the cities. The party was heavily in debt; in late 1997 it came within two days of being declared bankrupt. In many areas of the country the organisation was moribund, and the average age of party members was 62.

The party never agreed on the lessons of the crushing 1997 defeat. Detailed analysis of the 1997 election campaign by the British Election Study showed that the Labour and Liberal Democrat parties more accurately represented the issue preferences of their supporters' views (but not on the EU) than did the Conservative Party. The party was particularly out of touch on economic policies, such as further privatisation and giving priority to tax cuts over greater spending on public services. Some shadow ministers and Conservative Central Office strategists accepted the implications of these findings and thought that they had to recapture the centre ground. However, they never won the argument for projecting popular reforms on health and education and altering the image of the party.

Other advisers calculated that electoral recovery would come from adding to the 9 million loyal Conservative voters, the 2 million believed to have abstained and the 1 million anti-EU voters who had supported the Referendum Party and UKIP. Adopting populist policies and a tough line on Europe, plus the inevitable disillusion with the Labour government, could give the Conservatives victory at the next general election. They believed that the lesson from John Major's failure was that the party needed to be more right wing and Eurosceptic. A hidden majority of the electorate was waiting to be mobilised. Over the four years of the Parliament, however, there was little research to support this view. Indeed, there was much to confound it.[2]

For much of the year after the general election Hague and a few other leading figures struck a contrite note about the behaviour of the previous Conservative government. He apologised for joining the ERM and its aftermath in the form of Black Wednesday. He admitted that in government the party had not listened sufficiently to the public and had become remote. He wanted to break the popular identification of the Conservatives with the sleaze and divisions of the Major era. As he told the 1997 party conference: 'Our party as a whole was regarded as out-of-touch and irrelevant ... so we need to change our attitudes, change our organisation, change our culture.' Yet the public never perceived the party as having apologised enough, while many of his MPs, especially former ministers, thought he had apologised too much.

Some advisers recognised the wisdom of Blair's explicit break with Old Labour and his admission that his party had stopped listening to voters. They echoed the first of Philip Gould's ten campaign principles for the success of New Labour's project: 'concede and move on'. Hague in his first year seemed to be emulating Blair's leadership of his party in Opposition. He was a moderniser and in September 1998 he presented copies of Philip Gould's *The Unfinished Revolution* to senior shadow ministers, personally signing them: 'Know thine enemy'. But before the Conservatives could move on, they had to show voters that they had turned over a new leaf. As one insider put it: 'It was more than saying "sorry". We had to show that we understood the voters' critical judgement and that we accepted it; we had to internalise it.' Prominent among advocates of the so-called 'apology' approach were Andrew Cooper, in charge of political operations and strategy, Danny Finkelstein, in charge of policy development, and Rick Nye, recruited in 1998 from the Social

Market Foundation to be director of the Research Department. All were young, and had been together in the SDP in the 1980s before switching to the Conservatives. The first two had been closely involved in the Conservative general election campaign in 1997 and had felt the brunt of the voters' rejection of it. Some 3.5 million Conservatives from 1992 had switched to Labour or the Liberal Democrats. The image of broken promises on taxes, of incompetence, and of sleaze was still strong with too many voters.

On the other hand, some of the more experienced members of Hague's Shadow Cabinet, particularly Michael Howard and John Redwood, were strongly identified with the Major years. More damagingly, they had a high media profile and seemed to voters to be arrogant and unapologetic when they criticised Labour. This was not the tone Hague's new Conservative Party wanted to strike. Hague urged colleagues not to look back: 'I've seen the video of the 1997 election. No matter how many times you replay it, we get wiped out in the end.'

In July 1998 Peter Lilley, as Deputy Leader, launched 'Listening to Britain'. It was another exercise designed to open opportunities for MPs and local association officials to contact networks of voluntary organisations and professionals, identify issues for policy development, and show that they were 'listening' to voters. Before the 1992 general election, Labour had mounted a similar exercise of the same name, and for broadly similar reasons. Some 400 meetings were held around the country in which voters could raise concerns. Lilley's instruction that front-benchers should listen, not make speeches, was only partly followed. The exercise informed the policy document *The Common Sense Revolution*, published in 1999.

Many Conservatives conceded that they had been outclassed in the 1997 election campaign, notably in the deployment of party workers in key constituencies, use of technology, and in managing the media. Radical reform of the party was overdue. The National Union, the arm of the local associations, had become disillusioned by the behaviour of many MPs over the previous five years, and, realising that an election defeat would provide a good opportunity to set the agenda, it had arranged a meeting for the Friday a week after polling day. Hague had made party reform a key feature of his leadership campaign. He wanted to unite the different sections of the party into a single organisation, and to give individual members more say in leadership elections and in deciding policy. One of his first decisions as leader was to appoint the newly-elected MP, Archie Norman, chairman of the Asda supermarket chain and a friend from McKinsey days, as chief executive with the task of reforming the party. Norman had written Hague a memo soon after his election as party leader urging him to take drastic action.

Hague also recalled Lord (Cecil) Parkinson to be Party Chairman – a job that he had held from 1981 to 1983 – with a remit to sell Norman's reforms to the party and to help consolidate them. 'I was conscious that you could not have two revolutionaries at the head of the party', Hague said, explaining the twin appointments of Norman and Parkinson. Archie Norman's forceful management style did not go down well with many in Central Office. Other senior figures thought that they should have a key role in implementing reform, and expressed concern that Norman's proposals would be too expensive and offend the voluntary party. For his part, Norman was struck by the number of vested interests opposing change. The reform package was, however, effectively complete by Easter 1998 and presented as *The Fresh Future*.

The reforms amounted to the most significant restructuring of the party's internal structure since the Maxwell Fyfe reforms after 1945. They were controversial and MPs took time to be reconciled to losing their exclusive right to elect the party leader, just as for a time the National Union tried to resist its own abolition. The constituency organisations under the umbrella of the National Union were merged with MPs and with Central Office to constitute a single party. A newly created, 15-strong Board was set up to head the new organisation to decide all organisational issues within the party. It would also oversee a new Ethics and Integrity Committee, which had powers to suspend or expel any member judged to have brought the party into disrepute. The Treasurer, now a member of the Board, would at last be accountable to the party. A new Policy Forum was set up to consider details of policy together with a new National Party Convention of the voluntary party (the successor of the National Union) to discuss broader issues. Finally, revised rules were introduced for challenging a Conservative leader, the result of a complex and bruising battle between the National Union and the 1992 Committee Executive. In future, the process would begin with a motion of no confidence, activated at the request of at least 15 per cent of MPs. If this were carried, the leader would resign and take no further part in the process. MPs would ballot for a short-list of two candidates who would go forward to an election open to all party members.

The party leader appointed only 5 of the 15 members of the new Board and in theory he could be blocked by it. Although the reforms added to the internal democracy of the party, the views of the Policy Forum and the National Convention were only advisory; ultimately, the party leader could at any time call ballots of members to outflank critics and claim endorsement for his policies. The new rules also appeared to make it more difficult to challenge the leader.

Indeed Hague used ballots of members to win endorsement for his position as party leader and for his policy on the euro. This plebiscitarian technique of party management was only one imitation of what Blair had done inside the Labour Party. The creation of the war room in Central Office (see p. 49), the introduction of one member one vote, and the system for expelling members who brought the party into disrepute via the Ethics and Integrity Committee, were other examples.

Organisational reform, however necessary, was not enough; the party also needed a political strategy. In November 1998 Andrew Cooper, assisted by Finkelstein, presented his 4,000-word *Kitchen Table Conservatives* paper to Hague. The tone was set by its opening sentence:

> The fundamental problem of the Conservative Party is that it doesn't have a strategy – and hasn't had one for at least four years.

Cooper argued that electoral recovery depended on the leadership making it plain that the party had changed from being out of touch, divided and lacking a sense of direction, and on demonstrating that it had learned the lessons of its 1997 defeat. The party had to show that it was listening to the concerns of ordinary people, had policies to deal with them, and could speak in a language people understood. Cooper also advocated a '10,000-volt shock', equivalent to Blair's break with Clause IV in 1994, to dramatise Hague's change from the Major government. Indeed, the paper quoted liberally from Gould's *The Unfinished Revolution*. The party had to realise that Blair would constantly remind voters of the failures of Major's government. The paper was an implicit criticism of Hague's performance to date, as well as an explicit one of Major's time as Prime Minister.

Hague commended the strategy to the Shadow Cabinet in March 1999. He had for some time thought that the Conservative Party was concentrating too narrowly on economic issues. However, he quickly seemed to lose interest in it and the phrase, 'Kitchen Table Conservatism' was rarely heard again in Central Office. 'Telling politicians that they are part of the problem' was not helpful, said one supporter. This was particularly so when many Conservative MPs were reluctant to change and thought that the electorate had got it wrong. The supporters of change failed to win MPs over; they may have assumed that because Kinnock and Blair had crushed or marginalised their Labour opponents, Hague should and could do the same. The paper also coincided with the arrival of new people appointed to handle the media, Amanda Platell and Nick Wood, who were not sympathetic to the approach. A disappointed Cooper soon left Central Office.

The defeat in 1997 of so many Conservative ministers, together with the refusal of Kenneth Clarke and Michael Heseltine to join the Shadow Cabinet, meant that Hague's team lacked experience as well as public recognition. The leader, however, was privately relieved that Clarke refused: Clarke would have held a senior position (Hague had offered him the deputy leadership) and strained any attempt to unite the Shadow Cabinet against the single currency. Hague subsequently spoke of it as an extra birthday present. Successive Shadow Cabinet reshuffles meant that by mid-2000 Hague himself was the only survivor of John Major's Cabinet who had served continuously in it. He had gradually shed the old faces, regarding them as a barrier to making a fresh start. A number of newcomers emerged, notably David Willetts, Andrew Lansley, Theresa May, Liam Fox and Ann Widdecombe. Michael Portillo (who had returned to the Commons, winning the Kensington and Chelsea by-election in November 1999) joined the Shadow Cabinet in February 2000.

Hague was a collegial chairman of the weekly Shadow Cabinet. Each shadow minister submitted to Hague (copied to his Chief of Staff, Sebastian Coe, and to his PPS, first David Lidington and then John Whittingdale) a one- or two-page weekly report of what he or she had been doing (Hague had learnt this practice from his McKinsey days). Policy initiatives were sometimes collectively decided, but discussion was mainly dominated by the following week's business in Parliament. In late 1999 Hague introduced three Shadow Cabinet committees – one on the economy chaired by Francis Maude, and then Portillo, one on home affairs under Ann Widdecombe and one on foreign affairs under John Maples and then Maude. From late 1999 Hague responded to pressures and convened weekly strategy groups, in which he was joined by the senior shadows (Maude, Lansley, Portillo, Widdecombe, Norman, Michael Ancram and, eventually, Iain Duncan Smith).

Hague's public image was not something that the party could exploit. Indeed, it was a matter of concern and then of reluctant acceptance by the end of the Parliament. Supporters claimed that he 'needs time to establish himself', and made comparisons with the relatively low levels of popular approval for Ted Heath and Margaret Thatcher before they became Prime Minister; but these protestations became more half-hearted and unconvincing over time. Focus groups in the first year of the Parliament revealed that Hague was quite wrongly perceived as a southerner, upper class, and privately educated. Like Thatcher and Major before him, he tried to play the role of outsider against the metropolitan liberal elite, now represented by Blair. In his 1999 conference speech, he replied to Blair's attack on the Establishment and 'the forces of conservatism' which were holding Britain back:

> He's a 40-something, public school educated barrister from Islington, with a 200-seat majority in the House of Commons. Who does he think is the Establishment?

Hague was perhaps the party's best orator as party leader since Winston Churchill, but oratory mattered less to voters in the era of television, and the polls encouraged periodic media speculation about who would succeed him as leader. There were times during the Parliament when more Tory supporters were dissatisfied than satisfied with his performance. One concerned aide commented: 'In modern campaigns the message is largely carried by and through the party leader. You have to construct a narrative around him.' Unfortunately, Hague's standing in the polls was usually decisively worse than his party's – in contrast to the position under John Major in 1997, and under Tony Blair. The cartoonists' tasteless likening of Hague to a foetus resonated with some voters. Whatever the reason – his physical appearance, his youth, his voice, or his manner, or his lack of empathy – he was not an electoral asset.

Hague suffered for his own misjudgements, too. In the hours following the death of Diana, Princess of Wales, he appeared wooden, particularly in comparison with Blair's sure performance, and his suggestion that Heathrow be named after her was poorly received. He supported Jeffrey Archer as the party's candidate for the London mayoral election, in spite of warnings against this from senior staff. This backfired badly when the millionaire author was charged with perjury. In August 2000, the magazine *GQ* published an interview in which the leader recalled drinking 14 pints in one day as a student. The *Sun* ran a front page headlined 'BILLY LIAR'. Regardless of such unfairness, the episode did little to combat complaints that Hague lacked *gravitas* or advance his claim to be considered as an alternative prime minister. One influential member of the Shadow Cabinet admitted that the Conservative Party was often seen as a one-man band. He added: 'Unfortunately, that one man is William Hague.'

Sebastian Coe, who had lost his seat in the 1997 election, became Hague's Chief of Staff. The leader appreciated Coe's dedication, self-effacement and ability to help him to relax: Coe acted as a trainer, having regular judo sessions with Hague. He persuaded the leader that physical fitness and stamina were essential for an effective performance in modern campaigning conditions. No other political figure had as much private time with Hague. George Osborne became Political Secretary at the age of 25 and emerged as Hague's chief speechwriter. He had worked briefly in the party's Research Department, as a special adviser at MAFF, and then as a researcher for John Major in the 1997 campaign. In 1999 he was nominated for Tatton. David Lidington was Hague's PPS until his promotion to the front bench, and was replaced in 1999 by John Whittingdale who, before becoming MP in 1992, had been Mrs Thatcher's last Political Secretary at Number 10.

Like many party leaders before him, Hague endured regular complaints from colleagues about his political office – that it was young, inexperienced, lacked respect for senior party figures, and did not facilitate easy contact between himself and MPs and shadow ministers. Hague had a deliberately devolved management style and let shadow ministers get on with their portfolios in contrast to the central control that Blair's office had exercised when Labour was in Opposition before 1997. But some of Hague's colleagues thought that he was too hands-off and should have shown more interest in the work that they and their teams were doing.

Perhaps the major challenge to Hague's authority came over proposals for House of Lords reform. Hague authorised the party leader in the Lords, Lord Cranborne, to hold secret negotiations with Labour; but when he instructed Cranborne to end the discussions, the latter ignored him and made a private deal with Blair in November 1998. The substance of the agreement – retaining 92 hereditary peers on an interim basis until there was comprehensive reform – was not the main issue, but making it then would prevent the party from tabling amendments to government legislation. When he learnt of the deal, in December 1998, Hague abruptly sacked Cranborne (who said that had he been leader, he would have done the same) and went at short notice to the regular Wednesday meeting of the 1922 Committee to inform them of his action. He also attended and received a rough reception from the regular meeting of Tory peers. For a while the threat of resignation by the entire front bench team in the Lords hung over Hague, a step that would have made his position impossible. Only when Lord Strathclyde, the Chief Whip, was convinced by the seriousness of the situation did he agree to replace Cranborne and carried most colleagues with him. Yet the Cranborne deal stood.

During the 1980s Conservatives had divided between 'wet' and 'dry' on economic policy and in the 1990s between supporters and opponents of greater European integration. As the first issue declined, so new causes and alliances emerged. *The Times* (6 July 1998) characterised the two groups as 'mods' (modernisers) and 'rockers'. The former wanted the party to reflect society's changing values, particularly among the young, and to be more socially inclusive and tolerant of different lifestyles. Outside Parliament until November 1999, the new Shadow Chancellor, Michael Portillo, had emerged as a spokesman for this trend. Portillo, the rising hope of the Thatcherite wing of the party in the mid-1990s, was a much changed man since his defeat in the 1997 general election. Partly because of his admission of homosexual experiences before marriage, and partly because of his adoption of more socially liberal views, he was no longer the hero of the right. A year after his return to Parliament he resigned from the Thatcherite *No Turning Back* group over a mischievous leak of its proceedings. His more tolerant outlook was supported by many in the Shadow Cabinet, including David Willetts, Archie Norman and Francis Maude. Ann Widdecombe represented the so-called 'rockers' – defending a more populist, authoritarian stance. She could usually rely on the support of Iain Duncan Smith, and sometimes Hague, who had a foot in both camps. She led opposition to Labour's efforts to repeal Section 28 of the 1988 Local Government Act (which forbade the promotion of homosexuality by local authorities), and pursued a hard line on bogus asylum seekers, drug use, and the right of citizens to employ force in self-defence against burglars. The campaign to retain Section 28 was seen by some as hostile to gay rights; it was cited by two prominent defectors to Labour, the Conservative MP Shaun Woodward, and the gay millionaire businessman Ivan Massow.

Nowhere was William Hague's impact more apparent than over policy towards the European single currency. The issue had divided the Conservatives up to and during the 1997 general election, sapped John Major's authority and damaged the party's public image. Supporters and opponents of entry to the single currency had placed conflicting inter-pretations on John Major's 'wait and see' approach to possible British entry. Hague regarded a clearer line on this issue as 'the essential first step; unless I tackle this, I cannot do anything else' he told his aides. The policy of ruling out British membership for the current Parliament and the next was confirmed by a ballot of party members in September 1998 and this certainly reduced the intensity of internal arguments over the issue. He was also determined to have a more sceptical position, binding in the Shadow Cabinet, well in time for the 1999 European election. He wanted to attract the support of those who said 'never' to the euro, notably those who had voted for the Referendum and UKIP parties in 1997, as well as those who opposed it for the present. He had coined the well-tested title of the manifesto for the European elections, *In Europe, not run by Europe*, as long ago as the 1997 general election. Much of the party's rhetoric throughout the Parliament, however, emphasised 'Not run by Europe' rather than 'In Europe'.

The policy was driven by Hague's perceptions of the mood of the party rather than the mood of the electorate. Indeed, in October 1997 the party's private polls suggested that John Major's 'wait and see' line best met the swing voters' ambivalent mixture of scepticism, confusion, resignation and pragmatism on the euro issue. The new policy had some costs as well as gains for the party. It prompted the breakaway of a small faction of pro-euro Conservatives, who fought the 1999 European election but fared disastrously. It also meant, more importantly, that Kenneth Clarke, Ted Heath and Michael Heseltine (and, outside Parliament, Chris Patten) could not wholeheartedly back the party; they were waiting for another election defeat to move the party back to middle ground. Hague's line also cost some support among the City and business, but helped to harden the backing of the Eurosceptic press. He regarded the new-found unity on Europe of his Shadow Cabinet as his greatest achievement. 'They now say we are united on Europe, but divided on drugs', he commented to colleagues in September 2000. In contrast to the 1997 election he added 'We want to talk about Europe, Labour doesn't.' Hague felt vindicated by victory in the 1999 Euro elections, the party's first success in a nation-wide election since 1992 (admittedly on only 35.8 per cent of the vote). It also strengthened his leadership in the party. Later, he pledged that a Conservative government would renegotiate the Nice Treaty and try to ring-fence UK domestic law from incursions from the European Court of Justice.

Peter Lilley was relieved of duties as Shadow Chancellor in June 1998 so that he could concentrate on the review of policy. Lilley felt that it was foolish to make precise commitments too early in the Parliament and that bright ideas might be pinched by Labour. There was no coordinating machinery available and most shadow ministers failed to initiate detailed policy work. Lilley was impressed by reports of the voters' distrust of the party on the core public services. It was seen as unsympathetic on schools, health and social security and in favour of privatisation of these services. He decided to use the annual R.A. Butler Lecture in April 1999 to reassure voters that privatisation was not on the Conservative agenda and the services would remain as state responsibilities. Unfortunately the speech coincided with a dinner to celebrate the twentieth anniversary of Mrs Thatcher first becoming Prime Minister. To ensure ample media coverage, Nick Wood persuaded an initially reluctant Lilley, who in turn convinced Hague, that the speech should be 'spun' in advance as a significant change. Some newspapers (notably *The Times* and the *Telegraph*) as well as MPs read reports of the speech as a repudiation of Thatcherism and protested. Hague was startled at the hostility and came to the brink of resignation. This was a decisive event for him and the party (see p. 53). Lilley's position was weakened and he left the Shadow Cabinet in a reshuffle soon afterwards. Although deputy leader, he had not been close to Hague or to his inner circle, who were frustrated with the lack of progress on the policy front.

In June 1999, Andrew Lansley took over Peter Lilley's role in coordinating policy. Lansley had been elected to Parliament in 1997, and was a former director of the party's Research Department; he had played an important role in managing the 1992 general election campaign. He had also impressed Hague with his performance as the coordinator of the June 1999 Euro elections and was appointed Shadow Minister for the Cabinet Office and policy renewal.

On the policy front, there was nothing comparable to the policy exercises after 1945 and 1966 when the Conservatives had been the victim of landslides. After 1945, R.A. Butler and Harold Macmillan had forced the party to come to terms with the Attlee government's measures. They reassured voters that there would be no going back to the 1930s. Similarly, after 1966, Ted Heath instituted a wide-ranging policy review that aimed at renewing Conservatism after its 13 years in office. After 1997, however, Conservatives faced some difficulties because Labour had built so largely on the Conservative's own policies. Moreover the party was virtually bankrupt and lacked the resources to commission research. For the first two years after 1997 most shadow ministers had the equivalent of half a research assistant each. The position improved in summer 1999 when the so-called Short money available to Opposition parties was substantially increased to £3.5m annually. Although Labour MPs complained that Central Office was misusing the money, the Conservatives had in the course of negotiations with the Parliamentary Fees Office gained authorisation for this use of the funds. In an era of permanent campaigning, it must always be difficult to distinguish between parliamentary and campaigning research. In a compromise with the Shadow Cabinet, which allowed the money to be channelled through Central Office, each shadow minister had his or her own officer from the Research Department and a share of an officer employed by the media unit. This formed the basis of a much expanded war room. The Conservative Research Department was now effectively merged with the press department and mainly engaged in war room activity and in providing short-term tactical advice for shadow ministers.

There were few initiatives from the free market think-tanks that had helped Mrs Thatcher in the late 1970s. Although William Hague regularly made policy addresses at the Social Market Foundation, the Centre for Policy Studies, the Institute of Economic Affairs and Politeia, his aides complained that 'little came back'. His team looked abroad for ideas; the 'Common Sense Revolution' phrase was borrowed from the Conservative leader in Ontario, Mike Harris, and Governor George W. Bush's advisers worked out the theme of compassionate conservatism. Policies on 'free' schools and welfare reform reflected some ideas from the United States and had been worked up by Nye and Finkelstein in their earlier days at the Social Market Foundation. Interestingly, there was little reference to the ideas of European centre-right parties. Yet, compared with the radical changes to the party organisation and the operations in Central Office, on policy there was, to quote Archie Norman, something of 'an ideas fatigue'. In some desperation, Hague, helped by Lansley, Finkelstein and Osborne, wrote *The Common Sense Revolution*, for the 1999 conference. 'We have to have something', said one of them. The document provided a number of 'guarantees' (including one on tax) that would make for a 'smaller government, bigger citizens' society.

One difficulty for any Opposition is that it has to respond to a policy agenda largely set by the government of the day. Shortly after his appointment in February 2000 as Shadow Chancellor, Michael Portillo accepted the independence of the Monetary Policy Committee of the Bank of England and the minimum wage, both of which had been opposed by the party when Labour introduced them. These were regarded by the press as Portillo-inspired initiatives. In fact they had been discussed for several weeks beforehand – as Shadow Chancellor, Maude had established a committee to report on the Bank of England – and Portillo had favoured independence for the Bank when he was in government. But his announcement dramatised them. In July 2000, following lengthy discussions with Hague, he also extricated the party from Maude's 1999 'tax guarantee' pledge to reduce taxation as a share of GDP over the next Parliament.

Portillo was also determined to restore public trust in the party's economic policy by introducing his own macroeconomic disciplines. These included greater independence for the Bank's Monetary Policy Committee (its members would be appointed for seven years, not the lifetime of a Parliament, and a committee would oversee appointments) and establishing a Council of Economic Advisers to act as a fiscal policy watchdog on the Chancellor. At 'away-days' Portillo found that all spending shadows, except for David Willetts, pressed for larger budgets while supporting tax cuts.

Portillo mapped out a tax-cutting agenda for his party. Although Gordon Brown kept his 1997 pledge not to raise the rates of income tax, he steadily increased indirect taxes and national insurance contributions. By summer 2000 these so-called 'stealth taxes' were meeting public resistance, which culminated in the petrol blockade by farmers, hauliers and tanker drivers, starting in September. After some delay, Portillo promised a substantial cut in the duty on petrol and the abolition of tax on unearned income for those earning less than £32,785 a year. In response to Labour's announced plans to boost public spending on key services by £73 billion cumulatively between 2001 and 2004, he promised an increase of £65 billion (matching Labour spending plans on schools, health, and crime) and calculated that he could trim spending elsewhere to offer £8 billion in tax reductions. Although the policy allowed Labour to ask which services would be cut to pay for the reductions, Portillo was sure that the planned growth of public spending was not sustainable in the long term and promised to limit it to the rate of growth in the economy. Some commentators were unimpressed with the package of improved public services and tax cuts.[3]

The party opposed most of Labour's constitutional changes until they had been achieved. Hague continued to raise the 'English question' in the wake of devolution to Scotland and Wales, and promised to end the right of Scottish MPs to vote on English legislation. Theresa May was determined to establish new Conservative territory by promising to 'free' schools from local education authorities, allowing them to set their own standards on discipline, selection and staffing, and to give more financial autonomy to universities. Although Alan Milburn, the Health Secretary, eventually provided opportunity for cooperation with the private sector, Liam Fox received little encouragement in his plans to expand private insurance schemes. According to a party strategist: 'We want to take the politics out of health by converging with Labour. We want target voters to think there is not much difference between the parties.' Yet a sentence in *Kitchen Table Conservatives* – 'we have failed to get across what we will do about public services' – still held true. David Willetts, the social security spokesman, proposed that free TV licences for the over-75s, Christmas bonuses, and winter fuel allowances be consolidated into the basic state pension. But after Gordon Brown's promise of a substantial increase in the basic pension in late 2000 the policy had to be modified. Pensioners were given the option of retaining the additional 'perks' or having them consolidated into the basic pension.

Over the summer months of 2000, Andrew Lansley collated the reports from the party's various study groups. He and Danny Finkelstein wrote a follow-up to *The Common Sense Revolution,* which became effectively a draft manifesto, *Believing in Britain,* presented at the October party conference.

In the course of the Parliament the party revised a number of policies. These included pensions proposals, the guarantee to cut taxation as a share of national income, and the guarantee to reduce waiting time for NHS patients. Each was later abandoned on grounds of administrative practicality or because of lobbying. More embarrassing was drugs. When Ann Widdecombe unveiled a proposal to impose fixed penalty fines on drug users at the party conference in October 2000, there was widespread alarm about large numbers of middle-class young thereby being given a criminal record. Several members of the Shadow Cabinet quickly confessed, in response to allegedly planted press questions, that they had used drugs when younger. Although the policy had been cleared with Hague beforehand, it was now in ruins; the leader and his shadow home secretary had to beat a hasty retreat.

Colleagues were puzzled by Hague's mixture of social liberalism (for example, his vote in 1994 for reducing the homosexual age of consent to 16 as well as open support of multiculturalism), and authoritarianism (for example, retaining Section 28, and a tough stand on 'bogus' asylum seekers). They contrasted the symbolic significance of his attendance at the Notting Hill Carnival in 1997 and his calls at the outset of his leadership for the party to be inclusive with his controversial 'foreign land' speech at Harrogate in March 2001 (see p. 62). 'How can we create a coherent narrative from these different images?' asked one strategist. During the first two years, Hague sought to broaden the party's appeal in line with his interest in capturing the floating or 'swing' voters. But in the final two years of the Parliament, he was more interested in consolidating his core vote, expressing sympathy for Tony Martin's use of a gun, supporting the petrol protesters, and endorsing Ann Widdecombe's proposal to place asylum seekers in secure detention centres on their arrival in the United Kingdom. Had Hague changed his mind on social issues, did he deliberately alter electoral strategy, or had he not thought it through? The editor of *The Times* let Hague know that he felt 'betrayed' by the change. On 2 May 2000, Hague commented on the shift to aides: 'Have I done this the wrong way round?' But when questioned about the apparent contradictions, he was unapologetic. He saw no contradiction and thought that the alleged problem arose from the mutually exclusive stereotypes employed by his critics.

A number of events paved the way for the core vote strategy. One was the Lilley speech in April 1999. William Hague was already taken aback by the hostile reaction. His position was under threat, his public image was poor, his party languished in the opinion polls, and his activists were complaining. The Lilley speech, which was presented as a break with Thatcherism, was the last straw for many of them. Hague was so dismayed at his misjudgement that he thought of resigning. 'He had to protect his position; if ever the core voters defected, he was finished. We could not reach out for new voters until we had shored up our core vote', said one adviser. An aide added, 'I won't say he panicked – he's not that sort of person – but a big hole opened up before us.' Colleagues date the beginning of the shift in strategy to this period. It was the end of any serious engagement in 'Kitchen Table Conservatism' or any attempt to take on the right of the party. The term 'core vote' was used in a small circle in Central Office, and not for outside. Advocates of 'core plus' claim that the intention was to broaden the party's appeal once the core had been established.

Reinforcement came from Hague's visit to North America in February 1999. He was impressed at how Republican Governor Bush in Texas, as well as conservative leaders in New York and Canada, had used right-wing positions to win elections. When the anti-euro message of the European election campaign in June 1999 was crowned with an election victory, Hague felt that his concentration on the core vote was vindicated. He also believed that his opposition to the euro was a vote-winner.

Finally, mounting public concern about asylum seekers, the petrol blockade, and Tony Martin's arrest, provided opportunities for Hague to take strong positions and gain applause from the *Sun, Daily Mail* and *Daily Telegraph*. When Platell and Wood learnt of a forthcoming feature in a paper, one aide said that their message to Hague was: 'We've got to be in this story'. The strategy certainly seemed to be working in terms of getting coverage. But not all members of the Shadow Cabinet were pleased at the impression that the party's policy was being driven by the short-term news agenda of these papers. Archie Norman reflected, 'The core vote approach means that we were talking to ourselves and not to the voters we need to win over. The media strategy seems to be our political strategy'. David Willetts asked the Shadow Cabinet: 'Is there anything we will not do to get three paragraphs on the front page?'

Responding to this concern, Hague agreed to revive the 'reach out' approach, or at least to broaden the core vote strategy. This was the case, for example, at the Harrogate Central Council in March 2000 and at the party conference in October 2000. At the latter, Portillo, Maude and Hague tried to broaden the party's appeal and there was a focus on the regeneration of inner cities. However, the message was largely undone by Ann Widdecombe's controversial speech on law and on drugs, and by the 'confessions' of her colleagues. Advocates of the more balanced approach were disheartened. 'We agree on the approach but it somehow never seems to happen or the story gets "spun" in a different way', said one member of the Shadow Cabinet. Hague himself made major speeches on education and health in June and July 2000, but was struck by how little media coverage they received. There appeared to be a gap between the political strategy agreed at senior level and the spin doctors implementing it.

Attempts to consolidate a core vote of some 30 per cent were hardly likely to win a general election. They might pay dividends in local and European contests, which was a low turnout. The Romsey by-election in May 2000, however, showed that in elections with a high turnout and with anti-Conservative tactical voting, the party was still in trouble (see p. 20). The core vote strategy was most unlikely to recommend Conservative candidates to those Tory voters who had switched to Labour or Liberal Democrat in 1997. Tony Blair had taken great risks with his own core vote in his attempt to broaden the base of Labour Party support (and gain 'soft' Tories). Modernisers looked in vain for William Hague to follow suit.

Once the reforms to the party structure had been accepted, Parkinson departed as party chairman. Michael Ancram, shadow minister for constitutional affairs and Parkinson's deputy, took over in September 1998 and served for the remainder of the Parliament. At one time Hague had seriously thought of appointing Ann Widdecombe. Archie Norman, after delivering the reform of party organisation, became chief executive in April 1998 with a remit to sort out the party's finances. The task inevitably involved the dismissal of many staff. He left in June 1999 and his successor was the new Norfolk North MP and party vice-chairman David Prior. Prior was a cost-cutting chief executive overseeing the detailed functioning of Central Office. Although the party was £9 million in deficit and contributions were falling, he managed to balance income and expenditure by March 2000. Ancram dealt largely with the voluntary side of the party, and Andrew Lansley and Tim Collins oversaw the war room in Central Office. With Hague himself in Central Office part of the day, the result to an outside observer was a messy structure.

Michael Ashcroft was appointed as party treasurer by Parkinson. He contributed £1 million annually to the party, as well as making loans and providing guarantees to the bank. He kept a tight rein on spending, at one time insisting on personally signing cheques to the value of £100 or more. His position became embroiled in controversy as *The Times* reported that his business activities in Belize were being investigated by the US regulatory authorities and suggested that it was improper for the party to be beholden to an expatriate multi-millionaire who represented Belize at the United Nations. An embarrassing libel action threatened and for a while the Political Honours Scrutiny Committee blocked Ashcroft's proposed ennoblement.

Ashcroft acknowledged that, in the new climate created by the Nolan recommendations about party finances, the party should reduce its dependence on large donations, particularly if the donor demanded secrecy. His department compiled a mailing list of some 30,000 donors, who collectively raised £600,000 yearly. In addition, large contributors were rewarded with access to lunches and functions with leading party figures. These included the Renaissance Forum (for contributions of £10,000) and the Front Bench Club (for donations of £5,000). In early 2001, help arrived with a £5 million gift from the Chairman of I.G. Index, Stuart Wheeler. Known to very few was the fact that it was conditional on the party maintaining its campaign to save the pound.

William Hague and his staff spent mornings in Central Office, afternoons in the Commons. Each morning at 9 a.m. Hague chaired a 30-minute session with shadow ministers, party officials and his advisers, to review the daily press and decide on themes and lines for the day. Previous Conservative leaders, particularly when based in 10 Downing Street, had not shown much interest in Central Office as long as it won elections. The physical presence of the party leader and his team in Central Office certainly altered the chemistry of power relationships in the building. Officials reported to the chief executive and the politicians reported to Hague. There was a notable reduction in the standing of the party chairman, and directors went directly to the party leader when the opportunity allowed. Ancram, however, was popular with the constituency associations, and loyal to Hague. These reforms, however, failed to reverse the sharp decline in party membership during the 1990s. In spite of reduced subscriptions and ambitious targets, it remained around 320,000, and it was elderly and comfortably middle class. Hague's rash promise to double the membership was confounded.

Stephen Gilbert became director of field operations, in succession to Tony Garrett. Garrett opposed Norman's decision to downgrade the area offices and dismiss many staff and was sacked by Norman in July 1998. Gilbert's unit was in charge of the nuts and bolts of campaigning in the constituencies. He was helped by 28 area campaign directors (who were also constituency agents) and an agency service, over which the centre had at long last achieved effective control. Research commissioned from ICM, the party's polling agency, was used to identify likely swing voters, such as 1997 Labour voters who were thinking of defecting. Gilbert concentrated direct mail and telephone canvassing on swing voters in 180 target seats. By late 2000, the Central Office direct call centre (known internally as GENEVA) contained 60 terminals, staffed by volunteers, and by early March 2001 staff were making up to 10,000 calls a day and had reduced the target voters down to 1.5 million. In the target seats, ICM identified constituency neighbourhoods which contained voters with the demographic and lifestyle characteristics of swing voters. Callers contacted the voters and immediately deleted firm Conservative or Labour supporters as targets. The interviews were used to identify the issues of concern to respondents, who then received 'personalised' letters from William Hague. All-important campaigning activity was concentrated in the war room on the second floor of Central Office, where some 50 research and press staff worked closely together. Day-to-day control was exercised by Rick Nye, who in turn reported to Tim Collins as party vice-chairman.

The House of Commons did not present many opportunities for the party. Many Labour ministers took Parliament for granted and Conservative MPs were greatly outnumbered. A number of heavyweight ministers from John Major's government went to the House of Lords, and Michael Heseltine and Kenneth Clarke were quiet on the back-benches. The sense of impending election defeat may also have undermined the effectiveness of the shadow front bench. Neither Francis Maude nor Michael Portillo made much impression on the formidable Chancellor of the Exchequer. Only Ann Widdecombe as Opposition health and then Home Office spokesman had much success in advancing her position in Parliament.

Yet, throughout much of 1998, 1999 and 2000, Hague's debating skills at the Despatch Box, especially at Prime Minister's Questions, heartened supporters. On many occasions his combination of humour and aggression enabled him to outshine Blair, although it did little to improve his standing with voters. The two leaders exchanged soundbites, already tested in focus groups, across the despatch box. 'All mouth and no delivery', 'Tony's cronies' and 'stealth taxes' resonated with voters. But when Hague sprang to the defence of Tony Martin, and praised the petrol blockade protesters as 'fine, upstanding citizens', pledged cuts in the excise duty on petrol and complained about 'bogus' asylum seekers and interventions by the EU Commission, Blair countered effectively by attacking Hague's 'bandwagon' approach.

The party never recovered the scale of press support it had enjoyed until 1992. In 1997, six of the ten daily newspapers had endorsed Labour and a couple of the others offered only lukewarm support for the Conservative Party. Although the Eurosceptic press welcomed William Hague's decision to rule out membership of the single currency for two Parliaments at least, the party's lack of voter support was a dampener on more enthusiastic press endorsement. Hague maintained good relations with editors Charles Moore (*Daily Telegraph*), Paul Dacre (*Daily Mail*), David Yelland (*Sun*) and Dominic Lawson (*Sunday Telegraph*). Indeed his decision to bring forward the party leader's speech at the annual conference from Friday to Thursday was done at Moore's urging. But before the election campaign, the Conservatives never matched the Labour government's formidable communications machine.[4]

Initially, the party's media relations were handled by Gregor Mackay. In March 1999, in the hope of gaining a higher profile, Amanda Platell, a former *Sunday Express* editor, replaced him as head of media. She joined Nick Wood who had been recruited a few months earlier from *The Times* to handle the lobby on behalf of Hague and the shadow team. Their efforts highlighted right-wing policies and helped to improve media coverage, not least by the *Mail* and *Telegraph*. More cynical Conservatives reflected that the press, like the voters, turned its fire on the government without endorsing the Opposition. Platell did not concern herself much with the details of policy or even debates about strategy; some regarded her hostility to complaints about the lack of a coherent strategy for the party as misplaced loyalty to Hague. Her answer to such discussions was simply, 'Let William be William.' She acquired a reputation as a fierce guardian of the leader and as a force for driving suspected supporters of Portillo out of Central Office.

Platell was involved in the uneasy relations at the top of the party. Francis Maude reacted badly to the way that the media team handled his 1999 reshuffle from Shadow Chancellor to Shadow Foreign Secretary, and took some time to become reconciled to the move. He and Portillo were incensed by Platell's allegations that their aides, with or without their connivance, were plotting against Hague. One week after Portillo had joined the Shadow Cabinet, he and Maude confronted the leader and protested that Platell was destroying team spirit by briefing against them. They asked for her to be dismissed and also expressed concerns about Coe and Wood; by implication, if this was not forthcoming they would resign. Hague, sensing that his authority was under challenge, called their bluff and refused. When faced with a similar ultimatum later in the year, he warned that if they resigned, so would he.

Hague and his aides spent much time mending fences with Portillo and, more often, dissuading Maude from resigning. On one occasion the latter did submit a letter of resignation to Hague. Hague and some of his staff felt undermined by constant media speculation about leadership plots, although Portillo aides retorted that the speculation was encouraged by Hague's media team. There were significant costs in terms of mutual trust at the top, not least between Maude and Portillo, on one side, and Platell and Wood, and by association Hague, on the other. Hague himself found it all wearying and dispiriting. Along with the bad press and poor polls, it was another reason that periodically led him to think of giving up during 2000. Until the eve of the general election, Hague's team and Ancram were convinced that Portillo's supporters were poised to mount a post-election challenge for the leadership and thought that he could have acted more decisively to curb them.

Hard-pressed directors at Central Office looked back wistfully to the 1997 election campaign when the party had spent £27 million. Maurice Saatchi, who had handled all advertising campaigns for the party between 1979 and 1997, agreed with Central Office that his M&C Saatchi agency would not be involved in the future. The party managers looked for an agency that would be cheaper and over which they had more political control. William Hague himself was keen to appoint an agency that was, as Saatchi and Saatchi had been in 1978, relatively new and ambitious to make its reputation in the Conservative account.

Rick Nye drew up a shortlist of agencies which were given a remit to prepare a strategy to win the next general election and to recapture swing voters. The agency Yellow M, appointed in May 2000, was based in Newcastle and Edinburgh, and was appreciably smaller than Labour's TBWA. But it had made its reputation with aggressive advertising for the party during the Scottish parliamentary campaign when one of its posters carried the slogan 'BLIAR'. Its 34-year-old creative director, Ronnie Duncan, had voted Labour in 1997 and Liberal Democrat in local elections.

The agency's early advertisements were aimed at swing (or target) voters and designed to maximise dissatisfaction with the government and its failure to deliver better services. The initial theme was 'Pay more

---

(tax), get less (services)'. In January, the posters asked: 'You've paid the taxes, so where is … ?' In February the 'Can you wait four more years?' posters attacked the government's increase in red tape for teachers, nurses and the police. The ads did not mention Labour and only mentioned the word 'Conservatives' almost as a footnote. The poster campaign was negative, designed to put Labour on the defensive. The hopes of some Conservatives that the party would sell its own plans in later advertisements were not fulfilled. One person closely involved in this exercise could not see any ultimate benefit for the party without the last stage: 'The slogan certainly reflects the voters' mood, but they then say, "So what? The Conservatives will do even worse."'

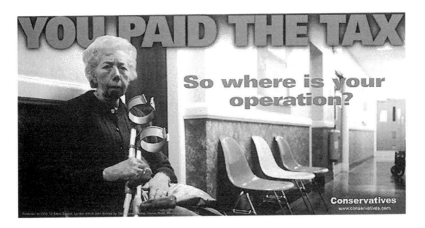

Conservative opinion polling remained with Nick Sparrow's ICM. Cecil Parkinson rebuffed an approach from Bob Worcester of MORI, made soon after the 1997 election. Quantitative polling was limited until the summer of 1999 because of lack of funds. For the first two years, Sparrow liaised with Andrew Cooper, who was in charge of polling and strategy at Central Office. At annual 'away-days', Sparrow's presentations reminded MPs and the Shadow Cabinet members how unpopular they and the party were. When Cooper left Central Office in summer 1999 his remit on political strategy and polling was absorbed by Rick Nye as Director of the Research Department. Sparrow wrote memos for Hague less frequently than Philip Gould did for Blair and, when he made his occasional oral presentations to Hague, the leader was usually accompanied only by his immediate aides. No other MPs were present.

Sparrow's focus groups with swing voters and his ad hoc surveys told a story similar to that of the public opinion polls. By mid-2000 the party had been stranded around the 30 per cent mark for some eight years, and Labour was comfortably ahead on all the key issues. Voters' disappointment with the government's record on delivery was not translating into significantly greater Conservative popularity. The party's support in the polls dipped in late 1999, when critical media stories affecting Jeffrey Archer, Michael Ashcroft, Jonathan Aitken, Neil Hamilton, and Shaun Woodward revived pre-1997 memories of sleaze and internal divisions. Andrew Lansley's paper for the Strategy Group in February 2000 commented on the downturn: 'This suggests that we do not have the change in image to distance ourselves from negative image factors. A continuing reduction in the likelihood of voting Labour is not being accompanied by an increasing likelihood of voting Conservative.' The opinion poll fillip that came with the petrol blockade in September proved to be short-lived.

Sparrow's research was used in helping to formulate David Willetts' original package of pension benefit changes in summer 2000 (see p. 52), and its subsequent modification in January 2001, as well as suggesting language for use in advertisements and shadow ministers' speeches. Some shadow ministers thought that Hague and his entourage relied too much on focus groups. Critics held them responsible for his gradual dismissal of some experienced members of the Shadow Cabinet, notably John Redwood.[5] But specific personalities were never directly a subject of research. Sparrow's research also showed that even when the swing voters agreed with Conservative views, the stumbling block was the party's image. 'The problem for them is the Conservative Party. They just do not like us', said one strategist.

Some Central Office advisers seized on parts of the research to propose an attacking Conservative agenda which centred on populist cultural and nationalist themes, as well as on the distrust of the government. They wanted to exploit the widespread view that ministers did too much spinning; had failed to deliver, particularly on health; tied people down by raising taxes too much and introducing regulations; were not standing up for Britain against the EU and against bogus asylum seekers; and were too soft on criminals and presided over a fall in police numbers. But before the election none of this translated into increased Conservative support.

From these calculations emerged, as much by default as design, the core vote strategy (see pp. 53–4). The trouble was that most of the issues relatively favourable to the Conservatives, notably tax, Europe, asylum and the euro, were of low salience to voters. The party therefore had to promote public awareness of these issues and emphasise the differences between Conservative and Labour. On issues unfavourable to the

Conservatives – notably pensions, education and health – the party should strive to depress their salience by matching Labour's spending plans, minimising the differences between the parties, and not talking about them too much. Andrew Lansley, Tim Collins and Nick Wood were strong supporters of this approach.

The thinking behind all this was similar to that in the successful 1992 election campaign in which Collins and Lansley had been closely involved. On that occasion, the Conservatives enjoyed the strong support of a number of tabloids and had managed to increase the salience of tax (a strong point for them) and lower that of health (then already a Conservative weak point). Supporters of the strategy argued either that the Conservatives simply could not compete with Labour on health and education – 'suicidal', Hague was heard to say – or that there was insufficient time before the election to work up strong policies. But in contrast to 1992, Labour in 2001 was more trusted on economic management and leadership than were the Conservatives, and the press was more pro-Labour.

Optimists, and Hague, pointed to the party's victories in the European elections and in a number of local elections. Because Labour had failed to score over 35 per cent in any of these elections, they argued that the opinion polls were wrong. The Conservatives – and parties other than Labour – did well in elections that had a few key issues and attracted a low turnout. But would this hold true in elections with a higher turnout and where the choice was for a party to form a government?

Some supporters of an alternative 'reach out' approach worried over the party's weak standing with the public on health and schools, and its failure to meet the expressed concerns of swing voters about public services and unhappiness that proposed tax cuts might undermine them further. In any case, voters were sceptical that any party would cut taxes, and worries about public services were more powerful than the appeal of tax cuts. The euro was not a salient issue for many, and Labour had promised a referendum on the issue and was preferred as the best party to manage European matters. Some strategists feared that the party was in danger of not appearing well rounded and a credible alternative party of government and of seeming to have nothing to say on the issues most important to voters. Even if it lost the coming election, the campaign would be an opportunity to shift perceptions of the party. Although they did not go public with their disquiet, it was an argument that they lost largely because they did not push hard enough for it.

The Conservative Party searched in vain for a theme. 'Thatcher had the Cold War, the over-mighty unions, and a hopeless Labour Party. We have none of them', said one strategist. Dissatisfaction with the state of public services, rising taxes, crime, and incursions from the EU did not translate into Conservative support. Expectations of an economic downturn in 1999 failed to materialise. Hague looked wistfully to Germany where the left-wing Social Democrats, having formed the government, suffered an economic downturn after six months. Moreover, the Conservatives were not given credit by voters for the economic reforms they had made before 1997 or for the success of the economy. Labour strategists had looked with interest on Hague's reforms of his party. But they dismissed comparisons with Tony Blair's modernisation of Labour. 'They have no message', was their verdict on the Tories.

Conservative leaders welcomed the annual spring conference over the weekend of 3–4 March 2001 as an opportunity to lift the spirits of MPs, candidates and party workers. Of all William Hague's speeches as party leader, none received more coverage, and none more criticism than this one. In making his familiar attacks on Labour's position on the euro, asylum seekers and constitutional changes, he warned that a second term of Labour government would turn Britain 'into a foreign land'. This echoed a theme from his 1999 conference speech, the peroration of which had been: 'Come with me and I will give you back your country.' *The Times*, in an editorial, condemned 'alien rhetoric' and warned that Hague should temper his language 'or lose his honour'. The *Sun* newspaper, more surprisingly, immediately damned it as xenophobic and extreme. A number of Conservative strategists and politicians were taken aback by the hostile reaction and blamed the 'spin' imparted by the media team. They claimed that the controversial passage was about the impact on Britain of a more integrated Europe, which would follow from another four years of a Labour government, not about asylum or race – although party spin doctors had apparently made the connection in briefing journalists. Many suspected that the *Sun*'s opposition to the Harrogate speech was a trailer for endorsing Labour in the coming election. They were correct.

By March 2001, William Hague could point to a number of achievements in his four years' leadership. He had created a new party structure, introduced a new leadership team, and united the Shadow Cabinet and much of the party on Europe. Labour's modernisation project had lasted for at least ten years before 1997, and had taxed three successive party leaders. In projecting himself and his team as a credible alternative government and in challenging Labour's huge lead in the opinion polls, however, Hague's efforts made little impact. He had failed to communicate a clear image of modern Conservatism or to establish its relevance to the country he sought to govern. Faced with this judgement, an aide said: 'I can't deny it, but in defence it could be said that nobody else would have done better. The mountain was too high to climb.'

Notes

1. For background on William Hague see J. Nadler, (2000).
2. See T. Hames and N. Sparrow, (1997) *Left Home: the Myth of Tory Abstentions in the Election of 1997* (CPS).
3. See P. Riddell, 'Hague's numbers game doesn't add up', *The Times*, 24 January 2001.
4. P. Oborne (1999); N. Jones, *The Control Freaks* (1999).
5. See Simon Heffer, 'Portillo's Militant Tendency', *New Statesman*, 14 February 2000.

4
Liberal Democrats and Others

Britain used to be seen as having a two-party system. As recently as 1959 there were only seven members of Parliament who did not take the Conservative or Labour whip. In 1997 there were 75. The advance of the Liberal Democrats, the Scottish and Welsh Nationalists and the various Northern Irish factions have incrementally complicated the simple picture, even though they have not won a proportionate share of London media coverage. In the 1999 elections for a Scottish Parliament and a Welsh Assembly, the nationalist parties had made a breakthrough in votes and, thanks to proportional representation, in seats. As the 2001 election approached, although the choice of forming a government was effectively confined to Conservative and Labour, the various other parties all had their own goals.

Liberal Democrats

The 1997 election gave the Liberal Democrats more representation in the House of Commons than any third party since 1929. But the election also had its disappointments. Although the party doubled its MPs, its actual vote fell to the lowest level since 1979. Moreover, the size of the Labour majority put paid to the dreams of the 'project', a Blair–Ashdown coalition of the left-centre. The 46 Liberal Democrat MPs had no serious leverage on a Labour Party of 419. The Government was carrying out some key policies that were largely in line with Liberal Democrat thinking, which made it hard for Paddy Ashdown and Charles Kennedy to give their party a distinctive image in the eyes of the public. But many inside the party as well as the wider electorate remained unclear as to whether there was a coherent strategy. Were the Liberal Democrats a party of the centre or were they trying to position themselves to the left of Labour? They seemed at times to be moving in both directions in their simultaneous pursuit of those disillusioned with the Conservatives and those disillusioned with Labour. Their large army of local councillors gave them a solid base but they had to please many other interests too. Fortunately each of the main parties found it politic not to attack the Liberal Democrats or dissect their main policies too seriously.

Yet the party was not forced into the margins. Paddy Ashdown maintained close contacts with Tony Blair. A Cabinet committee on constitutional matters was set up with Liberal Democrat members. In July 1997 Paddy Ashdown persuaded Tony Blair to agree to proportional representation for the 1999 European elections. The introduction of PR for the devolved assemblies in Scotland and Wales ensured for the Liberal Democrats a key role both in Edinburgh and Cardiff. A former party leader, Lord Jenkins, was asked to produce an alternative to first-past-the-post voting that might be put to a referendum. But the party felt frustrated that the Joint Cabinet Committee was something of a washout, especially in connection with Lords reform.

The party was considered to have fought a good campaign in 1997. The ruthless targeting of a limited number of seats had been rewarded with more victories than anyone expected. But its organisation had still smacked of the amateur approach that had so long characterised the party's efforts. After a couple of false starts a retired Admiral, Hugh Rickard, was found to take over as chief executive. Chris (later Lord) Rennard, who had made his reputation as a by-election wizard, further tightened up the party's campaigning machine. Lord Razzall became the non-executive Chairman of the campaign but left the great bulk of the work to Rennard. A veteran lobby journalist, David Walter, took over as publicity director. Richard Grayson, policy director, played a large role in drafting the manifesto.

The manifesto was offered as a 'pre-manifesto' to the Harrogate conference in September 2000 and then refined into a 20,000-word document by February 2001. This was intended to be a robust, fully-costed programme which could stand up to scrutiny, whilst also putting forward 'freedom' as the party's core value. Two issues were, of course, especially associated with the party in the public mind: euro-enthusiasm and, in a downplayed way, proportional representation. But the party still had to face the problem of getting its policies taken seriously as promises for a future government. It tried to make itself more appealing to environmentalists and civil libertarians, showing sympathy for the medical use of cannabis and crusading against the tough approach to asylum seekers shown by Jack Straw and Ann Widdecombe.

Across the country, from 1996 to 1999 the Liberal Democrats had more councillors than the Conservatives as well as having full or shared control in many more local authorities. This strong base in practical affairs helped the party to shrug off the old internal ideological struggles. The former fissures between Liberals and Social Democrats had virtually disappeared; indeed a majority of the 100,000 party members in 2000 had joined since the 1989 merger. The 46 MPs did not break up into tribes and any differences on Europe or education or foxhunting were muted. Some new back-benchers made a national impact – Evan Harris on health, Norman Baker on the Hindujas, Ed Davey on finance, Steve Webb on social security and pensions, and Paul Burstow on personal care for the elderly.

The 46 Liberal MPs had been formed into subject area teams under Paddy Ashdown but it was only under Charles Kennedy that a Shadow Cabinet was formally established. All the manifesto promises were approved by the Shadow Cabinet and discussed widely inside the party before being put to the Federal Policy Committee.

Among others the Liberal Democrats recruited Hugh Dykes, a long-serving Conservative ex-MP, and Bill Newton-Dunn, a newly returned Conservative MEP. Thanks to proportional representation, the party also secured 10 seats in the 1999 Euro elections. These, together with their 46 MPs and their balance-of-power representation in the Scottish and Welsh assemblies, meant that the party had a significant presence in every area of the country with suitable people readily available to appear on the ever more numerous regional media outlets.

Scotland and Wales presented a problem. Were campaigns for Westminster elections to be confined to the issues still decided in London, or were the regional manifestos to deal also with the matters that belonged to Edinburgh and Cardiff? The Liberal Democrats chose a broad front approach recognising that, inevitably, the campaign would be about the whole activities of government whether or not it was any business of Westminster.

There were strains in the North of England where, with the collapse of the Conservatives, Liberal Democrats had often become the principal opposition to Labour. They ousted Labour from control in their old strongholds of Liverpool and Sheffield City Councils. The Liberal Democrats had to woo tactical votes from Labour in the South and from Conservatives in the North.

The biggest boost to the party's morale came from the Romsey by-election in May 2000 when they won a safe Tory seat on an 18 per cent swing, aided by tactical voting which cut Labour support from 19 per cent to 4 per cent. If the Romsey performance could be repeated, it was argued optimistically, then another 50 seats lay within the party's grasp.

Paddy Ashdown announced in January 1999 that he was standing down. He was nearing 60 and a new leader was needed who would serve the full length of the next Parliament. The resignation was announced early so that his departure would not be seen as a reaction to whatever happened in the European contest in June of that year. Charles Kennedy and five other MPs put their names forward. On 9 August 1999, Charles Kennedy won easily over Simon Hughes.[1]

Paddy Ashdown had been a remarkable leader, exciting public esteem for his crisp, military bearing and his vigorous involvement in the Balkan scene. Since the 1992 abandonment of 'equidistance' between the two big parties, he had moved closer to Labour, especially after Tony Blair became leader. New Labour appeared unthreatening. However, the Liberal Democrats could distinguish themselves by their unfettered advocacy of proportional representation, European integration, and more spending on education. Labour found it expedient not to hit back.

Charles Kennedy had a more relaxed style of leadership than Paddy Ashdown. He seemed more cuddly and lightweight. He did, however, take a strong stand for a humane approach to asylum seekers, and he attacked William Hague far more vigorously than he attacked Tony Blair. He pressed for more spending on education and health, secure in the knowledge that neither of the other parties took the Liberal Democrats sufficiently seriously to dissect their policies. Indeed both Conservatives and Labour made strategic decisions against turning their fire nationally onto the Liberal Democrats.

The party stayed solvent. The increased Short money enabled the leader's office to be more adequately staffed. The headquarters in Cowley Street were refurbished and a sophisticated computer set-up and website were installed. By the end of 2000 Kennedy and his team were fully ready for the fray.

UKIP

The United Kingdom Independence Party was founded in 1993 by Alan Sked together with some members of the 1993 Anti-Federalist League; its simple programme was withdrawal from the European Union. In 1997 UKIP's efforts were overshadowed by the intervention of Sir James Goldsmith's Referendum Party, which put up 547 candidates. Where the two parties clashed, UKIP's 194 standard-bearers lagged behind in all but one seat.

However, after Goldsmith's death in July 1997, the Referendum Party submerged itself into the Democracy Movement, a lobbying group that would not put up candidates. UKIP had an open field. Alan Sked resigned from the party, troubled about some of its new recruits. He later supported the Conservatives. Michael Holmes and Nigel Farage took over the management of UKIP, which decided to fight on a broad range of policies. They drew the bulk of the Referendum Party activists under their wing.

The European Parliament elections in 1999 gave the party an unexpected boost. Under proportional representation they secured 7 per cent of the vote. They won seats in the South East, the South West and East Anglia, and their MEPs were able to funnel fresh resources to the party organisation.

But the party hierarchy fell out. The leader, Michael Holmes, quarrelled with some members of the National Executive. After a succession of no confidence motions had been passed against both him and the National Executive, Holmes left the party (which vainly claimed that his European seat should be transferred to his runner-up in the South West). Jeremy Titford, MEP for East Anglia, emerged as leader.

UKIP had negligible paid staff and no rich backers but it built up a membership of almost 10,000 and a network of local branches. However, the party found it hard to get attention; actor Leo McKern and the Earl of Bradford were their best-known public figures. By March 2001 there were 280 confirmed candidates; these interventions depended on the enthusiasm of local parties and were only targeted to a limited degree. In the end, thanks to the delayed election, 428 stood. However, the best-known Conservative Euro-enthusiasts were to be challenged as well as

Labour and Liberal Democrats MPs in marginal seats. In February 2001 it emerged that Lord Pearson and Lord Neidpath had privately approached Nigel Farage with a suggestion that £2 million might be given to the party in return for their withdrawing candidates who were standing against Eurosceptic Conservative MPs; nothing came of the initiative except for embarrassing headlines. In March Christopher Gill, the retiring Conservative MP for Ludlow, announced that he had left the Conservative Party and would campaign for UKIP. Roger Knapman, a former Conservative MP stood in North Devon. Paul Sykes, a Yorkshire millionaire, played a significant role in financing the party.

UKIP tried to discourage extremist infiltrators. Its supporters were mainly right of centre but it tried not to be a right-wing party. Fishermen and farmers and small businessmen provided its core support. Inevitably its central appeal was to people disgusted with Europe (and it claimed that this had brought them some recruits from the far left).

UKIP scorned the Conservative line 'In Europe, not run by Europe' and even those who argued 'Never' to the euro. However their popular appeal was limited by the basically Eurosceptic approach of William Hague's Conservatives.

The Green Party

After its tender beginnings in the 1970s first as People, and then as the Ecology Party, the Green Party made its great breakthrough in the 1989 European elections. It won 15 per cent of the national vote and came second in six seats. Its support quickly subsided to a negligible level in the next two general elections: in 1992 its 295 candidates secured an average vote of 1.3 per cent and in 1997 its 95 candidates secured an average vote of 1.4 per cent. However, it began to elect a smattering of local councillors, gaining a share of power in four local authorities.

The advent of proportional representation in 1999 offered new opportunities. The party elected two MEPs and one member of the Scottish Parliament as well as three Greater London councillors. It had only 4,000 members and a turnover of £120,000 but it began to draw increased coverage from the media.

The Greens tried to avoid being confined to ecological issues; they offered a comprehensive manifesto, broadly left-wing in tone. They were critical of European bureaucracy but they did not advocate withdrawal from the EU. They argued for more national self-sufficiency in food.

They claimed to be a political party not a pressure group but they maintained good relations with Friends of the Earth and Greenpeace. They sympathised with some forms of non-violent direct action but sought to avoid infiltration by anarchists or extremists. They wanted to escape past images of weird zealotry and to become part of the mainstream of politics, dreaming of the foothold that proportional representation for the House of Commons might offer.

The Greens on a modest scale sought the attributes of a national political party, but they could afford only two full-time employees – Chris Rose, the National Agent and Ffinlow Costain, the General Manager (although the MEPs and the London Councillors had their own teams). The party refused to have a leader. The National Executive had an annually elected chair. The two MEPs, Caroline Lucas (South East) and Jean Lambert (London), together with the two 'Principal Speakers', Mike Woodin and Margaret Wright, became the best-known representatives.

By early 2001 there were 110 prospective candidates; in the end the number of candidates reached 145. There was some strategy in their placing; where they stood depended partly on local enthusiasm (although in marginal Lewes, the party voted not to put up against the exceptionally green Liberal Democrat MP, Norman Baker). However, there was a conscious effort to ensure a regional spread (in order to secure local television coverage) and to build up local structures in areas where there was a chance of council gains or a possibility of advance if some form of proportional representation arrived.

The Scottish Greens, being independent of the English and Welsh Party, offered only four candidates. This denied the Greens a nationwide election broadcast on Channel 4 or Channel 5 because the rules provided that a party must fight a sixth of the seats in each region to qualify. The English Greens offered to guarantee the deposits of further candidates but their Scots colleagues insisted on reserving resources for the next Scottish Parliament election.

Although environmental issues were more talked about than ever the Greens had only limited scope for turning sympathy into votes. The Liberal Democrats had much greater opportunities to project themselves as the most seriously environmental party.

Scottish National Party

The 1997 election had been a disappointment to the SNP. It gained only two seats and its vote rose by only 0.6 per cent (to 22.1 per cent). But it was confirmed as the second party in Scotland and, when the devolved Parliament came into being in May 1999, its vote rose to 29 per cent. Thanks to proportional representation, it took more than a quarter of the MSPs. The party now had a watching seat at the process of government and a platform from which to preach the case for an independent

Scotland. But the SNP was still split between fundamentalists, focused on an independent Scotland, and realists who wanted to make devolution work through the Scottish Parliament. Some thought the party lacked a clear and agreed strategy.

Table 4.1   **Votes in Scotland (per cent) 1992–99**

	SNP	*Lab*	*Con*	*LibDem*
Gen. El.1992	21.5	39.0	25.6	13.1
Gen. El.1997	22.1	45.6	17.3	13.0
S. El. 7 May 1999[a]	28.8	38.8	15.6	14.2
S. El. 7 May 1999[b]	27.3	33.6	15.4	12.4
EU El. June 1999	27.2	28.7	19.8	9.8

[a] Constituency vote [b] National vote

All six Scottish National MPs became MSPs. Alex Salmond, who unexpectedly resigned as leader in September 2000 and was replaced by John Swinney, was the only MP who opted to stand again for Westminster in 2001. After the Scottish Parliament started, SNP members were largely absent from the House of Commons; but candidates were chosen early for all of the Westminster seats. In Chapter 6, James Kellas discusses the difficulties of fighting a UK election in Scotland when so much of Scottish politics now focused on Edinburgh.

Plaid Cymru

Plaid Cymru enjoyed a remarkable upsurge of support in the first Welsh Assembly elections in May 1999. Its vote jumped from 10 per cent to 31 per cent and it elected members of the Assembly in 9 of the 40 Westminster constituencies. In the late 1990s the party had very consciously changed its English label from Welsh Nationalist to 'the Party of Wales'. It ceased

Table 4.2   **Votes in Wales (per cent) 1992–99**

	PC	*Lab*	*Con*	*LibDem*
Gen. El. 1992	8.8	49.5	28.6	12.4
Gen. El. 1997	9.9	54.7	19.6	12.4
W. El. 7 May 1999[a]	30.6	35.5	16.5	12.5
W. El. 7 May 1999[b]	28.4	37.6	13.5	13.5
EU El. June 1999	29.6	31.9	22.8	9.8

[a] Constituency vote   [b] National vote

to be a separatist party, merely demanding for Cardiff the powers given to the Parliament in Edinburgh. It preserved its traditional style of trying to outflank Labour as the most left-wing party in the Principality.

In August 2001 Dafydd Wigley retired from the leadership which was taken over by Ieuan Wyn Jones. Karl Davies and a staff of five ran the Cardiff headquarters. Inevitably their activities focused largely on the activities of the new Assembly.

Socialists

Three left-wing groupings were heard from as the election approached. The Socialist Alliance was based on the old Militant tendency and had David Nellist, the former Coventry MP, at its head. The Socialist Labour Party had been formed by the miners' leader Arthur Scargill in 1996 and Scargill himself took on Peter Mandelson in Hartlepool. The Scottish Socialist Party had the support of Tommy Sheridan, who had won a Glasgow seat in the 1999 elections to the Scottish Parliament: it fought every seat in Scotland, cashing in on the idea that the SNP had become 'men in suits' as they cooperated with other MSPs in Edinburgh.

Others

The other candidates who drew some attention had no national organisation. The most notable was the Independent MP Martin Bell who (as promised) moved from Tatton and fought Brentwood, challenging a split Conservative organisation. Christine Oddy, a disgruntled ex-Labour MEP fought Coventry North-West. Dr Richard Taylor, disillusioned with the closure of units at the local hospital, mounted a serious challenge to Labour in Wyre Forest. Labour rebels in Hartlepool, Gloucester, St Helens South, and Perry Barr also attracted notice – but not much. Candidates were nominated by 75 registered parties.

Note

1. C. Kennedy 22,724, S. Hughes 16,233, M. Bruce 4,643, J. Ballard 3,978, D. Rendel 3,428. After reallocation of preferences: C. Kennedy 28,425 (57%), S. Hughes 21,833 (43%).

1. Tony Blair and David Blunkett arrive at St Olave's School

2. Tony Blair and Gordon Brown at a Millbank press conference

4. Peter Hyman, Douglas Alexander, Philip Gould, and Margaret McDonagh

3. John Prescott punches a protester in Rhyl

5. William Hague launches the Conservative manifesto

6. Michael Portillo

7. William Hague (Michael Ancram in background)

8. Francis Maude

9. Andrew Lansley and Liam Fox

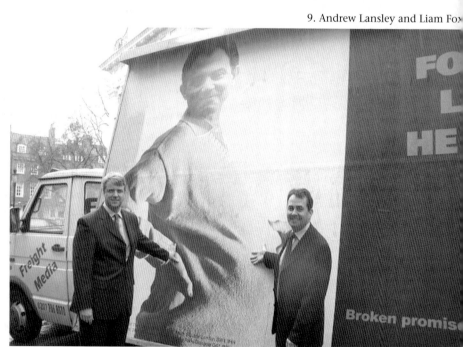

10. Charles Kennedy with (*clockwise*) Alan Beith, Menzies Campbell, Dr Jenny Tonge, Colin Breed, Don Foster, Malcolm Bruce

11. Paddy Ashdown hands over the Liberal Democrat leadership to Charles Kennedy

12. Lord (Chris) Rennard

13. John Swinney

14. Ieuan Wyn Jones

15. Peter Snow on the BBC's election night programme

16. The Electoral Commissioners (Glyn Mathias, Sir Neil McIntosh, Pamela Gordon, Sam Younger (Chairman), Professor Graham Zellick, Karamjit Singh)

17. Jeremy Paxman interviewing Tony Blair

18. Paxman interviewing William Hague

5
The Coming of the Election

Since 1987 parties, particularly in government, have usually undertaken what they call a 'near term campaign'. In the months before the calling of the election, party managers pursue what is, in effect, a dress rehearsal for the real thing. It supplements or replaces the old-style launch of the manifesto; this used to crowd the display of all their new promises into one day, but now they are unveiled one by one over several weeks. The parties can test themes, spokespersons, and press conference and war room arrangements. They also try to set the media agenda, with daily announcements, new policies and initiatives; these can be linked to activities in Parliament, to the leaders' tours and interviews, and to the ongoing work of government, including the budget. The governing party is at an advantage, partly because the greater resources of incumbency enable the government to make news, partly because it can still decide the date of the election. Yet the opposition parties cannot afford to be idle. In early 1997, Labour successfully nullified a number of Conservative initiatives by launching their own initiatives. In January 1992, however, Labour had been unsuccessful in trying to counter the Conservative tax bombshell campaign.

For much of the 1997–2001 Parliament, voters and politicians could be forgiven for campaign fatigue. In addition to regular local and by-elections, there were also referendums in Scotland, Wales, Northern Ireland, and London, to approve the various devolution proposals. These were followed by elections for the various new legislatures. The pro-active approach to the media by the Blair government, and the constant monitoring of the public mood through opinion polls and focus groups, as well as through radio and television phone-ins and talk shows, made it seem that Britain was witnessing a permanent campaign.

Gordon Brown's Budget speech was received more favourably than William Hague's references to Britain becoming a 'foreign land'.

Peter Brookes, *The Times*, 7 March 2001.

Although the government had been preparing for the general election since the beginning of the year, Gordon Brown's fifth budget on 7 March represented a significant change of gear. The government had a good story to tell on the economy, not least the surplus on the public finances. Brown prided himself on the economic stability that had been achieved during his stewardship. This would be the foundation for the policies designed to improve the public services. He was not prepared to offer what might be regarded as irresponsible tax cuts in a pre-election budget; these might imperil stability as well as limiting the room for spending. The broad outline of the budget had been foreshadowed the previous November in the Pre-Budget Report, which announced the increase in pensions and the cut in the duty on petrol. The budget also widened the 10p starting rate of income tax and set out further tranches of public spending on schools and hospitals over the next three years. There had been some discussion between Number 10 and Number 11 about tax cuts, but the policy on the 10p rate was Brown's. The unemployment numbers in March and April were the lowest for over 20 years. In the concluding remarks of his budget speech, Brown struck an electioneering note; having achieved economic stability, Labour was now able to rebuild the public services, and would invest heavily in schools and the NHS. These three themes would be the essential building blocks of Labour's election campaign. The budget, and Gordon Brown as Chancellor, received record opinion poll endorsement. MORI found 55 per cent approval for the Chancellor, well above most of his earlier ratings and far above the level achieved by his predecessors.

In a reminder of the final weeks of John Major's government, questions of standards and ethics of ministers were raised. Peter Mandelson's resignation of 24 January over alleged intervention to help a Hinduja passport application had its echo on 9 March with the report, by Sir Anthony Hammond, which cleared him of any improper involvement. The judgment in turn raised questions over the speed with which Blair had dismissed Mandelson. However, Keith Vaz, the Minister for Europe, was rebuked by the House of Commons Standards Committee for refusing to answer the questions of their Commissioner, Elizabeth Filkin. Former minister Geoffrey Robinson was also criticised for lack of candour about his financial links with the late Robert Maxwell.

Although a prime minster is virtually free to decide the date of a general election, the choice is subject to constraints. To call one less than four years into a government's life, and with a secure majority, might look opportunistic. In Tony Blair's case, the four-year watershed was May 2001. Margaret Thatcher in June 1983 and June 1987 had gone to the country after four years. John Major in April 1992 and May 1997 had waited five years, in the hope of an upturn in the opinion polls. Prime ministers know that the stakes are high since getting the date wrong means being ejected from power. Mrs Thatcher, in spite of favourable opinion polls in 1983 and 1987 and a divided Opposition, still waited for further reassurance from local election results and private opinion polls conducted in marginal seats, as well as the assent of senior colleagues, before she took her final decision.

A prime minister usually has a long-prepared list of preferred election dates. Tony Blair's entourage and the Millbank apparatchiks had for at least two years pencilled in 3 May 2001. He would have served for four years, it would follow a budget, which hopefully would be a tangible reminder of Labour's successful management of the economy, and, because it would coincide with shire contests, it would help to mobilise a Labour vote and avoid the embarrassment of adverse local election results. Opinion hardened during the autumn, as the party recovered its substantial lead in the opinion polls. Planning meetings until then had

Table 5.1   Chronology of the near term campaign

January

3 Jan.	Ld Hamlyn gives £2m to Labour.
	Sir W. Macpherson says Hague is not playing race card.
	Tories unveil plans to cut £425m from £11 billion housing benefit.
4 Jan.	US interest rates cut by 1%.
5 Jan.	Ld Sainsbury and C. Ondaatje each give £2m to Labour.
	Brown in *Times* interview rules out tax cuts.
	Blair says Labour close to keeping four of its five pledges.
6 Jan.	Report reveals at least 236 deaths due to Dr Shipman.
7 Jan.	Blair on *Breakfast with Frost* says joining euro 'sensible in principle'.
9 Jan.	Conservatives launch poster campaign.
	Blair launches 10-year battle on crime.
10 Jan.	Blair hit by a tomato in Bristol.
11 Jan.	Scandal of radioactive shells.
12 Jan.	Brown speaks about community volunteers.
	Hague backs Star Wars.
14 Jan.	Hague on *Breakfast with Frost*.
15 Jan.	Blunkett announces £4bn for the repair of schools.
16 Jan.	Metric law case begins.
17 Jan.	Scandal of adopted American twins.
	Stuart Wheeler gives £5m to the Conservatives.
	Blair rules out TV debate with Opposition leaders.
18 Jan.	Foxhunting ban passes 2nd Reading by 387 to 174.
19 Jan.	Gallup poll says 58% against parties' dependence on large donors.
20 Jan.	George W. Bush succeeds Clinton as US President.
21 Jan.	Tories announce plans to privatise Channel 4.
22 Jan.	Meacher revealed as owning nine houses.
	House of Lords approves controversial stem cell research by 219 to 92.
23 Jan.	Hague pledges to match Labour spending plans on social services and police.
	Labour launch national advertising campaign.
	Hague says he would be happy to see women fighting on the front line.
24 Jan.	Mandelson resigns as NI Sec. over Hinduja passports. Reid succeeds him.
28 Jan.	Portillo announces planned changes to the taxation of savings.
29 Jan.	UKIP allegedly demands £1m from Cons to drop challenge to 30 MPs.
	Kennedy describes Lib–Lab pact or tactical alliance as 'preposterous'.
30 Jan.	Alder Hey report on post mortem organ stealing.
31 Jan.	One Libyan found guilty in Lockerbie trial.
	Hague speaks about public service reform.

February

1 Feb.	Corus announce 6,050 steelworker sackings, more than 20% of workforce.
2 Feb.	Treasury Committee criticises Chancellor's dominance.
	Blair admits that sterling's strength can be a problem.
5 Feb.	One-day London Tube strike.
	Cook endorses euro in *Times* interview.
	Labour unveils its new 'cross my heart' logo.

	Jenkin announces Con plans to replace bus lanes with cycle lanes.
6 Feb.	Redwood says that Britain must cut its EU contribution.
7 Feb.	Blair promises euro decision in two years.
8 Feb.	Bank of England cuts interest rates by 0.25% to 5.75%.
9 Feb.	Gallup puts Lab 21% ahead.
10 Feb.	Cons change pensions plan.
12 Feb.	Blair announces plans to close 'bog standard' state schools.
13 Feb.	Inland Revenue criticises Con pensions plan.
14 Feb.	Hague vows to restore grammar schools.
15 Feb.	In Commons debate on Phillips Report, Con ex-ministers fend off blame for BSE.
16 Feb.	UK and US fighter planes bomb Iraq.
	Blair says euro is too big an issue to be wrapped up in election campaign.
17 Feb.	Ld Irvine criticised over Labour lawyers' fund-raising dinner.
18 Feb.	Blair tells Labour activiststs to 'fight for a second term on our terms'.
	Sir M. Rifkind rules himself out of Con leadership race.
19 Feb.	Prescott announces £200m subsidy for rural buses over three years.
20 Feb.	Cons announce plans for private medical insurance tax breaks.
	First foot and mouth case.
21 Feb.	Meat and dairy product export ban introduced because of FMD.
22 Feb.	Reports that Con left would back Portillo for the leadership.
23 Feb.	Blair has first meeting with President Bush in Washington.
	Home Office figures show 10% rise in asylum applications in Jan. 2001.
25 Feb.	Hague tells Cons to be ready for a 5 April general election.
26 Feb.	Dando murder trial begins.
	Countryside Alliance calls off its March protest in London.
	Straw announces 10-year plan to reform criminal justice.
	Dartmoor is closed to the public for the first time ever.
27 Feb.	Straw criticises lawyers for failing to fulfil social duty.
	US Ambassador to London rebukes Cons for using his name in fundraising leaflets.
28 Feb.	Rail crash at Great Heck on the East Coast Main Line.
	Government announces £1.5bn road-building plans.

March

1 Mar.	Hague backs Macpherson Report.
4 Mar.	Hague says a Lab election win will cause Britain to become 'a foreign land'.
	Heseltine will vote Tory, despite Eurosceptic policy.
6 Mar.	CPS accuses Chancellor of introducing 45 'stealth taxes' since 1997.
	Tories promise to protect homes of elderly savers.
	Government announces that minimum wage will rise to £4.10 from October 2001.
7 Mar.	Brown delivers his fifth budget.
9 Mar.	Report by Sir A. Hammond clears Mandelson over Hinduja passports.
10 Mar.	Gallup survey for *Telegraph* shows Brown is most popular post-war Chancellor.
12 Mar.	Vaz rebuked for refusing to answer questions of Parliamentary Commissioner.

Table 5.1   Chronology of the near term campaign *continued*

13 Mar.	Conservative Party membership reported to have hit post-war low of 300,000.
	Milburn offers GPs an extra £10,000 each to alleviate shortages.
14 Mar.	Unemployment falls below 1 million for first time in 25 years.
	Prince of Wales gives £500,000 to farmers.
15 Mar.	Back-bench Tory MPs call for general election delay.
19 Mar.	Blair 'opens war on voter apathy'.
20 Mar.	*Sun* declares that the general election will be on 3 May.
21 Mar.	Blair and Hague both speak at high-profile Islamic events this week.
	Blair heckled at Islamic community awards ceremony.
	Blair says election delay would signal Britain was 'closed for business'.
	Hague rebuked by Parliamentary Standards Commissioner.
	Prince of Wales reported as going 'into purdah for election'.
22 Mar.	Major calls for election delay.
	Labour–Liberal Democrat compromise on PR.
	MPs vote to introduce secret ballot for future elections of a Speaker.
23 Mar.	Labour rural MPs 'back May election', but polls show public opposition.
	Blair heard discussing election date with Romano Prodi in Stockholm.
25 Mar.	PLP reported as 70% for 3 May; 20% unsure; 10% against.
28 Mar.	MORI poll in *The Times* highlights urban–rural divide.
29 Mar.	Vaz collapses during interview.
	C. Gill, Con MP for Ludlow, resigns from party.
	Archbishop of York calls for election to be delayed until autumn.
	Blair launches bid for faith vote.
31 Mar.	*Sun* and *Times* reveal that the election will be delayed until 7 June.
April	
2 Apr.	Blair announces local elections will be delayed until 7 June.
4 Apr.	Bill to delay local elections in England until 7 June passed in one day.
5 Apr.	Hague demands extra payments for farmers affected by foot and mouth.
8 Apr.	*News of the World* publishes full transcript of Sophie Wessex tapes.
9 Apr.	Sunderland market trader convicted of not using metric measures.
10 Apr.	Parliament adjourns for Easter recess.
	Blair in talks to save Motorola jobs.
11 Apr.	Mandelson attacks Hague and Tories.
	March unemployment at 995,200 – a 25-year low.
13 Apr.	Good Friday.
15 Apr.	Easter Sunday.
16 Apr.	Con PPC for Torbay on firearms charge.
	Clarke denies moves to remove Hague as Con Party leader.
17 Apr.	Government accepts limited FMD vaccination in principle.
	Portillo says poor are getting poorer under Labour.
18 Apr.	Teachers' unions call for a 35-hour week.
	Tacticalvoter.net web-site launched.
19 Apr.	Cook speech on Britishness to the Centre for Open Society.
20 Apr.	Commisssion for Racial Equality publishes names of Con MPs who will not sign pre-election race pledge.
23 Apr.	Portillo claims tax for poorest 20 per cent has risen under Labour.

24 Apr.	Blair announces plans for urban regeneration.
	Downing Street denies plans to cut funding to Scotland and Wales.
	Con Party release 1,000th press statement of the year.
25 Apr.	Brown warns EU Commission against 'over-reaching itself' in budgetary matters.
	Report that government has spent £63m on advertising in the first quarter of 2001.
	Milburn announces NHS reforms.
	Hague accuses Labour of introducing 45 new 'stealth taxes'.
26 Apr.	'People's Peers' announced.
	Hague describes John Townend's views on race as 'totally unacceptable'.
27 Apr.	Lab rules out motorway tolls for ten years.
	Ld Taylor (Con) denounces decision not to expel Townend from party.
29 Apr.	2001 Census.
May	
1 May	May Day protests in central London.
2 May	Milburn offers incentives for former midwives to return to work.
3 May	Blair announces that foot and mouth is on the wane.
	Con unveil poster of pregnant Blair.
	Lab announce relaxing of pub opening hour restrictions by 2002.
4 May	Blair announces changes in asylum law.
6 May	Cons promise asylum 'hit squads'.
7 May	Ronnie Biggs returns to UK.
8 May	Blair announces election.

substantial lead in the opinion polls. Planning meetings until then had been rather desultory. Now they had a purpose.

For a few weeks in the new year Blair and Brown seriously entertained the idea of an April election, immediately following the budget. The political and economic indicators were so favourable and could not be guaranteed to last. But the foot and mouth crisis quickly killed the idea. William Hague, however, put Central Office on an election alert for a 5 April poll. He thought that Blair might announce it the day after the budget. He had noted that the day was blank in the Prime Minister's diary.

Foot and mouth disease is a dramatic example of an event that can scupper the best-laid plans. The first outbreak was confirmed on 20 February, and the swiftly rising number of cases soon dominated the news agenda. It also raised the town versus country tensions that had simmered throughout the Parliament. On 8 March, Jim Scudamore, the government's Chief Veterinary Officer, warned that the outbreak would last a long time. Claims by the agriculture minister, Nick Brown, that matters were under control were disputed by the National Farmers' Union and, as the number of confirmed cases rose, Brown's assurances appeared complacent. On

23 March, Professor David King, the government's Chief Scientific Adviser, said that the epidemic was out of control. Pictures of thousands of slaughtered animals being burnt in fields dramatically brought home the distress of the countryside. Tony Blair was genuinely shocked when he visited the worst hit areas in Devon and Cumbria, and by mid-March the possibility that the spread of the disease would rule out a 3 May election began to be canvassed.

At first it was Conservative-inclined newspapers, particularly the *Daily Mail* and the *Daily Telegraph*, and then William Hague, who urged delay. How could electioneering be conducted when many parts of the countryside were out of bounds? When Tony Blair became involved in detailed crisis management and pledged to devote all his energies to quelling foot and mouth disease, sceptics asked how he could do both this and hold an election. The whips found that urban-based Labour MPs, particularly those with large majorities, supported a 3 May election. Those in marginal seats, or in seats containing a substantial number of farmers, were more cautious. From the middle of March Tony Blair grew increasingly uneasy about a May election; he was concerned about acting

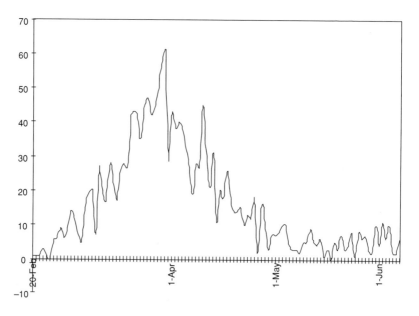

Figure 5.2   New cases of foot and mouth (daily reports)

Source: MAFF

Prescott–Blair–Campbell–Brown

The spread of foot and mouth in early March, with the consequent vast cull of sheep and cattle, put in doubt the favoured election date.

Peter Brookes, *The Times*, 14 March 2001.

in a way that would appear opportunistic and split town from country. Number 10 advisers were divided. Most suggested that if the disease was clearly seen to be contained, or if the government was perceived to have an effective strategy for containing it by the end of March, then a May election was still possible. Ministers and Labour MPs took to the airwaves, arguing that the disease was irrelevant to the decision about an election date and that delay might cause damage to the British tourist industry.

Trevor Kavanagh, political editor of the *Sun*, tipped off by Number 10, declared: 'MAY 3. ELECTION DAY: OFFICIAL' (*Sun*, 20 March 2001). This proved to be premature and a source of embarrassment to the newspaper. At a meeting of EU heads of government in Stockholm on 23 March, however, Tony Blair was filmed privately telling Romano Prodi that he had only ten days in which to make a decision about the election date.

The struggle for Blair's mind lasted for just over a week. On 26 March Clive Soley, Chair of the PLP, stated that 70 per cent of the Labour MPs he had contacted favoured a 3 May election. Many Cabinet ministers and

Alastair Campbell were of the same mind. In an editorial on 2 April, the *New Statesman* reflected an urban impatience with the countryside. 'The idea that an election should be postponed because of problems, no matter how grave, in a single industry is preposterous' (although in the same issue Jackie Ashley, the Deputy Editor, argued for delay). In Number 10, it was known that Anji Hunter, Blair's Special Assistant, and Sally Morgan, his Political Secretary, thought delay was the best choice, and that it would not damage Labour's election prospects. Gordon Brown was aware of the disadvantages of both May and of June, and left the decision to Tony Blair although, when it was made, he thought it was probably a mistake, perhaps fearing the afterglow of his budget might weaken. But Blair was by now convinced that an election should not take place, partly as a mark of respect for those who were suffering but also because he could get the right measures in place to eradicate the disease.

Blair's decision to postpone the local elections (and, by implication, the general election) from 3 May to 7 June was finally taken on Friday 30 March. The *Sun*, having been misled once was favoured with another leak. 'ELECTION OFF' was its front page splash the next day. Blair had listened to the views of colleagues and advisers, and had studied public and private opinion polls, which showed that while voters were fairly evenly divided over a May election, opinion was turning against 3 May. He read a note about a focus group held in Shropshire on 28 March that stated:

> On balance delay appears the right course. It is a gesture of respect, it does enable us to build up good will; it will enable us to build some confidence about the future.

But it was not a poll-driven decision. Blair simply felt that it would not be right. An election might be dominated by questions about the disease or the legitimacy of holding an election at all. His position was not dissimilar to Ted Heath's in January 1974, when he resisted strong party pressure to call an early general election for 7 February, in the face of the coal miners' strike against his government's statutory prices and incomes policy. For a fortnight Heath passed up the opportunity of an election in the search for agreement with the miners. Eventually he called an election for 28 February – and lost.

When Blair made his announcement to delay the election on Monday 2 April, he did not state that it would be held on 7 June. But he had decided to call it then 'even if our lead is down to six points' as he told an aide. In succeeding days, those close to Blair came to approve of his decision. One original May supporter said later: 'In the end no Prime Minister could

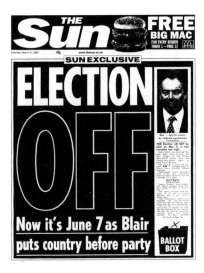

Sun front page, 31 March 2001

have gone in May'. But there were short-term costs. Cabinet ministers had seen their advice spurned, and some had gone public in arguing against delay on the grounds that it would send negative messages abroad about the state of Britain. It would also mean a lengthy campaign. Many ministers had also metaphorically cleared their desks and the Whitehall machine relaxed.

In all party headquarters there was a sense of anticlimax. Plans had to be hastily revised. Labour moved quickly to cancel a large poster campaign booked for April. Usually there are heavy cancellation charges involved in withdrawing from optioned poster sites. Labour managed to get sympathetic business groups and some government departments to take over these sites and to release others for later on. Party organisers, alerted by the *Sun* front page on 31 March, moved over the weekend to purchase on favourable terms 2,500 sites from mid-May to the end of the first week in June, and another 4,000 sites for that final week. The Conservatives did not make their dispositions until Monday 2 April, reselling the best of their sites and using the rest to relaunch the 'You Paid the Tax' poster campaign.

On 2 April, Jack Straw introduced an emergency bill in the Commons postponing the local elections until 7 June; the legislation, which was passed two days later, gave the government the power to reimburse local government for the extra administrative costs, and to cover the printing of ballot papers and the hiring of premises for use as polling stations.

Labour feared that the delay might weaken their favourable electoral position; Conservatives hoped that things could only get better. Labour enjoyed huge leads on virtually all the important issues and had actually increased its lead over the Conservatives from 1997. In mid-March Gould sent Blair a summary of the polling material:

> Tax and living standards have moved from issues of comparative vulnerability to issues of Labour dominance. Labour has effectively won the battle.

Even on the more pro-Conservative issues of Europe, asylum, crime and standing up for Britain, Labour was ahead, although narrowly. Among the switchers, however, Gould claimed that Hague was making some gains with his aggressive 'foreign land/standing up for Britain' message.

But, as foot and mouth abated, the underlying electoral mood did not change. Indeed, if anything, successive polls showed a hardening of Labour's lead. In contrast to the fuel blockade, Blair was determined to be seen to be fully engaged. Although Hague felt he had acted with restraint in his criticisms of the government's handling of the crisis, Labour's private polls showed a weakening in his ratings.

During March and April, Conservatives unveiled or restated policies at various launches. There were proposals to help the elderly with the costs of care, while allowing them to keep some of their assets. In the second half of March, the party launched the poster campaign 'Can you really wait another four years for improvements to public services?' Andrew Lansley calculated that by using the posters to highlight at this point the government's failures of delivery, the Conservatives might inhibit Labour from returning to these issues during the campaign. The Tories could then concentrate in the campaign on the preferred issues of Europe, crime, and tax.

In the vacuum that followed the postponement of the election, the Conservatives found themselves put on the defensive by the retiring East Yorkshire MP, John Townend. In remarks to his constituency, Townend blamed immigrants for the rise in crime in recent years. Hague speedily disowned him. However, because he did not want to give further publicity to the MP, he decided against expulsion. It was then revealed that Townend was one of a number of Conservative MPs who had refused to support a Commission for Racial Equality pledge not to exploit race in the forthcoming election. The pledge had already been signed by the three national party leaders, presumably on behalf of all candidates. But other prominent Conservatives, including Michael Portillo and John Gummer, refused to sign the pledge on the grounds that it pandered to political correctness and was not proof of disowning racism. Townend continued to speak out, on one occasion talking about the British becoming a 'mongrel race'. The black Conservative peer, Lord Taylor of Warwick, attacked Hague for not taking stronger action. The issue was becoming a question of William Hague's authority and a divided party. Finally, on 30 April, following his regular strategy group meeting, William Hague insisted that Townend withdraw his remarks or else face expulsion, while Taylor and others were asked to sign a letter pledging loyalty to the party. Townend apologised and Taylor stayed in the party.

The whole incident had lessons for the two main parties. Labour's private polls showed that, if anything, it lost support from the row. Conservatives were reminded of the subtle distinction between the public's hostility to bogus asylum seekers and more tolerant outlook on race. One Conservative strategist said: 'We should draw a clear line between bogus asylum seekers and race. William does this, but some nasties in the party don't. We need to speak with one voice.' Conservative leaders also decided that they could not talk too much about the asylum issue in the coming election.

The gloomy opinion polls added to Conservative difficulties. William Hague felt the pressure that came from a mix of MPs and candidates who saw their prospects of returning to the House of Commons fading, from shadow ministers who feared that they faced another lengthy spell in opposition, from those who supported either a more positive or a more critical Conservative stance on the EU, and from those who thought that Hague was an electoral liability. The press still carried stories about plans to challenge Hague after the anticipated election defeat. One, which ran over the Easter weekend, involved an alleged agreement between Portillo and Clarke. In the course of an interview in *The Times* on 23 April the Shadow Minister, Archie Norman, questioned whether his party had struck the right tone in recent months. Was it too hectoring and carping to impress voters as a would-be government? Could it be more measured? He was perhaps referring to some of his party's rhetoric on asylum, on Section 28 and on the euro. One of William Hague's aides dismissed the advice: 'Fine if you're 20 per cent ahead, but not if you're 20 per cent behind.' Others, who agreed with Norman's point, doubted the wisdom of so public a criticism of Hague.

What could the Conservatives do? In opposition, they had traditionally relied on two themes – 'Time for a change', and 'Labour isn't working.'

It was too soon to make an effective argument for change when Labour had been in office for only 4 years while the Conservatives had enjoyed 18. And the voters' cynicism about politicians was such that debunking Labour would not increase Conservative support. Labour was ahead – often by large margins – in polls on which party was the best on living standards; on economic competence; on which was moderate not extreme; and on which represented all sections of the community, or had the best leaders. Hague admitted to colleagues, 'Our strategic position is not a happy one.' One senior strategist said: 'Because Labour is so far ahead on the economy and health and education, much is closed off for us. Therefore we have to create our own battleground. Crime is obvious ground for us, although people regard rising crime as a fact of life and do not think a government can do much.' The party's best issues, where it was on level or near level terms with Labour, were asylum, crime, Europe and taxes. It would run an aggressive campaign with these issues, mainly the last three. On Europe, it would claim that this was the last chance to save the pound, protect our way of life and retain powers to set interest rates. The party would stress tax cuts in an attempt to neutralise the sense that the economy was doing well.

In early March, in a presentation to the Shadow Cabinet, and later to MPs, Andrew Lansley identified the issues and themes, mostly on the public services, on which the party would have to fight defensively. He wanted these matters to be raised before the campaign proper, so that Conservatives could then concentrate on their chosen issues. Lansley and Collins drew up a grid of daily election activities and themes. When the grid for a 3 May election was presented for approval to the strategy group of the Shadow Cabinet, one member objected about the neglect of schools and health, and asked: 'Are we really saying to people that we are not interested in schools and hospitals?' In contrast to Blair, Hague's team planned for him to appear for only one photo opportunity at a school and for none with an NHS connection. Organisers feared that such visits would attract protesters, yielding images that would dominate media coverage and boost the salience of these issues.

The Conservative approach would be a challenge to those who believed that British general elections are won in the middle ground and on those issues which most concern target voters. Under Blair, Labour had accepted a number of John Major's policies and this move to the political centre narrowed the scope for Conservative strategists. The Conservatives hoped to nourish and profit from the voters' dissatisfactions and grievances. In an echo of Labour's left-wing manifesto in 1983, Hague and his team were clearly aiming at the party's core vote, as well as working-class voters disillusioned with Labour, emphasising those issues which enthused activists and on which they could draw a line from Labour. In a low turnout, this might not be enough to achieve victory (as it had been in the 1999 Euro elections), but they could do well. Very few expected to win but some Central Office strategists believed that at least a 35 per cent share of the vote was achievable and that this would be a good result, particularly when compared with the low expectations set by the media and the opinion polls.

Since February, as part of the so-called 'Next Steps' programme, Labour ministers had been unveiling draft manifesto policies and initiatives for the next Parliament. Once Tony Blair had passed up the May election option, the exercise was renewed at Easter. For all his determination to remind voters of his economic record, Gordon Brown believed that people voted prospectively, not retrospectively. In the course of an interview, he said: 'The great danger for an incumbent is lack of momentum. We have to gain momentum, like Thatcher did in 1987 and Clinton did in 1996. It can't just be a referendum on us. You have to show a positive vision for the future.' He thought the task of a party in modern campaigning was to 'draw lines between the parties to your own advantage'. As the campaign strategist, Gordon Brown intended to warn voters not to 'go back' to the economic recession of the early Major years. Hard-hitting posters and broadcasts would warn of the dangers of change, the classic cry of the incumbent. Brown and Blair would argue that economic stability had been for a purpose – to allow the second-term manifesto to have a distinct and essential focus; the renewal of public services.

Labour's campaign team agreed the themes of the manifesto, *Ambitions for Britain*. There was some top-level discussion of the wording to be used on tax policy. Blair and Brown finally agreed to a repeat of the 1997 promise not to increase income tax rates: to fail to repeat it would look inconsistent and might frighten the 1997 Labour converts. Brown was determined to deliver his spending programme, but not at the cost of raising income tax rates. Although some advisers wanted a pledge not to increase income tax to be made before the campaign started, Brown insisted that it be delayed until the manifesto. In 1997 the pledges had been designed to reach new voters. They were specific and costed. Advisers had doubts whether the device was suitable for a party in government; it might suggest limited ambitions. Eventually they agreed on specific pledges and a general sentence emphasising the difference between Labour and Conservatives. They rejected a suggestion of starting with plans for improving the public services, fearing that an emphasis on public spending might appear to vindicate Conservative warnings about the need for tax increases. The party's target audience was first the 1997 converts, second the loyalists who had to be motivated, and third the post-1997 switchers. Gould concluded his strategy note for Blair: 'We do have remaining vulnerabilities, but our core position remains one of overwhelming strength. The electorate is poised to give us another chance.'

By the end of April, ministers felt confident that the foot and mouth outbreak was under control. When Tony Blair told a Downing Street press conference on 3 May that 'we are on the home straight', he removed any remaining doubts about a June election. Ministers announced cash handouts to different areas and groups, including teachers, doctors and consultants. They also unveiled some of Labour's more attractive policies, including the baby bond, although the details were left vague. Blair cancelled a weekend trip to Berlin for a meeting of European Socialist Party leaders on 5–6 May. On Bank Holiday Monday, 7 May, he convened a political Cabinet meeting to approve the final version of the election manifesto and campaign plans.

Tony Blair had a slightly different, if complementary, agenda to Brown. He regarded the coming election as a good opportunity to seek a mandate on his own terms. In 1997 he had been campaigning in the shadow of the Thatcher revolution and the failure of old Labour. 'Then we had to provide reassurance to new supporters', said a close adviser, 'but now he is more confident and wants it to be his victory'. On 21 April he sent a 15-page memo on the election to his 'office group' of close advisers, stating his determination to make a break both with Thatcherism and old-style social democracy. He wanted a mandate for reform of the public services, a more positive engagement with the EU and for creating a post-Thatcherite political order, one that restored the importance of community over individualism – a mandate that he could wield against opponents, within as well as outside the Labour Party. The emphasis on investment over tax cuts would be a break from the 1980s while reform of the public services would be a break with 'old' Labour.

The Conservatives had feared that the large number of special advisers that Labour had recruited to Whitehall and the Downing Street machine would be available for the election campaign and financed by the taxpayer. They knew the electoral value of such a network from their own time in power. Sir Richard Wilson, the Cabinet Secretary, made an effort to check this. He ruled that all special advisers who planned to resign to work on the campaign would have to leave their posts once the election was called. They would also have to return their pagers, mobile phones and laptops, and they were forbidden to contact officials or their advisers who carried on working in government. The special advisers would not be allowed to log on to the Number 10 Knowledge Network database, which gave a constituency breakdown of information (which briefly remained on the Labour website), and must return any material that they had taken from it. In the event 62 advisers resigned, most of them on 8 and 9 May, and only 14 remained in Whitehall.

The general election had been anticipated and the parties had been on election alert for several weeks. Campaign managers used the delay to review their grids of issues and activities for each campaign day, to refine themes, to redraft speeches and newspaper articles, to finalise posters and broadcasts, and to consolidate research on the rival parties. On the basis of their own surveys into each party's strengths and weaknesses, and knowledge of the politics of the previous four years, party strategists had a good idea of how their opponents would campaign.

The Conservatives did not enter the campaign in good heart. The transition from government to opposition four years earlier had left its mark. In conversation, in early 2000, a Conservative had likened the slow progress of his party's electoral recovery to 'the coastal erosion of the chalk face'. The electoral system, as in 1992 and 1997, was now massively biased against them. To deprive Labour of its overall majority they needed a swing of 7.2 per cent, and a lead over Labour of 8 per cent; and to gain an overall majority they needed a record swing of 11.5 per cent. Yet on many issues the Conservative standing vis-à-vis Labour had worsened since May 1997. It would be William Hague's campaign. How the party performed, and how far he reduced Labour's lead, would determine whether he had a future as party leader. Labour, for the first time in 22 years, entered a general election as the government. Even the most cautious Labour campaigner was hard-pushed to point to an area of weakness that the Conservatives could exploit.

The Liberal Democrats, like every other party, had prepared for a 3 May contest and disliked coming off the boil. But they were able to put extra effort into their narrow band of the targeted seats and into having a decent Easter holiday before the strenuous final five weeks. UKIP and the Greens used the pause to recruit more candidates than they had ever expected to field.

In the early months of 2001 not much happened in the outside world to affect the British political scene. Overseas George W. Bush took office and had a brief honeymoon before setting other leaders against him over Star Wars and global warming. At home the railways, all too slowly, got back to normal timetables as they coped with the aftermath of the Hatfield crash. The collapse in the dotcom sector and decline in share prices prompted mild speculation about a possible recession. But none of the politicking of the extended near term campaign seemed to have had much impact on electoral prospects.

Sun front page, 2 May 2001

Daily Express front page, 8 May 2001

6
The National Campaign

Election campaigns are more carefully orchestrated than ever before. Each party prepares a grid, setting out the agenda for each day's press conferences and for leaders' tours and broadcasts – and, on the whole, the plan is closely followed. Each party conducts similar focus groups and gets the same message about public reactions – or non-reactions – to the campaign. Each party tries to lead the media to cover the themes that are most favourable to them. And each party communicates by fax or e-mail or website daily – or hourly – with all their spokesmen and candidates, priming them with the message of the day and supplying the agreed line to take on any new developments. Yet, because the efforts are all so prepared and stylised, spontaneity tends to disappear from the campaign and, especially when the outcome is seen as a foregone conclusion, it becomes increasingly difficult to excite the public's interest. The 24-hour media schedule, coupled with more use of helicopters and battle buses, means that the coverage is more continuous and the campaign ever more exhausting for the leaders and their teams, even if it is less listened to by voters.

Tony Blair had warned a political cabinet, held on Bank Holiday Monday, 7 May, not to be overconfident but on 8 May the *Daily Express* filled its front page in huge type with the prediction 'BLAIR BY 250'. When, at 1 p.m. that day, he went to Buckingham Palace to ask the Queen for a dissolution, he cannot have had much doubt about what would happen a month later. At 3.15 he told a Catholic girls' school in South London that the election would be on Thursday 7 June and that the new Parliament would meet on 13 June. The locale of the announcement and its partisan style ('Never since 1983 has there been so wide a gap between the parties') excited criticism, even from the hosting headmistress and from Clare Short, a Cabinet colleague. Columnists condemned it as 'cynical' and 'tacky'. The respected Peter Riddell wrote in *The Times*:

> Tony Blair began his campaign in the most nauseating and emotionally explosive way. Everything about the event was a reminder of what is most objectionable about New Labour, its obsession with symbols and presentation and, above all, its lack of shame.

Previous elections had been announced in a press statement or from the steps of 10 Downing Street. Tony Blair wanted to demonstrate his enthusiasm for education, but it was odd to reveal his political news between hymns and to an audience too young to vote.

Six days elapsed from the announcement to the actual dissolution on Monday 14 May – comparable to the four days in 1983 and the seven days in 1987. In effect the election date had been clear since 2 April with the postponement of the shire council elections from 3 May to 7 June. No one could complain of surprise.

Announcement of Election	Tuesday 8 May
Dissolution of Parliament	Monday 12 May
Close of nominations	Friday 25 May
Polling Day	Thursday 7 June
Meeting of Parliament	Wednesday, 13 June
Queen's Speech	Wednesday 20 June

There was some hurried clearing of the parliamentary decks, though the Conservatives were not very helpful in allowing pending legislation through. Among the casualties were bills on adoption, leasehold reform, foxhunting, international development and tobacco advertising.

The Conservatives implemented their 'fast start' plan instantly, delivering 10,000 leaflets to target voters in each marginal seat. They then produced the first surprise of the campaign by the swift issuing on Thursday 10 May of their manifesto, *Time for Common Sense*. (If, as they had suspected, the announcement had been delayed two days, they had been ready to launch the manifesto on Sunday 13 May). The actual document[1] offered an £8 bn cut in taxes, even though it promised to match Labour's spending plans on health, education and the police. The manifesto came out against any further transfer of power to Brussels and against a European defence force outside NATO. It made radical promises on freeing head teachers from local education authorities and on the funding of universities. It demanded a tougher policy on asylum seekers and an end to the early release of convicted prisoners. Its most notable surprise was a promise of a 6p per litre cut in fuel duty. It also offered a married couple's allowance, a tax cut of £1,000 per couple and a tax credit of £200 for children under five as well as an increased state pension. In blessing his proposals William Hague stressed:

> Above all we will keep the pound ... It is time to choose between a Labour party that trusts government instead of the people and a Conservative party that trusts people instead of government.

The campaign soon settled towards a familiar routine of press conferences and leaders' tours. The Liberal Democrats met the media at 8 a.m. in the Local Government Association building in Smith Square (once Transport House, the Labour Party's old headquarters). At 8.30 a.m., breathless from a quarter-mile walk, the media were received by Gordon Brown at Millbank Tower and at 9.15 a.m., it was expected, the Conservatives would be at home back in 32 Smith Square. However, the Conservatives were not ready to submit to this routine, so convenient to the media. They only held four 9 a.m. press conferences in the first two weeks and William Hague was present at only two of them; they wished to show themselves a party for the whole of Great Britain with their leader enjoying photo-opportunities in all parts of the country. They thus forewent a lot of reporting in the continuous live coverage of all press conferences on the 24-hour channels provided by Sky Television, by *BBC News 24*, by *BBC Parliament* and by ITN, and much monitored by journalists across the country. However, in the last days of the campaign, the Labour Party in their turn took three of their four final press conferences out to the provinces.

The leaders' tours to target seats and rallies and regional media outlets were hampered by the demands of security. For two reasons they could not be announced in advance; the Special Branch had to worry about terrorism and the party managers were equally troubled about organised heckling and poster-waving opponents. 'You can't have a genuine walkabout nowadays – embarrassments are too easy to engineer', was a strategist's comment. One party leader regretted that they had not sent a posse to follow Charles Kennedy and submit him to the treatment that Blair and Hague were receiving.

In his Sedgefield constituency on Sunday 13 May, Tony Blair delivered what he regarded as his most important speech of the campaign, an expression of personal faith:

Let us lift this election up. Let it be about the bread-and-butter issues. But let it also be about values, conviction and belief. I stand as New Labour, seeking for the first time in a century of British politics to marry together a well-run economy and a just and fair society, where life's chances are given to all not just a few.

When Tony Blair attended a Labour press conference he would arrive in time for the 7 a.m. briefing meeting, chaired by Gordon Brown. He would then depart in the battle bus accompanied by his aides. These included Anji Hunter, Hilary Coffman from the press office in Number 10, and Bruce Grocott, his long-serving parliamentary private secretary. Also on the bus was an old friend, Tom Dibble, who acted as an office manager. His wife Cherie accompanied him on about ten days. The bus was equipped for e-mail and conference calls. Contact was maintained with Number 10 on government business (of which there was very little) and with Gordon Brown in Millbank. Much of Blair's time was spent in giving interviews to reporters from the regional press who were collected and dropped off at lay-bys. At the end of the day he would usually return to Millbank for an hour or so and then retire to Downing Street.

On Tuesday 15 May the Liberal Democrats released their manifesto, *Freedom, Justice, Honesty*. It promised a 1p rise in the basic rate of income tax and a 50 per cent top rate for incomes over £100,000. This would pay for more doctors and nurses and teachers and policemen, and finance the abolition of university tuition fees. The manifesto stressed environmental issues and opposed US Star Wars. Charles Kennedy reiterated his mantra, 'Freedom, Justice, Honesty'.

On Wednesday 16 May the Labour leadership assembled at the Birmingham International Conference Centre for the launch of their manifesto, *Ambitions for Britain* (an odd echo of the Liberal Democrats' 1997 manifesto, *Ambitious for Britain*). The document contained no surprises. It stressed keeping to a 2.5 per cent inflation target and it promised not to raise income tax or VAT. It envisaged further expenditure on transport and urban renewal. It talked of smaller class sizes and set a target of half the population going into higher education; it promised the recruitment of 10,000 more teachers, 20,000 more nurses and 6,000 more policemen, as well as a £4.20 minimum wage and a continuation of winter fuel payments. In launching the manifesto Tony Blair raised the prospect of a greater role for the private sector in the management of public services. He ended:

As long as there is one child in poverty, one pensioner in poverty, one person denied their choice in life, this is one Prime Minister and one party, who will have no rest, no vanity in achievement, no sense of mission completed.

The coverage of the Labour manifesto was swamped by other events. William Hague had to call off a walkabout in Wolverhampton because of crowd pressure and Jack Straw was slow handclapped when he addressed the Police Federation in Blackpool (Ann Widdecombe was wildly cheered by the same body the following day). The television showed these episodes but more sensational pictures were captured when the Prime Minister was lengthily waylaid outside a Birmingham hospital by a very angry woman, Sharron Storer, protesting at delays in treating her partner, a cancer patient.

This cartoon of John Prescott, after his punch, mocks the 1997 'Demon Eyes' Conservative poster, and depicts Prescott as a threat to the carefully-spun image of New Labour.

Garland, *Daily Telegraph*, 18 May 2001

Still more memorable footage was produced later in the day when the Deputy Prime Minister punched an egg-throwing farmer in Rhyl. In Millbank strategists were coming to terms with the bad news from Birmingham when one of them suddenly interrupted, 'There is worse to come. John Prescott has just punched a member of the public.' John Prescott's violent reaction excited both admiration and distaste but most observers concluded that it was a plus for Labour. Mr Prescott refused to express contrition and wisely, but against advice, Tony Blair laughed it off at the next day's press conference, 'John is John.' There is no doubt that the episode produced the most memorable shots of the whole campaign. As Chapter 9 shows, this extraordinary image stole all the front pages the next day and led Margaret McDonagh to protest, without much evidence, against TV crews inciting protesters to yield good pictures.

Table 6.1   Chronology of the campaign

Tue 8 May	Blair announces election.
Wed 9 May	Last PM's Questions. Lab issues Pledge Card.
Thu 10 May	Con manifesto.
Fri 11 May	Tapsell's 'Never'.
Sat 12 May	Hague suggests Lab means £6 a gallon petrol.
Sun 13 May	Blair at Sedgefield. Woodward selected at St Helens.
Mon 14 May	Parliament dissolved. UKIP manifesto. Lab claims business vote.
Tue 15 May	LibDem manifesto. Letwin's £20 bn cuts.
Wed 16 May	Lab manifesto. Straw heckled. Prescott punch.
Thu 17 May	'John is John'. No foot and mouth outbreak.
Fri 18 May	SNP manifesto. Green manifesto. Hague on asylum seekers.
Sat 19 May	Lab woos pensioners.
Sun 20 May	Heath on need for Con defeat.
Mon 21 May	Con claim business votes. McDonagh letter.
Tue 22 May	Thatcher 'never'. Argument over Nat. Insurance.
Wed 23 May	EU document on tax-harmonisation.
Thu 24 May	MORI: 25% Lab lead.
Fri 25 May	Nominations close. Archbishops ask for moral campaigning.
Sat 26 May	Hague's 12 days to save £.
Sun 27 May	Oldham riots.
Mon 28 May	Referendum as issue. Jospin speech.
Tue 29 May	Prodi on EU-wide taxes. LibDems claim Opposition role.
Wed 30 May	ICM puts Lab 19% ahead. Last day for claiming postal votes.
Thu 31 May	MORI: 16% Lab lead.
Fri 1 June	Con raise landslide fears.
Sat 2 June	Peerages for retiring MPs.
Sun 3 June	Polls show increasing LibDem support.
Mon 4 June	Hague's plans for office. Ladbrokes close books.
Tue 5 June	Final rallies Rasmussen: 11% Lab lead.
Wed 6 June	ICM 11% Lab lead.
Thu 7 June	Polling day MORI 15 % Lab lead; Gallup 17 % Lab lead.

Tony Blair had spent much time before the election preparing a series of major speeches to spell out his own personal vision of where he wanted to take the country. A number of outsiders contributed sections, which were coordinated by Peter Hyman and Alastair Campbell. The last two, along with Blair himself, wrote up the final drafts. Blair made six speeches including:

13 May Our Core Beliefs (Sedgefield)
15 May Economic Stability and Prosperity (Leeds)
16 May Ambitions for Britain (the manifesto launch at Birmingham)
21 May Public services (Gravesend)
25 May Britain's role in Europe and the world (Edinburgh)
30 May The Strong Society (Newport, Shropshire)

William Hague convened a leader's team meeting on most mornings in Central Office at 8.15 a.m. This was attended by Central Office officials, his office staff – Michael Ancram, Andrew Lansley, Michael Portillo and Francis Maude – and whichever other shadow minister was appearing at that morning's press conference. Hague would then take the press conference or set off in his battle bus. On his travels he was accompanied by Seb Coe, Mark Parsons and Ed Young from his staff together with his wife, Ffion, who was helped by Shana Hole.

At Central Office Michael Ancram and Andrew Lansley took it in turns to be present to give direction to staff. Michael Portillo and Francis Maude took many of the press conferences. At the end of the day, usually at 9 p.m., Hague gathered in Central Office with Ancram, Lansley, Maude and Portillo (on their pagers they referred to themselves as the 'Gang of Four') and Coe. This meeting reviewed the events of the day and the grids for the next seven days, received private polling and focus groups results, and approved themes and press releases for the next day. Compared with the original grid, Europe (and the euro) was downgraded and in the last week Hague warned of the dangers of a Labour landslide and put more emphasis on Conservative plans for the public services.

At the Central Office call centre thousands of contacts were made to the swing voters. The results were available to Stephen Gilbert the next morning. The findings were not encouraging. Conservative support never reached 40 per cent in any of the target seats. There was more positive news from candidates and regional officials.

On Monday 14 May, there came accidentally a key development to reinforce Labour's central campaign against the Conservatives' position on taxation and the social services. The *Financial Times* reported that an unnamed shadow minister had spoken of a £20 bn cut in public spending by the end of the next Parliament. The Shadow Chief Secretary to the Treasury, Oliver Letwin, was quickly unmasked as the source. (He had made the same point in a letter to the *Daily Telegraph* two weeks earlier.) He went into hiding and the Labour Party put up 'wanted' posters and engaged in further teases, sending Andrew Smith, the real Chief Secretary, to Dorset to look for him. Letwin finally emerged a week later to confirm his support for the official Conservative line – that the party was only promising £8 bn in cuts. Later Lord Saatchi, another shadow economic spokesman, spoke of £50 bn cuts.

Wanted!
Oliver Letwin

Last wherabouts unknown
Reward
£20 Billion
for schools, hospitals and police
if this man is stopped

There can be no doubt that the Letwin episode drove the Conservative 'tax and spend' attack off course. Gordon Brown was determined to press his claims that stability had been hard won over the past four years and it would be undermined by a Conservative government. All Labour press conferences in the first week were devoted to the economy and to the Conservatives' tax plans and their likely spending cuts. The Letwin-inspired figure of £20bn was a gift to Brown and threw the Conservatives into disarray.

They were not even able to exploit fully Gordon Brown's refusal on 21 May and several times thereafter to rule out any increase in National Insurance contributions – the 10 per cent bombshell so effectively used against Labour in the 1992 campaign. Gordon Brown dismissed the suggestion of a planned increase as 'a typical Tory slur' but, although he went on equivocating, the Conservatives were handicapped by their reluctance to make absolute commitments about specific taxes.

Europe came up constantly as an issue. On 11 May Sir Peter Tapsell drew headlines for likening the plans for the single currency to Hitler's attempts to unify Europe. As the number of Conservative candidates who said 'never' to the euro instead of following the party line 'not in the next Parliament' grew to 101, Labour publicised a running tally.

In repeated interviews (notably in the *Financial Times*, 25 May) Tony Blair indicated sympathy for joining the euro but he always took refuge behind the necessity of Gordon Brown's five conditions being met (see p. 6). The media hinted at strains between Prime Minister and Chancellor on this issue, particularly about Tony Blair's readiness to speak about Europe, but neither could be pinned down to any conflicting utterances.

On 22 May, in a *Daily Mail* interview, Margaret Thatcher rejected 'multiculturalism' – a concept that William Hague had explicitly endorsed. Michael Portillo, according to Amanda Platell, wanted William Hague to repudiate the Thatcher statement publicly. But, fortunately for the Conservatives, journalists failed to spot the off-message sentence. However, that evening Thatcher, in her one major public speech, deviated from her prepared text to say 'never' to joining the euro and received a tumultuous reception for the remark. This rumbustious intervention in Plymouth, including her joke about 'The Mummy Returns' (the title of a newly released film), drew mixed comments and cartoons. William Hague remarked breezily that her euro comment was, for her, 'rather restrained' but there was consternation in Central Office because she was conveying the wrong image. Many Conservatives certainly felt that their campaign was not helped by the 'return of the Mummy'. Labour's private polls reported that her intervention had only fired enthusiasm among Labour supporters and Conservative canvassers reported adverse reactions. Central Office had engaged in delicate negotiations with the offices of previous prime ministers about platform appearances. It was agreed that Lady Thatcher and John Major would each speak for six minutes at rallies. The build-up to the Thatcher appearance was nerve-racking for the Hague team. John Major's one speech at a Brighton rally on 29 May was more on-message. After paying warm tribute to William Hague and castigating Labour spin doctors he ended: 'Polls suggest that the nation is sleepwalking to catastrophe. Our job is to wake them up.'

Nominations closed on Wednesday, 23 May. There were 3,325 candidates nationwide compared to 3,724 in 1997. The three main parties fought every constituency in Great Britain except the Speaker's Glasgow seat and Wyre Forest where the Liberal Democrats allowed a clear run to a hospital closure protest. UKIP put up 428 candidates and the Greens 145. The Scottish Socialist Party contested every seat in Scotland.

Party election broadcasts drew even less attention than in the past (see Chapter 8). The parties used more photo-montage and fewer talking heads. But two Conservative efforts did stand out as the most extreme

examples on negative campaigning, so much less used in Britain than in the USA. The first Conservative broadcast on 15 May dealt with law and order and, using acted scenes, implied that under Labour criminals were let out of jail early to commit more crimes; the third on 24 May painted Labour's education policies as leading to truancy and disaster. Both evoked strong protests. On 25 May, in an unusual move, the Archbishops of Canterbury and York issued a joint appeal to the politicians to show restraint. 'We all sense how tempting it can be, especially in an election season, for the short term, the negative and the self-serving to dominate the political scene.' The Archbishops stressed they were non-partisan but some took the statement as an especial reaction to the first Conservative election broadcast.

The election was generally portrayed as a bore. The press showed repeated pocket cartoons portraying the tedium or the hostility of the voter. The opinion polls made their contribution by constantly repeating the grinding leads which pointed to another landslide for Labour – even though the lead wobbled implausibly between 28 per cent (*The Economist* 18 May) and 11 per cent (*Guardian* 23 May). ICM provided the lowest leads and it was a particular blow to William Hague when, on 31 May, ICM, the Conservatives' own pollster, suddenly put Labour 19 per cent ahead.

There was some frustration in the Blair and Hague camps about how little of their campaign arguments were being reported. The entourage of Tony Blair complained that media criticisms that he was not meeting 'real' people were wide of the mark. On most days he held question and answer sessions which were organised by constituency parties and which also included non-party members, often recruited by local newspapers.

NOT ALL PARTIES ARE THE SAME

TAX

TAX

Vote for common sense. Vote **Conservatives** ✗
www.conservatives.com

Although the media were present, these meetings were rarely reported. Journalists only seemed interested in confrontations or embarrassing incidents. One aide said they seemed to be on 'tomato watch'. William Hague was similarly frustrated. His question and answer sessions in private homes were rarely used by broadcasters. Instead he was usually shown on a soap box shouting above noisy interruptions. He avoided being filmed in schools and hospitals, in part because he considered that these were likely to attract protestors and that the resulting confrontation would then dominate media coverage.

Both leaders also had to endure tough sessions with broadcast interviewers. Hague's team felt bruised after a particularly abrasive encounter with Jeremy Paxman on *Newsnight* and Blair's team reacted similarly after a *Today* interview with John Humphrys which concentrated on sleaze and reports that there was a 'deal' for Blair to hand over the leadership to Gordon Brown in due course. On 24 May the *Independent*

headlined a front-page report; 'Frustrated Blair Accuses Media of Ignoring "Real" Election issues'. He had attacked reporters for concentrating on such matters as sleaze, the campaign process, and the certainty of a Labour landslide. He told a newspaper; 'I have never heard such rubbish in all my life.'

Apart from the punch by John Prescott and the intervention of Margaret Thatcher, the parties offered nothing much to enliven the campaign. There were none of the scandals of 1997. Moreover no unexpected outside events or economic statistics intervened to distract the media from the election. There were no major Royal stories. The Jill Dando murder trial continued throughout the period and the Archer perjury trial began on 30 May. On election eve, England faced a critical World Cup qualifying match against Greece and there were fears of a negative reaction to defeat. England, however, won 2–0.

On Sunday, 27 May, there were serious race riots in Oldham, but few, except the British National Party, appear to have exploited them, though Simon Hughes did blame the Conservatives. However, the John Townend affair (see p. 84) seems to have inhibited any serious development of the issue of asylum seekers (where the Conservatives' hard line had some popular appeal). William Hague, who had vetoed a hard-hitting election broadcast on asylum seekers, felt he had to get the vexed question out of the way early in the campaign. He said in Dover on 18 May 'We will clear up Labour's asylum mess. Conservatives will ensure that Britain is a safe haven and not a soft touch.' Charles Kennedy responded that Hague combined 'the instincts of Alf Garnett with the electoral appeal of Michael Foot'. Lord Razzall, the Liberal Democrat campaign manager, was even harsher on the Conservative approach: 'Enoch Powell was sacked for making the sort of speech that Ann Widdecombe makes every week.'

In the outside world the only events with a serious bearing on the British electoral scene were two European speeches. On 28 May, Lionel Jospin, the French Prime Minister, while rejecting a federal Europe, argued that corporate taxes would have to be harmonised. Francis Maude attacked his remarks, commenting 'Labour is happy to take Britain into an EU super-state but wants to do it by stealth.'

On 29 May, the European Union President, Romano Prodi, explicitly asked for a more centralised European economy and toyed with the idea of an elected President of the EU and some form of EU tax. His ideas were speedily repudiated from both sides. Robin Cook and Tony Blair talked about winning the argument against an over-centralised EU from within, while Francis Maude and William Hague spoke of the need to renegotiate the Rome Treaty and threatened to institute safeguards against an extension of EU competence.

Conservatives were disappointed that the Eurosceptic press did not utter more outrage over these interventions. Although 'keeping the £' was a key theme in the Hague campaign and was often used as a backdrop at his press conferences, it was not made the theme of the day until the third week. There was, however, much anticipation in the media that Conservative fortunes hinged greatly on the issue. But despite the coverage the theme did not seem to be working for the Conservatives. By the end of the campaign the strategists concluded that there was no appetite for yet more on Europe among voters, as opposed to journalists. This was a significant reverse for the original campaign strategy and left the Tory attack on Labour somewhat rudderless.

The Liberal Democrats won kindly coverage from the media for their energetic but narrowly targeted campaign. Their poll rating crawled up from 13 per cent to 17 per cent and finally, in one poll, to 19 per cent. The television news constantly showed Charles Kennedy, hitherto ignored by the media, in his battle bus and helicopter, eager and friendly – and remarkably uncriticised. During the campaign his image seemed to grow from 'a lightweight couch potato' to a formidable leader. By the final week he was emboldened to suggest that the Liberal Democrats should be supported as the party most likely to provide the real opposition to Labour in the next Parliament. 'Don't waste your vote on the Tories.'

One factor working for the Liberal Democrats was the increased attention given to tactical voting. Billy Bragg, a Labour-supporting pop star, opened up a website for vote exchanges in Dorset where Lib–Lab cooperation could, potentially, secure each of the four Conservative seats. Charles Kennedy, while formally urging everyone to vote Liberal Democrat, pointed out that each citizen had to decide for himself, joking that tactical voting was 'do-it-yourself PR'. Interestingly, the Liberal Democrats did not spend much effort on their traditional theme of proportional representation, although they must have felt annoyed when, in an off-the-cuff answer on 5 June, Tony Blair expressed his fundamental doubts about PR for Westminster.

UKIP made far less splash than the Referendum Party had done in 1997. More generally it was plain that ordinary candidates from major parties, as well as the minor parties collectively, were failing to attract any serious national attention. Less was heard of the 145 Greens than of Martin Bell in his white-suited attempt to represent Brentwood or of the miscellaneous dissidents challenging Shaun Woodward in St Helens and Peter Mandelson in Hartlepool.

Soon after the election was announced, there were two last-minute retirements by MPs. David Miliband, head of the Number 10 policy unit, was uncontroversially chosen for David Clark's South Shields seat. But when Gerry Bermingham's St Helens South party, by 81 votes to 77, selected as his successor the floor-crossing and wealthy Shaun Woodward, there was an outcry against Millbank 'fixing' for one of 'Tony's cronies'. Woodward's campaign replaced Peter Mandelson's as the focus for media sniping. On 24 May Lord Stoddart, a Eurosceptic peer, was 'expelled' from the Labour Party for endorsing one of Shaun Woodward's socialist opponents. Labour also suffered from the way that the much accused Keith Vaz used his ill-health to avoid media questioning.

The Conservative assault on the Labour government's failure to deliver was countered by emphasis on how the growing expenditure on hospitals and schools was beginning to take effect, with the reiterated slogan: 'The Work Goes On'. Candidates were supplied by Millbank with a detailed list of the latest central government spending in their constituencies.

William Hague campaigned eloquently to the end, showing no sign of defeatism, despite the negative opinion poll verdict on his personal appeal, not to mention the disloyalty of a few colleagues (though some noted his visible tiredness after the 31 May ICM findings). On 10 May Ted Heath described him to the *Spectator* as 'a laughing stock' and John Horam, a veteran MP, said 'William does not appeal to some of our traditional supporters. There is a snob thing about William. They took the same view of John Major.' Even loyal front-benchers gave the game away; Tim Yeo admitted to having a bet on a Labour victory and Bernard Jenkin talked explicitly of the next Labour government. The media (and, privately, Conservative candidates) tried in vain to analyse why Hague, smiling confidently to the cameras beside his sympathetic Ffion, made, if anything, a negative impact. Was it his baldness? or his Yorkshire monotone? or was it simply that he was a messenger bearing an unacceptable message?

If the election was boring for the public, there was no lack of serious issues. Each of the parties launched carefully timed mini-manifestos on health, education, agriculture, youth, women, Scotland, Wales, London and other subjects. But the assiduously researched proposals drew little coverage or refutation, although they were doubtless mailed out to specialist groups. The *Guardian* ran articles on 'Debates that Nobody Wants', treating neglected issues such as culture, the environment, gay rights and missile defence.

Questions of political propriety arose from time to time. Tony Blair's use of a school for his election announcement was harshly criticised. So too was the transfer of 62 of the 76 political advisers from their ministries to campaign in Millbank. Their redundancy payments more than covered their salaries until they were, mostly, reappointed after the election. Conservatives complained to the Electoral Commission, in particular about the large subsidy to Alastair Campbell, obviously a key figure in the Labour campaign. Sam Younger, the Commission Chair, referred the matter to Sir Richard Wilson, the Cabinet Secretary, who had already sternly reiterated to civil servants and ministers the traditional guidelines on neutrality in the weeks between the election announcement and the vote.

There were unexpectedly few threatened lawsuits or complaints of local unfairness. But the new postal vote facilities came under scrutiny; there were stories of intimidation in the search for proxy and postal votes in Bradford and a BBC reporter showed how easy it could be to collect postal votes for dead people in Torbay.

The Conservatives launched their carefully prepared countdown 'twelve days to save the pound' on 26 May. They argued that, if Labour won the election, their promised referendum on the euro would provide no real safeguard because, under the new *Political Parties, Elections and Referendums Act,* more expenditure would be allowed to the pro-euro side and because the government would determine the timing of the vote and the wording of the question. Since the referendum would not be fair, it was argued, this election was effectively the key vote on saving the pound. Although the 'x days to save the £' was not consistently headlined, William Hague still stressed at Perth on 4 June:

Three days to save the £. Three days to decide whether our children and grandchildren will inherit the same freedoms that we inherited. ... Come with me and I will give you back your country.

In Edinburgh on 26 May, Tony Blair, in the fifth of his six major campaign orations, turned to foreign policy. It was said that he did not

want to be accused later of not having faced up to the problems of relations with Europe – and with the United States. His theme was 'Isolationism or marginalisation in Europe is not patriotic.' Blair deliberately talked about the EU and the world, rather than just about the euro. This speech created some differences of opinion at Millbank. The speech was on the grid but Gordon Brown wanted to soft pedal the theme. Lady Thatcher's intervention at Plymouth four days earlier had exposed divisions in the Conservative Party and he wished to take advantage of this.

However, as the opinion polls showed, the public (and particularly the floating voters) did not put Europe high among their priorities or feel scepticism about the idea of a referendum under a re-elected Labour government. The Conservative's focus on the euro at this stage of the election smacked of desperation. On 2 June a senior strategist was reported in *The Times* as saying rather pathetically that 'William has energised and shored up the core vote. We are now reaching out beyond the core.' There was a defeatist ring to William Hague's cry: 'If Labour wins the election, Tony Blair, by hook or by crook, would try to get us into the euro.' And, indeed, the theme was not wholeheartedly pursued over the last week – contrary to the original grid plan.

The Conservatives had a problem. All the surveys showed that voters were much more interested in the Labour issues of health and education than in the Conservative issues of Europe and tax. Indeed, on 28 May Alastair Campbell revealed, in the hope of creating instability in Central Office, a Labour private poll which showed how out of touch the Conservative campaign was with the public. Europe was not working. In the last week William Hague admitted to aides that his neglect of the public services 'is becoming an issue in itself'. Ignoring the issues was not helping the party. More attention was therefore given to these matters in the last days. The Conservatives also decided to concentrate resources on the closer target seats that they had neglected, anticipating that they would fall to them on even a small anti-Labour swing.

On 31 May Gordon Brown stressed other themes: 'For the final week we are going hard on public services. ... People will want to cast their votes for hospitals and schools.'

On 2 June the Conservatives launched an advertisement widely picked up by the cartoonists. 'Pricking the bubble' showed Tony Blair in an inflated bubble with the electorate posed with a pin.

A more pessimistic line developed in the final stages when even Conservatives expressed worries about the dire consequences of a Labour

A Conservative poster, putting Blair's head in a bubble, pricked by a pin, and warning of Labour arrogance and the threat of a landslide, was widely satirised.

Steve Bell, *Guardian*, 4 June 2001

landslide. This tactic had been discussed for some weeks. The key question was how to launch it without seeming defeatist.

It was Margaret Thatcher who on 31 May agonised publicly in the *Daily Telegraph* about the 'elective dictatorship' that would result. Aware of the impending Thatcher article, William Hague decided to use an interview with the BBC's Andrew Marr to raise the issue. That night Yellow M prepared the bubble ad which ran the following Saturday.

Tony Blair's response was to talk about the Tory ruse of trying to get in by the back door with talk of a landslide, thus encouraging Labour supporters not to vote. William Hague said on 4 June that a Labour landslide would mean that 'the brakes would be off for the most arrogant, aggressive and intimidating government in modern history'. However, on the same day he boldly listed the actions that he would take in the first fortnight after assuming office at the end of the week. But his final cry was:

Issue by issue, we have made and won our case. We have put forward answers that Labour is unable to question and we have put forward questions that Labour is unable to answer. ... Vote Conservative tomorrow and Britain will again become a place we can be proud to call our home.

Blair in the last week was also concerned about a low turnout and a reduced majority. In 1997 he had coined the phrase, 'this is not landslide country' to warn against complacency. This time he said in reply to a question by Channel 4's Elinor Goodman, 'The polls do not decide the election, the press do not decide the election – the British people are the boss.' Hard-hitting posters superimposed Margaret Thatcher's hair on top of William Hague's face and warned, 'Get out and vote. Or they get in.' At his press conferences Gordon Brown urged people to vote for hospitals and schools.

Tony Blair's last appeal contained these words:

This election really matters because it can, if the people decide, mark a real and historic turning point – a clean break with the politics of the eighties which left behind so many of our people.

As the campaign ended, the press and some politicians began increasingly openly to look beyond the campaign. There were stories of pro-European Tories, who had been silent so far, preparing to speak out and also of Labour left-wingers preparing to flex their muscles. There was also extended speculation as to what would happen to the Conservative leadership after a defeat. At the same time Labour was securing the endorsement of an unprecedented proportion of major national newspapers. Only the *Telegraph* and, ambivalently, the *Daily Mail* produced editorials in support of a Hague victory. *The Economist* of 1 June had a cover showing Tony Blair with Margaret Thatcher's hair (mimicking a Labour poster showing Hague as Thatcher), and argued that he was the best Thatcherite available.

The weather on Thursday 7 June was clement throughout most of the country, though there were heavy downpours in Buxton and Scarborough, as well as rain in parts of Scotland. But certainly meteorological conditions provided no excuse for the very low turnout that was being reported as the day advanced. When the booths closed at 10 p.m. all the networks quoted exit polls predicting a handsome Labour victory. At 10.46 p.m. Sunderland South was once again the first constituency to produce a result. Over the next hour returns from 20 other safe Labour seats confirmed a small swing to the Conservatives and a precipitous drop in participation. It was 1 a.m. before the first Conservative return (Poole) was reported and

The Economist front page picture of Blair (2 June) echoed a Labour poster depicting Hague in a Thatcher hair-do.

it was at 2 a.m. – with 236 results already in – that Romford provided the first Conservative gain of a seat. All but 5 British constituencies were counted on the night but only 21 changed hands and there were no celebrities among the casualties, although Sir Malcolm Rifkind's failure to recover Edinburgh Pentlands excited wistful comment.

Table 6.2   Party Gains and Losses

	Gained	Lost	Total seats
Labour	2	8	413
Conservatives	9	8	166
LibDem	8	2	52
Nationalists	1	2	9
Other	1	1	1
N. Ireland parties	7	7	18

It was different in Northern Ireland where the votes were counted on Friday. On an increased turnout 7 of the 18 seats changed hands and it was the extremists who advanced. The DUP moved nearer to the UUP in votes and seats. Sinn Féin overtook the SDLP in both votes and seats.

The most remarkable result was Wyre Forest where a local doctor, fighting solely on the issue of the closure of an Accident and Emergency facility at Kidderminster Hospital, secured 58 per cent of the vote and became the first MP to get to Westminster since the Second World War without any previous party history or any support from either of the main parties.

Blair heads for second landslide

The Times, 7 June 2001

Blair on brink of electoral history

Tories face longest period out of power since 1920s as opinion polls predict Labour majority

Financial Times, 7 June 2001

Blair cruises to victory

Guardian, 8 June, 2001

Blair strides to a place in history

Independent, 8 June 2001

Blair's back with a landslide

● Exit polls give Labour another huge majority   ● Tories slump to defeat amid lowest turnout for century

Daily Telegraph, 8 June 2001

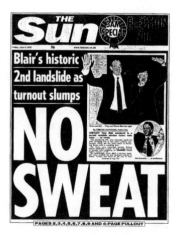

Sun and *Mirror* front pages, 8 June 2001

UKIP and the Greens, together with the miscellaneous socialist groupings, fared disastrously, though a few saved their deposits (see p. 301). The 16 per cent for a BNP candidate in riot-torn Oldham was ominously noted. The votes in the elections for the English shire counties (affecting a third of the total electorate) were not counted until the Friday.

There was a nationwide swing of 2 per cent from Labour to Conservative but Labour had a net loss of only 6 seats. The 12 per cent fall in turnout to 59 per cent was greatest in safe Labour seats where it affected few outcomes. It is discussed at length in Chapter 13 and in Appendix 2. Behind an election that seemed to make little change were far-reaching changes in the working of the electoral system.

Annex:

The Campaign in Scotland

James G. Kellas

The first general election since the advent of devolution in 1999 had many voters, politicians and observers confused. Among the first group, as vox pop interviews showed, were some who thought that the election was for the Scottish, not the British, Parliament.[1] That is not surprising since many of the politicians leading their party's campaign were actually Members of the Scottish Parliament (MSPs) who were not standing for Westminister. John Swinney, the SNP leader, was seen on TV more than Alex Salmond, the former leader who was still standing for the House of Commons. Similarly, David McLetchie, the Scottish Conservative leader in the Scottish Parliament, Jim Wallace the Scottish Liberal Democrat leader and Deputy First Minister in the Scottish Executive, and Henry McLeish, the Labour First Minister in the Scottish Executive were prominent. The latter was reported to be 'totally absorbed' in the campaign,[2] and Wendy Alexander, the Enterprise Minister in the Scottish Executive, was Labour coordinator of the campaign in Scotland, alongside her brother Douglas Alexander who ran the British Labour campaign. Apart from Douglas Alexander, none was standing in the election. News reports and TV election specials covered these Holyrood politicians as much as those who were actually standing.

Although the Scottish Parliament continued to meet during the campaign, First Minister's Question Time was rescheduled to Wednesday 6 June from Thursday 7 June, and the Parliament did not meet on election day. According to one report, Labour used the Scottish Parliament as a headquarters in breach of Holyrood rules issued to MSPs and parliamentary staff in March 2001. These state that 'e-mail accounts, the Parliament's telephone system and postal address should in no way be used for ... any party activity related to elections'. The SNP promised to raise this later in the Scottish Parliament's Standards Committee.[3]

Although devolution had been up and running since May 1999, the division between devolved and reserved functions was hopelessly blurred in the 2001 election. As in the rest of Great Britain, voters in Scotland rated health, education, and law and order as the most important issues.[4] However, for Scotland these functions have been devolved, and it could reasonably be asked what the Westminster Parliament could do for Scotland in these areas. The answer to that question is not straight-forward, something which appears to be appreciated by the electorate in Scotland. When asked 'Who do you think has most influence over the quality of the NHS and schools in Scotland?', voters rated Westminster highest (38 per cent), Holyrood second (27 per cent), and both equally (27 per cent), with Don't Know at 8 per cent.[5] This is no doubt related to the fact that the Scottish Parliament at present receives all its income from a grant paid by London on the basis of the 'Barnett Formula'. This formula was to become an issue in the election in Scotland, at least as far as the politicians and the media were concerned, if not the public.

Another feature of this aspect of politics in Scotland is the merging of party policies across the devolved and reserved functions. Thus the British party leaders and the party manifestos often assumed that devolution did not exist, and committed the parties to British-wide policies, even in devolved matters. Some unscrambling took place in the separate Scottish manifestos of the British parties, but the overall impression was of a British policy agenda. This could get the parties into a tangle at times: Henry McLeish, the Labour First Minister of the Scottish Executive, had to distance himself from Tony Blair's policy of privately-run surgical health units treating NHS patients,[6] and this policy was not mentioned in the Scottish Labour manifesto.[7] Of Labour's 'Five pledges for the next five years' in that manifesto, three related to devolved matters ('1,000 extra teachers in Scotland's schools; biggest ever hospital building programme; new powers to seize the assets of drug dealers'). The two remaining pledges ('Mortgages as low as possible, low inflation and sound public finances; Pensioners' winter fuel payment retained, minimum wage rising to £4.20') were indeed matters reserved to Westminster under the Scotland Act. The five pledges were subtitled 'Working with Labour in the Scottish Parliament', but this aspiration for 'joined-up government' could not disguise the fact that Labour in the Scottish Executive was already committed to different policies from Labour in the British government. Fees had already been abolished for Scottish-domiciled university students, and maintenance grants reintroduced for less wealthy students; free personal care for the elderly had been promised; education and health policies were different at several points. The pledge at the 1997 election to reduce hospital waiting lists by the next election by 10,000 was rescheduled by Labour in Scotland to run on past the 2001 election to April 2002.

The Conservatives in Scotland were just as muddled. When Ann Widdecombe was questioned on BBC Radio 4's *Election Call* (22 May) about Scotland's free personal care for the elderly, she attacked the policy and predicted an outflow of elderly people from England to Scotland to reap the benefit of free care. She had apparently forgotten that the Conservatives in the Scottish Parliament had voted for free care, as indeed they had for the abolition of student fees. Neither of these policies was supported by Conservatives in England.

Only the Liberal Democrats managed to keep a united policy front across Scotland, England and Wales. What they had achieved in coalition with Labour in Scotland was trumpeted as evidence of their success in forcing their policies through, and they hoped to do the same in England and Wales. Their problem in Scotland and Wales was that having joined with Labour in coalition government in these countries, they were now fighting against Labour in Westminster elections. They had therefore to find issues which divided them at a British level. Since the main issues according to voters were devolved matters where the parties were in coalition, that was not easy. The position of Charles Kennedy, the British Liberal Democrat leader, illustrated the party's problem. As a Scottish MP, Kennedy was intimately tied into Scottish politics, but he was not a member of the Scottish Executive, where Jim Wallace was Deputy First Minister. Kennedy and Wallace accompanied each other on tour in Scotland, as did the other party leaders both British and Scottish. But their view of politics differed because of the different power bases they appealed to. In the case of British leaders, London was that base; in the case of Scottish leaders, it was Edinburgh.

The fact that Scottish voters rated health, education and law and order as priority issues in much the same way as English and Welsh voters had implications for the Scottish parties, which were to tell in the election results. The SNP's platform of independence for Scotland, while continuously raised in the media, did not rate as an important issue for voters. Nor did the Barnett Formula, the powers of the Scottish Parliament, or the relationship with the EU (including the euro). Yet these were the issues that clearly distinguished the SNP and the Conservatives from the other parties. That left the parties to fight over the priority issues, where there was little to choose between them in a Scottish context. Even the Conservatives had moved to a left of centre position on these issues, unlike the Conservatives in England. That ought to have helped the Conservatives a little in Scotland, but it was not easy for them to distance themselves from the 'British' party's more radical right-wing stance. At the election the Scottish Conservative vote dropped from 17.5 per cent in 1997 to 15.6 per cent, although they gained Galloway and Upper Nithsdale from the SNP, their only Scottish seat.

It is little wonder that commentators were also bemused by all this, and some were irritable. Dr Peter Lynch of Stirling University, author of *Scottish Government and Politics. An Introduction* (Edinburgh University Press, 2001), wrote in the *Sunday Mail* (20 May), 'I'm confused ... the political parties are "disinventing" devolution and pulling the wool over our eyes on what this election is actually about ... The parties are seeking mandates that do not exist and wrecking any notion of a link between policies and what happens after the election.' For Lynch, 'Voters will have to wait for the 2003 Scottish election to have a say in those areas [education, crime, housing, health] here.'

Gerry Hassan, co-author of *The Almanac of Scottish Politics* (Politico's Publishing, 2001), wrote in the *Sunday Herald* (3 June) that the 2001 election 'is possibly the last British election', since at the next general election Scottish, Welsh and English politics would be more clearly distinguished, leaving Westminster with a remnant of the vital policy issues. The journalist Jason Allardyce in *Scotland on Sunday* (27 May), wrote under the headline 'THE REAL VOTE IS 2003, STUPID', that by then 'Scotland's money will be the dominant theme.'

Scotland's money was in fact a theme in the 2001 election. The notorious 'Barnett Formula' whereby Scotland, Wales and Northern Ireland are allocated funds by Westminster, was in fact first raised by the Deputy Prime Minister, John Prescott, Peter Mandelson and some other Labour politicians back in April, before the campaign had officially started. Prescott voiced the view, shared by many in England, that the Formula gave Scotland more than its fair share of public expenditure, and should be renegotiated, especially as the English regions were on train for some devolution themselves. What Prescott did not appear to realise was the strong commitment of Scottish Labour leaders to the Formula, in particular, Helen Liddell, the Scottish Secretary in the British Cabinet, and Henry McLeish, the First Minister of the Scottish Executive. Tony Blair quickly moved to quash this incipient policy move by Prescott, and no more was heard of it during the campaign. However, the issue did not go away in Scotland, and it was one of several 'devolution/constitutional' issues that surfaced, mainly at elite level, but spread into the media as well. (Another was the future position of the Secretary of State for Scotland. This was widely predicted to disappear after the election. However, a Scottish Labour and Scottish Conservative backlash led to both Blair[8] and the Scottish Conservatives[9] announcing that they would retain the position.)

Curiously it was a letter to the *Scotsman* (21 May) by 12 economics professors at Scottish universities that sparked the 'Barnett' controversy. The subject was the rather arcane one of 'fiscal autonomy' for Scotland, but the political effect was immediate and strong. What the learned correspondents proclaimed was no less than the statement that 'It, therefore, gives us some pleasure, but no surprise, to learn that Scotland actually subsidises England to the tune of £1.2 billion each year' (quoting as source a letter from a London accountant to the *Financial Times*, 1 May). The lesson of this revelation was that Scotland could well afford to go it alone, or at least operate 'fiscal autonomy', meaning raising all its own revenue, and sending a contribution to London for non-devolved services. This hoary old debate, which goes back to the nineteenth century, was clearly designed to set the constitutional issue alight again, in effect to the SNP's advantage and to the discomfiture of Labour, though that was not intended by all the signatories. For not only was Labour's embarrassment over the Barnett Formula revisited, but the ball was placed firmly in the SNP's court regarding the viability of an independent Scotland. Recriminations were not slow in coming about the credentials and motives of the professors, some of whom quickly denied any sinister nationalist motive. But, from Labour's point of view, the damage was done, and all branches of the media pounced on the debate, while the SNP referred continuously from then on to the 'expert' backing for their case for Scottish independence.

In the event, there is little evidence of the SNP gaining anything electorally from this. Its vote fell from 22.1 per cent to 20.1 per cent and it lost one of its 6 seats to the Conservatives. From the SNP's point of view, the strategy of contesting Westminster seats was a failure. Its strength was in the Scottish Parliament, where it had achieved 28.7 per cent of the vote in the first ballot and 27.3 per cent in the second (party list) ballot and won 35 seats (28 under the second ballot). It would be likely to do even better in the next Scottish elections in 2003, when Labour might be facing unpopularity and when the only alternative government was the SNP. The achievement of independence would follow from that, and from a Scottish referendum, not from Westminster, according to the SNP.

The election results in Scotland reflected the general confusion and apathy. Turnout was marginally lower (at 58.1 per cent) in Scotland than in the UK as a whole (58.8 per cent), and was almost exactly the same as at the Scottish Parliament elections in 1999. Would the trend downwards continue at the next Scottish Parliament elections in 2003, or would the turnout increase to a level higher than in 2001? That would test the voters' opinion of the importance of the Scottish Parliament as compared to Westminster.

The media tried valiantly to inject enthusiasm into their coverage of the campaign but BBC Scotland admitted that its ratings were down on 1997, although one of its programmes reached an audience of 250,000. There were various opt-outs from London programmes, some of them on BBC1 and some of them on BBC2.[10] Scottish Television claimed a 2 per cent increase in its share of the audience in the month before the election,[11] and it ran five *Scottish 500* hour-long discussion programmes with featured party leaders, as well as several *Election Face to Face* programmes. Party Election Broadcasts came in two formats, British and Scottish, with the latter predominating. Some of these were essentially British with Scottish voice-overs, and Scottish captions. The Scottish Socialist Party merited one PEB, since it put up candidates in all of the 72 Scottish seats. Produced and directed by professional film-makers who produced the film *My Name is Joe,* and scripted by actor Peter Mullan, it was a highly watchable if rather horrific piece. The Scottish Green Party, on the other hand, had no PEB, as it put up only 4 candidates. The UK Independence Party got a PEB on the basis of its British-wide candidatures, not its 10 in Scotland (maximum vote 1.6 per cent in Roxburgh and Berwickshire). Viewers to Channels 4 and 5 could receive the same PEBs as those in England and Wales (including Plaid Cymru!), but viewers there (except in the north of England) could not receive the Scottish PEBs.

The press in Scotland is divided into purely Scottish titles, Scottish editions of British papers, and British papers with no substantial variation in Scotland. The first two categories are by far the best-selling papers, especially among the broadsheets,[12] with the second relying heavily on a Scottish identity (for example, *Scottish Sun* 380,537, *Scottish Daily Express* 88,352, *Scottish Daily Mail* 125,158, *Scottish Mirror* 51,719, *Scottish News of the World* 338,079).[13] Coverage of the campaign was extensive, with many feature articles by Scottish journalists (all papers have resident

Scottish political correspondents). When the crunch came to recommend how to vote there was more confusion than usual, especially in the purely Scottish titles. The *Scotsman* (92,648), 'Scotland's National Newspaper' (so-called) endorsed a selection of 20 individual candidates (8 Labour, 4 Liberal Democrat, 4 Conservative, 4 SNP): 'A vote for the person who will work best for the country'[14] not a party. No doubt this was because the editor-in-chief, Andrew Neil, is Conservative, while the paper generally leans to Liberal Democrat and Labour. The *Scotsman's* sister paper, *Scotland on Sunday* (99,604), editorialised that it supported 'Labour, on a warning', the warning being that it would be judged on its fulfilment of its election promises.[15] Scotland's other broadsheets, the Glasgow *Herald* (93,434) and *Sunday Herald* (59,965), part of the Scottish Media Group which also owns Scottish Television and Grampian Television, were explicitly anti-Conservative, but it was not clear who they were for. The *Herald* wanted 'An election to end timid government'[16] and the *Sunday Herald* said 'We need Blair to make a commitment that his second administration will be significantly different',[17] quoting a Scottish 500 survey of voters in which 55 per cent trusted Blair less after four years. The Scottish daily papers outside the central belt are the Dundee *Courier and Advertiser* (90,431) and the Aberdeen *Press and Journal* (102,100: 1999 figure). The former is owned by the old Scottish family firm, D.C. Thomson (which also owns the high-selling (631,161) *Sunday Post*), while the latter is part of Associated Newspapers, the *Daily Mail* group. Both are Conservative-leaning, but in the election were not explicitly so. The *Courier* editorialised, 'The spectre of an electoral dictatorship is again stalking the land',[18] while the *Press and Journal* said that no party was worthy of support in this election and the reason for electoral apathy was that 'blame lies with the poor quality of political candidate being foist [sic] on the country'.[19]

The Scottish tabloids are all part of British publishing groups. The only purely Scottish titles are the *Daily Record* (601,544) and *Sunday Mail* (708,781), in the Trinity Mirror Group. Like the other Mirror group titles, both are staunchly Labour. The Scottish Socialist Party leader, Tommy Sheridan, planned to sue the *Daily Record* because of what he claimed was a smear campaign against him. The *Record* for its part banned any mention of him for its pages.[20] The Scottish editions of the *Mirror* (51,719), *Sunday Mirror* (28,941), *Daily Mail* (125,158), *Mail on Sunday* (112,759), *Daily Express* (88,352) and *Sunday Express* (66,660) (all with 'Scottish' in front of their titles) conformed to their editors'/proprietors' voting preferences, but the Scottish editions' editorials were altered to take account of Scottish circumstances, with references to the SNP, devolution and independence.

The papers with purely British titles and editors adhered to the line taken by the London papers, and were much more partisan than the purely Scottish titles. This may be because the party choice and electoral support in England is less varied than in Scotland, especially with the absence of the second party in Scotland, the SNP.

No paper in Scotland supports the SNP (although the *Scottish Sun* did between 1992 and 1997, but not at the election of 1997). This is certainly an anomaly in terms of a representative press, but it should be pointed out that some papers carry regular columns by SNP politicians. The most notable of these is Andrew Wilson MSP's full-page column in the mass circulation *Sunday Mail,* and Alex Salmond's full-page column in the *News of the World.* These ran throughout the election campaign, with a combined circulation of almost a million copies. The brief campaign visit of Sean Connery in support of the SNP was also given extensive coverage in the tabloids. Despite these SNP inputs in the media, the SNP's vote fell in the election.

This was an inconclusive election as far as Scotland was concerned. To a large extent Scottish politicians and the public were looking to the Scottish Parliament, not Westminster, for a solution to Scotland's problems, although they were disappointed in its record to date.[21] Voter turnout in Scotland in 2001 matched almost exactly that at the Scottish Parliament election in 1999. Voting behaviour in these elections was however different, although 2001 was similar to the 1997 British general election. Seats won were almost identical in these elections, except that the Conservatives gained Galloway and Upper Nithsdale from the SNP. This has been attributed to foot and mouth disease and the obscurity and youth of the SNP candidate. It was certainly not a 'seat to watch' in the media, and the result came as a complete surprise (the SNP holds it for the Scottish Parliament).

Scottish and English voters were similar in their apathy towards politics and politicians in 2001. But their views on some major issues (for example the duty of the state to supply employment and to redistribute income) were divergent.[22] These were matters mainly for Westminster, not 'Holyrood'. At the same time, devolution has been responsible for several divergent policies in Scotland – in education, health, social policy and law reform (for example, the repeal of 'Section 28' = Section 2A in Scotland) – and has forced all the parties to support different policies in Scotland from those presented to voters elsewhere. And behind all the debates in Scotland is the agenda of nationalism and independence, and the future position of the SNP. The 2001 election did not (and could not)

Daily Record front page, 8 June 2001

deal properly with these. The 2003 Scottish Parliament election certainly will.

Notes

1. There were two Scottish Parliament by-elections held on the same day, for Banff and Buchan and for Strathkelvin and Bearsden. The former was the result of the SNP's Alex Salmond resigning to stand for Westminster, and the latter because of the resignation from the Scottish Parliament of former Executive Minister Sam Galbraith. There was no change in either seat, but the voters discriminated between the two Parliaments by casting their votes somewhat differently. For example, the SNP vote in Banff and Buchan was 50.1% for Holyrood and 54.2% for Westminster. In Strathkelvin and Bearsden, Labour won with 37% for Holyrood, but with 46.4% for Westminster. An Independent (who did not stand for Westminster) came second in the by-election with 18.2% of the vote.
2. 'Anger as McLeish admits Blair election campaign is Labour MSPs' top priority', *Sunday Herald*, 6 May 2001.
3. 'Labour's election HQ breaks Holyrood rules', *Sunday Times Scotland*, 20 May 2001.
4. 'What matters most to the voter, on a scale of one to ten': The NHS (9.22); Education (9.03); Law and order (8.84); Environment (8.35); Taxes (7.87; Plight of countryside (7.69); Fuel duties (7.52); Third world debt (6.23); Europe (6.19); GM food (5.26); Genetics, including cloning (4.83) (ICM/*Scotsman*, 15

May 2001). 'What issues matter most to voters?': Health (71%); Education (54%); Law and order (40%); Unemployment/jobs (40%); The economy (28%); Taxation (27%); Transport (11%); European issues/single currency (8%); Immigration/asylum seekers (7%); Foot and mouth (5%) (System Three/*Herald*, 24 May 2001).

5. ICM/*Scotsman*, 15 May 2001.
6. 'McLeish defies Blair on health', *Sunday Times Scotland*, 20 May 2001.
7. *Ambitions for Scotland. Labour's Manifesto 2001*, pp. 19–21.
8. 'Pledge to maintain cabinet post for Scottish secretary', *Herald*, 26 May 2001.
9. Scottish Conservative manifesto: *Time for Common Sense in Scotland*, p. 44.
10. 'Electorate gave small screen a big switch-off', *Sunday Times Scotland*, 10 June 2001.
11. *Ibid.*
12. The 'British' broadsheets sell in derisively low numbers in Scotland (*Times*, 34,517; *Daily Telegraph*, 24,771; *Guardian*, 13,803; *Independent*, 6,785. Sunday equivalents are somewhat higher: *Sunday Times*, 81,372 – but this is actually a Scottish edition, *Sunday Times Scotland*; *Sunday Telegraph*, 33,946; *Observer*, 25,445 (also a Scottish edition); *Independent on Sunday*, 8,234. Source as for note 13.
13. All press circulation figures are average net circulations, November 2000–April 2001. *Scotsman*, S2 Monday, 18 June 2001, p. 5.
14. *Scotsman*, 5 June 2001.
15. *Scotland on Sunday*, 3 June 2001.
16. *Herald*, 7 June 2001.
17. *Sunday Herald*, 20 May 2001.
18. *Courier and Advertiser*, 4 June 2001.
19. *Press and Journal*, 7 June 2001.
20. *Sunday Times Scotland*, 20 May 2001.
21. 'Voters lose faith in Holyrood', *Scotland on Sunday*, 24 June 2001. This story is based on the first Scottish Social Attitudes Survey, and is analysed by John Curtice in the same issue. 'Nearly three-quarters still believe the Scottish Parliament ought to be the body that has most influence in Scotland. Only one in eight think that the UK government should actually hold that position.' Nevertheless, 'the predominant mood in the country is that having the Parliament is simply not going to make any difference, either to life within Scotland or to Scotland's position in the UK'. Curtice concludes, 'the Scottish Parliament does indeed face a real danger of becoming as much of an embarrassment as the Dome'. Given the responses as a whole, however, Westminster might appear to be the 'second-order' Parliament in the opinion of most Scots.
22. John Curtice, 'The Sunday Essay: Devolution's Second Birthday', *Scotland on Sunday*, 24 June 2001.

7
Public Polls and Private Polls

Opinion pollsters are now major players on the electoral scene. Their findings shape the mood of protagonists and of voters. In a competitive world their commercial success in the market research trade depends significantly upon their accuracy in indicating the likely division of the vote. Election forecasting is not their main source of income but it is their most publicised activity.

The polls indicated the outcome of the 2001 election long before it began. From 1997 onwards, except for a brief period following the fuel protest crisis, they always reported Labour as comfortably ahead of the Conservatives (see p. 16). Although many suspected that both sampling methods and the prevailing political mood had long caused the polls to overstate Labour's support, the margin was too big for doubt. The findings lay like a cloud over all the Conservatives' efforts at revival. They may also have reduced media interest and depressed turnout.

Only 31 nationwide polls were published compared to 44 in 1997 and 57 in 1992. Only 3 per cent of front pages had a poll as their lead story, compared to a fifth in 1987 and 1992. When on 31 May *The Times'* MORI survey cut the Labour lead from 25 per cent to 16 per cent following a change in methodology, it was not splashed on the front page as planned. Moreover the papers made less play with their own focus groups than in previous campaigns, despite some ingenious work by Andrew Cooper for *The Times*.

Four pollsters dominated the political scene. The surveys that the politicians followed were MORI in *The Times*, Gallup in the *Daily Telegraph*, ICM in the *Guardian* and NOP in the *Sunday Times*. The Harris Poll, once prominent, produced only occasional reports. In 2001 the *Independent* used Rasmussen, an American company, employing a new telephone

121

technique, with random dialling and automated voice questioning; the questions were prepared by the *Independent*, the questions recorded by a British actor, and the phone calls made from America.

Sophisticated comment on the polls was provided by Peter Kellner in the *Observer* and *Evening Standard*, Peter Riddell in *The Times*, Anthony King in the *Daily Telegraph*, Alan Travis in the *Guardian* and John Curtice in the *Independent* and elsewhere.

The 2001 election was the first in which random digit dialling was used for the great majority of polls. Only MORI continued face-to-face interviewing. This means that quasi-random sampling has become the norm of British polling rather than the quota sampling that has been dominant since its inception in 1937.

Some pollsters claimed that the 1997 election showed that they had put their house in order following the disaster of 1992. In 1997, when the actual Labour lead was 13 per cent, the final surveys ranged between 10 per cent and 18 per cent. This was a relief since in 1992 they had collectively underestimated the Conservative lead by about 8 per cent. However, there had been an ominous warning during the European Parliament election of 1999. The polls had found that only 30 per cent said 'certain to vote'. Confining their forecasts to this category, Labour was still expected to win handsomely – by 14 per cent (MORI), 13 per cent (Gallup) or 7 per cent (ICM). The Conservatives ended up 7 per cent ahead and the turnout proved to be only 23 per cent. During the 2001 campaign the polls agreed in putting Labour well ahead but the margins varied considerably. ICM had long been reporting a smaller lead than its competitors. There was general agreement that this was mainly due to the fact that 'how will you vote?' was asked later in the interview after respondents had been reminded of the existence of the Liberal Democrats.

During the 2001 contest, the differences between the polls became more significant. Early on Labour's lead varied from 28 per cent (MORI, 18 May) to 13 per cent (ICM 23 May). Each of the polls was fairly consistent but at a different level. Only MORI gave the impression of a trend in either direction between the major parties (though all polls agreed in indicating the Liberal Democrat advance).

Behind these stable figures there was a lot of 'churning'. Panel studies in past elections have shown 25 per cent of the electorate changing their voting intention during the campaign. A MORI panel suggests that as many as 36 per cent reported different action on 7 June from their answers in early May; 19 per cent moved to 'did not vote' (5 per cent from Labour and 3 per cent from the Conservatives) and 6 per cent refused. But 10 per cent actually switched parties.

Table 7.1   Labour lead (per cent) in weekly tracking polls

	Week 1	%	Week 2	%	Week 3	%	Final	%	Average
MORI	17 May	26	24 May	25	31 May	18	7 Jun	15	22
Gallup	17 May	16	24 May	16	31 May	16	7 Jun	17	16
ICM	16 May	15	23 May	13	30 May	19	6 Jun	11	15
NOP	13 May	17	20 May	19	27 May	19	3 Jun	17	18
Rasmussen	15 May	14			29 May	12	5 Jun	11	12
Average	18%		18%		18%		14%		

Result Labour lead 9%

Every election must expect one or two rogue polls, suddenly out of line due to the chances of sampling. ICM's jump to 19 per cent (*Guardian*, 30 May) must be put in this category (possibly the ICM result could be due to interviewing during a Bank Holiday). But, unfortunately for Conservative morale, none erred in their favour.

In their main time-series each poll had a distinctive pattern. But the variations within and between the polls hardly suggest a consistent measuring instrument. There were significant changes in technique during the campaign. On 17 May Gallup introduced a turnout filter: by confining their figures to those most certain to vote this cut the Labour lead by about 3 per cent. MORI (which was alone in conducting face to face interviews) confronted voters in their 31 May and 7 June polls with a full list of the candidates in their constituency (just as they had done in 1997); this seems to have led to a sharp reduction in Labour's lead. They also introduced, in their final survey, some further adjustment based on telephone re-interviews with some respondents and also making allowance for refusals and likelihood to turn out. Each pollster had its own rules about adjusting for refusals and 'don't knows'.

Each of the polls managed to put the Conservatives within 3 per cent of their final level of support and all but one put the Liberal Democrats within 1 per cent of theirs. But it is important to note that all of them overestimated the Labour vote – in the case of NOP and Gallup by 5 per cent.

Was the fall in participation the explanation? The polls often reported the likelihood of a low turnout. Up to 10 per cent fewer were saying 'certain to vote' than at the comparable moment in 1997. But virtually no one suggested that the actual turnout could fall to 59 per cent, 12 per cent down from 1997. A private Labour Party study at the end of May explored what would happen if turnout fell to 55 per cent and came up with a prediction that exactly matched the 42/33/19 outcome that actually

Table 7.2   **Voting intentions during the campaign**

Date of field work	Sample size	Date of publication	Polling org / Newspaper	Con %	Lab %	LibDem %	Other %	Lab Lead%
8 May	1,046	10 May	MORI/*Times**	30	54	13	3	+24
10–11 May	1,003	13 May	NOP/*S.Times*	32	49	13	6	+17
10–11 May	1,011	13 May	ICM/*Obs*	32	48	15	5	+16
10–12 May	1,021	13 May	MORI/*S.Tel*	31	51	13	5	+20
11–13 May	1,437	14 May	ICM/*E.S*	32	48	14	6	+16
12–13 May	1,030	15 May	Rasmussden/*Ind¢*	32	46	13	9	+14
13–14 May	1,004	16 May	ICM/*Gdn*	31	46	16	7	+15
10–14 May	1,846	18 May	MORI/*Econ**	26	54	14	6	+28
14–15 May	1,004	17 May	Gal/*D.Tel*+	32	48	13	7	+16
15 May	1,019	17 May	MORI/*Times**	28	54	12	6	+26
17–18 May	1,107	20 May	NOP/*S.Times*	30	49	14	7	+19
19–21 May	1,000	23 May	ICM/*Gdn*	32	45	17	7	+13
21–22 May	1,931	25 May	Rasmussen/*Ind¢*	32	44	16	8	+12
21–23 May	1,439	24 May	Gal/*D.Tel*+	32	48	15	5	+16
22 May	1,066	24 May	MORI/*Times**	30	55	11	4	+25
24–25 May	1,001	27 May	NOP/*S.Times*	30	49	14	7	+19
26–27 May	1,227	29 May	Ras/*Ind¢*	32	44	17	7	+12
26–28 May	1,000	30 May	ICM/*Gdn*	28	47	17	8	+19
29 May	1,013	31 May	MORI/*Times***	30	48	16	6	+18
28–29 May	1,462	31 May	Gal/*D.Tel*+	31	47	16	6	+16
30 May–1 Jun.	1,007	1 Jun.	ICM/*C4*	31	43	19	7	+12
31 May–1 Jun.	1,105	3 Jun.	NOP/*S.Times*	30	47	16	7	+17
31 May–1 Jun.	1,005	3 Jun.	ICM/*Obs*	34	46	15	5	+12
31 May–2 Jun.	1,010	3 Jun	MORI/*S.Tel*	27	50	17	6	+23
2–3 Jun.	1,381	4 Jun.	ICM/*E.S*	30	47	18	5	+17
2–3 Jun.	1,266	5 Jun.	Rasmussen/*Ind¢*	33	44	16	7	+11
2–4 Jun.	1,009	6 Jun.	ICM/*Gdn*	32	43	19	6	+11
5–6 Jun.	1,967	7 Jun.	MORI/*Times***	30	45	18	7	+15
6 Jun.	2,399	7 Jun.	Gal/*D.Tel*+	30	47	18	5	+17

ᵃ * Face-to-face poll

¢ Computer Automated Telephone poll

** Secret ballot for voting intention – also based solely on those intending to vote

+ Figures based only on responses of those believed most certain to vote (66%)

Source: MORI

occurred. A post-election study by ICM found that the abstainers, if they had voted, would have divided 57 per cent Labour to 19 per cent Conservative.

The pollsters professed themselves to be pleased with their performance, even though it would have been a major achievement to get wrong the broad outcome of so one-sided an election. As in 1997, APOPO, their

Table 7.3 **Final polls (per cent)**

	Lab %	Con %	LibDem %	Lab Lead %	Error on Lab Lead%
MORI *Times* 7 June	45	30	18	15	+6
Gallup *D.Tel* 7 June	47	30	18	17	+8
ICM *Guardian* 6 June	43	32	19	11	+2
NOP *S.Times* 4 June	47	30	18	17	+8
Rasmussen 6 June	44	33	16	11	+2
Average	45	31	18	14	+5
Actual Result	42	33	19	9	

association (from which ICM had withdrawn in 2000), quickly issued an undeservedly self-congratulatory statement:

> Confounding their critics, especially those within the Conservative Party who had poured scorn on them throughout the campaign, the opinion polls conducted in the last week of the campaign proved the most accurate since 1987, and the exit polls performed remarkably well. This level of accuracy in the polls was achieved despite the record low level of turnout, which made forecasting far more difficult.

Robert Worcester of MORI commented on his website that:

> the worry for pollsters is that once again a late swing confounded them. In every election save one, 1983, the party ahead in the polls ends up with fewer votes than forecast.

This is no proof of a late swing and other pollsters contended that the only net movement was the Liberal Democrat advance and a small late switch to non-voting. ICM conducted a poll for the BBC in the last week of the campaign and recontacted respondents on election day to find out how, if at all, they had voted. Of those originally saying they were certain to vote Conservative, 98 per cent said they had cast a vote and 93 per cent had voted Conservative (3 per cent had switched and 2 per cent refused to answer). The figures for Labour were very similar – 97 per cent said they had cast a vote, 91 per cent for Labour and 2 per cent for another party. Nick Sparrow claimed that Labour lost a maximum of 1 per cent in the last few days because of 'late swing' and failure to turn out. The problem lay more in polling methodology, with low response rates and imperfectly representative sampling than in late swing.[1]

Critics pointed out that, if the election had been close, the variations during the campaign and the divergences at the end would have excited reproach. Some were troubled about sampling. A MORI panel poll for the Electoral Commission found 80 per cent claiming to have voted. A post-election survey for the Labour Party found 78 per cent saying the same. If 78–80 per cent of respondents claimed to have voted when the actual turnout was only 59 per cent, this suggests either false memory by the public or imperfect sampling by the pollsters. In a 1987 study, the only one of its kind, Swaddle and Heath found, after checking the electoral records, that only 4 per cent of those who told a post-election survey that they had voted, had in fact failed to do so.[2] Unless there has been a great change in public veracity since 1987, it does seem that a significant tranche of the public must have been escaping the pollsters' attention in 2001.

Because they were sampling in predominantly marginal seats the exit polls did not venture figures for turnout or overall party percentages. But the estimates for seats were as close as could reasonably be expected.

Table 7.4   Exit polls
(Seats projection at 10 p.m. on 7 June)

	Lab	*Con*	*LibDem*	*Other*	*Majority*
BBC (NOP)	408	175	44	30	157
ITN MORI	417	155	58	30	175
Result	413	166	52	28	167

At the constituency level, only a few professional polls were reported. An ICM poll of the 137 most marginal seats for the *News of the World* was very accurate about party gains; six constituency polls were reported in Scotland and all suggested the correct winner – but almost all underestimated support for the Conservatives – and for the Liberal Democrats. There were also five Scotland-wide polls which ended not too far in error even though they tended to be too optimistic for the SNP and too pessimistic for the Liberal Democrats. There were also two polls in Wales.

Although the polls on voting intention were fewer and less publicised than in previous contests, polls on issues were more reported in the press than ever before. By contrast, broadcasters were interested in the horse race. A study of the coverage of the polls by the ITV's *News at Ten* and BBC's *Ten o'clock News* by a team at Cardiff University revealed that fewer than one in five references to the polls reported public opinion on issues or policies. The fact that the public consistently put health and education as top influences in their voting decision, with law and order and Europe far behind, was constantly cited as an explanation for the failure of the Conservative campaign to make much impact. It was notable that, while the public divided 67/33 per cent against joining the euro, they divided only 39/25 per cent in favour of the Conservatives when asked which party had the best policies for Europe. A change in economic optimism was also noted; when MORI asked in late April whether economic conditions would get better or worse, pessimists prevailed by 40/18 per cent; by late May they only led by 24/20 per cent. And by 71/16 per cent they felt that the government had done a good job at managing the economy over the past four years.[3]

Tony Blair steadily led William Hague as 'best prime minister' by about 50/15 per cent. The only significant campaign effect on leaders' images was the rise of Charles Kennedy from 8 per cent to 14 per cent, virtually equal with William Hague. In April 1997 by 55/33 per cent the public agreed that Labour was ready to form the next government; in May 2001, by 25/6 per cent, they thought that the Conservatives were not ready.

As in 1997, Labour's opinion research was more wide-ranging and continuous than the Conservatives'; it also influenced the themes of every party's campaign. Philip Gould had been associated with the party continuously since 1985; in late 1997 he formed his own research company, GCGNOP (the acronym was based on Gould, together with the two American campaign advisers, Stan Greenberg and James Carville, using the long-established British polling company, NOP under Nick Moon to do their fieldwork). Gould and Greeenberg, helped by Greg Cook at Millbank, took over surveys for the party. As noted on page 33, his work had been important before the campaign in reassuring Blair of the strength of the party's position on tax and investment in public services.

Tracking surveys were planned and analysed by Stan Greenberg. He had polled for Bill Clinton in the 1992 presidential campaign, for Al Gore in 2000, and had worked with Gould on Labour Party surveys since 1996. The picture he provided was reassuring on many of the key themes. During the campaign the party conducted two to three polls a week, with a sample of 1,000. Greenberg found increasing Labour leads on voting intentions reaching 22 per cent in the third week and 21 per cent on 5 June. Even assuming a low turnout (57 per cent) the lead was still 17 per cent. On the key attributes which the polls tracked, Labour's lead over the Conservatives was stable but improving on leadership, tax and standing up for Britain.

Philip Gould personally conducted focus groups in London some six nights a week during the campaign. A note interpreting the findings was available for Gordon Brown and Tony Blair at the end of the day. One observer of the groups commented that people took the view that Labour should be given time to deliver on schools and hospitals. 'It is a conditional vote of approval', he added. In the middle of the campaign Gould shifted from studying 'switchers' and concentrated on the weakening core of Labour voters, particularly working-class women under 45. Many felt that Labour was abandoning them for the middle class and business. He reported a worry among core Labour voters about the pound. Focus groups were also conducted in marginal seats in the Pennines, Scotland and Wales and on the Kent coast about voters' reactions to the euro and asylum seekers by the party's advertising agency, TBWA.

Parties usually guard their private research jealously. When they reveal a few select findings, it is usually for tactical reasons. Considering that Tony Blair wished to prevent complacency and combat the poll-inspired view that a Labour victory was foreordained, it was extraordinary that his Press Secretary publicised details of the party's research. On 28 May Alastair Campbell called a lobby meeting to report Labour's commanding leads on voting intention and on many policy areas. The reasons for this were largely tactical but the effect was to induce even more confidence about the result. At this time other aides were talking freely to reporters about a possible 'melt down' in the Tory vote.

Gould was closely involved throughout in shaping Labour's campaign thinking and shared the central desk in Millbank with Campbell, McDonagh, Hyman, Ed Miliband, McFadden, Alexander and Sally Dobson. Like other key aides Gould received strategy memos from Tony Blair and was in frequent face-to-face contact with him. Blair and to a lesser extent Brown liked to talk at length about the findings of the opinion polls and focus groups and tease out the strategic implications. This was a different relationship from that which Conservative leaders had with their pollsters.

As noted on page 60, ICM had polled for the Conservative Party on a modest scale throughout the Parliament. It had pre-tested ideas for advertising and policy changes, and identified likely 'swing' voters. In the build-up to the campaign this research was still limited and a programme of research and a budget were only agreed between Central Office and ICM in March 2001. As in 1997, the party did not commission national polls, but decided to take advantage of the many polls published in the media.

Conservative supporters of the polling operation hoped that one effect might be to convince Conservative politicians how out of touch and unpopular they remained with the public after the 1997 election. They regarded this as an important first step in achieving the modernisation of the party. Nick Sparrow spoke of his task as trying 'to get shadow ministers to think themselves into the lives of ordinary people'. There was some resistance. At one Shadow Cabinet meeting early in the Parliament John Redwood claimed that he conducted his own focus groups – on the doorstep in Wokingham every week!

During the election ICM conducted focus groups five nights a week, concentrating on issues of crime, the euro, asylum and tax. The findings were available for Rick Nye and William Hague at the end of the evening. The gist of the reports was that neither tax or the euro were working, in the sense of winning over non-Conservative voters, although people certainly brought these up as concerns. The promise of tax cuts raised fears about cuts in public services and many voters took the view that the future of the pound could be decided at the promised referendum. When ICM asked voters what themes the parties were talking about, the swing voters correctly identified the Conservative themes, as well as Labour's emphasis on schools, hospitals and crime. But when the interviewers further asked which issues mattered to the voters personally, respondents were much more likely to mention Labour themes. When asked how they knew that Labour was talking about schools and hospitals, many replied that they frequently saw pictures of Tony Blair at a school or hospital.

In addition, ICM conducted weekly surveys with samples of 500 in a selection of 180 target seats. The original intention had been to move quickly from the 28 seats that were most likely to fall to the party on a modest pro-Conservative swing. This did not happen. Hague and his aides were disappointed that the ICM findings in the target seats were as discouraging as those in the national polls. Hague himself was perplexed that his opposition to the euro was not gaining votes. In the last week the survey was disaggregated into Conservative–Labour and Conservative–Liberal Democrat marginals, to assess whether the Conservatives should concentrate more fire on the Liberal Democrats.

ICM also did extensive political polling for the media as well as other interest groups. Because of its adjustments (see p. 122) ICM usually reported lower Labour leads than other polling organisations. The ICM poll in the *Guardian* on 31 May, which reported an increase in the Labour lead to 19 per cent, therefore achieved quite an impact. Michael Portillo, under questioning at the morning press conference in Central Office, dismissed the finding and added that the party had cut back its private polling. It had not, and Nick Sparrow maintained a dignified silence throughout the campaign as William Hague and other leading Conservatives regularly dismissed the accuracy of the opinion polls.

When party strategists are challenged about the extent to which their private polls influenced their strategy, they tend to be ambivalent. Often they find difficulty in pointing to a specific change of direction attributable to a poll finding. But at times they value polls for the reassurance they can give that they are addressing the right issues and they use them to check colleagues advocating impractical courses of action.

This cartoon seemed as true in June 2001 as when it was published in November 1997.

Garland, *Daily Telegraph*, 28 November 1997

ICM findings, however, were not reassuring for Conservative strategists. They showed that swing voters were more concerned about poor public services than tax cuts and that they did not identify with William Hague and other leading Conservatives. As in Labour's focus groups Hague was often seen as too negative, too 'knocking'. Sparrow thought that his research suggested that the Conservatives could have been even more radical in proposing reforms of the NHS and of schools, providing more opportunity for the private sector and more experiments in delivery. The work suggested that the party should neutralise Labour charges of 'cuts' by matching Labour's proposed spending and making the issue one of management of the services. Traditionally, the Conservatives had been seen as more competent managers than Labour.

It is doubtful that the Conservative Party made the best use of its polling. Given William Hague's personal opposition to the euro as well as the hostility of many of his MPs and activists, and the party's determination to find room for tax cuts, the scope for changing the strategy was limited. 'This campaign is one-eighth research seven-eighths dogma', said one who was closely involved. Over the course of the Parliament, Nick Sparrow made periodic presentations to William Hague and his advisers (usually Seb Coe, George Osborne, Rick Nye and Danny Finkelstein). During the campaign the Gang of Four also received a summary report of all the focus groups. In contrast to Gould, Sparrow had few face-to-face meetings with the leader and made only one presentation to him in the six months before the election campaign. But more important than the question of the pollster's face-to-face time with the leaders was that the polling was never a structured part of the political decision-making process.

The Liberal Democrats lacked the means to do as much private polling. But they employed Martin Hamblin to conduct research on policy, as well as focus groups and in-depth interviews. Most of their work was in key marginals where they conducted a quarterly survey on issues. During the campaign they had a rolling poll based on a hundred interviews each day. They also relied heavily on a systematic analysis of canvass returns.

The public polls create pressures for the politicians by creating expectations. At the start of the campaign, Labour strategists would have considered a majority of 100 or so sufficient. By the end they felt under pressure to achieve at least 150. Anything less would be a setback and would be interpreted as a success of sorts for Hague. Indeed, after the election, some Conservatives claimed a limited success because they had done better than the polls predicted.

Notes

1. See N. Sparrow, 'Faulty Psephology' *Guardian*, 10 Sept. 2001.
2. K. Swaddle and A. Heath 'Official and reported turnout in the British General Election of 1987' (1989) *British Journal of Political Science*, 19, 537–70.
3. For more data see figures in R. Worcester and R. Mortimore, *Explaining Labour's Second Landslide* (2001).

8
Politics on the Air

Martin Harrison

The campaign opened with ritual and innovation. Ritual: helicopter cameras tracking Tony Blair to the Palace and back live into the lunchtime news. Innovation: the choice of a school, rather than Downing Street, for the formal announcement, excited schoolgirls greeting the Prime Minister, the choir singing *Kumbayah*, the churchy setting, the announcement, a clip of upbeat speech, jacket donned and purposeful departure. While criticism by people who were there or watched the rolling news made this into a Labour gaffe, it came across well enough in the edited version carried by the evening news programmes. Even there, however, a teacher's criticism of exploitation was an early intimation that Labour's touch with the media was not what it had been in 1997.

The years since 1997 had been cruel to coverage of politics on the air. ITV now carried no regular current affairs in peak time. *Panorama* had been relegated to late on Sunday evening with fewer editions. *News at Ten* had been shunted to 11 p.m. and shortened, then induced to return to the earlier time on three nights a week. Meanwhile, the BBC had moved its main news to 10 p.m. during the week, to angry noises from ITV and apprehensions about restricted choice and poorer audiences. (The combined audience actually increased slightly.) Critics maintained that what politics survived had been dumbed down – an allegation vigorously denied by broadcasters.

From the summer of 2000 it was increasingly apparent that a spring election was on the cards. The perennial suggestion of a televised leaders' debate had an early airing following musings by Alastair Campbell. As always it came to nothing, amid much irrelevant talk about the principles of the constitution. Campbell may well have set the hare running simply to dispose of it well before serious electioneering got under way. From the turn of the year the broadcasters were in 'election imminent' mode with 3 May the assumed date until fate decreed otherwise. Other factors counselling delay apart, could one imagine election coverage running alongside nightly scenes of devastated farmers and animal carcasses silhouetted against funeral pyres? References to the election practically vanished, only returning a day or so before the May Day holiday.

The postponement caused no little disruption to broadcasters' holiday plans and Western Europe had to be scoured for outside broadcast units for election night, replacing those committed elsewhere on the new date. But, with few exceptions, the coverage planned for May went ahead with a month's delay.

This was a particularly challenging election for the broadcasters. They had to produce comprehensive and balanced coverage of an event that a largely apathetic electorate considered a foregone conclusion, while contending with the new constitutional arrangements arising from devolution. They had limited success with devolution. Every channel explained who was now responsible for what, usually more than once, but politicians and broadcasters were prone to forget, particularly on health and education. Many voters must have remained confused.

By contrast, the broadcasters had a long experience of maintaining balance. Guidelines recently produced by the BBC's Chief Political Adviser comprehensively set out how balance was to be achieved and clarified lines of responsibility. They were mostly a slightly more relaxed version of existing practice among the broadcasting organisations generally. Also, a change to the Representation of the People Acts meant that candidates could no longer veto constituency reports or debates. This was to come as a nasty shock to some veteran obstructionists.

The revised guidelines allowed daily sequences to achieve balance over a week rather than on a daily basis. This greater flexibility was welcome, though not fully exploited. Doubtless for convenience's sake reports on the activities of the party leaders still tended to run within a second or so of one another. 'Balance' did not imply absolute equality. As Table 8.1 shows, the party split of coverage varied somewhat from channel to channel.[1] Overall, Labour got most attention – probably because, as the governing party, it was slightly more newsworthy, as the Conservatives were in 1997. The Liberal Democrats lost ground but, more important to them as the third party, they nevertheless featured in almost every bulletin. In aggregate, minor party coverage was down in national news but parties judged to be significant players in Scotland, Wales or Northern Ireland had full status there.[2]

Table 8.1   **Parties' share of news coverage**

	Con %	Lab %	LibDem %	SNP %	PC %	Green %	UKIP %	Others %	%
BBC1	36.1	35.0	19.9	3.1	1.9	0.7	1.1	2.4	100.2
ITV	34.7	36.5	24.3	1.7	0.5	0.7	0.4	1.2	100.0
C4	33.9	36.1	19.6	1.5	0.8	2.1	2.4	3.7	100.1
C5	26.2	36.1	28.1	2.2	0.5	2.1	2.4	3.0	100.0
R4	32.2	37.0	20.9	3.2	2.2	2.1	1.8	3.0	100.0
All 2001	34.3	36.1	21.1	2.5	1.5	1.0	1.3	2.2	100.1
All 1997	35.3	31.3	25.0			8.4			100.0

[N.B. in the last row, 8.4 is a cumulative figure for SNP + PC + Green + UKIP + Others]

Some questioned the commitment to balance, arguing that, with Labour's victory a racing certainty, time spent on Conservative proposals, let alone the LibDems', was wasted. Instead, it should be used for a closer examination of Labour's record and plans. It is doubtful if any senior broadcaster seriously contemplated going down that path, not least because the journalistic pitfalls and political perils were so instantly apparent. In the event, not least to avoid undermining their own output, news coverage treated the contest as if it was genuinely undecided, while emphasising the immense task facing the Conservatives.[3]

By far the biggest challenge was apathy. This was frequently referred to as 'the apathy election'. 'They're off, but how many people really care?' asked *Channel Four News*. ITV's controller of news and current affairs described this as 'the most difficult election we have had to cover', for that reason.[4] So how was it tackled? Essentially by offering less of the same. But there were exceptions: Radio 1's *Newsbeat*, which appointed a reporter from the Westminster staff to put politics across to its predominantly young audience. The result was in every respect a world away from the sedate agenda and language of Radio 4: news cheek-by-jowl with pop, youth venues and one-minute mini manifestos. It remained to be seen how successfully this reached younger voters. Commercial radio stations ran a Use Your Voice campaign aimed at rousing the youth vote – again with uncertain success.

Five News also targeted a young audience. Its relatively 'popular' agenda gave the arrest of the entertainer Michael Barrymore pride of place over the election. It alone reported that Tony Blair had topped a poll for 'the sexiest bottom in politics'. Its pace was faster, its style colloquial, its presenters youthful – newsreader Charlie, 'agony aunt' Charlotte providing potted summaries of the parties' proposals in response to viewer requests,

Richard and Lucy, the casually dressed, fresh-faced couple looking as if they were on day-release from college, who conducted a phone-in and discussion of the day's topic. A panel of 'virgin voters' indicated which party's policy they preferred; the studio audience whooped and cheered as if at a game show. The programme's 'man in the white suit' specialised in wheezes like hiring a stretch limousine to follow the Blair campaign, champagne lunch included, for less than Labour was charging hacks on its battle bus. On another occasion, volunteers were wired up to see which was more exciting, watching the election or paint drying. The paint won. The 'eminent American politician', Jerry Springer, made a cameo appearance lauding British elections because paid-for political commercials are barred. (Presumably he found the party broadcasts a higher form of discourse.) *Five News* was very hit and miss – more miss than hit. But, like *Newsbeat*, it squarely raised the question of whether new ways could be found of engaging those untouched by more established means.

Mindful of the audience collapse in 1997 the BBC added only 7 minutes to the main news during the week, giving a net length of roughly 30 minutes.[5] *News at Ten* returned temporarily to its old slot on weekdays with approximately 21 minutes of national news. *Channel 4 News* ran its customary 40 or so minutes and extended its weekend coverage. Against the tide, *Five News* went to about 50 minutes at 5.30 p.m. and Radio 4's *World at One/World This Weekend* were extended to 40 minutes and 60 minutes respectively.

Paradoxically, the election was both omnipresent and downgraded. All the 364 news programmes monitored carried reports. There was no escaping it. Yet coverage was down almost everywhere. The election took 57 per cent, 50 per cent and 56 per cent respectively of the lunchtime, early evening and main news on BBC1. The corresponding 1997 figures were 62, 54 and 67 per cent. ITV returned 45, 46 and 49 per cent against 60, 48 and 57 per cent. One ITN insider reportedly felt that their biggest single contribution to the election was 'not inundating the viewers with politics'. Channel 4 dropped from 78 per cent to 59 per cent. Channel 5 went from 46 per cent to 60 per cent, but with less demanding content. Radio 4's half-hour news at 6.00 p.m. and midnight carried 38 and 29 per cent respectively (1997 figures not available). The bulletins in *Today*, *The World at One* and *The World Tonight* ran about 25, 36 and 34 per cent election content. (However, the 'magazine' sections that followed were heavily electoral.) This slimming down may explain why audiences held up fairly well. Even so they were below the 1997 level.

With apathy ever in mind, editors were readier to lead on other stories than in 1997. The BBC did so with the main evening news on 5 of the

Table 8.2   Headlines of BBC1 and ITV main evening news

BBC	ITV
May	
8 Tony Blair finally names the day	Blair chooses London school to confirm election date
9 Opening shots in the campaign	Row as Blair launches 5 new election pledges
10 Tories promise £8 billion tax cuts	Hague promises big tax cut if he wins
11 Lab's going to promise not to raise income tax in next parliament	Blair's tax plan challenged by Hague
12 Cons say stealth taxes will go up under Labour	(2) Blair woos pensioners but is attacked again on tax
13 Party leaders step up the pace	Lab and LibDems prepare to launch manifestos
14 William Hague's under pressure after the Tories hint of huge tax cuts	Hague battles to contain row over Tory tax plans
15 A major row tonight over the Tories' first election broadcast	Hague under fire for failing to discipline rebels
16 Prescott involved in a fight	Prescott hits out after egg attack by protester
17 John Prescott regrets his brawl but calls it self-defence	All smiles now as Prescott defends that punch
18 William Hague gets tough on asylum	Hague's controversial plan to detain asylum seekers
19 (2) Pensioner power at the ballot box	The battle is on for the grey vote
20 Law and order has dominated the election campaign	Protecting children against paedophiles – the fight to be tough on crime
21 Lab and Tories slug it out over tax and spending	Row over future tax rises – Brown responds
22 Lady Thatcher joins the election fray, backing Hague	(2) Thatcher weighs in with challenge on Europe
23 Europe and tax have dominated today's election campaign	(2) New election row as Blair says patriots can embrace Europe
24 Who'll do most for schools and hospitals? Blair says it's the great divide	Blair put on spot as public services take centre stage
25 (2) Blair takes on Thatcher over Europe	(4) Battle lines finally drawn on Europe and the euro
26 Cons step up their attack on the euro	Thatcher hits campaign trail in Tories' bid to save the pound
27 (2) Fears of fraud with big rise in postal vote	(2) (Controversy over Hughes'comment on Oldham riot)*
28 EU competition: Blair hits back over claims euro will cost billions	(2) Hague's anger over call for British tax to match Europe's

29 Election gets personal: Tories accuse Blair of barefaced deceit	Lab under fire as campaign gets personal
30 (2) Hague strategy under fire on euro	(2) Hague denies retreat on campaign to save the pound
31 A week to go. William Hague warns against Lab landslide	(2) Blair's crusade runs into criticism
June	
1 Family doctors drop an election bombshell	(2) Doctors threaten mass resignation
2 (3) 3 party leaders, one call: get out and make sure you vote	(3) Blair: next few days are crucial
3 William Hague talks about Lab landslide, warns of danger to democracy	Blair says Tories have admitted electoral failure
4 Just two days of campaigning left. Leaders step up pace	No let-up as leaders prepare for home stretch
5 The final push for votes and the leaders agree it's a turning point for Britain	Passion and surprises at final rallies tonight
6 It's nearly over. Leaders' final appeals	Leaders' final appeals as the nation prepares to vote

* Not a headline.
Number in brackets indicates the position of the story in the bulletin. The story was first unless stated otherwise.

30 evenings before polling compared with 1 in 1997. ITV did so no fewer than 10 times (7 in 1997). Both channels' early evening news led on the election on 14 of the last 28 days compared with 22 and 24 days respectively out of 30 in 1997. Channel 4 dipped from 28 election leads in 30 days in 1997 to 18 out of 28. Some editors regretted there had not been more strong stories to warrant moving the campaign down the running order more often. Those that did included the Middle East conflict, riots in Oldham, a massacre in Nepal, a disaster in Israel, fresh outbreaks of foot and mouth, and the trial of Jeffrey Archer. Even so, with the campaign no longer swamping the bulletins, the news was more varied than in some recent elections.

Whichever channel people took their news from they would have gained very similar understandings of what and who the election was about, presented (Channel 5 apart) in the customary mix of salami-sliced sound bites, briefings, polls, constituency reports, commentary and analysis. Table 8.2 shows the way the campaign was perceived to develop, as displayed in the headlines of BBC1 and ITV main evening news. Essentially the same story topped their election package every evening but two – both occasions when the main election story was relatively weak. Also, as usual, many headlines were safely bland, carefully balanced, or partly neutralised by a subsidiary headline not shown in the table. However, the Conservatives had a slight edge on both channels. Be that as it may, all channels ranked campaign issues very similarly (Table 8.3).[6] From one standpoint, the high measure of convergence might appear reassuring, but might it not also be just a shade disquieting?

Table 8.3   **Relative prominence of issues in news coverage**

	BBC1	ITV	C4	C5	R4	All	All 1997
Europe	1	2	1	1	1	1	1
Taxation	2	1	4	2	2	2	5
Health	3	5	2	4	3	3	6
Public Services	6	4	3	9	4	4	N/A
Tax & Spend	4	3	7	7	5	5	N/A
Education	5	9	5	3	9	6	4
Law & Order	7	6	9	6	6=	7	10
Asylum	8	7	6	5	8	8	N/A
Pensions	9=	8	14	8	6=	9	7
Race	9=	10	12	10	11	10	N/A

While the principal issues were in greater or lesser measure present throughout the campaign, due to the Conservatives' sprint start the opening skirmishes were preponderantly fought on what they considered 'their' terrain of taxation and public expenditure. But these fell away in the final fortnight, in part because the Letwin indiscretion on a shift in public attitudes meant that tax cuts played less well than the Conservatives had hoped. Also, editorial restlessness makes it very difficult to sustain any issue for a week let alone a full month without something new to feed it. That did happen with Europe, which came to the fore in the middle period and was sustained by Lady Thatcher's intervention, speeches by Romano Prodi and Lionel Jospin and a bogus scare about tax harmonisation. Labour's priorities, health and education, grew as the campaign progressed. Although parties are aggrieved when 'their' issues appear to be downgraded, 'balance' means their assertions will usually be juxtaposed with their opponents' – not necessarily to their advantage. Their 'strengths' may be undermined in unforeseen ways, such as the confusion over Conservative tax-cutting plans or Lady Thatcher's 'Never!' The Sharron Storer episode, the threat by GPs to resign, and the angry noises emanating from the teaching unions' conferences took some of the shine off Labour's claims on health and education.

Race was not on any major party's agenda until the riots in Oldham forced it there. As soon as was decent it dropped off the bulletins and remained unvoiced for the rest of the campaign, together with the inner cities, urban decay and the north–south divide. The problems of the countryside, transport and the environment appeared fitfully. Post-devolution, constitutional issues – ranked second in 1997 coverage – now had only a tiny place. The controversial missile defence system, overseas aid, globalisation, GM crops, drugs policy, or electoral reform featured vestigially, on the initiative of minor parties. In short, there was consensus on non-issues as well as issues. Nothing was heard about the new economy or the arts. Mostly this was because the politicians were not talking about them, but sometimes they were and were not reported. Tony Blair's Edinburgh speech on Britain's role in the world was picked up for his contention that one could be both patriotic and have a positive attitude towards the EU but not for what he said about relations with the rest of the world. The most striking silences followed publication of the employment and trade figures – respectively the best and worst for years. Time was when these would have been seized on with joy and horror, according to taste. Curiously, they now appeared without a word of campaign comment. The most striking omission from earlier agendas was the charge that Labour was unfit to govern. That dragon, it seemed, had been well and truly slain.

The similarities between the various channels in the number of times the leading politicians were quoted (Table 8.4)[7] owe something to newsroom consensus and the requirements of 'balance', but they also reflect the parties' ability to confine exposure to people they could rely on to stay on-message. They were obviously not entirely successful: Clare Short, who was ever so slightly critical of her party's launch, and the Europhobic Tapsell were obvious exceptions; Thatcher was arguably another. Prescott's prominence was almost wholly due to the confrontation at Rhyl. Most of the 'others' in the table were candidates enjoying their 15 seconds of fame in constituency reports. Despite the liberalising of constituency coverage, the number of representatives from the major parties reported in the national news was down on 1997. Those receiving little or no recognition included a majority of the Cabinet and Shadow Cabinet. There were admittedly one or two rare birds who worked hard at avoiding the cameras and microphones. One of the jollier episodes was the hunt for Oliver Letwin following his embarrassing enthusiasm for tax cuts. Camera crews roamed the West Country in pursuit and Labour symbolically mustered bloodhounds and a 'Sherlock Holmes' in front of Central Office. Keith Vaz was elusive almost throughout. Ostensibly

Table 8.4 Politicians quoted in radio and television news (number of times)

	BBC1	ITV	C4	C5	R4	Total		BBC1	ITV	C4	C5	R4	Total
Labour							*Conservatives*						
Blair	101	89	30	26	98	344	Hague	103	87	29	28	112	359
G. Brown	28	17	6	5	21	77	Portillo	22	29	9	4	21	78
Milburn	11	5	3	3	11	33	Thatcher	7	10	5	4	10	36
Straw	11	6	2	1	5	25	Widdecombe	12	9	3	1	6	31
Prescott	4	6	7	–	6	23	Maude	6	5	4	2	6	23
Darling	7	3	3	3	5	21	Ancram	5	4	4	2	4	19
Boateng	3	1	–	1	2	6	Fox	4	2	1	1	6	14
Short	2	3	1	–	–	6	Tapsell	6	2	1	–	3	12
Woodward	1	2	2	–	1	6	Major	4	1	3	1	3	12
35 others	10	17	17	5	14	63	Rifkind	–	6	2	–	–	8
							Lansley	2	–	2	–	3	7
							37 others	8	8	10	2	18	46
Liberal Democrats							*Other parties*						
Kennedy	93	92	31	30	103	349	Swinney (SNP)	18	15	5	4	25	67
Hughes	13	10	3	1	10	37	Wyn Jones (PC)	7	7	1	1	7	23
Campbell	1	5	2	–	2	11	Trimble (UU)	5	1	1	–	3	10
Bruce	2	2	–	–	3	7	Farage (UKIP)	2	3	1	–	3	9
Harvey	4	2	–	–	1	7	Adams (SF)	2	1	1	–	2	6
Taylor	3	1	–	–	2	6	58 others	27	12	18	12	37	106
32 others	9	–	18	–	23	50							

ailing, when eventually tracked down he seemed unable or unwilling even to say whether or not he was well.[8] Kenneth Clarke, though readily visible, remained resolutely mute on national issues. Geoffrey Robinson apparently avoided national exposure to the very end.

In contrast to these shrinking violets Blair, Hague and Kennedy accounted for over half of all news citations.[9] This presidentialised presentation of campaigns is by now 'traditional'. It has advantages for broadcasters and parties and, in some measure, the public; it is simpler, easier to understand and more economical on resources – but it sits oddly with Blair's dismissal of debates between leaders on the grounds that Britain does not have a presidential system. The disadvantage is that the news can be locked into carrying three consecutive reports from the teams following the leaders, irrespective of whether there is anything to say – mechanical, repetitive, excluding other possibilities and, ultimately, boring. One Hague walkabout, one Blair school visit, even one clip of Kennedy reading 'brown bear, brown bear, what do you see?' to winsome tots looked very much like another. Was it imagination or were the photo opportunities even duller and more repetitive than usual? The nadir was Blair's excursion to a construction site near Inverness, said to be 'the biggest hole in Scotland'. Viewers never actually saw the hole because cameras were kept at a distance and accompanying hacks had to follow the ensuing exchange of banalities by radio. There was a Blair visit to Microsoft that degenerated into a product launch, a desperately stilted 'tea party' with a young couple highlighting lower mortgages and a man-of-the-people dive into the Happy Haddock chippy. As Jon Snow remarked from the set of *Brookside* on one such occasion, 'Has it really come to this?' The only place for such material was the cutting-room floor; was there really no place during an election for strong-minded editing? Where radio scored was in not being burdened with all this clutter.

The parties claimed the media wanted photo opportunities; the media denied this. Regional news, resenting being patronised by London as a soft touch, paid them less attention. The politicians became interesting only when things went wrong, as in the Sharron Storer incident. This ran live on *Sky News* and *BBC News 24* and was reported and repeated countless times on all channels. An ordinary woman, incensed by the delays in treating her partner, a cancer patient, unstoppably vented her fury when she chanced on the Prime Minister who was visiting the hospital's new wing. Probably oblivious of the cameras, she implacably brushed aside his apology with: 'If you was sorry you would do something.' Blair had no choice but to take it for the several minutes the incident lasted. Unlike so much shown during the campaign, this was raw, real, un-spun, and instantly comprehensible, and it connected with a central issue in the campaign. It was well reported but, local television apart, not so well followed up. The caravan had moved on.

Even photo opportunities occasionally produced moments of pure serendipity. Visiting a hospital, Charles Kennedy encountered a patient about to be wheeled into the operating theatre, who greeted Kennedy with, 'I want to pay more tax.' Even Kennedy was momentarily speechless. (The man later said the pre-med must have made him light-headed – but why spoil a nice story?)

If one image of this campaign lingered in people's memory it was John Prescott's left hook landing on an egg-throwing protester. The handling of the incident brought out the best and the worst in the coverage. Unquestionably newsworthy, this was screened rapidly and repeatedly from a variety of camera angles. Together with the Storer encounter it elbowed Labour's carefully choreographed manifesto launch off the top of the coverage. Unlike the Storer incident its wider import was negligible. This did not prevent it being milked at inordinate length, with much waffly opining about whether Prescott should be sacked or whether the 'apathy election' had become the 'antipathy election'. The excited reaction by journalists contrasted with the relaxed attitudes of the leaders of all political parties.

Photo opportunities and compilations of mutually cancelling sound bites – what Andrew Marr aptly termed the ping-pong packages – were by no means the whole coverage. Among the most valuable were the issue briefings by specialist correspondents assisted by contributors from nonpartisan bodies like the Institute for Fiscal Studies and The King's Fund. These set out and compared the parties' policies clearly and fairly, cutting through the fog of claim and counter-claim, particularly on whether the figures 'added up' or setting the argument about £8 billion of public expenditure in some sort of context. Constituency surveys lent visual variety, even flashes of illumination – the personal antagonisms at Hartlepool, the fallout from the Woodward selection at St Helens, or the intensely local issue at Wyre Forest. (One of the most telling moments of the campaign came in a Midlands piece on Wyre Forest. The reporter asked a succession of locals, 'What is the main issue here?' All replied in two words: 'the hospital'.) As usual, the opinion polls were regularly updated, invariably well down the bulletin, not least because they barely budged. It became increasingly difficult to offer even crumbs of hope to the Conservatives. One commentator concluded: 'We're talking about the difference between a disaster and a rout.' Channel 4 deployed a Message Poll, a technique of analysing ways of fine-tuning language for maximum voter impact. It also tracked the standings of the party leaders – Kennedy emerging as the great beneficiary of the campaign, as Liberal Democrats often do – and the changing salience of key issues, notably an increase in the perceived importance of the euro from its initial very low level.

Significantly, a record number of items, including constituency reports, dispensed with politicians. Channel 4's touring battle bus featured several gatherings of voters talking with a presenter and among themselves. This looked like an attempt to engage viewers by featuring people rather like themselves. While confirming that ordinary people can be sensible and articulate when not compressed into the stultifying, demeaning five seconds normally accorded to vox pops, there was not much more to be gained from them. A substantial crop of reports focused on apathy, whether among young people, ethnic minorities or in the inner cities. Having looked around a sink estate in Leeds and interviewed disillusioned inhabitants, George Alagaiah reflected that he could understand why so few felt voting worthwhile. But he encountered many of the same sentiments in rural West Yorkshire, concluding: 'It's not that people don't care, but they feel shut out.' In Liverpool Riverside 'people feel let down by all the parties'. And so on. Ignorance, indifference and cynicism about politics and politicians abounded, with feelings that 'they're all the same', that it 'would make no difference who won'. Widespread sentiments – but some reports fitted just a shade too comfortably into the 'apathy election' pigeonhole.

The most extensive strand in election coverage was the election itself. This absorbed far more time than any issue. The largest single element was the reports from the correspondents accompanying the leaders. These carried a substantial amount on movements and photo-events but frequently became two-ways between newscaster and reporter about the 'mood' in the appropriate camp or the tactical implications of recent developments. It was not as if the news was otherwise short of comment. This was also the year of the political editors. The BBC's new political editor, Andrew Marr, was one of the campaign's stars. One awoke to him on *Today* and went off to bed with his piece (surely recorded?) on the midnight news. Here was a man who was actually enjoying the election, bringing to it a sharp mind, a sense of humour and a quirky turn of phrase that kept one wondering what he might say next. He was by no means always right but he was always worth listening to. Adam Boulton at *Sky News* was equally tireless and enthusiastic. John Sergeant and Elinor Goodman performed a similar service for ITV and Channel 4, according to their differing personalities and the characteristics of their channels.

They played a crucial role in expanding understanding of what was happening. Yet one was left with a slight unease. Taking Marr as exemplar, he was seen or heard in the news more than any politician, possibly more than all the party leaders combined. Their thoughts as often as not came over in reported speech; in direct speech they rarely exceeded 20 seconds. Marr always spoke directly and usually for over 20 seconds. He and his peers strained every nerve to be evenhanded. Yet was it healthy for so few individuals to loom quite so large in shaping perceptions of what was happening and what it signified? Cumulatively, the two-ways from the field and the interpretative asides in top-of-bulletin reports were arguably excessive. No less arguably, this surfeit of comment on the calculations lying behind almost every utterance and action risked further deepening distrust of politics and politicians. Yet electioneering is at times so devious and reporting so fragmented that we would fare even less well without the commentators.

While most of the coverage looked much as in 1997, there were also changes. Reporting was a shade more robust, if not robust enough. Juliet Bremner, with William Hague, remarked on 'a day of what passes for campaigning' while George Meany, after Tony Blair opened a runway at Manchester, spoke of 'the politics of symbol rather than substance'. There were pointed comments about politicians meeting only hand-picked crowds, though Blair insisted he did meet 'real people' – off camera. But these scattered remarks scarcely amounted to a considered editorial strategy. There were a few more black and brown faces among the reporters and appreciably more women, though they still had to achieve full recognition. One of the few hilarious moments occurred at Labour's press conference when male journalists held back, obliging Gordon Brown to call a woman. Jackie Ashley of the *New Statesman* asked Estelle Morris, Minister of Education, why female spokespersons never got to answer questions. Brown instantly cut across the reply and the whole room collapsed in mirth – but everyone knew that a telling point had been made. Changes in the press corps were slow; in the political elite they were glacial. All but one of the politicians given substantial news coverage were white; all but three were male.

Happily, there was more to coverage than the news. Broadcasting's more valuable contribution lay in the diversity of other offerings: daily reportage and analysis from *Today* (Radio 4), *The World at One* (Radio 4) and *Newsnight* (BBC2), cumulatively criss-crossing a wider range of issues, some briefly and some at greater length; old election standbys like *Election Call* (Radio 4 and BBC2) and *On the Record* (BBC1), specials like *Politics Isn't Working* (Channel 4) and *Panorama* (BBC1) and, regionally, *The Scottish*

500 (STV) or *It's Your Call* (BBC and local radio).[10] Unhappily, even the most successful attracted only a fraction of the news audience. Those who had most to gain from them were probably least likely to see them, not least because so much went out off-peak. This must have been the first campaign in which *Panorama* has run just one programme, albeit a blockbuster. 'The Labour Years' subjected key areas of the government's record to detailed scrutiny. It went out against objections from Labour's director of communications, Lance Price, a former BBC journalist, who contended (incorrectly) that by dealing with the government alone it contravened the guidelines. Yet, while Labour was not surprisingly unhappy at being found wanting in some respects, this was just the sort of serious approach to issues Tony Blair had called for.

Channel 4's series title, *Politics Isn't Working,* suggested it might pander to the ambient cynicism. Instead it took a long look at issues like the power of global corporations, the challenge of street protest to conventional politics and the politics of inequality. Another Channel 4 offering, 'The Party Crashers' aroused the ire of the parties by planting young people as volunteers at their headquarters to see what they got up to during a campaign. Unfortunately one of them bonded so successfully with her team that she owned up and the other two were also withdrawn prematurely. Ironically, conceivably the most influential election programme was not seen until over a month after polling day: *Amanda Platell's Secret Diary* (Channel 4), implying disloyalty by supporters of Michael Portillo, might just have swayed the single vote by which his post-election leadership bid was to fail.

Question and answer formats were greatly favoured, whether one-on-one interviews, phone-ins, studio audiences with moderator and, sometimes, 'debates' among the politicians. All offered opportunities for politicians to elucidate and defend their party's positions on a whole range of issues – often including some they may have preferred not to address. The UK party leaders, the SNP and Plaid Cymru were, with one exception discussed later, interviewed on every major outlet and quite a few minor ones. *On The Record* featured senior ministers and their shadows taking questions and discussing on health, the economy and law and order. Inevitably there were occasional clashes. Blair was called a liar on *Newsbeat* and Baroness (Shirley) Williams a hypocrite on *Election Call*. She rounded passionately on the caller – an intending abstentionist – recalling her grandmother's struggle for women's suffrage. (The caller eventually agreed to vote – Conservative.) Margaret Beckett encountered a woman on *Election Call* who had suffered mis-diagnosis and medical delays. Her 'I'm 37 years old and I don't want to die' lingers in the memory. Beckett's recital of the Millbank mantra cut no ice there. Similarly, Blair had a tricky encounter on *Question Time* with a determined couple whose child suffered a rare bone marrow disease.[11] There were quite a few more such occasions, whether on phone-ins or in studio questioning. These were what other media seized on. But they were untypical. The vast majority of exchanges were polite yet firm, undeferential but civilised. Obviously many questioners disliked the answers they received, but at least the politicians had been required to answer and to have the answer judged by a wider audience. And, perhaps, on occasion, the politicians were made to think.

However, some subjects called for sustained questioning in formal interviews. There were many such. The ones that attracted wider notice were usually the aggressive confrontations; Jimmy Young's deceptively gentle probing of Tony Blair on Radio 2 on reform of the public services was revealing but little noticed. Some interviews did a service by exposing inadequate thinking – David Willetts was driven by Jeremy Paxman virtually to concede that plans for public expenditure were unworkable, while Robin Cook was totally nonplussed by a question from Jeremy Paxman on what political benefits might arise from joining the euro.[12] Paxman brilliantly exposed the illogicality of Hague's position: against the euro in principle, unable to envisage any circumstances in which he might favour joining, yet committed to opposing it for only a single Parliament. (The political logic of holding a divided party together could of course not be admitted.) Sometimes even persistent questioning was unsuccessful. Neither ministers nor their shadows would say anything substantive about the implications for their plans of an economic slowdown, nor could they be drawn on how to deal with a putative funding gap after 2004. Ministers were unable or unwilling to explain the manifesto commitment to reform the public services. Nor were they forthcoming about the process of reaching a recommendation on entering the euro. Interviewing the Prime Minister, Paxman sought his views on the widening gap between rich and poor. Blair knew what answer many of his supporters expected but explicitly substituted his own anodyne alternative, leaving Paxman unanswered. While politicians cannot be forced to answer, at least their evasions and stonewalling may be exposed. Yet aggressive interviewing could be misused – witness Alistair Darling being pressed five times for an instant judgement on the Prescott punch. When we hear a newsreader looking forward to an interviewer 'doing battle with Tony Blair' it is perhaps time to give pause. Aggression by interviewers, while necessary at times, may also be a turn-off for many.

Every election brings friction between broadcasters and politicians. This was no exception. The BBC established a central unit to handle complaints.

It seems to have been kept busy. For years Conservatives had complained of bias at the 'Blair Broadcasting Corporation'. Come the election, though, the main difficulties between them and the broadcasters were over their inability or unwillingness to provide timely information about their plans. Labour was a different matter. Ominous rumblings preceded the campaign. 'Senior' Labour officials reportedly intended to launch 'a war of attrition' during the campaign; Alastair Campbell complained that the *Today* programme was following the *Daily Mail*'s agenda and a 'senior minister' accused the BBC of wanting to focus on 'Tory issues' – asylum and Europe rather than health, education and the economy.[13]

Matters deteriorated. Labour refused *Panorama* accreditation to its press conferences because of the 'huge demand'. BBC and ITN journalists took umbrage when Labour officials implied that if they agreed to put soft questions at the manifesto launch their chances of being recognised would be improved. In an interview on the *Today* programme, Tony Blair was plainly annoyed at John Humphrys' emphasis on 'sleaze' and the possibility that he would make way for Gordon Brown during the next Parliament. Humphrys drew more Labour ire for his questioning of Yvette Cooper about using lottery money for health projects. Blair did not appear for the interview each party leader customarily gives to *The World This Weekend*. Gordon Brown did not appear for *On The Record*'s edition on the economy, sending Andrew Smith in his place. Labour insisted it had never agreed to either appearance. Maybe, but it had received the BBC's requests some weeks earlier without signalling any difficulties.[14] Another time, Humphrys took the unprecedented step of apologising for the lack of balance in the programme because Labour had not been prepared to put up any speaker on any issue. Chris Smith and Clare Short had been asked for but the party had apparently not passed the invitations to either. According to the editor of *Today*, Rod Liddle, when he sought an explanation the response from Millbank was 'Well, it's not our fault you've got John Humphrys presenting the programme every day.'[15]

Margaret McDonagh's complaint that broadcasters were inciting and colluding with anti-government protesters came in the midst of this. In the absence of sustaining evidence Blair made a speedy withdrawal. However, he returned to the attack in the *Independent*, accusing broadcasters of ignoring the 'real' issues and playing the Tories' game by encouraging cynicism.[16] He singled out the BBC's 'incredible' morning bulletins on 23 May, for giving prominence to Tory allegations about EU plans to harmonise taxes throughout Europe. On the particular instance he had a point: the Conservatives' contention rested on a dubious reading of a 'secret document' that was in fact on the brink of publication. While there was countervailing input from Robin Cook and Brussels the story scarcely warranted lead position, even on a slow morning. However, Blair's call for debate and dialogue and his belief that there was 'a real hunger' to hear what the parties had to say were not easily reconciled with refusals to put up representatives, or with episodes like dragging the media to view a hole (or rather not to view it). Labour never explained why the BBC, with a Labour-supporting director-general, might wish to impose a Conservative agenda. The BBC clearly felt, not without reason, that Labour was trying to bully it into covering politics according to its dictates though it was conceded that some episodes may have reflected inefficiency rather than intent. The wrongs were, without doubt, not totally one-sided. Yet, however convinced Labour was of its grounds for complaint, responding with empty chairs and obstruction scarcely advanced its cause.

Inquests follow every campaign. The broadcasters were in chastened mood. 'How much of it was our fault?' headlined the BBC's newspaper, *Ariel*,[17] adding that it was 'clear at the Royal Television Society's post-election conference that it's not only the Tories who are worried about what went wrong this time'. 'We do have a problem', admitted Mark Damazer, Deputy Director of BBC News. While they found much to praise, what most dismayed broadcasters was that many things they (rightly) thought had worked attracted disappointing audiences; Tony Blair's *Question Time* was watched by only 2.6 million. The middle-aged, middle-class audience had responded, but substantial numbers beyond that had not been engaged. Many things had not worked – the reporting from the battle buses, the 'cosy chat' among those within 'the bubble', the photo-opportunities, the 'sterile set-pieces in which the cameras colluded', the absence of imagination or humour. 'This isn't journalism, it's nonsense', argued the BBC's Director of News, Richard Sambrook. 'Too much coverage giving too little added value', concluded another. These occasions usually attract some exaggerated breast-beating, but this time there was a greater readiness to acknowledge that the broadcasters themselves could be part of the problem and a feeling that they must try to do things differently next time. Nigel Dacre, Editor of ITN, thought they must be more sceptical – but an already sceptical public might be better served by tougher editing. Which network would be the first to bin duff photo-events? Sambrook looked for greater imagination and a different tone, but what would that tone be? The mood of self-criticism in the immediate wake of the dismal turnout could well prove transitory; the problems the low turnout signalled would not. How to handle the 2005 campaign could wait a while. The more pressing question was what the broadcasters might do in the meantime to reach the unreached. This was not a challenge to them alone. It also depended on the readiness of politicians to raise their game and speak more in terms people could understand and to which they could relate.[18]

The party broadcasts

Tony Blair had at least half a point when he complained of the media discussing what politicians meant rather than reporting what they actually said. Time was when politicians had ample time to speak to the voters without anyone interpreting or interrupting, in election broadcasts lasting up to 30 minutes. What they made of that opportunity was variable, to say the least, and the electorate scarcely rejoiced in its good fortune. But election broadcasts have been wasting away for many years. Now none ran to more than 5 minutes; many lasted less than 3.[19] Even so, how the parties chose to present themselves in these broadcasts said much about how they saw both themselves and the voters.

Labour opened with a celebration of its first term. Backed by the campaign theme (*Lifted*, an undemanding nineties number by the Lighthouse Family), key fact captions interspersed sunny scenes of happy children, smiling NHS patients, and jolly policemen, with a voice-over by actor Kevin Whately (replaced by a Scottish voice north of the border). The keen-eyed may have glimpsed 'Dickie' Bird, the former English cricket umpire, but what set all the media a-flutter was the heavily trailed appearance of former Spice Girl, Geri Halliwell. She was seen for all of two seconds, silently serving tea to pensioners. Twelve million people reportedly watched; millions more would have seen news clips. Labour hoped that they took in its message along with Ms Halliwell. Maybe.

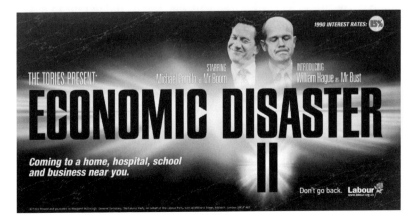

'Economic Disaster II' was a pastiche of every disaster movie trailer you have ever seen. Opening with a mock classification certificate, 'Tory Policies Will Hurt U', it depicted terrified crowds running to escape nemesis in the form of Tory economic policies as the voice-over recalled the 1990s depression. There was even a poster for the forthcoming 'Towering Interest Rates'. William Hague and Michael Portillo featured as Mr Boom and Mr Bust. Proud Labour reportedly gave it a press showing in a Soho cinema, plying journalists with tie-in T-shirts, popcorn and the video in an old-style film reel case. In Scotland, Labour ran a more straightforward piece: 'What Would a Tory Government at Westminster Mean for Scotland?' with captions of cuts in schools, police, nursery places and the like over stills of self-satisfied Tory leaders, while Rod Stewart sang 'The First Cut is the Deepest Cut' (though the Tory cuts would be even worse). The third programme was in direct line from that 1987 classic, 'Kinnock the Movie'. Directed by Jack Price, better known for a film about a woman obsessed to the point of illness by Nike products, it presented 'the real Tony Blair' reading to schoolchildren, being greeted by screaming teenagers in Scotland, relaxing over a pint in the local Labour Club, reflecting on the opportunities education had given him and declaring himself an optimist who believed in the power of politics to change things. To critics recalling Blair's criticism of the media's preoccupation with personalities Alastair Campbell gravely replied, 'Leadership is a big issue in this campaign.' So that was all right.

Next, Blair presented 'the real heroes who are building the future of Britain' – young couple, nurse, teacher, retired policeman, ex-serviceman still doing voluntary work – with pledges relevant to each on mortgages, medical services, education and pensions. It was competent, clear and straightforward, so ignored by other media. Which did not mean it was ineffective. Following it, Blair and other ministers took a phone-in that reportedly attracted a significant number of callers. The last broadcast was a call to get out and vote. With *Lifted* in the background, this playlet featured a young couple (she an actress from *Hollyoaks*, a Channel 4 soap) slightly reluctantly deciding to go and vote – 'not always the most fun thing to do', commented Kevin Whately's voice-over (again replaced in Scotland). They ran into a heavy shower but, in true cinematic fashion, she arrived at the polling station with her coiffure immaculate. (Now if New Labour could deliver that … .) They voted – Labour of course. While returning they were thanked by schoolchildren, teachers, medical staff and police. A pleasant if highly unlikely little tale that might just have encouraged the mildly disappointed that Labour deserved a second chance.

The Conservatives were unremittingly negative. Every image was dark, every sound filled with menace. Their first broadcast, on crime and tax, depicted men leaving prison under the early release scheme and immediately going on to commit fresh crimes. It included a scene of a woman about to be mugged and a tally of crimes committed by prisoners released early, including two rapes. (The men concerned in fact had no previous record of sex offences.) This recalled the notorious Willie Horton advertisement used against Michael Dukakis in the 1988 Bush presidential campaign – though that linked crime and race; the criminals here were all white, avoiding any hint of the race card. A second, no less depressing, segment depicted the mute misery of people, captive in their homes, unable to afford petrol at £6 per gallon, which 'could' be the price under Labour – a classic example of using language which was strictly accurate to convey a wilfully misleading message.

Another shocker tackled Labour on education. Made by the Yellow M agency under the supervision of Andrew Lansley and Tim Collins, it asked: 'What are your children *really* learning under Labour?' It showed a school on a four-day week due to staff shortages, pupils unable to learn, classrooms empty because the children had bunked off. When the children were not shoplifting they were burning cars, spraying graffiti, and using or dealing in drugs. This created as great a reverberation as the Willie Horton piece, all of it hostile. Reputedly, negative campaigning is unpopular but effective. But when even the *Daily Mail* says a Tory broadcast is in the gutter and a *Daily Telegraph* focus group finds it 'too extreme' it seems a fair bet it has gone too far. The second half of the broadcast offered a scary vision of a Britain-dominated Brussels, with a declining economy, rising interest rates, additional taxes, and the pound consigned to a glass case in a museum. The Scottish Conservatives used some London-based material but also ran a segment on Labour's broken promises to Scotland, including a ghastly clip of a desperately ill old lady vainly summoning a nurse, police unable to get backup, and those delinquent youngsters again, but in a presentation which was less likely to raise teachers' hackles. The third broadcast repeated the £6 gallon and EU spots, the fourth brought crime and the EU back. The series ended with crime and the £6 gallon yet again, and the merest hint of salvation – William Hague's promise, 'I will give you back your country.' Apart from this brief passage, the series had not provided as much as a glimpse of the party's leaders. That omission spoke volumes.

The Liberal Democrats opened with a biopic by the man who made *Billy Elliot*, the hugely successful story of another unlikely lad making good. In a lovely, tranquil Highland setting Charles Kennedy spoke of the early influences of his teachers and parents. He came across as at ease with himself and easy to relate to. His commitment to 'freedom, justice and honesty' was as close as it came to policy. It may have made some friends; it could certainly have made no enemies. (But when did a Liberal Democrat broadcast ever make enemies?)

The programmes which followed, presented by Kennedy, used the concerns of 'ordinary' people about the public services as cues for pledges on the NHS, pensions and crime in the first, on education, public transport and student fees in the second – the last an illustration of what Liberal Democrats achieved when they had power, as in Scotland. The Conservatives would be a 'disaster' for the NHS; Labour had simply been a 'disappointment'. The final broadcast aimed to create a bandwagon feeling. Taking the proposition that everyone wanted better public services it featured 'typical' people – a nurse, a student, a former policeman, and a pensioner – assuring that many more like them would be flocking to support the party on polling day.

The SNP's first broadcast was a dire variation on ancient speculation about what lies under a Scotsman's kilt: a woman with three kilted men – 'Labour', 'Conservative', and 'LibDem'. The kilt of each lifted in turn and was found to have nothing to offer Scotland. 'SNP-man' was then inspected (off-screen) and had exactly what Scotland requires. Oh dear. The SNP's other offering flashed up a rapid sequence of captions and cuttings about slights, cuts and setbacks at Labour's hands and fleeting glimpses of SNP members of the Scottish Parliament fighting the good fight. A caption 'Don't it make you want to shout' (sic) introduced a succession of snatches of cleaning ladies, cooks, fishermen, bus passengers, people on a park bench, and building workers chanting in approximate unison, 'Shout' and then 'Shout, shout it out aloud' with an incomprehensible backing track, leading to the closing caption, 'Make Scotland's voice heard at Westminster.'

There was no problem grasping Plaid Cymru's appeal. Their modest, quietly spoken programme presented Plaid as the party of every facet of Welsh society. It was particularly aimed at people disappointed materially or in their ideals by New Labour, which was depicted as a prolongation of Thatcherism. Its resonances were much Old Labour. As Ieuan Wyn Jones put it: 'Labour has turned its back on the people of Wales and the traditional values of equality and social justice.'

Socialist Labour and the Socialist Alliance appealed to a harder, disillusioned left. The SLP offered a mix of a play-within-a-play, with Arthur Scargill and actor-activist Ricky Tomlinson ostensibly chatting while making an election broadcast, and short to-camera attacks by activists on Labour's record on health, education and pensions, with pledges to fund improvements by slashing the defence budget. The Socialist Alliance broadcast, directed by Ken Loach, featured six of its candidates angrily attacking Labour on education, health, pensions, asylum seekers and public transport, and assuring, 'there *is* an alternative'. This could have been a Labour broadcast a decade ago. The Scottish Socialist Party made the most savage attack. Scripted by actor-director Peter Mullan and Martin McCardie, the writer of *Tinseltown*, it showed an impoverished family's frantic search for money for the meter – for air. Unable to find it, they were cut off by officials of the Scottish National Oxygen Company and boarded into the flat, their suffocating screams muffled by the hammering of nails into the plywood. 'Let's face it', said Tommy Sheridan, the SSP leader. 'If they could sell us back the air that we breathe, they would.'

Plaid, Socialist Labour, the Socialist Alliance and the Scottish Socialist Party all took their stance with relation to Labour. The UKIP implicitly took its in relation to the Conservatives. Its opening sequence – as doom-laden as anything the Tories offered – led to the warning that, 'slowly and relentlessly the UK's independence is being stolen'. Even greater loss of sovereignty lay ahead. But all this was not inevitable: we should not be tied to a failing EU; Britain could stand on her own feet outside the EU. And graphics rained down pell-mell to prove this.

The Green Party went one better than the parties that presented few or no recognised politicians: it banished adults too. The screen was filled with appealing tots struggling to articulate solemn little speeches about 'pesticides' and the like. They were our future, but they were being brought up in towns and cities unfit for them through pollution and bodily danger. This broadcast was almost alone in explicitly recognising an international dimension.

Any prize for the least seen broadcast went to the Pro-Life Alliance. It put up the six candidates required to qualify for a party broadcast in Wales. In a re-run of 1997, senior broadcasters judged its pictures of aborted foetuses incompatible with their guidelines or codes. The Alliance took them to court and lost. After further to-ing and fro-ing it provided a tape with the offending material occluded in red, which went out to Wales, unheralded, on the last Saturday of the campaign.

The verdict

And so to election night, that great quadrennial climax for broadcasters as for politicians, with its vast, expensive sets, its gadgetry and its pundits, backed by armies of technicians and journalists. In addition to the huge

London operation, devolution spurred more ambitious efforts than ever in 'the nations'. If there were any lingering doubts about how the result would go they were dispelled by the exit polls on the stroke of ten. For anyone with hopes resting on the fallibility of past polls Sunderland South pointed to the night's inexorable trend. And so on through long hours of the predictable and the predicted, scarcely enlivened by one of Peter Snow's more manic performances with the swingometer and ITV's innovative computer graphics, dramatic music and reporters racing around in helicopters. ITV had the edge on speed, leaving the BBC muttering darkly about underhand methods, but the BBC had strength in its in-depth analysis. Both sides could claim some kind of victory, though the largest audience, as ever, went to the BBC.

Just under 20 million people watched between 10 p.m. and 1 a.m. – 18 per cent down on 1997. Nothing matched 1997's Portillo moment. The nearest contenders were Peter Mandelson's graceless victory speech and the BNP candidate at the Oldham count, who was gagged in protest at the returning officer's veto on speeches to avoid aggravating racial tension. Breakfast, though, brought William Hague, accompanied by a funereal Ffion, mute to the last, with a dignified resignation statement that was as much news to the party workers within Central Office as to the country. Later, and with equal unanimity, the cameras switched to Downing Street. No excited crowds, no flags, just a few Downing Street staff listening with folded arms as the Prime Minister addressed the cameras. In conscious contrast with 1997's epiphany, this scene spoke of getting down to the formidable task of delivery ahead and a new aspiration – victory in 2005.

Notes

1. Unless otherwise stated all data relate to main news programmes on BBC1, ITV, Channels 4 and 5 and Radio 4 for 10 May–6 June inclusive. ITN supplies news to ITV and Channels 4 and 5; to avoid confusion the output is discussed in terms of the channel where it appears – for example, 'ITV news'. *Sky News* and *BBC News 24* are not discussed as their audience share was below 1 per cent, albeit with substantial blips following moments like the Prescott incident. However, their role was by no means unimportant. They were monitored continuously by election professionals and, together with Radio 5, they often provided extensive coverage of events like press conferences and speeches that were otherwise seen only in heavily edited form. Rolling news also reported some people who were not heard on the other channels, or carried them at greater length. In short, it provided significant variety and choice.
2. The SNP in Scotland, Plaid Cymru in Wales, and the Ulster Unionists, SDLP, DUP and Sinn Fein in Northern Ireland. A study of broadcast coverage by a team from Loughborough University, which also included *Sky News* and *Newsnight*, found that quotations from the three main parties came 43.9 per

cent from Labour, 37.8 per cent from the Conservatives and 18.3 per cent from the Liberal Democrats. *Guardian*, 12 June, 2001.

3. Andrew Marr described Hague as 'the man with the hardest job in Britain' (BBC1 22.00 10 May). With greater latitude on *Newsnight* (8 May), Jeremy Paxman put to Michael Ancram, 'Are you seriously suggesting there is the remotest chance of your winning this election?'

4. Steve Anderson, *Ariel*, 26 June 2001.

5. Excluding headlines, opt-outs, commercials and trails.

6. Although the categories appear quite distinct reality was more complex. The 'Europe' of 1997 and the 'Europe' of 2001 differed appreciably; 1997 was mainly about a Conservative split but now the main focus was the euro. Material classed as 'public services' often mentioned health, education and/or law and order. (Many sound bites contained phrases like 'doctors, nurses, teachers and police'.) The LibDems' 'penny for schools and hospitals', with pensions added for good measure was classed as 'tax and spend' while also referring to the specific services. So did much of the argument about the implications of the Conservative cuts under 'taxation'. Even 'asylum' includes argument about the implications for public expenditure.

7. The BBC used a somewhat different measure involving the number of clips. It reckoned that Blair and Hague came out almost exactly equal.

8. For the text see 'Vaz displays his unique mastery of the art of not answering questions', *Guardian*, 27 May, 2001.

9. In keeping with this, the Loughborough study reckoned that Blair appeared in 29.3 per cent of election news items and Hague in 27.4 per cent.

10. It would be remiss to overlook *Tonight With Trevor McDonald*'s contribution on ITV, 'When Tony met Cherie: the Blairs uncovered'.

11. Blair subsequently invited the couple to Downing Street and promised greater efforts to tackle the condition.

12. While *Newsnight* was widely praised for its heavyweight interviews it was also responsible for one of the more engaging contributions – Jeremy Vine working his way down the country from the furthermost tip of Scotland in a decrepit VW Dormobile, stopping off at politically interesting and, at times, unfashionable points on the way. The series did not take itself too seriously. Part of the interest was in seeing whether the VW would make it to the next day's destination (not always) and finally to Land's End (just).

13. *Observer*, 15 April, 2001 and *Sunday Telegraph*, 6 May, 2001.

14. There were other such episodes, including one where Labour, late in the day, proposed a virtual unknown against senior figures from the other parties and the programme was replaced by a repeat. A further complication arose from Labour's dilatory behaviour: 'balance' requires equality in 'trails'. Sometimes this proved impossible and, on occasion, an inaccurate trail was run.

15. *Guardian*, 5 June, 2001. Apart from the Humphrys interviews that so annoyed Labour, *Today*'s most notable contribution was a report demonstrating how easily a postal vote could be improperly acquired.

16. *Independent*, 24 May, 2001.

17. *Ariel*, 26 June, 2001.

18. For a politician's view on this see Roy Hattersley, 'Humphrys and his kind', *Guardian*, 21 May, 2001.

19. Some Labour advisers favoured the parties having greater flexibility in dividing their allotted time, apparently opening the way to 30-second spots.

9
The Press Disarmed[1]

Margaret Scammell and Martin Harrop

In 2001, Labour achieved a record level of support in the national press. The party improved on its previous best performance in 1997 as *The Times* and the *Daily Express* declared for Labour for the first time. The *Sunday Times* and *Sunday Express* also switched to Labour. Conservative support was reduced to just the *Daily Telegraph* and the *Daily Mail*, and their sister Sunday papers. In recent times, only the Conservatives under Margaret Thatcher in 1983 could claim more overwhelming support (see Tables 9.1 and 9.2).

Yet Labour's moment of press glory passed by, if not unremarked, then hardly trumpeted. One reason for this limited response is that it was still possible to read the transformation in the press as de-alignment rather than re-alignment. Paralleling the mood of the electorate, the papers endorsed the inevitable Labour victory, but – bar the *Mirror* among the dailies – without gusto. More titles voted Labour but support was generally subdued, often qualified and sometimes critical. Indeed Echo Research recorded a significant increase in negative coverage of Labour compared with 1997.[2] Tony Blair commanded respect, especially among the tabloids, but any praise was restrained, and fell far short of the adoration of Maggie that had accompanied the Conservative successes of the 1980s. New Labour had disarmed and contained the press but not converted it.

For the press as for the public, 2001 was a low-key and passionless campaign, a dull sequel to the blockbuster result in 1997. Such a tepid election was an apt finale to four relatively quiet years for the national daily press. There was some churning among editorships, and one change of ownership (the *Express* stable), but no new titles emerged and none disappeared. There were skirmishes with the government over spin, splits and sleaze but no sustained battles. Even the perennial threat of privacy legislation slipped off the horizon as, in the aftermath of the death of Princess Diana, the tabloids exercised greater voluntary restraint on intrusions into celebrities' lives. Much like the election itself, the period from 1997 contained intriguing detail for the cognoscenti but little to excite a wider audience. The great media stories were elsewhere: the internet revolution and the rapid strides of satellite and digital television.

The main changes in the press were threefold. First, national newspaper circulation declined by nearly 5 per cent between April 1997 and March 2001 (Table 9.1). The tabloids took the heaviest losses, with the *Sun* slipping by 8 per cent, the *Mirror* nearly 10 per cent followed by the *Star* (15 per cent) and the *Express*. Second, the *Daily Mail* continued to strengthen its position in both absolute and relative terms. Its circulation expanded by an impressive 11 per cent while its competitors lost some 2 million readers between them. This was easily the biggest growth of any paper, apart from the *Financial Times*, whose increase came from a much lower base and was largely overseas. For the first time in over 50 years, the *Mail* outsold the *Mirror* in England and Wales, becoming the second most important paper politically, after the *Sun*. It was rumoured that Blair and his advisers tested every potentially controversial action against the question, 'how will this play in the *Mail*?' The *Mail*'s success was based on a formula of lifestyle journalism, less partisan Conservatism and the championing of consumer issues. It effectively set the agenda for the tabloid market. The *Mirror*, the *Express* and even the *Sun* followed its lead into more middle-brow territory.

The third major change in the press was the sale in November 2000 of the *Express* and *Daily Star* to Richard Desmond, whose Northern & Shell group publishes several magazines including *OK!* and an assortment of soft-porn titles. The *Express*, traditionally the most loyal of Conservative supporters, had switched to Labour after the 1997 election, reflecting the influence of its then owner, Lord Hollick, a Labour peer. In April 1998, Hollick appointed the former *Independent* editor, Rosie Boycott, to transform the *Express*'s identity from an ailing Conservative mouthpiece to the 'voice for the new millennium'. Hollick admitted defeat by putting Express Newspapers up for sale in July 2000. Desmond's takeover prompted some high-profile departures, including Boycott herself, the respected political editor Anthony Bevins and the right-wing columnist, Peter Hitchens. However, Desmond's *Express* continued to support Labour while it also aggressively targeted *Daily Mail* readers. The rivalry exploded into print in February 2001, when an *Express* editorial condemned the hypocrisy of the Harmsworth dynasty, the aristocratic proprietors of the

Table 9.1   Partisanship and circulation of national daily newspapers

Name of paper Ownership group (Chairman) Editor Preferred result	Circulation[1] (1997 in brackets) (000s)	Readership[2] (1997 in brackets) (000s)	% of readers in social grade[3] (1997 in brackets)			
			AB	C1	C2	DE
Mirror						
Trinity Mirror PLC	2056	5733	12	22	30	37
(Sir Victor Blank)	(2390)	(6389)	(10)	(23)	(31)	(36)
Piers Morgan						
Labour victory						
Express						
Northern and Shell	929	2168	29	35	20	17
(Richard Desmond)	(1208)	(2878)	(24)	(34)	(23)	(19)
Chris Williams						
Labour victory						
Sun						
News Corporation	3288	9591	11	22	31	36
(Rupert Murdoch)	(3935)	(10211)	(8)	(22)	(30)	(40)
David Yelland						
Labour victory						
Daily Mail						
Daily Mail and General Trust PLC	2337	5564	30	34	20	16
(Viscount Rothermere)	(2127)	(5159)	(28)	(38)	(18)	(16)
Paul Dacre						
Conservative victory						
Daily Star						
Northern and Shell	585	1460	9	18	31	41
(Richard Desmond)	(660)	(2089)	(7)	(19)	(34)	(40)
Peter Hill						
Labour victory						
Daily Telegraph						
Hollinger International Inc.	989	2235	57	29	8	6
(Conrad Black)	(1126)	(2542)	(56)	(28)	(9)	(7)
Charles Moore						
Conservative victory						
Guardian						
Scott Trust	362	1024	57	31	7	5
(Hugo Young)	(402)	(1274)	(57)	(29)	(5)	(8)
Alan Rusbridger						
Labour victory[4]						
The Times						
News Corporation	667	1575	61	27	7	6
(Rupert Murdoch)	(772)	(1904)	(57)	(27)	(8)	(8)
Peter Stothard						
Labour victory						

Name of paper Ownership group (Chairman) Editor Preferred result	Circulation[1] (1997 in brackets) (000s)	Readership[2] (1997 in brackets) (000s)	% of readers in social grade[3] (1997 in brackets)			
			AB	C1	C2	DE
Independent Independent News & Media PLC (Tony O'Reilly) Simon Kelner Not Conservative[5]	197 (256)	571 (867)	59 (52)	30 (31)	7 (8)	5 (9)
Financial Times Pearson PLC (Lord Stevenson) Richard Lambert Labour victory	176 (304)	598 (717)	70 (63)	22 (26)	4 (5)	3 (6)

Notes:
1. Source: Audit Bureau of Circulation (May 2001).
2. Source: National Readership Survey (April 2000–March 2001).
3. Calculated from National Readership Survey (January 2000–December 2000), which classifies the population aged over 15 as follows:
    AB (professional, administrative, managerial) – 23% (1997: 21%)
    C1 (other non-manual) – 27% (1997: 28%)
    C2 (skilled manual) – 22% (1997: 22%)
    DE (semi-skilled or unskilled, residual) – 27% (1997: 29%)
4. Also increased number of Liberal Democrats.
5. 'Overall, the Government's successes outweigh its failures ... A large presence of Liberal Democrat MPs will be needed as a bulwark against one of the most insidious tendencies of the Government – its steadily creeping authoritarianism' (*Independent*, 6 June 2001).

Mail. A series of double-page spreads, with the injunction 'show this to a *Daily Mail* reader', contrasted the *Mail*'s public preaching of family values with unwholesome episodes in the Harmsworth family history. The *Mail* responded by denouncing the 'pornographer' Desmond. The papers' owners soon agreed a truce, but for a fleeting moment the personal abuse recalled the 1930s battles between the papers' godfather press barons, Beaverbrook and Rothermere.

So the papers entered the 2001 election lightly shuffled and scrapping furiously in a diminishing market. Aside from the *Express* and *Star* there were other changes of editorship – in most of the Sundays and at the *Independent* as well as, more significantly, at the *Sun* where David Yelland took over, assigned to stem the slide in sales. Yelland launched a price war in the *Sun*'s traditionally weaker market in Scotland, at the expense of the *Mirror*'s stablemate, the *Daily Record*. By virtue of its large circulation,

Table 9.2   **Partisanship and circulation of national Sunday newspapers**

	Preferred winner 2001	(1997)	Circulation[1] (000s)	Readership[2] (000s)
News of the World	Lab	(Lab)	3675	10244
Sunday Mirror	Lab	(Lab)	1761	5719
Sunday People	Lab	(Lab)	1277	3392
Mail on Sunday	Con	(Con)	2238	5979
Sunday Express	Lab	(Con)	870	2224
Sunday Times	Lab[3]	(Con)	1206	3228
Observer	Lab[4]	(Lab)	408	1039
Sunday Telegraph	Con	(Con)	767	2002
Independent on Sunday	Lab[5]	(Lab)	211	646
Sunday Business	Lab	–	53	N/A

1. Source: Audit Bureau of Circulation (May 2001).
2. Source: National Readership Survey (April 2000–May 2001).
3. Labour 'deserves to win, but with a reduced majority. Intelligent readers will cast their votes accordingly. A Labour landslide would be bad for parliament and bad for Britain' (*Sunday Times*, 3 June 2001).
4. Vote tactically for 'a stronger Liberal Democrat representation in the House of Commons' (*Observer*, 3 June 2001).
5. 'We hope people vote tactically and that, with sizeable votes for Greens, Liberal Democrats – even for the sane wing of the Tory party ... – the Opposition backbone will be strengthened after Thursday' (*Independent on Sunday*, 3 June 2001).

the *Sun* remained the paper to watch most keenly during the election, but now followed closely by the *Mail*, while the *Express* under Desmond looked less predictable than at any time since the war.

Table 9.3   **Profile of press content**

	Daily Telegraph	Guardian	The Times	Financial Times	Independent
Mean number of pages					
2001	53	121	79	63	49
(1997)	(52)	(84)	(67)	(61)	(56)
Front pages lead stories on election					
2001, 21 days	15	15	18	17	17
(1997, 27 days)	(25)	(23)	(25)	(21)	(17)
Editorials on election					
Number/out of	37/56	29/55	23/59	13/56	20/60
Per cent	66	53	39	23	33
(1997, per cent)	(49)	(49)	(41)	(55)	(21)

Note: Front-page leads and editorials analysis covers the period 15 May–7 June. Page count

How individual papers covered the campaign

On 8 June the *Daily Mail* generously saluted Blair's 'stunning' victory, then added, 'but the real winner is apathy'. The topic of voter apathy and boredom framed the papers' coverage of the campaign from start to finish. However, it would be neither fair nor accurate to describe the press's own attitude as apathetic. There was considerable variation between the titles but across the press as a whole the election commanded very nearly as much attention as it had in 1997; the proportion of front-page leads dedicated to the campaign barely altered (Table 9.3). All the broadsheets devoted several pages each day to campaign reports and analysis, frequently supplemented by additional opinion on the comment pages. Given the near-certainty of the result this was an almost noble allocation of resources. If the tone was low-key, it was also serious and substantial. To paraphrase Hugo Young in the *Guardian* (1 June), let nobody say of this campaign that the papers did not take politics seriously. We might have expected a significant drop in tabloid interest in a campaign routinely characterised as dull. In fact, attention was sustained close to 1997 levels; only the *Express* dramatically reduced the priority it gave to the campaign.

The *Sun* claimed to have swung it for Blair in 1997 but in the following four years it had been a critical commentator; its warm praise for William Hague's leadership ensured that its continued backing for Labour was not a completely foregone conclusion. In the event, however, the *Sun* declared its hand on 8 March, the day after the budget. 'IT'S IN THE BAG, TONY' ran its front-page headline over a gushing editorial lauding the government's 'astounding' economic achievements and pledging the *Sun*'s support for a second term. The paper hailed the announcement of

	Mirror	Express	Sun	Daily Mail	Daily Star
Mean number of pages					
2001	59	76	56	84	53
(1997)	(42)	(78)	(46)	(76)	(40)
Front pages lead stories on election					
2001, 21 days	12	2	9	9	4
(1997, 27 days)	(13)	(14)	(6)	(14)	(1)
Editorials on election					
Number/out of	33/61	28/62	38/54	31/37	19/61
Per cent	54	45	70	84	31
(1997, per cent)	(76)	(37)	(51)	(77)	(37)

based on Monday to Friday issues only.

the election with the headline, 'Hague hasn't got a prayer' yet according to a MORI poll 48 per cent of regular *Sun* readers did not know whether or not their paper was supporting Labour. The *Sun's* campaign was deeply ambivalent. Although it never seriously threatened to withdraw its endorsement, it also followed a broadly orthodox conservative agenda, far closer to the *Mail* than the *Mirror*.

On 9 May, the day after Blair called the election, the *Sun* issued its own 'manifesto', demanding tax cuts, tough policies on crime and asylum, more teachers, doctors and nurses, and of course saving the pound. As the campaign progressed, the *Sun* peppered Labour with some low fire on sleaze (Europe minister Keith Vaz and his connections with the Hinduja brothers); hypocrisy (the parachuting of Tory defector Shaun Woodward and his butler into the safe Labour working-class constituency of St Helens); and splits (the 'helicopter gunship politics' of confrontation between Blair and his Chancellor). On the single currency and the danger of a European superstate, the tone became increasingly testy. Europe dominated the *Sun's* political world for the last two weeks of the campaign. Its editorial of 24 May confidently predicted that Labour would not lead Britain into the euro-zone during the course of the next Parliament. However, amid mixed signals to other newspapers from Blair and his advisers, the *Sun* began to appear nervous that it had fallen victim to the government's spin doctors. The editorial on 28 May came as close as the *Sun* managed to thunder during the entire election. If Blair called a referendum, it warned, 'our opposition wouldn't just be unprecedentedly ferocious – it would be deeply, even mortally damaging to Tony, Gordon and everyone connected with the project. Don't make us do it, Prime Minister.'

As usual for the last 20 years, the *Sun* was unmissable during the campaign. However, on this occasion it offered little of the stunning and brilliant populism which had become its trademark. Rather, its value lay in its insider knowledge. The paper decided, not unreasonably, that the real interest of the campaign lay in the shape and direction of a second Labour government. It announced exclusively and accurately on 16 May that David Blunkett would be the next Home Secretary ('he'll blitz asylum cheats'). It also broke the story that Estelle Morris ('a great advert for New Labour') would be the new Education Secretary. If in the past, the *Sun* had boasted of its ability to move votes, this time it flaunted its inside track with government and its capacity to lead the press. On the eve of poll, it proudly quoted the *Wall Street Journal's* reference to Trevor Kavanagh as the most powerful political journalist in Britain. All the press had been following the *Sun's* lead only with thousands more words, the *Sun's* editorial claimed. 'DON'T LET US DOWN TONY' was its final front page of the election. Labour had done enough to merit a second chance but now it had to deliver.

If the *Sun* could be characterised as *Daily Mail*-lite, the *Mail* itself was in less than vintage form. It started off brightly enough, setting out its own agenda of Europe, asylum, tax, welfare and crime. For the first two weeks it launched robust attacks on Labour, criticising the threat of tax increases, the 'ticking timebomb' of National Insurance contribution hikes and the continuing 'sleaze storm' of Vaz and the Hindujas. A succession of editorials condemned Labour's 'arrogance', its trivialising and cynical campaigning and its 'contempt' for the electorate. However, as the campaign ground on with no opinion poll cheer for the Conservatives so the *Mail* increasingly seemed to be going through the motions. Overall, the paper significantly reduced its front-page commitment to the election compared with 1997; by the last week it seemed to have virtually given up. Most unusually, the *Mail* did not put the election on its front page on polling day.

As with other traditional right-wing papers, the *Mail* was not inspired by the Conservative offer, particularly in comparison to the confidence and commitment that had characterised the party under Margaret Thatcher. On the eve of poll, its editorial admitted that 'this paper understands why so many voters remain resolutely unimpressed by the Tories'. Moreover, despite Labour's 'frightening arrogance', disturbing toleration of corruption and willingness to manipulate the truth, it was still able to admire Blair's rejection of socialist ideology and the Chancellor's competence in managing the economy. The *Mail* concluded that the election was really about whether we live in an elective dictatorship: Labour 'is destroying the vibrant message of Thatcherism that people should make their own choices, this government pretends it can do everything … if the Tories haven't done enough to win, surely Labour with this track record doesn't merit an overwhelming victory'.

Alone among the tabloids, the *Mirror* launched into the election with genuine relish. Its 9 May front page 'BRIDGET HAGUE'S DIARY', a spoof of the popular fictional *Bridget Jones' Diary*, was easily the most memorable – probably the only memorable – newspaper cover of the campaign. Just as Ms Jones laments the alcoholic units and calories consumed, so William (Bridget) Hague confesses the pints downed and the votes lost. 'Note to self', his diary said. 'Remember inner poise and find proper career. Job prospects v.v. bad.' To the *Mirror*'s delight, its parody was the talk of the many media-on-media reviews elsewhere in the press. The Bridget Hague mock diary became a campaign fixture, although rapidly diminishing in both prominence and wit.

Increasingly the *Mirror* turned to the tabloid's stock weapon: fear of the enemy. It chose a quiet Bank Holiday Monday (28 May) to run a seven-page 'nightmare fantasy' of Hague's Britain under the front-page banner, 'VOTE TORY ... AND SEE WHAT WILL HAPPEN TO BRITAIN'. In a pale imitation of the *Sun*'s infamous 1992 'nightmare on Kinnock street' spoof, the *Mirror* portrayed an economy in ruins, the country expelled from the European Union, unemployment back at 3 million, civil war in Ireland, pensioners freezing to death and asylum seekers in detention camps. An accompanying editorial explained that the paper feared that too many of its readers were hesitating about voting Labour this time or thought it unnecessary. Any vote not cast for Labour would benefit Hague's Conservatives, it warned. As the 'tedious' campaign wore on, the *Mirror* clearly decided that fear of the Conservatives was the strongest motivation for Labour supporters. 'X MARKS THE CLOT' was its polling day front-page lead over a picture of William Hague. This Conservative Party, 'extreme and inward-looking', was not fit to oppose, let alone govern.

Richard Desmond's *Express* devoted fewer front pages to the election than any other paper, including the unashamedly downmarket *Star*. The election provided the *Express*'s main story just twice during the formal three-week campaign. Its coverage was slight but its position consistent: lukewarm support for Labour. This attitude was confirmed with a front-page endorsement on polling day: 'OUR VOTE IS FOR TONY'. There was only one leader capable of turning Britain into a better country to live in, and that person was Tony Blair: 'that is why after 100 years of support for the Conservatives in every general election since 1900 we urge you to vote Labour today'. The paper's break from its Conservative past was complete. Blair was right, it said, to consign Thatcherism to history, and that was long overdue. While democracy did demand a strong opposition, this required total reconstruction of the Conservative Party. The Conservatives had 'been hi-jacked by extremists and oddities for long enough. The in-fighting must stop and the rebuilding begin. Only then will democracy remain a winner.'

The *Star* supported Labour on similar grounds; Blair deserved a second chance while the Conservatives were an unelectable rabble. The *Star* waited until 6 June to formally declare its support, although by then there was little element of surprise. The paper had found virtually nothing to admire in the Conservatives, and from the start it was bored with the 'elect-yawn'. Its main interest was in the fortunes of its very own model, 'superbabe' Jordan, who was standing in the Manchester constituency of Stretford and Urmston for a bigger, bouncier Britain. The change of ownership made little difference to the paper's outlook, although if anything the new *Star* revelled even more joyfully in its downmarket status. The *Star* however was one of the few papers capable of surprise, as with its succinct editorial on the vexed question of the euro, asking 'what's so special about the pound, anyway?'

The broadsheets largely repeated the basic format of 1997. However, replay was bolstered by the press equivalent of the sporting world's multiple camera-angles. Across all the papers there was much to admire: informative policy analysis, balanced assessment of parties' claims and counter-claims, attention to minor parties and neglected issues, and much taking of the public pulse through focus groups, voters' panels and reporters' treks through the key constituencies. There were 'truth watches', 'ad watches' and 'media watches', both quantitative and qualitative, in abundance. In case the diet seemed too heavy, the dough was leavened with 'infotainment': 'gaffe of the day', 'website of the day', two-minute interviews and much else. The *Telegraph*, the *Guardian* and to a lesser extent *The Times* reduced the prominence of the election on their front pages but there was no slacking on the inside. This election may have been strictly for political junkies but the broadsheets were happy to supply.

Above all, though, the expert analysts and star columnists dominated the broadsheet campaign. This was the pundits' election. Too often in 1997 the battle of the commentators had been an irksome distraction from the real business of political journalism. Now the pundits' columns seemed to define serious electoral journalism. All the papers, bar the *Financial Times*, exploited their glittering arrays of columnists to attract readers to their election coverage. The star writers increasingly defined newspapers' political identities and in the process the special place of the editorial became marginalised. The leader comment was once the clear, authoritative voice of the paper, striking a distinctive tone above all other opinion on its pages. Now the editorial seems to be merely holding the ring between the powerful voices of its columnists, or is even undermined by the star performers. Amid the acres of dross from the pundits, there were many examples of thoughtful and sometimes sparkling writing. By contrast, few editorials passed the memory test.

The Times was the clearest example of this phenomenon. There was interesting opinion aplenty from its experienced team, especially Peter Riddell and the over-stretched Matthew Parris. However, there was only one leader of note, and that came on 5 June when the paper announced portentously that, for the first time in its history, it was endorsing Labour. 'In our time,' said the editorial, 'it is Labour that deserves the votes of reformers'. It reasoned that the key task for today was to consolidate the core achievements of Thatcherism. Labour had been lacking in the areas of education, health and civil liberties. 'For all that, we feel comfortable as never before with the case for Labour. Mr Blair is likely to blend Thatcherite means with social democratic ends in a manner which will benefit the public services.' This momentous shift in party allegiance actually seemed a relatively small step in the context of the campaign. *The Times* in 1997 had made the euro its decisive issue, but now, like its sister paper the *Sun*, it was persuaded that Labour was unlikely to hold an early referendum. Moreover, it had not been impressed with Hague's Conservative Party, which 'will have to be hit hard by voters for a second time before it provides a full alternative to Labour'.

The *Daily Telegraph* pitched its resistance to Labour on the grounds that the party aimed to destroy rather than consolidate the Thatcherite legacy. It would be a disaster if Labour secured another landslide, said the eve-of-poll editorial. 'For all the studied moderation, there is a hunger for political, ideological and cultural control that is really quite frightening. New Labour wants to make Toryism literally unthinkable and to uproot our deep-rooted political culture of robust debate.' Under Charles Moore's editorship, the *Daily Telegraph* proved to be the Conservatives' strongest and most consistent supporter. The paper was unique in finding nothing to like about Labour; not even the *Mail* was so single-minded. Even so, the *Daily Telegraph* again offered some of the most digestible coverage of the campaign: generally fair reporting, sharp analysis, lively commentary. All admirable qualities but they seemed to be a source of mounting frustration to Moore's leaders. At times the editor seemed to do battle with his own paper. While an editorial on 23 May encouraged the Tories to emphasise the euro issue, the celebrity columnist David Hare wrote that nobody understood why not being given a referendum was superior to being given one: 'on present form Hague looks like a man doing butterfly stroke in an emptied swimming pool. The only person he is hurting is himself.' Another editorial denounced the paper's own focus group when the results showed that voters disliked Tory advertising. As criticism of Hague's campaign grew, and even *Daily Telegraph* pundits told of their spouses turning Labour, Moore exploded. 'Tories versus the Rest' proclaimed an editorial on 1 June. The liberal-left project was about more than victory, it was about remoulding the Conservatives into their pre-Thatcherite state of ideological passivity: 'Like a lynch mob attack in the Middle East, mere execution is not quite enough, the steaming heart of the slain victim must be held aloft for all to see ...'

Repeating its 1997 formula, the *Guardian* ran an eight-page daily election pull-out. It was awash with pundits, and befitting its status as the paper of choice for media students, it devoted considerable space to analysis of the media and advertising. In Polly Toynbee and Hugo Young it possessed two of the press's more original analysts, who in an engaging debate between themselves came to different conclusions as to how to vote. Young urged a Liberal Democrat vote, to keep Labour honest. Toynbee offered a spirited defence of Labour, which, she said, had done more for the poor than any government in 50 years. There was never much doubt that the paper itself would go for Labour, nor any surprise that its endorsement fell between the views of its most respected columnists. It made clear its reasoning on 6 June, arguing that the most important question in politics was the reconstruction of the public services. Labour was the only party fully committed on this issue and 'for that reason alone we want to see Labour back in office on Friday'. However, it added: 'As a newspaper living with Labour's apparently sleepless desire to intimidate and interfere with news and observing by contrast their often cringeing and unprincipled wooing of the rightwing tabloids it is inevitable that our endorsement of Labour will take the form of a "yes, but" ...'

Under Andrew Marr's leadership, the *Independent* had supported Labour in 1997. Under Simon Kelner it returned to more familiar ground, declining any positive alignment. Its final leader on 6 June was headlined 'Why Britain should reject this Conservative Party'. Labour, it said, was entitled to a benevolent assessment of its record and the government's successes outweighed its failures. However, more telling for the *Independent* was the performance of Hague's Conservatives, 'offensive and illiberal' on asylum and nowhere near sharing the paper's own vision of Britain as a modern European country. It concluded 'with regret that the Conservative Party on this occasion does not deserve to be elected'.

As in 1997, the *Financial Times* made fewest concessions to the election of any broadsheet. Its campaign reports were confined to two or occasionally three inside pages and it devoted considerably fewer editorials to the election than did its rivals. Yet its coverage was all the more pertinent as a result. Its early exposure of confusion in the Tory camp on the magnitude of tax cuts, based on an interview in which Oliver Letwin suggested larger reductions than those proposed in the manifesto, was the most telling press intervention in the campaign. The *Financial Times* was also quick to spot the hospital protest brewing in Wyre Forest. On the question of which party to support, the Conservatives' Euroscepticism was always likely to be decisive for the pro-European *Financial Times* and so it proved. On 5 June, and for the third successive election, the paper of business offered its support to Labour. On the central issues of Europe, the economy and public services, Labour was the better choice, but not without qualification:

There is much that is unappealing about Mr Blair's government. It has been arrogantly dismissive of those who challenge it. It has colluded with the Conservatives in a grubby illiberal approach to crime and asylum. In many respects it has lost the goodwill of voters. But elections pose a choice. Labour has governed with competence. Mr Blair has earned his second chance.

The campaign in progress

The news agenda in 2001 showed marked similarities to 1997 (Table 9.4). The European Union and party strategies and prospects headed the list in both elections while there were only three changes in the top 10. Northern Ireland, manifestos and sleaze went out; the Prescott punch, asylum and public services came in. Bread-and-butter questions of unemployment, inflation and economic prospects that once dominated British elections have now slipped off the agenda. Foot and mouth, the issue which delayed both the general and the local elections, was conspicuous by its absence.

Table 9.4   **Front-page lead stories and editorials about the election, by topic**

	Front-page lead stories			Editorials		
	2001		*(1997)*	2001		*(1997)*
	Number	*%*	*(%)*	*Number*	*%*	*(%)*
European Union	21	18	(22)	33	12	(16)
Party strategies/prospects	16	14	(19)	18	7	(9)
Prescott	16	14	(–)	11	4	(–)
Opinion polls	11	9	(5)	3	1	(8)
Taxation/public spending	7	6	(2)	14	5	(4)
Public services	6	5	(–)	12	4	(–)
Asylum/race	5	4	(–)	21	8	(–)
Exhortation to vote/advice on voting	4	3	(2)	17	6	(8)
Health	3	2	(2)	18	7	(2)
Party leaders	3	2	(–)	15	6	(–)
Manifestos	2	2	(7)	14	5	(8)
Thatcher	–	–	(–)	6	2	(–)
Northern Ireland	–	–	(3)	6	2	(4)
Tactical voting/strong opposition needed	–	–	(–)	5	2	(–)
Constitutional reforms	–	–	(–)	5	2	(–)
Other	24	20	(37)	73	27	(41)
Total	118	99	(99)	271	100	(100)

In front-page leads and in the editorials, Labour was the prime focus of attention (Table 9.5). In the *Sun* 22 of the 38 editorials during this campaign concerned Labour while just 8 were about the Conservatives.

Echo Research found that 86 per cent of election articles in the national press covered Labour compared to 68 per cent the Conservatives, reversing the situation in 1997 when, of course, the Conservatives were still the governing party.[3] With Labour so clearly set to win, its proposals were simply more newsworthy. They were not a better story than Prescott's punch, however, which made as many front-page leads as health, taxation and public services put together.

Table 9.5   Coverage of major political parties in front-page lead stories and editorials about the election in daily newspapers

	2001 Number	2001 %	(1997) (%)
Front-page lead stories			
Conservative	26	22	41
Labour	64	54	22
Liberal Democrat	–	–	1
Other	2	2	–
More than one party	26	22	36
Total	118	100	100
Editorials			
Conservative	45	17	26
Labour	142	52	32
Liberal Democrat	8	3	1
Other	6	2	–
More than one party	70	26	40
Total	271	100	99

For all the censure of Labour's attempts to manipulate coverage, its press in the opening phases of the campaign was far from favourable. In particular, the decision to announce the election date during assembly at a girl's school attracted virtual ridicule. The Prime Minister's image, piously framed by a stained glass window, hymnbook in hand, provided a picture for almost every front page. 'Here beginneth Blair's crusade' was the *Telegraph*'s headline. In its tangible expression of the moralising element in New Labour, the event was a gift for the broadsheet sketch writers. They united in condemning Blair's 'cynical' choice of venue. Labour's exploitation of a schoolgirl audience was close to 'child abuse', said the *Telegraph*'s Frank Johnson; '... if the Prime Minister sanctioned the arrangements for this dire event, and if there is a hell, he will go to it', wrote Matthew Parris.

A week later came Prescott's brawl with Craig Evans and Labour's 'nightmare day' when Sharron Storer harangued the Prime Minister

Table 9.6 Front-page lead stories, 15 May–7 June 2001

Date	Mirror	Express	Sun	Daily Mail	Daily Star	Daily Telegraph	Guardian	The Times	Independent	Financial Times
May 15	(Help me die, Dad)	(The day I had to kill my darling daughter)	(One winner scoops £20m)	(Why I killed my daughter)	(Geri Halliwell)	Blair counters 'spin' claims	Hague denies £20bn handout	Private health 'factories' to rescue NHS	Voters reject Tories tax cuts	Business influence cut by Labour shake-up
16	(Catherine Zeta Jones)	(Medicine prices slashed)	Blunkett next home secretary	Campaigning really getting dirty	Britney backs Labour	(Medicine prices slashed)	Secret reform agenda revealed	(Chemists at risk as prices slashed)	Blair risks wrath of left in public-sector reforms	(Fed makes half-point cut)
17	Manifesto: Prescott in street brawl	(Fergie's aide Jane Andrews guilty of murder)	Two jabs: Prescott punch up	Two jags floor show	(Survivor TV show)	Prescott punches a protestor	Secret Labour plans to reform prisons	Prescott lashes out at protestor	Prescott attack ruins Labour's day	Prescott's fracas takes shine off launch
18	Forget Rocky, meet Labour's champ – Stocky	I'll fight on says thumper Prescott	Two bibs v. Two jabs	(Company pension funds run out of cash)	Prescott jabs: Lennox would be proud	Prescott calls in the minders	Ranks close around Prescott	Prescott refuses to apologise	Prescott row derails campaign	Prescott to face police questioning over brawl
19	(Alex Ferguson)	(Million holiday flights for £1)	(David Beckham)	(Police told: fine more motorists)	(Big Brother TV show)	(Israeli jets strike back after bomb)	Hague stirs row over asylum	(Cricket still suspected of match-fixing)	Labour memo: 125 seats at risk	(Alcatel and Lucent hold merger talks)
21	I'll end evil on net	(Tears of drugs women jailed for life)	(Lottery winner's £50,000 nicked)	(House prices 'sure to plunge')	(Chris Evans)	Blair under fire from boardrooms	(Heading for disaster)	Tory grandee shatters Europe truce	Tory cuts will total £25bn, says Labour	Tories vow to rein in regulators and cut business taxes
22	(Survivor TV show)	(Britain in Fear)	(Angel of death to wed vampire)	The ticking N1 timebomb	(Survivor TV show)	TV to blame for protests, says Labour	TV inciting protests	Labour fury at TV 'setting up' protests	(Shock at growing number of foreign nurses)	Brown aims to boost productivity
23	(Cop-out: Fury as police walk free)	(Philip: my son's unfit to be King)	(Executed by the police)	(Philip's rift with Charles)	Jordan stands as MP	Labour wriggles over 50pc tax	Blair asks French: be quiet on EU	Thatcher stretches Tory line on euro	Brown rules out big rises in tax	Blair to base euro case on patriotism
24	Meltdown: euro row shatters Tories	(Scandal of the lottery fat cats)	My hair-do	Postmen: back to the bad old days	Jordan: I've got 'em by the ballots	(Millions of letters delayed by strike)	Tory tax ploy misfires	Record lead for Labour	Blair accuses media of ignoring 'real' issues	Brown aides raise concerns on ECB
25	Kids are vile (say the Tories)	(Don't drink the water)	(ITV poach Lineker)	(Car insurance set to rocket)	(Jonathan Ross)	Parties draw battle lines over Europe	(Deficit of £6bn sparks new rail crisis)	Archbishops decry cynical campaign	Voters against Blair plans for public service	Blair says he can win euro debate

Date										
26	(Twins at 56)	(Mum jailed for leaving kids alone)	(Coronation Street)	(Cancer fear over milk)	(Big Brother TV show)	(MAFF reveals 1500 more virus farms)	(Leaked spy report names UK)	Two weeks to save pound, says Hague	Hague says UK is 'highly likely' to vote for euro	(Interbrew wins Bass reprieve)
28	Vote Tory ... and see what will happen to Britain	Petrol set to hit £4 a gallon	(David Coulthard)	Petrol to rise 30p a gallon after the election	(Big Brother TV show)	Race riot town on a knife-edge	Racial tension blamed for riot	Riots put race on poll agenda	Bitter race row after Oldham riot	Business spurns key Euro role
29	We've lost: top Tory admits bet on election defeat	(Copycat race riot warning)	(Hospital cleaner snatches baby)	Labour: it's in the bag	(Big Brother and Survivor TV shows)	Jospin reveals 'superstate' plan	(Mugabe faces coup plot)	Jospin fuels Europe row with Labour	Prodi undermines Blair on Europe	Labour vows to ease mergers
30	EU silly Billy	(Train fares set to double)	(Survivor TV show)	Now the poll is getting personal	(Big Brother TV show)	The campaign turns personal	Tories face poll meltdown	Hague rows back on euro deadline	Tories break ranks over Europe	Brown re-buffed on call for ECB reform
31	(Jeffrey Archer)	(Jeffrey Archer)	(Panties put on parade)	(Jeffrey Archer)	(Big Brother TV show)	(Jeffrey Archer)	(Post office services to be sold off)	(Jeffrey Archer)	(Jeffrey Archer)	Polls fail to daunt Tory leaders
June 1	Tatty bye Tories: euro poll tickles 'Doddy' Blair	(Jeffrey Archer)	Blair does a Becks: Mohican look for PM	NHS: fantasy and reality	(UFO: is this best proof yet?)	School and health chiefs attack Blair	Tories: the cracks begin to show	Blair looks to business for Whitehall fix	Clarke attacks Tory leader over Europe	Blair faces union backlash
2	(I was kidnap baby Alex)	(Anti-fat pills on the NHS)	(Amanda's at it again)	('Torture' of Briton facing a flogging)	(Hear'say)	(Euro police HQ raided in fraud inquiry)	Private role for best schools	Hague turns left to avert landslide	(Mystery over third black man found hanged)	Tories to warn against a landslide
4	(Michael Barrymore)	(Poison in our food scandal)	The Tory's way out in front	Fury as Labour faces TV attack on NHS	(S Club Dad in sex limo shame)	Blair tries to counter new Tory tactics	(Israeli forces await order to act)	Blair in last push as Tories warn of landslide	Hague accused of spoiling tactics	Hague links euro with future public spending
5	PS: exciting isn't it?	(Innocent drivers in fines fiasco)	How come there's a big swing to the Tories?	(NHS to ration dental braces)	(Ronnie O'Sullivan)	Waiting lists are fiddled - official	Left plans assault on Blair	Labour row as Brown blocks youth pay rise	(Coroner tells jury of 'horrific' racial harassment)	Blair pledge on high tax rates
6	It's official, this election is ... pants!	(I love you Mum but I need to love my Daddy too)	Exposed: Labour TV babe	(Jail warders payout storm)	(Kebab'em for us lads)	Hague's last hurrah for Tories	Hague to get survival ultimatum	Brown vows: I am ready to be unpopular	Blair gets date for euro campaign	(Railtrack shares plunge 17%)
7	X marks the clot	(Michael Barrymore)	Don't let us down Tony	(Michael Barrymore)	(Michael Barrymore)	It's all over bar the voting	'You hold the key ...'	Blair heads for second landslide	The spin is spun, punches thrown. Nation decides	Blair on brink of electoral history

about NHS funding on the same day as Labour launched its manifesto (see Table 9.6). 'LABOUR'S BIG DAY IS SCRAMBLED', said the *Independent* headline; 'MANIFISTO' said the *Mirror*. Others could not resist the pun on Prescott's 'two jags' nickname: 'TWO JABS' was the *Sun*'s headline, while its leader, 'Thrilla in Rhyla', pronounced that the people were fighting back. However, Prescott received considerable support from the red-tops. The *Mirror, Sun* and *Star* all claimed considerable public backing for his 'lethal left hook'. The *Mirror* ran a 'tribute edition' to Stocky, the East Hull stallion. Only the Conservative papers were wholly unsympathetic. For the *Mail*, the fracas was another sign of Labour's 'demeaning of democracy'. For the *Telegraph,* the episode symbolised the entire government's inability to cope with criticism. Prescott 'showed a boiling, brutish, ignorant nature, a man made instinctively aggressive by his long training in trade union militancy ...'. In the *Mail on Sunday*, Norman Tebbit adopted a similar line: Prescott's 'loss of control' reflected his 'deep unhappiness' in knowing that 'if Labour wins he will become Minister for Nothing At All. On his way to the backbenches Prescott's left hook landed on Craig Evans, but it was aimed at the Prime Minister.'

The significance of these unspun events exercised the columnists for the remainder of the week. They had given the campaign its metaphor, was David Lister's view in the *Independent*. 'At last a moment of authenticity punctuates the sheer bloody awfulness of this election', wrote fellow columnist David Aaronovitch. The *Mirror* concurred, claiming that the most boring election ever had burst into life. It may not have been pretty 'but it sure beats the banal activities the spin doctors prefer'. Prescott's punch was 'in a weird way a blow for freedom' said Nicholas Wapshott in *The Times*, a blow against 'control freakery'. It told us something important about the British political mood, said the *Guardian*: people were not apathetic but angry and frustrated. For others, all this pontificating was too much to bear. 'What a punch', said *Independent* sketch-writer Simon Carr. 'Semiotically, the significant gesture of the last five years ... On the face of it, we may assume it is disastrous for the Government. But when we have had it properly explained, we will see that it means an increased government majority.'

The Conservatives were first off the mark with their manifesto, impressing the press with their speed but failing to completely satisfy. According to the *Daily Mail*, the programme was coherent and sensible but 'have the Tories been too timid?' The *Daily Telegraph*, too, was not over-generous, although it did find some relief in the 'Tory vision of lower taxation for individuals ... and the consequent development of a freer, more responsible society'. The *Sun* liked the proposals but distrusted

Conservative competence to deliver. For the *Financial Times* the manifesto was 'vague on detail and disturbingly inconsistent ... Taxes cannot be cut significantly without affecting public services.' *The Times* complained that Hague seemed to be running on 'B-list' issues, too much on tax, crime, asylum and the euro; overall, a work in progress rather than a programme for power.

'Too timid' was also a common reproach in press reaction to the Liberal Democrat manifesto. It was more social democrat than liberal, said the *Financial Times*: 'Charles Kennedy has not yet defined a mission for his party. It should and could be a more vibrant force of liberal economic and social values in Britain.' The *Daily Telegraph* did not trouble its leader writers but columnist David Hare found the manifesto 'a howling missed opportunity'. The *Independent* adopted a similar tone; while there was much for a liberal paper to like, it was 'worryingly flaky' on Europe and 'Mr Kennedy seems to have let his laid-back approach get the better of him'. However, for the *Guardian* and *The Times*, the programme represented shrewd positioning in the space vacated by Labour's move to the right.

Labour's programme, when it came, also failed to excite. For *The Times* it was 'a technocratic manifesto that leaves key questions unanswered' and contained no real surprises. For the *Independent*, Blair was asking for a doctor's mandate on all the big issues: 'Trust him, because he is a pretty straight sort of guy.' The *Guardian* agreed that the programme contained little that was new but still the 'Labour manifesto is a focussed and formidable document. It is a manifesto for active government ...'. The tabloids generally welcomed Labour's commitment to the public services while demanding fast delivery in the second term. The *Daily Mail* said that the Dome was the perfect symbol of the party's manifesto, 'shiny on the outside, full of beguiling gloss, but with worrying questions about the quality of its contents'. The real question was: can Blair deliver on his promises, and based on performance since 1997 'voters have every right to feel cynical ...'.

After the first full week, the press judged Labour's campaign to be the one that seemed to be struggling, its fabled presentation machine spluttering amid tales of disagreement between Blair and Brown. The papers analysed the campaign mishaps: the school launch, the punch, the Sharron Storer harangue, the bullying of journalists and Labour's unsubstantiated complaint that the press was colluding with demonstrators to set up confrontations. Brown's rigid management of the campaign was said to be at fault. Blair and Brown must stop rowing, wrote the *Sun*. They were the 'Lennon and McCartney' of British politics and for the good of the country it was essential that their relationship was strong. The *Guardian* criticised Labour's 'Rose Garden' strategy: Labour seemed more worried about opponents' attacks than attacking opponents.

With the manifestos done and discussion of unscripted events finally running out of steam, press coverage began to concentrate on specific issues. Tax, National Insurance contributions, asylum, investment and privatisation of public services moved up the agenda but increasingly Europe took top billing. The trigger here was Margaret Thatcher's intervention with her irresistible soundbite that she would 'never' sacrifice the pound for a single European currency. The papers divided on predictable lines. At last the *Daily Mail* rediscovered some fighting spirit: the core issues were sovereignty and democracy and it was a scandal that Labour refused to debate them. The *Sun* warned that Britain's 'golden future' would be destroyed if we 'scrapped the pound'. The *Daily Telegraph* took a harder line still, raising the prospect of leaving the EU altogether. However, for most commentators Thatcher's speech had simply highlighted the fault line in Conservative policy on the single currency. As the *Express* put it, her intervention had underlined the irrevocable Conservative split on the euro. 'Thank you Maggie,' wrote the *Mirror*, 'for all you are doing to get Labour elected'. *The Times*, so vigorously opposed to the euro in 1997, adopted a milder tone this time, contenting itself with the thought: 'The pound is likely to be much safer under Labour than the Prime Minister in his perfect world would like it to be.'

The euro remained the predominant headline in the penultimate week. As the *Daily Telegraph* noted, the parties drew battle lines over Europe, with Blair proclaiming the patriotic case for engagement and Hague starting the clock on the 'countdown to save the pound'. Speeches from across the Channel by Lionel Jospin and Romano Prodi also attracted critical press attention. The single currency signalled the 'death of our nation', said the *Sun* over a double-page spread on how the EU superstate would 'swallow up Britain'; our embassies would close and the EU would take control of tax, law and the police. 'Sleepwalking into the superstate', was the *Daily Mail*'s warning in its leader comment. Intriguingly though, the same day's *Mail* splashed on its front page the story of Labour's private poll showing a 20-point lead over the Conservatives: 'It's in the bag'. And for most of the press it seemed that Hague's gamble on the pound had backfired. People simply do not share Hague's euro obsession, said the *Mirror*, while the *Daily Express* wondered if Hague 'lacks the intelligence' to grasp the simple fact that this was a general election and not a referendum on the pound. As the *Guardian* reported that Tory elder statesmen were lining up to condemn the Eurosceptic strategy, a feature by James Fenton summed up the overwhelming verdict on William Hague's own political future: 'dead man walking'. On the campaign trail with the Conservative leader, the *Mail*'s Quentin Letts struck an equally funereal note; he wondered if his experience was 'what it was like in the briefing room for the kamikaze pilots'.

In the campaign's final days, the press reported that Conservative strategy had shifted again, this time to the public services. However, the move was deemed to be too little and too late. Newspapers began to speculate on the election result and its aftermath, examining the consequences of electoral apathy, differential turnout and another landslide. Baroness Thatcher again intervened with a piece in the *Telegraph* warning of the danger of 'elective dictatorship'. Fear of a landslide was the Conservatives' last roll of the dice and this theme, at least, did strike a chord across the press. As the papers one after another declared for Blair, few relished a massacre. Ironically, the *Independent*, which did not endorse Labour, was also the least concerned about the size of Labour's majority. Those genuinely worried about a landslide should focus on electoral reform, said its leader, and not start whingeing when it was too late about the democratic choices of their fellow citizens. Polling day dawned with the papers exhorting readers to vote and united in confident prediction of a second landslide: as the *Daily Telegraph* headline put it, 'It's all over bar the voting'.

Like the dailies, the Sunday press entered the campaign with circulation and readership well down on 1997 levels; only the *Mail on Sunday* showed a significant increase (Table 9.2). Perhaps reflecting commercial anxieties, the Sundays were reluctant to give priority to the election. The popular press found other topics while the special sections in the quality papers, although extensive and detailed, seemed to be a way of containing the election rather than highlighting it. Indeed, the *Sunday Times* was reduced to opening one of its election specials with a full-page analysis of why the public had lost interest in the whole business.

In their final editorials, the Sundays generally struck a moderate pro-Labour tone. Labour, yes, but not with great passion and (except for a few) not by a landslide. In the main, the uncompetitive state of the Conservative Party was treated as a matter for regret rather than exaltation. The small-circulation *Sunday Business* summed up the mood in commenting that 'this newspaper concedes that Labour is the only party currently demonstrating an ability to govern ... but a second landslide and a weak opposition would not be healthy for Britain'. As in 1997, the Sundays showed more enthusiasm for Labour's leader than for his party. The overriding issues were health and education; the dominant assessment was that Tony Blair deserved another chance – according to some, a final chance – to deliver on his genuine commitment to modernisation. Real enthusiasm for Labour may have been lacking but the extent of the party's dominance in the Sunday papers was remarkable and surely unparalleled. With the *Sunday Times* and the *Sunday Express* each moving into Labour's camp, the total readership of the pro-Labour Sundays amounted to 26.5 million compared with 9.4 million for the Conservatives (see p. 160).

Among the broadsheets, the only paper to change its stance was the *Sunday Times*. In 1997, it had endorsed the Conservatives 'warts and all'; this time, it preferred the imperfections of New Labour. Under the headline, 'THE LEAST WORST PARTY', it argued that 'Labour has grown arrogant with power and needs checking by an alert House of Commons. It deserves to win, but with a reduced majority.' By contrast, 'the Tories are unelectable in their current state … Mr Hague's followers have frittered the past four years away in sniping and sloganising. They wasted an opportunity to reorganise and rethink, which is why they have failed to make their case in this campaign.' The *Independent on Sunday* also endorsed Labour but again with anxieties about a landslide: 'after four years of better-than-the-Tories administration, the party of devolution and the minimum wage just about deserve their second term. But we do not welcome the prospect – as now seems near-certain – of another massive Labour win.'

The *Observer* was the most pro-Labour broadsheet. Under the heading 'GIVE LABOUR A SECOND TERM', it suggested that Tony Blair's government had 'set in motion a stunning programme of constitutional change', 'been truer to its obligations to the poor than Tony Blair and his ministers allow themselves to earn credit for' while 'abroad Labour has been enlightened and mostly liberal too'. However there were shortcomings: the state of the public services, poor delivery on the environment and illiberal treatment of asylum seekers, welfare claimants and criminals. Partly for these reasons, the paper urged a tactical vote for the Liberal Democrats where they were second to the Conservatives. Unusually, another massive Labour win held no qualms for the *Observer*: 'If a landslide victory means the extinction of a brand of Tory politics that stigmatises difference, enthrones self-interest and delights in authoritarian repression while indulging every base instinct, Britain would benefit from it.'

The landslide threat offered a natural escape route for the Conservative papers and both the *Sunday Telegraph* and the *Mail on Sunday* took full advantage. Under the heading 'VOTE FOR DEMOCRACY', the *Sunday Telegraph* dutifully listed 'the many good reasons to vote Conservative on Thursday: love of liberty, hostility to over-taxation, fears for the countryside, disillusionment with Labour's public service reform, a belief that the market works better than the state, a devotion to a strong and successful currency. Over-arching all these concerns, however, should be an awareness that the nation is electing a legislature, not a president.' The paper continued, 'Nobody can blame Mr Blair for seeking the largest majority he can get. But the polls' evidence that this is what he is most likely to achieve on Thursday is one of the most powerful arguments – in the national interest – for voting against him. This is not only a battle to decide who governs, but who is left to oversee them once the last vote is counted.'

The *Mail on Sunday*, now the Sunday paper with the highest readership after the *News of the World*, presented the same argument in more cataclysmic terms: 'a majority of the sort which Mr Blair is now seeking would be a blank cheque for a change so radical that it could turn Britain into something alarmingly close to a one-party state with much of its fate decided elsewhere. Those who would like to be rid of Mr Blair may – regrettably – have to wait until time. Those who believe that there ought to be a real democratic choice next time should vote Conservative.' In both the *Sunday Telegraph* and the *Mail on Sunday*, praise for the Conservatives was not entirely absent. The former noted that William Hague's 'guts and determination have never been in doubt' while the latter referred to 'the talents and integrity of Mr Hague' and the 'cautious and responsible Tory manifesto'. But the tone was muted; more obituary than coronation.

Like its daily sister paper, the *Express on Sunday* switched allegiance to Labour. But again the endorsement fell short of an embrace: 'BLAIR WINS OUR VOTE BUT HAS YET TO WIN OUR TRUST', ran a headline that summarised the predominant view across the press. And again the landslide theme was prominent: 'this newspaper would welcome an increased Liberal Democrat presence in the next House of Commons if that helps to hold a rampant New Labour to account'. But the Conservatives were not currently an alternative: 'a small clique now holds sway in the Conservative Party whose deep-rooted and blinkered Little Englander posturings find expression in hostility to Europe and asylum seekers but do not address the real concerns of the electorate'. So 'the Conservatives deserve to lose by a landslide even if Labour doesn't deserve to win by one, but like it or not, there is no alternative so we urge readers to vote Labour on Thursday'.

The traditional Sunday tabloids, the *Sunday People*, the *Sunday Mirror* and *the News of the World*, all again endorsed Labour, with varying commitment but a common focus on public services, notably health and education. The *People* provided a rare example of traditional class-war passion: 'This is probably the most important election you'll ever vote in. First, another Tory rout will drive their party into oblivion for at least a generation and probably for ever ... They will no longer be a danger to the ordinary working people of this country. Second, every extra Labour seat will give Tony Blair the platform he desperately wants to bring about the total revolution in the NHS and Education that he knows this country needs.' The *Sunday Mirror's* theme, 'TIME TO DO MORE', was more measured: 'Tony Blair talks a good game. His vision for Britain is one in which we all want to live [including] a Britain where our trains run on time and don't kill you. But after four years of New Labour, Tony's vision remains largely just that. A vision.' The *News of the World* focused even more intensely on 'DELIVERY, DELIVERY, DELIVERY': 'despite great advances, our schools are still short of teachers, and our teachers are still short of the best schools'. Similarly, 'despite four years of effort hospitals are still a mess'. The paper recognised that landslide majorities can promote arrogance but trusted Tony Blair in his crusade to modernise the nation. Labour 'remains the best choice for all of us'.

In the weekly political journals, the main story was *The Economist's* decision to support Labour. 'VOTE CONSERVATIVE' proclaimed the cover of its 2–8 June edition over a picture of Tony Blair, crowned by Baroness Thatcher's permed hair and pearl earrings. That was their point: 'Tony Blair is the only credible conservative currently available.' He deserved a second term, not a standing ovation. The real Conservatives, for their part, were hopelessly divided on Europe and 'shockingly illiberal' on asylum and immigration. The *New Statesman* felt outraged by the government on civil liberties, immigration, the Kosovo war and much else besides. However, it was more critical still of the Tories. 'Take a deep breath, grit your teeth', it urged; there was no alternative but to vote Labour. The conservative *Spectator* left its editorial view to a signed column by Boris Johnson, its editor who was about to depart for a seat in the Commons. 'Just say no to Blair', was his advice. The journal's editorial was unusually mild, with little to say about the Conservatives and a warning that a vote for Labour would prove costly.

Advertising

Political advertising in the national press continued its long-term decline (Table 9.7): the total number of pages purchased was less than a third of the 1997 figure. Labour was the only major party to advertise nationally, with a last-minute campaign exhorting its own supporters to turn out.

As at the last election Unison purchased more space than did the Labour Party, its advertising defending the value of public services such as health. With new national spending limits now in force, there was no realistic prospect of a return to the Saatchi-inspired extravagance of 1987 when the parties were among the heaviest press advertisers during the campaign.

Table 9.7 Political advertising in national daily and Sunday newspapers

| | 2001 | | 1997 |
	Number of insertions	*Number of pages*	*(Number of pages)*
Pro-Labour			
UNISON	10	8.5	(16)
Labour Party	7	7	(12.5)
Other			
Charter 88	2	6.7	(–)
UK Independence Party	6	5	(–)
British Democracy Campaign	3	3	(–)
Total	28	30.2	(99.4)

Conclusion

Overall, 2001 produced the most subdued press overage for an election for 30 years, exulting neither at the result nor its part in the outcome. There was no trace of 'the *Sun* wot won it' swagger of 1992. The size and consistency of Labour's opinion poll lead not only rendered the outcome predictable but also seemed to diminish the tabloids' belief in their own influence. For tabloid readers, as for the electorate at large, partisan allegiance shifted little (Table 9.8). Penned into Labour's Big Tent, and reduced to arguing for four more years of competent government, the popular press lacked the verve and passion of the Thatcher era. With their readership in decline, and apathy reigning supreme, it no longer seemed to matter so much what the tabloids wrote. Ironically, Labour's triumph in the press occurred at a time when the direct value of the prize had fallen.

Certainly, Labour achieved unprecedented support from both daily and Sunday papers. Yet in many cases this was a cool embrace, an affair without passion founded on the absence of a credible alternative. Tony Blair's achievement in disarming the press is remarkable in itself but it remains to be seen whether he has brought about a permanent realignment of newspaper loyalties. A clear answer will only emerge after a closer election in which the government faces a revived opposition;

then we will discover how many papers were flying a flag of convenience in this campaign.

Table 9.8   **Party supported by daily newspaper readers**

Newspaper		Party supported by readers		
		Con	*Lab*	*LibDem*
		%	*%*	*%*
Daily Telegraph	2001	65	16	14
	1997	57	20	17
Daily Mail	2001	55	24	17
	1997	49	29	14
Financial Times	2001	48	30	21
	1997	48	29	19
Express	2001	43	33	19
	1997	49	29	16
The Times	2001	40	28	26
	1997	42	28	25
Sun	2001	29	52	11
	1997	30	52	12
Daily Star	2001	21	56	17
	1997	17	66	12
Independent	2001	12	38	44
	1997	16	47	30
Mirror	2001	11	71	13
	1997	14	72	11
Guardian	2001	6	52	34
	1997	8	67	22

Note: Whole sample: Con 33%, Lab 42%, LibDem 19%. Non-readers: Con 27%, Lab 45%, LibDem 22%.

Source: MORI General Election Aggregate. Base: 18,657 British adults interviewed during 2001 British General Election.

However, it is clear that the tone of political coverage has changed over the last decade, particularly in the tabloids, and that newspaper endorsements have become more pragmatic and businesslike. For many papers, flags of convenience are all that are left. Acutely sensitive to changes in the popular mood, most newspapers no longer position themselves directly within the traditional frameworks of class and party. As late as 1992, the *Mirror* could discover homeless youths wandering the streets of the capital with only a puppy for company while the *Sun* found a miner with three cars who couldn't 'afford to vote Labour'. A decade later, such stereotyping appears old-fashioned. Today, the most successful papers are the consumer-friendly *Daily Mail* and the business-friendly

Financial Times; neither places politics at its core or expresses much interest in class divisions. Further, the main issues of this campaign – Europe, the NHS and education – were by nature regulatory rather than distributive; they were not conducive to the traditional simplicities of tabloid treatment.

It is a different matter in the broadsheets. As the era of vigorous tabloid propaganda fades, so the quality press continues to perform its age-old function of providing comment and interpretation for the political elite. In an era when politics has become less ideological and more technical, the views of commentators who combine specialised expertise with political judgement become more relevant. Particularly on the issue of private provision of public services, there was a sense in this campaign of a genuine debate opening up in the broadsheets, a discussion prompted but not dominated by cautious statements in Labour's manifesto. Lengthy articles in quality newspapers offer a forum for informed reflection which is unmatched by the tabloids, the broadcast media or even the leader columns of the broadsheets themselves. In that sense, the significance of the quality press to elite political debate may be increasing.

Notes

1. The authors thank Will Dinan of the University of Stirling for contributing the section on Scotland, Ana Langer of the LSE and Derek Bell for preparing the tables in this chapter.
2. Echo Research, June 2001, at www.echoresearch.com/election
3. Echo Research, op. cit.

10
MPs and Candidates
Byron Criddle

In 2001, the disengagement of the electorate was mirrored in a decline in the number of candidates, which fell from 3,724 in 1997 to 3,318, or 5.0 candidates per seat compared to 5.6 in 1997. One reason for this was that the duplication of minor Eurosceptic parties was removed in 2001 with the UKIP's 428 candidates covering the terrain which in 1997 had been covered by 641 candidates, either of the UKIP or its rival, the Referendum Party. In addition the Natural Law Party, which had fielded 196 candidates in 1997, withdrew completely in 2001. The Green Party, however, persevered with a modest increase of candidates from 95 in 1997 to 145.

Of the main parties, Labour and the Conservatives contested all the mainland seats except the Speaker's at Glasgow Springburn. The Liberal Democrats withdrew not only from the Speaker's seat, but also from Wyre Forest where they supported the Independent candidate, Dr Richard Taylor. The SNP ignored the traditional all-party truce in seats occupied by Speakers and, like the Scottish Socialist Party, fought all 72 Scottish seats. Plaid Cymru contested all 40 seats in Wales.

The new intake of MPs numbered 99, or 15 per cent of the House of Commons, a very much lower figure than in 1997 when 260 (40 per cent) MPs were new. The 99 comprised 38 Labour, 33 Conservative, 14 Liberal Democrat, 4 SNP, 2 Plaid Cymru, 3 DUP, 2 UUP, 2 Sinn Féin and 1 Independent.

Labour's new MPs comprised a mere 9 per cent of the PLP, the Conservatives' 20 per cent of their parliamentary strength, and the Liberal Democrats' 26 per cent of theirs. Amongst the 99 new MPs were 7 – all Conservative – who had previously sat as MPs, until losing their seats in 1997;[1] 23 other former MPs (21 Conservative and 2 Labour) also sought, unsuccessfully, to return to the House.[2]

In an election in which only 27 seats changed hands between parties – fewer than at any election since 1955 – the turnover in parliamentary personnel was principally dependent upon the number of retirements, 80 in all: 41 Labour, 23 Conservative, 7 Liberal Democrat, 5 SNP, 2 Plaid Cymru and 2 UUP.

Most of Labour's retirements were explicable in terms of age and infirmity, though a significant minority were attributable to the exit of dual mandate MPs opting for the devolved Scottish Parliament or Welsh Assembly to which they had been elected in 1999, rather than Westminster.[3] A few others were leaving out of disillusion, and two after having been expelled. Labour's most senior departing MP was Tony Benn (b. 1925) who had first entered the Commons as Anthony Wedgwood Benn at a by-election in November 1950.[4] Following Tony Benn into retirement was Sir John Morris (elected 1959), Labour's only other survivor from the Parliaments of the 1950s, and another former Cabinet Minister, having served as Welsh Secretary in the Callaghan government before ending up as Attorney General in Tony Blair's. Other long-serving retirees were Robert Sheldon (who had served for 37 years), former Junior Minister Ted Rowlands (34 years), Joe Ashton (33 years) and Barry Jones and Tom Pendry (31 years each). The bulk of Labour's elderly retiring MPs were of the 'lost' generation who had entered the Commons during the locust years of the Thatcher hegemony, and so been denied hope of office: Dale Campbell-Savours, Peter Snape, John Maxton, Alan Rogers, Maria Fyfe, Llin Golding and Robin Corbett. The retirement of Giles Radice, who had served 28 years, and who would almost certainly have graced any Labour Cabinet during the eighties, removed – in the steps of Cripps, Gaitskell, Jay and Crossman – the last of Labour's Wykehamists; and the departure of Eric Clarke and Lawrence Cunliffe, two of its last former mineworkers.

Some of the unorthodox were leaving following expulsion, as in the case of Ken Livingstone who had run against the official Labour candidate in the London Mayoral election, and Tommy Graham who had been dropped following fratricidal strife in the Renfrewshire Labour Party. One other, Peter Temple-Morris, was leaving for a peerage after 27 years in the Commons, but only 3 as a Labour MP, following his defection from the Conservatives in 1998. Rather than copy fellow defectors, Alan Howarth (before 1997) and Shaun Woodward (after 1997), he prudently chose retirement instead of an undignified trawl through safe Labour seats.

Labour retirements in Scotland and Wales were boosted by the eight MPs who had been elected to the devolved bodies, one of whom, Ron

Davies, had (like his English colleague, Joe Ashton) also been the subject of adverse press coverage of his private life.

Less orthodox was the withdrawal of four of Labour's women MPs: Mo Mowlam, Judith Church, Jenny Jones and Tess Kingham. Mo Mowlam (b. 1948) was the only serving Cabinet Minister to be leaving the Commons, and was doing so out of a mix of disillusionment and poor health. Judith Church (b. 1953), who had been elected in a 1994 by-election as a high-flying NEC member of whom much was expected, had achieved little during her six years as an MP and was giving up for personal reasons. Jenny Jones (b. 1948) and Tess Kingham (b. 1963) were even more surprising: both were from Labour's large female intake of 1997; it was claimed that Jenny Jones had never intended serving more than one term, whilst Tess Kingham was vocal in explaining her dislike of Westminster's arcane practices and its incompatibility with family life. Having won the barometer seat of Gloucester in 1997, she had joined five other women MPs of that intake in having babies. Finding combining the role of MP and nursing mother difficult, she complained that Parliament was 'not geared to anyone who has any kind of family life', and criticised the Whips, the 'yah-boo nonsense, point-scoring and silly games' of 'a male bastion', with its 'public school fagging system' and aura of 'a gentlemen's club', where one was required to 'sit up all night for schoolboy politics'. She had also been one of the handful of 1997 entrants to join the Campaign Group.

A number of Labour's retiring MPs were also leaving late in the day, announcing their departures in the last few months, weeks – or even days – before the election, in order to facilitate the leadership's insertion of favoured replacements from centrally-imposed shortlists. Most notorious in this case were the late withdrawals of Gerry Bermingham (St Helens South) and the former Cabinet Minister, David Clark (South Shields), on the eve of the election campaign in May.

All but two of the Conservatives' 23 retiring MPs were over 60 or (in one case) very close to being 60. The two exceptions were the former Prime Minister, John Major (b. 1943), leaving Huntingdon after 22 years, and much more surprisingly David Faber (b. 1961) who was not yet 40, had served only in two Parliaments, and was vacating a safe seat as Harold Macmillan's grandson and last serving member of the long-running Cavendish/Macmillan parliamentary dynasty. He was doing so for family reasons.

The most prominent of the Conservative retirements was the former Prime Minister (1970–74), Sir Edward Heath, who was both the oldest (b. 1916), and longest-serving (since February 1950) MP, and who had been Father of the House since 1992. His continuous 51 years' service was exceeded only by David Lloyd George's 55 years (1890–1945), although Winston Churchill served interruptedly (1900–22 and 1924–64) for a total of 62 years. With Labour's Tony Benn he was the last MP to have served in the Second World War. Sir Edward's retirement also meant the House was for the first time in 56 years without a former Prime Minister among its members.[5]

Accompanying Sir Edward into retirement were three other Conservative MPs who had also entered the Commons in the 1950s. Sir Richard Body (b. 1927) who was first elected during Sir Anthony Eden's premiership in 1955, had served for a total of 39 years; and from 1959 Sir Geoffrey Johnson-Smith (b. 1924) had served 41 years, and Sir Peter Emery (b. 1926), 39 years. Leaving too were the last remnants (bar Kenneth Clarke and John Selwyn Gummer) of Margaret Thatcher's Cabinets in the form of Tom King, John MacGregor, Sir Norman Fowler, and the ex-Deputy Prime Minister, Michael Heseltine.

Two of the Conservatives' retirements were late in the day and somewhat discordant. Charles Wardle was the victim of a virtual deselection at Bexhill & Battle, and Christopher Gill, a disaffected Eurosceptic, acrimoniously vacated his Ludlow seat.

The Liberal Democrats saw 7 of their 47 MPs retire – a number which in the 1950s would have wiped out the entire parliamentary party. The leading retirement was that of Sir Paddy Ashdown who had led the party for 10 years (1989–99) and held the Yeovil seat for 18 years. Robert Maclennan (b. 1936) was ending 35 years as an MP, initially as Labour and then SDP. Two other Liberal Democrats – Jim Wallace and Donald Gorrie – were leaving for the Scottish Parliament.

The minor parties contributed nine of the retirements, seven of them Scottish or Welsh Nationalists leaving for the devolved assemblies. These included the SNP's new leader, John Swinney who had only entered the Commons in 1997, and Plaid Cymru's recently elected leader, Ieuan Wyn Jones. Also retiring was the former leader of Plaid Cymru, Dafydd Wigley, whose 27 years (1974–2001) as a Nationalist MP had been exceeded by only one other, the Irish Nationalist MP, T. P. O'Connor, who represented Liverpool Scotland for 44 years from 1885 to 1929. The Ulster Unionists, John Taylor and Ken Maginnis, also retired.

Very little innovation was evident in the parties' candidate selection procedures before the 2001 election, but most – as always – came from Labour. If Labour's preoccupation before 1997 had been with 'feminising' the PLP by way of all-women shortlists, after 1997 it was with converting the party to a culture of government by means of a more professional candidate screening process and the creation of a 'National Parliamentary Panel', or list of approved eligible candidates. In the words of one Millbank official, the intention was 'to remove the need for the NEC to refuse endorsement' of certain candidates, as in the messy case of Liz Davies, the left-wing candidate for Leeds NE who was barred in 1995. Candidates for the list were required to attend training and assessment weekends, to submit full CVs to a standardised format, and to be interviewed by a panel involving at least one MP. A senior MP involved in the process defended the system as one designed to 'weed out the charlatans' who had come through the old system of CLP selection conferences, to secure more women candidates, to improve the quality of candidates, and to eliminate those who 'appeared not to have a pragmatic line on policy disagreements' or who could 'not avoid sounding divisive and combative if disagreeing with party policy', or who showed 'an unpreparedness to listen to the Whips'. The same MP denied that this represented a quest for 'Blairite clones', indeed voicing his own reservations about such an outcome and claiming that candidates were sometimes tested by being invited to react precisely to having the 'Blairite clone' point put to them. Naturally enough, the left-wing Campaign Briefing – active on the fringe of the annual party conference – saw the process as designed to 'promote identikit middle-class, on-message, New Labourites of whom we already have enough'.

Those aspiring to get onto the candidates list were issued with a 'How to be a Candidate' pack comprising an application handbook, application form and a 'nominees monitoring form'. This latter requested information on gender, age, ethnic background (with ten different options listed), disability, occupation (with distinctions made between 'manual, clerical and other') and experience as a local candidate or councillor. The application form required information on party experience, other experience, knowledge of policy issues, skills and a personal statement on the reasons for seeking selection. The application handbook provided guidance for applicants about demonstrating their experience and abilities and specifically sought evidence of the applicant's 'commitment to equal opportunities'. Most revealingly it contained statements from four model MPs from the 1997 intake, all orthodox loyalists – Hazel Blears, Oona King, Jim Murphy and Stephen Twigg – a group covering in their personal characteristics a full spread of race, gender and sexual orientation. Between them these four advised keeping in touch with the Whips as 'a source of helpful information', the importance of networking for aspiring women candidates, 'a strategic plan for working with the media', and getting to know 'key opinion leaders in local community organisations'. None of them referred to policy issues. The ethos of a highly professionally produced pack was that of a party of government seeking to induct orthodox professionals into its ranks.

Screening for the National Parliamentary Panel began in spring 1999 and the Panel was published at the end of the year, with seat selections starting early in 2000. Access to the panel was also available to candidates screened separately by affiliated bodies such as Unions and the Co-operative Party using their own methods, and of the 681 names on the Panel published at the end of 1999 – a figure whittled down from 886 original applicants – 103 had arrived by way of the Union route.

Labour made two other changes, one to placate those who opposed the ending (in 1996) of all-women shortlists: all bodies (wards or affiliates) nominating candidates must nominate both a man and a woman, and all shortlists must have equal numbers of men and women. The other change, which was designed specifically to restore security of tenure to sitting MPs, was to reduce from two-thirds to 50 per cent the number of nominations an MP required to avoid going through a contested reselection. No OMOV (one member, one vote) ballot would be required in such circumstances. This was the definitive end of 'mandatory reselection' in the style discussed by Chris Mullin in his 1981 *How to Select and Reselect Your MP*, the radical activists' manual for sacking loyalist MPs. The new system was officially termed 'affirmative nomination'. Those MPs whose tenure was now in doubt were now a handful and were the targets not of CLP activists but of the party leadership equipped with Whips' Office reports on the Member's record.

There was little grass-roots resistance to any of this. Unsuccessful attempts were made by a handful of CLPs at the 1999 conference to challenge the leadership's right to refuse endorsement other than on procedural grounds, and to permit the selection of candidates whose names were not on the Panel, but the culture had changed. CLPs were presented with very extensive sets of guidelines on candidate selection including a 'job description' and a 'person specification' identifying what was expected of a candidate. The entire thrust was towards a pro-fessionalised, loyalist PLP. The NEC produced limited evidence of CLP responses to the changes, showing approval for restricting eligibility for selection to Panel members only, for disallowing 'chicken-running' of MPs from marginal to safer seats, and for providing CLPs with MPs' voting records, though it appeared, even on the NEC's admission, that more CLPs favoured OMOV-style ballots over merely counting nominations received, to determine whether an MP be given a free run instead of a contested reselection.

Few of the cases where Labour MPs came unstuck between 1997 and 2001 had very much to do with any of this. Three MPs fell foul of the leadership and were expelled from the party: Dennis Canavan (Falkirk West), Tommy Graham (Renfrewshire West) and Ken Livingstone (Brent East). Dennis Canavan, a Scottish left-winger from the nationalist end of the party, was refused access to the approved list of candidates for the Scottish Parliament elections of May 1999. He retaliated by standing against the official Labour candidate in Falkirk West and winning. He was automatically expelled from the party and, after abortive attempts to mend his fences with the leadership, he resigned his Westminster seat provoking a by-election, which Eric Joyce narrowly won for Labour in December 2000. Joyce, a serving Army Major who had provoked controversy by publishing his criticisms of alleged elitism and racism in the Army, subsequently restored the seat to safe Labour status at the general election.

Ken Livingstone's offence was akin to Canavan's; having lost Labour's selection contest for the London Mayoral candidacy to Frank Dobson, he ran against Dobson and was automatically expelled from the party. He had claimed that Labour's selection process for the Mayoral nomination had 'set a new standard in ballot-rigging', with Dobson allowed privileged access to party membership lists well in advance of his rivals, Livingstone and Glenda Jackson, and with the use of an electoral college in which Union block votes, and the votes of London Labour MPs valued at 1,000 times the votes of ordinary party members, could be mobilised against the votes of the individual members (OMOV). Expelled immediately on submission of his nomination papers in April 2000, he went on to defeat Frank Dobson in the election for London Mayor and was replaced as Labour candidate in Brent East by local Brent Council leader, Paul Daisley, who claimed to have turned a famously discordant council into 'a model Labour authority'. Ken Livingstone's expulsion and loss of his Brent East seat in exchange for a London mayoralty of seemingly indeterminate powers, ended an impotent parliamentary career marked by a conspicuous failure to win the confidence of successive Labour leaders from the time of his Commons entry in 1987.

The third expellee was Tommy Graham. An MP since 1987, he was expelled in September 1998 following a long investigation into allegations that he had 'brought the party into disrepute' with unpleasant factional infighting in Renfrewshire and Paisley. In May 1997, shortly after the election, Gordon McMaster, MP for Paisley South, committed suicide, leaving a note in which he blamed Mr Graham for blackening his name with reports alleging alternately homosexuality and an affair with the MP for Paisley North, Irene Adams. Mr Graham in turn denied he had called Mr McMaster homosexual, but accused Mrs Adams of being 'lazy' and of 'milking' Mr McMaster's suicide for publicity. The Chief Whip, Nick Brown, cleared him of responsibility for McMaster's death, but he was duly expelled. His replacement as Labour candidate and MP was the local CLP ex-chairman and Renfrewshire councillor, Jim Sheridan, like Graham a former manual worker.

Two other Labour MPs were accused of electoral malpractices; Mohammed Sarwar, the first Muslim MP, had won Glasgow Govan in 1997 after a long disputed selection involving allegations of postal vote irregularities. On election as MP he was immediately embroiled in *News of the World* allegations that he had paid £5,000 to a rival Asian candidate in Govan to 'ease off' his campaign. An NEC enquiry found he had acted in a way 'grossly detrimental to the Party' and 'unbecoming and totally inappropriate for a Labour MP', and he was suspended in June 1997 pending police investigations. At a subsequent trial he was acquitted of charges of fraud, attempting to pervert the course of justice and contravening the *Representation of the People Act*; his suspension from the party was lifted in March 1999. At the election he was one of Labour's ethnic minority MPs who increased his vote share (in his case by 5 per cent).

Fiona Jones, elected for Newark in 1997, spent most of her time as MP under a cloud, with allegations of over-spending on her election campaign. In March 1999 she was duly found guilty of falsely declaring her election expenses, her seat was declared vacant, and she was sentenced to 100 hours community service and barred from holding public office for ten years. But at her appeal against the sentence, the Lord Chief Justice, Lord Bingham, quashing her conviction, described the Newark CLP as 'riven by personal animosity' and suggested that faction fighting had led to her conviction and that her enemies in the local party had leaked information about her campaign finances to the Liberal Democrats who had then initiated the complaint against her. She was fully reinstated as an MP, but the factional disputes had led to the suspension of local branches by the NEC and her reselection in 2000 had to take place by a ballot of the membership, and not by a counting of nominations, as under the reformed rules for sitting MPs. She was, however, duly reselected by a OMOV ballot, but the discordance surrounding her court case and local infighting had damaged her position and in June 2001 she was to be one of only eight casualties among sitting Labour MPs, with Newark falling to the Conservative, Patrick Mercer.

Bob Wareing, MP for Liverpool West Derby since 1983, also fell foul of the leadership. In June 1997 he was suspended from the PLP pending a Parliamentary Standards Commission enquiry into his non-disclosure of a directorship of a company (Robert Wareing Ltd) which had received a £6,000 retainer in August 1993 for consultancy services with a Serbian firm. The Standards and Privileges Committee found he had made a false declaration and that he should have declared his company's consultancy fee from Metta Trading, and recommended a week's suspension from the House in July 1997. In his subsequent apology to the Commons he launched into an attack on the Chief Whip, Nick Brown, for reporting him to the Standards Commission in the first place and for 'making a scandal out of an oversight', without ever allowing him a hearing, and was informed by Nick Brown that his apology was 'grudging, and fell well short of what was required'. He took part in a number of subsequent rebellions against the government, notably opposing NATO's bombing of Serbia, and by November 1999 was being ranked as Labour's seventeenth most dissenting back-bencher. In October 1999 he failed to get enough nominations to be reselected without a ballot, having received 12 nominations but with 18 against him. His supporters claimed Millbank had orchestrated the opposition with five USDAW branches having withdrawn their support for him, but with all five branch decisions having been signed by USDAW's Manchester-based political officer and all sent in the same envelope – a case of 'one person, five votes'. The AEEU also withdrew its backing for Mr Wareing, but in May 2000 he was narrowly reselected in an OMOV ballot by a four-vote majority, the only Labour MP to face a contested reselection ballot, and he duly retained his very safe seat in June 2001.

Race-related disputes featured in three other Labour-held constituencies, in two of which where Labour MPs had retired. In Birmingham Perry Barr the selection was very drawn out, culminating in the replacement of Jeff Rooker, who was leaving to continue his ministerial career from the House of Lords, by the Kashmiri Khalid Mahmood in a seat where (on 1991 Census figures) 38 per cent of the residents were non-white, but where there were intense inter-community rivalries between Muslims, Sikhs and Hindus. The Perry Barr CLP had been the scene of factional conflict and legal action for many years. The Kashmiri Muslim and former councillor, Khalid Mahmood, faced seven rivals for the nomination, but finally squared up to his main opponent, a Sikh woman, Sukhvinder Stubbs, who had the backing of Jeff Rooker; he beat her by 196 votes to 82. She however alleged postal ballot fraud but lost an appeal to the High Court. Mr Mahmood's controversial record as a one-term councillor, during which time he had allegedly spent a prolonged period out of Birmingham, as well as the fact that his name was not on Labour's National Parliamentary Panel, was also cited against him, but the election was imminent and his selection was endorsed. In retaining the seat in June he saw Labour's vote share fall from Rooker's 63 per cent in 1997 to 46 per cent in 2001.

In Gloucester the selection of the Sikh, Parmjit Dhanda, in a seat comprising 5 per cent non-whites drew an attack from the local paper, the *Citizen*, which ran an article on 10 April, 2001, suggesting that Mr Dhanda was 'doing himself no favours by getting himself selected in a cathedral city in the West Country which has a five per cent ethnic population most of which are of West Indian or Gujurati origin, and very few Sikhs'. Mr Dhanda denied he was threatening to sue the paper, and comfortably retained the seat at the election, albeit on an above average swing to the Conservatives.

A similar 'wrong kind of Asian candidate' row flared up at Northampton South, where the narrowly elected Labour MP Tony Clarke faced the only Conservative non-white candidate – Shailesh Vara, a City lawyer – selected for a winnable marginal seat. In this seat where non-whites also numbered only 5 per cent but were mostly Pakistani or Bangladeshi Muslims, Mr Vara was, in Tony Clarke's words, 'a Ugandan Hindu'. Mr Clarke also alluded to a minority of 'quite racist' voters in the rural part of the constituency. He was duly accused of playing the race card, but held the highly marginal seat with a majority up from 744 to 885 – a negligible gain compared to most of the other fresh victors of 1997.

Considerable attention was paid to Millbank's attempt to secure selection in Labour-held seats for favoured party-staffers. This led to complaints in Leigh where the selection had been long delayed but which finally occurred in January 2001, with a Whitehall political adviser, Andy Burnham, prevailing amid allegations of his having a head start by access to the membership list for over a year, and that he had overdone distribution of glossy election address-style leaflets to the membership – a form of canvassing used by many successful aspirants in pursuit of safe seat nominations.

Attracting more publicity was the eve-of-campaign parachuting into St Helens South of the ex-Conservative MP Shaun Woodward, who had crossed the floor in December 1999 despite a highly partisan history as a Central Office propagandist in the 1992 election and as an aggressive Labour baiter in his two-and-a-half years as a Conservative MP after 1997. Much mocked for his Oxfordshire mansion and Sainsbury heiress wife, he was imposed on St Helens South by means of an NEC-devised shortlist excluding strong local candidates such as St Helens Council leader Marie Rimmer (selections left until February 2001 were, under an NEC ruling, to be conducted by the NEC without the normal process of ward or affiliate nominations at constituency level). On the same day that Shaun Woodward was being awkwardly forced into St Helens the most senior of Labour's Whitehall insiders, David Miliband, Head of the Downing Street Policy Unit, was deftly inserted into South Shields, meeting rather more approval than Woodward had received. But by no means all of Millbank's efforts on behalf of apparatchiks were successful. At least four of the new intake (David Miliband, James Purnell (Stalybridge & Hyde), Andy Burnham and Jon Cruddas (Dagenham)) were from Whitehall backgrounds, but some who had been pencilled-in for safe seats came unstuck. The late retirement of the Prime Minister's PPS, Bruce Grocott, in Telford did not lead to the selection of a favoured metropolitan, but of a relatively unknown local councillor, Dave Wright. Nor did Derek Scott, a Number 10 adviser, win selection – as mooted – at Birmingham Erdington. And at Ashton-under-Lyne another local man, David Heyes, narrowly defeated a Millbank-favoured nominee. Nor was Ed Balls, a Treasury adviser, dropped as long-predicted into Bill O'Brien's Normanton seat. Mr O'Brien (b. 1929) remained *in situ* after the election as Labour's third oldest MP. Other old members of the awkward squad made their views clear: Gwyneth Dunwoody (b. 1930) spoke of the 'naked ambition of a small number of people, some of whom have not been in the Labour Party for very long, who believe they have a God-given right to be not only Labour MPs, but ministers as well; I'm going to keep going until I'm 110 on sheer bile!'

There was also some perception that the Unions were operating to ensure safe seat successes for their favourite sons. Certainly a good number of Labour's selections in seats where MPs were retiring went to high-ranking union officials such as the AEEU's John Mann (Bassetlaw), Mark Tami (Alyn & Deeside) and Tom Watson (West Bromwich East); to the GMB's Kevan Jones (Durham North), to MSF's Dai Havard (Merthyr Tydfil & Rhymney) and to UNISON's John Lyons (Strathkelvin & Bearsden) and Ann Picking (East Lothian). *The Times* reported in February 2000 a secret deal between the unions to avoid competing for the same safe seats.[6]

About a fifth of Labour's 38 new MPs were union officials, and about a third former party staffers – including those such as Kevin Brennan (Cardiff South), Hwyel Francis (Aberavon) and David Cairns (Greenock & Port Glasgow) who had worked for MPs. A further third of new Labour MPs in safe seats had backgrounds in local government as long-running councillors or as council leaders, as in the cases of Mark Lazarowicz (Edinburgh North & Leith), Iain Luke (Dundee East), Paul Daisley (Brent East) and John MacDougall (Fife Central). These latter were the true sons of OMOV: known and respected local leaders.

Responsibility for Conservative candidates passed after the 1997 election from Dame Angela Rumbold to Lord Freeman, who as Roger Freeman had lost Kettering to Labour at the election. An immediate problem he faced was the very large number (126) of Conservative MPs who had lost their seats in the 1997 election, many of whom wanted to return. Only about 40 were allowed back onto the candidates' list with the rest retiring or thwarted in their attempts to get back either by the Candidates Committee or in the Parliamentary Selection Board system. Even those ex-MPs who made it on to the list were discouraged by Lord Freeman from 'chicken-running' to better seats, enjoining them 'to stand in your old infantry trenches'. So it was that of the class of 126 defeated MPs in 1997, only 27 got themselves reselected in 2001, 20 fighting their former constituency (only 2 winning) and only 7 migrating elsewhere (5 winning).

Lord Freeman reconstituted the candidates list to comprise some 600 names, reduced from about 1,400 original applicants, 1,000 of whom were put through selection boards. The resultant list was – in his terms – 'a regular army rather than a territorial army', and, with some 470 non-Conservative seats to fight, provided a good ratio of candidates to constituencies.

Apart from dissuading the would-be retreads, Lord Freeman had other preoccupations. He sought to be more proactive in seeking candidates who had 'no political footprints' or political experience as councillors, but came from non-political professions, such as the army or business. (In the event at least four former serving officers were selected for Conservative-held seats.) He introduced additional tests for candidates at the by now well-established parliamentary selection boards, designed to test 'listening skills', believing that 'we were said not to be listening in 1997', and to inculcate TV interviewing skills. Caroline Spelman MP was also drafted in to push for higher numbers of women candidates from the 20 per cent share of the 600-strong candidates list. A revamped version of Central Office's long-running succinctly phrased 'Rules for the Selection of Conservative Candidates' was reissued outlining traditional selection procedures, but was also expanded to suggest criteria by which candidates should be judged and to define 'the ideal candidate' – with support expressed for older candidates ('it is better to have a good MP for ten years than a mediocre one for twenty'). Little of this reflected significant innovation and doubtless disappointed those who had been encouraged by Archie Norman MP, who occupied Vice or Deputy Chairmanships at Central Office between 1997 and 1999, to expect measures involving a quota of 25 per cent for women candidates on every shortlist before the next election, and as well as efforts to seek more ethnic minority and homosexual candidates.

Europe and 'sleaze', the two issues that had done so much to destabilise the party before 1997, rumbled on as a basis for certain local difficulties in the constituencies. Most prominent was the virtual deselection of the former Junior Minister Charles Wardle at Bexhill & Battle. Shortly after his reselection in January 2000, it was announced that he was taking a £120,000 a year two-day-a-week directorship from the Harrods owner, Mohamed-Al-Fayed. He reacted dismissively to the *Daily Telegraph's* leader dubbing him 'the MP for Harrods' and their accompanying cartoon depicting him diving into a cash-filled envelope, but facing calls for his deselection from elements in his Conservative Association, he resigned, declining 'to scrap with the shrill, deeply unpleasant faction inside and outside Westminster who are in danger of dislocating the Party from the wider electorate'. He was duly replaced by Gregory Barker who was himself soon the object of dissension in the local Association over his allegedly inaccurate CV, but he retained the safe seat comfortably in 2001, despite Charles Wardle's support for the local candidacy of the UKIP's leader, Nigel Farage.

An abortive attempt to deselect the Europhile MP, Ian Taylor, at Esher & Walton failed in December 2000. Mr Taylor was prominent among the two score of Conservative MPs who were resolute in their commitment to European integration and who – in his case – had resigned from the front bench in October 1997 over the increasingly anti-euro and Eurosceptic stance of the Hague leadership. His survival at Esher & Walton involved a public intervention by Central Office and by Kenneth Clarke who warned of 'the very severe consequences' if Conservative Associations sought 'to force a narrow nationalism onto our MPs'. Mr Taylor retained the safe seat with a virtually unchanged vote share in June 2001.

Euroscepticism surfaced at Henley in opposition to Michael Heseltine's continuing enthusiasm but he was intending to retire in any event. However at Ludlow the Europhobia of the sitting MP, Christopher Gill, flared into a late retirement at the end of 2000, and the subsequent loss of the seat to the Liberal Democrats.

Liberal Democrat candidate selections involved no innovation. At the 1998 party conference Jackie Ballard, one of the party's three women MPs, sought to introduce discrimination in favour of women by twinning seats to ensure that one in two constituencies would select a woman. In the 1999 European Parliament election the party adopted 'zipping' of its lists of candidates to give alternate positions to men and women. But for the general election it reserved its practice of merely shortlisting a woman wherever one applied for a seat. A further problem for the party was its paucity of available safe seats in which to place women candidates, the young men who were elected in the party's large expansion of 1997 being unlikely to retire for many years. Two of the party's high-profile women, Jackie Ballard MP (Taunton) and Rachel Oliver, the candidate in Totnes, both lost in rural seats.

The gender of candidates, which had been so emblematic of the 1997 election with the phalanx of women candidates which the Labour Party produced largely from all-women shortlists, caused some concern in both major parties. In Labour's case the issue certainly went off the boil with the party being securely in government and with there being no polling evidence at any point after May 1997 that the party was in any real danger of losing seats at the next election, whenever held. Whilst the party replaced all-women shortlists with 50–50 ones after 1997, only four women were selected in 40 seats from which Labour MPs – six of them women – were retiring. Many of Labour's vacant seats were in Scotland or Wales where dual mandate MPs were opting for devolved assemblies, but only one of these seats went to a woman candidate, Anne Picking at East Lothian. It was possible that Labour had used up its best women candidates in the Scottish and Welsh elections in May 1999. It was possible also that the unions were mobilising in favour of favourite-son candidates. It was even suggested that there might have been a backlash against selecting more of 'Blair's Babes' given their reputation for loyalism since 1997, with only a handful of the 65 new women MPs of that year rebelling against the government. For some observers the 'critical mass' of women MPs had turned out to be somewhat uncritical. In eight major rebellions during the 1997 to 2001 Parliament a total of only eight of Labour's 1997 intake of women MPs voted against the government.[7] There were complaints too, from female aspirants, of the party slipping back into macho habits. At Dagenham, where retiring Judith Church was replaced by a Downing Street adviser – if of allegedly independent bent (Jon Cruddas) – another candidate, Teresa Pearce, described the selection process as 'hellish', claiming that 'we have gone back to the old ways of favouring the male trade union candidate', and complaining that 'they brought out four cans of Carling Black Label to the women candidates; they just had a way of making you feel you shouldn't be there'.

Meanwhile the Conservatives continued rather complacently to regret the reality of the continuing refusal of the celebrated blue-rinsed matrons of Virginia Water to select women as candidates, without actually doing anything about it. Leading women figures in the party defended the status

Table 10.1   Women MPs 1997–2001

	1997	By-elections	2001		New Total
Lab	101	−1	−9	+4	95
Con	13	+1	−1	+1	14
LibDem	3	+1	−2	+3	5
SNP	2	–	−2	+1	1
Speaker	1	−1	–	–	–
SF	–	–	–	+1	1
UUP	–	–	–	+1	1
DUP	–	–	–	+1	1
Total	120	–	−14	+12	118

quo: Ann Widdecombe dismissed 'Blair's Babes' as sub-standard by virtue of the favourable method of their selection; Julie Kirkbride MP challenged the Labour women's assumption that women MPs were there specifically to 'represent women' and not the whole population; and whereas reforming noises were heard from Vice Chairman Steve Norris and from Tessa Keswick, whose report 'Conservative Women' urged quotas; even pragmatic figures like Gillian Shephard dismissed the call of Labour's Julia Drown (one of half a dozen MPs who had babies after their election in 1997) for breast-feeding on demand at Westminster, as equivalent to women lawyers demanding to be permitted to breast feed in court, and school-teachers in the classroom.

So it was that the number of women MPs fell (by two) in June 2001. The origin of the changes is shown in Table 10.1, with the fall from 120 (in 1997) to 118 being attributable to Labour losses.

Labour still remained the only party with a substantial number of women MPs, its 95 comprising 23 per cent of the PLP, the Conservatives' 14 only 8 per cent, and the Liberal Democrats' 5, 10 per cent.

The three parties had fielded a total of 381 (360) women candidates (with 1997 figures in brackets): 148 (155) Labour, 93 (66) Conservative, and 140 (139) Liberal Democrats. The figures represented 23 per cent (24

Table 10.2   Women candidates 1997–2001

	Total	Lab	Con	LibDem
1997	360	155 (24%)	66 (10%)	139 (21%)
2001	381	148 (23%)	93 (15%)	140 (22%)

per cent), 13 per cent (10 per cent) and 22 per cent (21 per cent) respectively of each party's candidates.

The number of women MPs fell from 120 to 118 because of a failure to place women in winnable seats. Labour, not expecting to make seat gains in 2001, had selected women in only 5 of the 16 Conservative marginals vulnerable to a 2 per cent pro-Labour swing, and none was successful. The Conservatives ran women in only 9 of their top 84 target seats vulnerable to a 5 per cent swing, and only 1 – Angela Watkinson (Upminster) was elected. Only 4 other women had been selected in statistically more winnable seats than Upminster. The Liberal Democrats selected women in only 5 of their 23 marginal target seats vulnerable to a 5 per cent swing, and in 3 of these seats they were successful: Annette Brooke won Mid Dorset & North Poole, Patsy Calton, Cheadle, and Susan Doughty, Guildford.

That Labour's 95 women MPs comprised only 23 per cent of the parliamentary party was a source of concern to aspiring women and to organisations such as the Fawcett Society. But it could also be noted that of 681 names on Labour's National Parliamentary Panel, 193, or 28 per cent, were women. Of those applying to get onto the Panel a higher proportion of women (70 per cent) had been successful than men (65 per cent), thus implying that it was less a question of a low demand for women candidates than of a short supply. There was too a certain symmetry between the 28 per cent of the Panel comprised by women and the 23 per cent of the PLP who were women. The Parliamentary Party was approximately mirroring the pool of eligibles.

A total of 66 (up from 42 in 1997) ethnic minority candidates fought the election for the 3 largest parties. The figures for each party were: Labour 22 (13 in 1997), Conservative 16 (10) and Liberal Democrat 28 (19). The increase in numbers was of no practical effect since only 3 of the 56 black or Asian candidates who were not already MPs were located in seats that were either already held by their party or were winnable, namely, the 2 Labour-held seats of Birmingham Perry Barr and Gloucester, and the highly marginal Labour seat of Northampton South, statistically winnable by the Conservatives. None of the other ethnic minority candidates had any prospect of election, not least the 28 Liberal Democrats.

MPs from ethnic minorities now numbered 12,[8] all Labour: Diane Abbott (elected in 1987), Paul Boateng (1987), Parmjit Dhanda (2001), Mark Hendrick (2000), Piara Khabra (1992), Oona King (1997), Ashok Kumar (1991–92, 1997), David Lammy (2000), Khalid Mahmood (2001), Mohammad Sarwar (1997), Marsha Singh (1997) and Keith Vaz (1987). In the space of a single year (2000–01) Labour had elected 4 new ethnic minority MPs, having lost 1, Bernie Grant, through death in 2000. Clearly, if demographic representativeness is the objective, the 5.5 per cent (at 1991 figures) of the population comprised by ethnic minorities is 'under-represented' by the 12 (or 2 per cent) of MPs drawn from those communities, notably so in the case of a large Muslim population 'represented' by only 2 MPs. Yet of the 681 names on Labour's National Parliamentary panel, 78 (or 11 per cent) were black or Asian (formally categorised for Labour's purposes as 'Bangladeshi, Black (other), Black African, Black Caribbean, Chinese, Indian, and Pakistani'). Thus the proportion of Labour's pool of eligible black or Asian candidates was twice that of the proportion of the population comprised by such ethnic minorities. The paucity of numbers of candidates selected would thus suggest that, in contrast to women candidates, the problem was one less of poor supply than of weak demand.

The *Jewish Chronicle* listed 21 MPs as Jewish, though because the newspaper's criterion is self-identification, it is likely that the number is an underestimate, excluding MPs, of whom at least 2 in the 2001 intake had Jewish parents but presumably wished not to be so categorised. Labour MPs (13) predominated over the Conservatives (7) and Liberal Democrats (1). One senior Labour MP – Robert Sheldon – had retired; 1 new Conservative, Jonathan Djanogly, had arrived. Of Labour's Jewish MPs, 2 of the 1997 intake, Ivan Lewis (Bury South) and Louise Ellman (Liverpool Riverside), had emerged as vocal defenders of the state of Israel and of other concerns of the Jewish community.

The retirement of Sir Edward Heath had removed the Commons' sole octogenarian, leaving the distinction of being the *doyen d'age* to Labour's Piara Khabra about whose date of birth there was some disagreement, but whether born in November 1922 or 1924, he was clearly the oldest MP. Only 3 other MPs had been born in the 1920s: the DUP's Revd Ian Paisley (1926), and Labour's Sir Ray Powell (1928) and Bill O'Brien (1929); 6 other MPs – all born in 1930 – had turned 70 by the start of 2001: Sir Peter Tapsell (Conservative), and Tom Cox, Gerald Kaufman, Bob Wareing, Alan Williams and Gwyneth Dunwoody (all Labour).

The median age of incoming Labour and Conservative MPs was 40 and 38 respectively; 4 Labour MPs were coming in in their fifties; as were 3 Conservatives, 2 of them retreads, the other, Angela Watkinson, elected at the age of 59. The rejuvenation of the Liberal Democrats in 1997 by the influx of many young MPs was partly balanced by the arrival of 5 MPs who were in their fifties, but the party's MPs had the lowest median age and no MP over the age of 70. The Independent MP, Dr Richard Taylor

(b. 1934), was embarking on his parliamentary career at the age of 66, the Commons' seventeenth oldest MP.

Table10.3   **Age of candidates**

Age*	Labour elected	Labour defeated	Conservative elected	Conservative defeated	Liberal Democrat elected	Liberal Democrat defeated
20–29	4	29	1	79	–	64
30–39	39	84	25	195	14	139
40–49	152	65	64	118	14	178
50–59	165	46	57	69	23	149
60–69	44	4	18	13	1	51
70–79	8	–	1	–	–	6
Median Age						
2001	50	40	48	38	47	45
1997	48	41	50	41	46	45

* at January 2001

In contrast to 1997 the absence of unexpected gains meant fewer new MPs at the lower end of the age range. Only 5 MPs (4 Labour and 1 Conservative) were under 30: David Lammy (b. 19 July 1972) – the baby of the House since his entry at a by-election in 2000, Christopher Leslie (b. 28 June 1972), Claire Ward (b. May 1972), the incoming Parmjit Dhanda (b. September 1971) and the Conservatives' new entrant George Osborne (b. May 1971). Two other Labour MPs were born in 1970, both new entrants: James Purnell (b. March 1970) and Andy Burnham (b. January 1970); as was the youngest Liberal Democrat, the incoming Matthew Green (b. April 1970). Michelle Gildernew, the new Sinn Féin MP (but in common with her 3 colleagues, not taking her seat), was believed also to have been born in 1970. The age profiles of the 3 main parliamentary parties were not essentially dissimilar, though a rather higher proportion (53 per cent) of Labour MPs were over the age of 50 than of Conservatives (45 per cent) or Liberal Democrats (44 per cent).

The election saw the return of only one MP who had first been elected in the 1950s – Sir Peter Tapsell (1959–64, 1966–), whose career began with the capture from Labour of Nottingham West in 1959. He remained in 2001 the sole survivor of Harold Macmillan's landslide win of that year – the high-water mark of One Nation Conservatism in the years of the post-war Butskellite consensus. Only one other Conservative MP – Sir Teddy Taylor (1964–79, 1980–) – remained from the intakes of the 1960s, and only a further 15 predated Margaret Thatcher's arrival in the leadership in 1975. Only 6 Labour MPs remained from the big intakes of the 1960s: Tam Dalyell (elected 1962), who with the longest continuous service became the Father of the House, Alan Williams (1964), Kevin McNamara (1966), and – all with broken service – Donald Anderson (1966–70, 1979–), Gwyneth Dunwoody (1966–70, 1974–) and David Winnick (1966–70, 1979–). In mid-2001 only 1 Conservative MP from the early 1970s, Kenneth Clarke, still remained in front-line politics; and in Labour's case only 4: John Prescott and Michael Meacher (both elected in 1970) and Margaret Beckett and Robin Cook (both 1974). A majority of Labour MPs had no experience of Westminster earlier than 1997.

Table 10.4   **Parliamentary experience of MPs**

First elected	Labour	Conservative	Liberal Democrat
1950–59	–	1	–
1960–69	6	1	–
1970–74	16	15	2
1975–79	14	8	–
1980–83	22	31	4
1984–87	51	22	3
1988–92	73	29	3
1993–97	182	29	25
1997(July)–01	48	30	15
Total	412	166	52

The family connections of MPs remained modest; 18 were the sons or daughters of MPs: Hilary Armstrong, Charlotte Atkins, Hilary Benn, John Cryer, Mark Fisher, Lindsay Hoyle, Ian McCartney, Estelle Morris and Dari Taylor (all Labour), James Arbuthnot, Dominic Grieve, Douglas Hogg, Bernard Jenkin, Francis Maude, Andrew Mitchell, Nicholas Soames and Bill Wiggin (all Conservative) and Annabelle Ewing (SNP). Nine were the grandchildren of MPs: Hilary Benn, Fiona Mactaggart, Peter Mandelson and Mark Todd (all Labour); Geoffrey Clifton Brown, Douglas Hogg and Nicholas Soames (all Conservative), and Sir Robert Smith and John Thurso (both Liberal Democrat).

Two sets of sisters remained: the Eagle twins, Angela and Maria, and Sylvia Heal and Ann Keen, and there were five married couples: the Conservative Bottomleys and Wintertons, and Andrew Mackay and Julie Kirkbride, the Labour Keens, and the DUP's Iris and Peter Robinson. Ann and John Cryer comprised the only mother and son pair.

Even though the House was virtually denuded of aristocrats, there were four baronets *in situ* as well as the Earl of Ancram, heir to the 12th Marquess of Lothian, but flying under a flag of convenience as 'Michael Ancram'. The baronets – all but one of whom were Etonians – were Sir George Young, sixth baronet; Sir John Sinclair, sixth baronet and third Viscount Thurso – known as 'John Thurso'; Sir Robert Smith, third baronet; and Sir Tam Dalyell, eleventh baronet (who established his claim to the title in 1973, but did not use it). It is also somewhat eccentric that of these four aristocrats, only one – Sir George Young – is a Conservative.

The House was also graced by five MPs, one of whom is mentioned in the foregoing paragraph, of undoubtedly dynastic standing, in the sense of belonging to families whose parliamentary service extended back at least four generations and in some cases far more. All Etonians, they were: Geoffrey Clifton Brown, Douglas Hogg and Nicholas Soames; and two newcomers, David Cameron and John Thurso. Seven members of Geoffrey Clifton Brown's family had been MPs since the mid-nineteenth century, as had four out of five generations of Hoggs. Nicholas Soames was the possessor of the longest political pedigree of them all as the great, great grandson of the seventh Duke of Marlborough, and as the latest representative, albeit in the female line, of his mother's Spencer-Churchill family, no generation of which had been absent from the House of Commons since 1790. John Thurso, the incoming Liberal Democrat MP for Caithness, Sutherland & Easter Ross, following three of his ancestors in representing the area, was the first hereditary peer to stand and gain election to the Commons following the expulsion of the hereditaries from the Lords in 1999.[9] Lest it be thought that the process whereby the composition of the House of Commons has been rendered prosaically democratic by a Labour-led march of the common man, it should also be noted that in Hilary Benn the House had the fourth generation of a political dynasty which extended back to the nineteenth century and had supplied five MPs since that time.

The knights of the shire, once so visible a feature of the Commons, continued to decline. In the 2001 House, there were (excluding baronets) only 8 Conservative knights, and 1 Labour (Sir Ray Powell).

The educational characteristics of MPs and candidates are shown in Table 10.4. The Conservative Party continues to rely for two-thirds of its MPs on the public schools, though its reliance on the privately educated as candidates in less hopeful seats has fluctuated. The Liberal Democrats' reliance on public school products has declined as the parliamentary party has expanded, but in 2001 a third of their MPs, and a fifth of their unelected candidates, were still public school people. The PLP's significant minority of public school products remains (17 per cent), and was even higher among the new intake (20 per cent). What was changing, however, was the type of public school from which the candidates were emerging. The most famous school, Eton, still produced more politicians than any other, but by 2001 that figure was reduced to 28: 18 MPs (14 Conservative, 2 Labour, 2 Liberal Democrat)[10] and 10 unelected candidates (8 Conservative, 1 Labour, 1 Liberal Democrat). Of the 8 unelected Conservative Etonians, only 4 were young enough to be construed as seed corn for the future. The percentage of Conservative MPs drawn from Eton had fallen by 1 per cent at each of the past four general elections, and by 2001 stood at 8 per cent. The political decline of Eton is symbolic of a move away from the grander public schools to the minor ones. No longer are the upper or upper-middle class attracted to political careers which have become more arduous because full time, lower in status, and badly paid, nor is the traditional vehicle for the advancement of public school men – the Conservative Party – any longer a certain route to political office.

The occupational classification of MPs and candidates is more an art than a science. Increasingly more candidates have had a variety of jobs

Table 10.5   **Education of candidates**

	Labour		Conservative		Liberal Democrat	
	elected	*defeated*	*elected*	*defeated*	*elected*	*defeated*
Elementary +	2	–	–		–	– –
Secondary	46	19	3	50	4	84
Secondary + poly/coll	83	55	9	99	8	158
Secondary + univ	213	119	48	151	22	231
Public School	2	1	6	15	1	4
Public Sch + poly/coll	4	8	10	26	3	21
Public Sch + univ	62	26	90	133	14	89
Unknown	–	–	–	3	–	–
TOTAL	412	228	166	474	52	587
Oxford	43	13	42	39	9	38
Cambridge	22	10	37	27	5	23
Other univs	210	122	59	218	22	259
All universities	275	145	138	284	36	320
	(67%)	(64%)	(83%)	(60%)	(70%)	(55%)
Eton	2	1	14	8	2	1
Harrow	–	–	–	2	–	–
Winchester	–	–	1	1	–	1
Other Public Sch	66	34	91	163	16	112
All public schools	68	35	106	174	18	114
	(17%)	(15%)	(64%)	(37%)	(35%)	(19%)

and it is hard to classify a Liberal Democrat MP who has managed record shops, taught at language schools, been a bag-carrier for another MP and run a railway station, or the Labour candidate who spent half his working life as a teacher and half as a builder.

The occupational profile of Labour MPs remains much as it was in 1997 (Table 10.6). The largest categories are the public-sector professionals (teachers, administrators), political staffers, union officials, journalists and lawyers. Despite being in government, firmly positioned in the centre ground and supposedly business-friendly, the party's parliamentary ranks still lack any substantial component drawn from the world of business, a mere 8 per cent of the PLP. Labour's candidate base has yet to mirror the government's embrace of the market. Meanwhile its working-class base continues to erode, with only 12 per cent of Labour MPs drawn from manual occupations (excluding a few categorised as union officials) and with only 14 manual workers among its 228 unelected candidates. A handful of the new intake were ex-manual workers, including the miner David Hamilton, the painter Jim Sheridan, the engineer John Lyons and the boilermaker John MacDougall, though the latter 2 came to the Commons as a union official and a council leader respectively. Labour MPs, of course, remain closer to working-class origins than all other MPs, but increasingly even they – as in the case of one new Labour MP – are obliged to recall their coalminer *grand*fathers. The new intake of Labour MPs, as already noted, essentially reinforced the ranks of 'professional politicians' – whether party staffers or union officials (the latter now totalling 33 and included under 'miscellaneous white collar'). Few of Labour's new MPs were 'other professionals' such as lawyers (of whom 4 in the new intake) or educators (of whom 3), moving over into politics.

The Conservatives remain the party of private-sector professionals, bankers and businessmen. The largest professional component, the law, remains paramount with 93 Conservative candidates drawn from it (compared to 53 of Labour's candidates). The party staffer category among MPs continues to grow – now providing 18 MPs, and the party retains its one link with the working class, in the person of the former coalminer, Patrick McLoughlin (West Derbyshire). Among new Conservative MPs were 5 bankers, 5 lawyers, 4 journalists, 4 party staffers and 3 military officers.

As implied by their educational profile Liberal Democrat candidates are the most diverse occupationally, ranging indeed from two former mineworkers to an ex-director of the Abbey National. Interestingly, with Labour's manual base among its unelected candidates virtually exhausted, the Liberal Democrats are now the more proletarian party, with 28

Table 10.6   **Occupation of candidates**[11]

	Labour		Conservative		Liberal Democrat	
	elected	*defeated*	*elected*	*defeated*	*elected*	*defeated*
Professions						
Barrister	13	12	18	28	2	7
Solicitor	18	10	13	34	4	19
Doctor/dentist/optician	2	1	3	7	3	13
Architect/surveyor	1	2	4	9	1	3
Civil/chartered engineer	5	5	1	12	1	14
Accountant	2	3	3	22	1	30
Civil service/local govt	30	21	2	13	3	23
Armed services	1	1	11	9	–	8
Teachers: University	18	6	1	1	2	15
Polytech/coll.	31	11	–	5	1	16
School	49	32	6	19	9	66
Other consultancies	3	6	2	12	–	24
Scientific/research	6	4	–	1	–	5
TOTAL	179	114	64	172	27	243
	(43%)	(50%)	(39%)	(36%)	(52%)	(41%)
Business						
Company Director	5	5	18	57	6	23
Company executive	10	9	31	66	7	42
Commerce/insurance	2	8	6	46	–	33
Management/clerical	12	2	2	12	1	21
General business	4	4	3	23	–	27
TOTAL	33	28	60	204	14	146
	(8%)	(12%)	(36%)	(43%)	(27%)	(25%)
Miscellaneous						
Miscellaneous white collar	73	35	2	29	1	90
Politician/pol. organiser	44	16	18	29	4	39
Publisher/journalist	32	19	14	18	4	20
Farmer	–	1	5	12	1	4
Housewife	–	–	2	2	–	4
Student	–	1	–	3	–	14
TOTAL	149	72	41	93	10	171
	(36%)	(32%)	(25%)	(20%)	(19%)	(29%)
Manual workers						
Miner	11	–	1	–	–	2
Skilled worker	37	13	–	4	1	16
Semi–skilled worker	3	1	–	1	–	9
TOTAL	51	14	1	5	1	27
	(12%)	(6%)	(1%)	(1%)	(2%)	(5%)
GRAND TOTAL	412	228	166	474	52	587

manual worker candidates, one of whom was elected. Liberal Democrat candidates range across the public-sector–private-sector divide, with a high representation of teachers and lecturers, but with a deep penetration of the world of business. It is an occupational profile arguably more appropriate to a party of government than Labour's, simply by nature of its diversity.

In 2001 the role reversal of the Labour and Conservative parties appeared complete. Labour, the fractious oppositional force of the fifties, seventies and eighties, was transformed into a disciplined government party of loyalist MPs and with a Millbank machine the envy of Smith Square. The Conservatives, once the natural party of government, had become elderly, demoralised, and absorbed with the intractable issue of Europe.

Reservations expressed in 1997 about possible activist resistance to Labour's rolling back of the left's gains in the 1980s, and the docility of the PLP, proved unfounded. A hardcore of 40 MPs had led rebellions against the government but it comprised only 10 per cent of the PLP and received little consistent backing from more than a handful of the large 1997 influx of MPs. The leadership had centralised and sanitised the process of candidate selection, and even if the activist-marginalising system of OMOV had as one consequence the selection of some municipal low-fliers instead of favoured metropolitan insiders, they were at least reliable. A PLP periodically topped up with party staffers, union officials and local councillors, was not one to cause trouble – unless the public-sector unions decided to confront a process of wholesale privatisation. Nor was Labour unaware of the need to restore positive discrimination in favour of women candidates, as promised in the Queen's Speech in June 2001, for this was essentially an apolitical issue approved by the voters if not by the politically ambitious and more numerous men who would be obliged to step aside.

Notes

1. The seven were (with their new and former seats): Alistair Burt (to Bedfordshire NE from Bury N), Henry Bellingham (again in Norfolk NW), Derek Conway (to Old Sidcup & Bexley from Shrewsbury & Atcham), Charles Hendry (to Wealden from High Peak), Andrew Mitchell (to Sutton Coldfield from Gedling), Robert Spink (again in Castle Point) and Greg Knight (to Yorkshire East from Derby N).
2. The 18 former Conservative MPs seeking unsuccessfully to return to their old seat were: Jacques Arnold (Gravesham), Vivian Bendall (Ilford N), Matthew Carrington (Hammersmith & Fulham), David Congdon (Croydon C), Simon Coombs (Swindon S), Tim Devlin (Stockton S), Robert Dunn (Dartford), Roger Evans (Monmouth), David Evennett (Bexleyheath & Crayford), Phil Gallie (Ayr), Lady Olga Maitland (Sutton & Cheam), John Marshall (Finchley &

Golders Green), Elizabeth Peacock (Batley & Spen), Sir Malcolm Rifkind (Edinburgh Pentlands), Iain Sproat (Harwich), Robin Squire (Hornchurch) and John Sykes (Scarborough & Whitby); 3 moved to new seats without success: David Martin (to Rugby & Kenilworth from Portsmouth S), Raymond Robertson (to Eastwood from Aberdeen S), David Shaw (to Kingston & Surbiton from Dover). One other, Alan Amos, who had been Conservative MP for Hexham 1987–92, was now standing for Labour at Hitchin & Harpenden. The 2 former Labour MPs seeking, unsuccessfully, to return were: Reg Race (to Chesterfield from Wood Green (1979–83)) and Dave Nellist, who had been Labour MP for Coventry SE (1983–92), but was now standing for the Socialist Alliance at Coventry NE.

3. A total of 17 MPs left Westminster for the devolved bodies: 8 Labour, 2 Liberal Democrat, 5 SNP and 2 Plaid Cymru.

4. Tony Benn's length of service (1950–61, 1963–83, 1984–2001) was rivalled by only two other former Labour MPs: George Strauss (1929–31, 1934–79) and John Parker (1935–83).

5. There had been former prime ministers in the Commons continuously since July 1945, as there had also from February 1906 to January 1945, during which period Arthur Balfour (from 1906 to 1922) and David Lloyd George (from 1922 to January 1945) continued to sit. Lloyd George's elevation to the peerage in January 1945 interrupted the sequence.

6. Union influence was less measurable following the removal of sponsorship of MPs in 1995. In the Register of Members' Interests in October 1997 only 33 MPs had declared contributions in excess of 25 per cent of their election expenses from trade unions.

7. Ann Cryer, Janet Dean, Eileen Gordon, Jenny Jones, Tess Kingham, Christine McCafferty, Julie Morgan and Betty Williams.

8. The Anglo-Indian Conservative MP, Jonathan Sayeed, is not included amongst ethnic minority MPs.

9. John Thurso was not the only hereditary peer to contest the election: Viscount Exmouth (Teignbridge) and the Earl of Bradford (Stafford) stood for UKIP. The *Removal of Clergy Disqualification Act* 2001 was passed to allow Roman Catholic priests to sit in the Commons. This legislation was specifically designed to enable the former Catholic priest, David Cairns, to take his seat at Greenock & Port Glasgow where he had been selected in place of the retiring Norman Godman. His election and that of the former Anglican priest, Chris Bryant (Rhondda), brought the first ex-clergymen to the Labour benches since the former Baptist minister, Sir Thomas Williams, retired from Warrington in 1981.

10. The Etonians elected in 2001 (with new MPs asterisked) were: Conservative – James Arbuthnot, *Henry Bellingham, *David Cameron, Geoffrey Clifton Brown, David Heathcoat Amory, Douglas Hogg, *Boris Johnson, Oliver Letwin, Nicholas Soames, *Hugo Swire, David Tredinnick, *Bill Wiggin, John Wilkinson and Sir George Young; Labour – Tam Dalyell and Mark Fisher; Liberal Democrat – David Rendel and *John Thurso.

11. Identification of occupational categories has been assisted by reference to the coding index of occupations published by the Office for National Statistics (The Stationery Office, 2000). In order to permit comparison between elections we have continued to use the same classification of occupations as used in all editions of this publication. However, as a result of technological change

there are now some occupations which did not exist, or barely existed, 10 or 20 years ago (e.g. 'call centre manager') and they have had to be identified and classified in order to place them within our categories. This has particularly had the effect of expanding (a) the 'engineers' section of the 'Professional' group to include the increasing number of professional computing/electronic engineers (b) the 'other consultancies' section to include the increasing number of business and statistical professionals, and (c) the 'miscellaneous white collar' section of the 'Miscellaneous' group, to include the increased number of personal and public service, and voluntary sector occupations.

11
The Local Battle, the Cyber Battle

Chris Ballinger

The campaign in the constituencies

For all the centralisation of the national campaign, most campaigning takes place on the ground in the constituencies. The national campaign, directed from London, differed markedly from the day-by-day realities of campaigning on the ground. In 2001, the candidates were busy throughout the 659 constituencies in an attempt to persuade each of the 44.4 million electors to vote at one of an estimated 46,500 polling stations. But fewer seats changed hands than at any election since 1955. What follows is based not only on press reports but also on interviews with candidates and their agents, on talks with central party officials, and, above all, on a sample of replies from over a hundred candidates to a comprehensive questionnaire.

The postponement of polling day from the long-expected 3 May to 7 June meant that this general election was, in effect, the longest campaign on record. Many Labour MPs were worried about a possible deflation of spirit. One Labour member commented that 'delay caused extra anxiety – we just wanted it over'. But such an MP was happier by 8 June. Some Conservatives felt that they might have fared better on 3 May – either because of a backlash against the government in foot and mouth-hit areas, or because the delay gave the opportunity for distractions. One candidate commented: 'The month's delay led to a row about John Townend and race relations, which was very damaging.'

The postponement made it harder to keep activists motivated. One problem was fatigue: 'Both party workers and the electorate were more exhausted because of the delay.' Another, in a three-way marginal, felt that five more weeks meant 'just exhaustion. We built for a crescendo in May, and then we had to start all over again.' One Conservative said that 'the timing of the election meant the exclusion of my usual keen young supporters from sixth forms' who had to take exams. A Labour opponent mourned polling day coming after the end of the university year in his town, since undergraduate voters had gone home for the summer. Others complained of the disappearance of activists on holiday.

Nevertheless, most candidates, from all parties, felt that the election would not have been better on 3 May than 7 June. Candidates in areas hard-hit by foot and mouth were naturally relieved at the pause, although some questioned whether five weeks was long enough. Those in other areas were grateful for the chance to refine their campaign plans. Given the long-held expectation of a general election on 3 May, it was somewhat surprising that they needed this extra time.

The election came too soon for Penrith and the Border, the constituency which had been most beset by foot and mouth. David Maclean, the Conservative incumbent, did no canvassing and announced in his one (and only) 'funereal' election address that: 'In these circumstances, I have decided that I will not campaign or electioneer as normal.' Instead, he simply held surgeries throughout his constituency. He increased his majority by over 4,000, on a reduced turnout.

Even in areas not beset by foot and mouth , June was too early for some voters. 'This was the election that nobody wanted, and many refused to take part in it. It was like asking people at half time in a football game to go out and pay at the turnstiles again to see the second half, and so many refused', said one Labour MP. Other candidates found 'a collective resistance to change. Blair's government was not too bad, and Hague's not exciting enough.' 'The voters', said a Conservative, 'were disengaged from politics. They were disappointed with Labour, but thought that we were not credible.' There was a sense that after 18 years of Conservative rule, the public had elected the Labour government on an 8-year term.

When the campaign arrived it saw several changes to electoral law and practice, affecting the electoral register, the registration of political parties, and postal voting, as well as expenditure by parties, candidates, and 'third parties'.

The *Representation of the People Act 2000* introduced 'rolling registration' from 16 February 2001. The electoral register, compiled on 10 October each year, had an initial inaccuracy estimated at 8 per cent, which increased over the course of a year. The system of rolling registration was designed to reduce inaccuracy by allowing for the updating of the electoral register on a monthly, rather than an annual, basis. But, outside of London, rolling registration made little difference in 2001 – only a fraction of 1 per cent. In rural seats, only 200 names were added. Even in Westminster, the borough with allegedly the highest turnover in the register, only 2,400 were added to the register and 700 removed up to the deadline of 5 April. Returning Officers thought that the effectiveness of rolling registration would increase as public awareness of the procedure improved.

In order to vote on 7 June, people had to apply for inclusion by 5 April, so as to be included on the register finalised on 1 May. Hence, despite rolling registration, it was already a week too late to get names added by the day upon which the election was officially announced, 8 May. The 'small but important minority of voters'[1] who were prompted to get on the register by the announcement of the election were, in effect, disenfranchised.

Since 1970, candidates had been able to append up to six words of political description to their names on the ballot paper. However, this opportunity was restricted by the new regulations concerning the registration of political parties. The new controls on party income and expenditure meant that only those parties registered with the Electoral Commission could put up candidates for election. The law did, however, allow for the candidate's political description on the ballot paper to differ from the party's registered name where the difference was unlikely to cause confusion with the name of another registered party. In some areas, variations were permitted, such as 'The Conservative Candidate' instead of 'Conservative and Unionist Party', and 'Scottish Labour Party' instead of 'Labour Party'.

The new regulations, designed to prevent misleading party names (such as Richard Huggett's 'Literal Democrat' in the 1994 Euro election), meant that candidates who did not belong to a registered party could describe themselves only as 'Independent' or give no description on the ballot paper. (Some campaigners thought that this inability to provide any additional self-description unfairly disadvantaged Independent candidates where they were unwilling or unable to pay £150 for registration as a political party.) Any potential confusion over candidates was further reduced by the inclusion of party symbols on the ballot paper. Symbols had been present for the first time in a national election at the 1999 Euro elections, but this was their first use at a general election.

Simplified regulations greatly decreased the restrictions on voting by post. The number of postal votes cast, which had risen slightly from 1992 to 1997, almost doubled from 738,614 in 1997 to at least 1.4 million (5.3 per cent of all voters) in 2001.[2] The last day for the receipt of postal and proxy voting applications was Wednesday, 30 May, eight days before polling day. MORI's investigations suggested that postal voters divided Conservative 39 per cent, Labour 39 per cent, Liberal Democrat 19 per cent. The traditional bias of postal votes towards the Conservatives disappeared. Of those issued with postal ballots, 82 per cent seem to have returned them. But, despite the efforts of the Home Office, 23 per cent of voters remained unaware of the increased availability of postal ballots.

The extent of postal voting varied considerably – from under 1 per cent to over 30 per cent of electors. The range largely reflected the proactivity, or otherwise, of Electoral Registration Officers. Cardiff County Council wrote to all 235,000 electors in the four Cardiff constituencies, informing them of their right to vote by post. In the end it issued 33,318 postal ballots, a 700 per cent increase. A leafleting campaign by Stevenage Borough Council led to over a third of those voting doing so by post. 11,177 postal votes were cast in Norwich South and 9,014 in Newcastle North (in each case a quarter of all votes). Even in areas where the increase in postal voting was less marked, there were a few reports of Electoral Registration Officers (EROs) being overwhelmed by the number of requests. The resources of EROs were strained, and might have broken down if a much higher number of postal vote requests had been received as some expected. Consignia reported to the Electoral Commission that a 'significant minority [of postal ballots] were posted on polling day itself or after', which meant that they arrived too late to be counted.[3] But the scare stories about the potential for widespread fraud in postal voting seemed overstated. An experienced campaigner observed that 'it would have been easier to vote fraudulently in person than by post' because of the absence of identity checks at polling stations.

There must have been about a hundred seats where the postal vote exceeded the majority but, given MORI's figures, it probably made less difference than in past years, when it had given the Conservatives a significant advantage.

In key seats, Labour was particularly energetic in encouraging known supporters to vote by post. Some would have voted anyway, but voting by post meant that the party did not need to remind them on polling day, and resources could be deployed elsewhere.

Following the *Bowman*[4] case, the limit for spontaneous 'third party' or pressure group spending in a constituency had been raised from £5 to £500. However, the main political parties were not much worried about these groups. One candidate found that 'the Democracy Movement intervened, as did a small group of anti-gay campaigners (Concerned Parents)'. Another candidate was criticised by the Society for the Protection of the Unborn Child, which 'did its usual leafleting attacking me and my pro-choice stand, with extensive deliveries'. But in neither case did these third parties have a discernible effect. The Democracy Movement targeted a number of pro-European Conservatives, but, as Appendix 2 shows, pro-European Conservatives fared no worse than their Eurosceptic counterparts. One Conservative reported that 'the Democracy Movement targeted me by way of distributing literature around the whole constituency saying that I wanted to scrap the pound and was a pro-European. This had no impact on the campaign whatsoever and the UKIP candidate received only 600 votes.'

Locally, candidates were, on average, able to spend about £9,000.[5] Some campaigners from the major parties argued that it was unfair to have an expenditure limit so low that it prevented a candidate placing advertisements in local newspapers. But it was usually only in marginals that the parties spent at or near the limit, and a Labour MP from a safe seat commented that 'election spending limits seemed generous, as the cost of printing has plummeted'. New accounting regulations for election expenditure came into force in 2001, although changes to the definition of candidate and election expenses, which promised to be important to local campaigns, did not come into effect before the election. These placed a large burden upon constituency accounting officers, mostly the candidate's agent, many of whom were well-intentioned volunteers. Full-time professional agents were in evidence – Labour had 150, the Liberal Democrats 80 – but these were directed to target seats. The 2001 election was the first at which full details of constituency expenditure were to be published by the Electoral Commission.[6]

One main lesson of the 1997 election had been that targeting seats could be effective. Labour sought to retain the seats that it had won from other parties in 1997, but found that defending demanded a marked change of approach after years of attacking, not least because incumbents in key seats were busy being MPs in the run-up to the election campaign proper. The Conservatives aimed to regain much of their lost ground. The Liberal Democrats sought to hold on to their gains, and also to break into new territory. Party headquarters left safe seats almost completely alone.

The focus of campaigning was on target voters in target seats. The Conservatives identified 1 million potential switchers across 180 key constituencies. More of the voters were telephoned from the call centre in Smith Square than were rung by local activists. Labour had, since January 2001, made over 1.5 million contacts through its call centre in North Shields, where 250 telephone operators worked. 'Regional and national phone banks did help, and we did better than 1997 in phone canvassing', said a Labour MP who increased her majority. A Conservative complained that 'Labour was almost invisible during the campaign – the constituency party did virtually nothing, yet Labour did an almost 100 per cent telephone canvass, almost entirely from Tyneside', although he did admit that Central Office had canvassed 'about 10,000 voters' on his behalf. Labour was pleased that its candidates experienced reverse swings in very few of the seats which they had gained in 1997. The highly targeted nature of the campaign caused a Liberal Democrat to remark that 'In effect this wasn't a general election but a series of by-elections in a few marginal seats.' As Appendix 2 demonstrates, incumbents were exceptionally successful in doing better than the rest of their party colleagues.

Campaign activity was at a lower level than in 1997. As Table 11.1 shows, only 19 per cent of voters reported being called on or telephoned – a new low. The amount of canvassing varied according to the geography of the constituency, the number and age of activists, the importance of the seat as a target, the existence of a council election (which ensured a ready team of would-be councillors for canvassing), and the impact of foot and mouth. Predictions of low turnout meant that canvassing for the purpose of producing a marked register could be particularly important, since there was more scope for getting out the vote and gaining a seat on differential turnout. Some candidates claimed to have attempted to canvass 100 per cent of their electorate, but even they admitted to 30 per cent or more non-contacts. But in many constituencies, parties approached only known identifiers and potential switchers.

Labour's Operation Turnout had concentrated on target seats. It built to a crescendo over the last three weeks of the campaign, as Millbank workers who had finished their duties in headquarters were deployed on the ground. Canvassers changed their canvass codes, and made a 'contract' with electors: party identifiers were asked at what time of day they were likely to vote, and were reminded at that time. The operation was thought by the party to have had some success.

The extent of public engagement with the campaign is shown by MORI's survey, reported in Table 11.1. However, this does not give the complete picture of activity. Formally, no constituency was uncontested, but in many seats candidates ran only nominal campaigns, and their workers were drafted into nearby marginals. The difference between peaceful territory and the theatres of conflict was marked: 'the flood of mail and telephone calls from the parties means that voters know when they're in a key seat', said a Conservative. In some areas, seats were twinned, a safe seat being paired with a target seat next door for campaigning purposes.

Table 11.1   Campaign experiences of the electorate

Q. During the past few weeks, have you ... ? (If Yes) Which party was that?

	All (1997)	Con	Lab	LibDem
Received leaflets	69 (89)	43	40	23
Saw TV PEBs	58 (73)	39	43	28
Saw posters	50 (70)	31	35	7
Saw leaders on TV	43 (36)	32	32	23
Saw press advertisements	37 (na)	23	25	11
Heard radio PEBs	16 (15)	10	10	7
Was called on	14 (24)	6	7	2
Received letter	12 (20)	6	6	2
Was telephoned	5 (7)	2	3	0
Helped party	3 (4)	1	1	1
Visited party website	2 (na)	1	1	0
Used internet	2 (na)	1	2	0
Attended meeting	1 (2)	0	1	1
Received party video	1 (na)	0	1	0
Received party e-mail	1 (na)	<1	<1	0

Source: MORI 24–30 May

The flurry of activity in target seats was not just a short-term election campaign strategy. Key seats had been the subject of permanent campaigning over four years. In a classic marginal seat, voters would have received a party newspaper three or four times a year. At an election in which 74 per cent of voters had decided how to vote before the campaign began, the four-year effort was more important than ever. (Appendix 2 offers an assessment of the efficacy of targeting.)

As Table 11.1 shows, 1 per cent of Labour's voters reported having received a video. Labour had sent out 1 million videos, and they had evidence that 84 per cent of the videos were actually played. Videos cost much less in 2001 than previously – at only 33p per video, hardly more than a very good glossy pamphlet. They had sent out 1,000 videos to first-time voters in 1997 when videos had not been very important. This time, however, it was thought that the videos might be very influential in helping to alleviate low turnout amongst Labour new voters.

Campaigning was more tranquil than in 1997. Conservative candidates were mistakenly heartened because this time they did not find on the doorsteps the public resentment and hostility with which they had been greeted, even in relatively safe constituencies, in 1997. 'The figures derived from our canvassing were hopelessly optimistic', said one Conservative. But others found warning signs: in some areas which once had been solidly Conservative, Tory candidates sometimes reported finding unenthusiastic Conservatives and enthusiastic Labour identifiers.

Table 11.2   The persuasiveness of election campaigning

Q. *Please tell me how much influence, if any, each of the following had on your decision about what you would do on the day of the General Election.*

	Great deal	Fair amount	Not v. much	None at all	Don't know
Election coverage on TV	13	36	20	30	1
Election coverage in the papers	8	30	22	39	1
Parties' leaflets or letters	4	22	25	49	<1
PEBs on TV	6	16	20	57	1
Election coverage on radio	5	17	18	58	3
Views of friends or family	6	14	20	60	<1
Opinion polls	2	11	21	65	1
Billboard advertisements	2	8	17	72	1
Personal calls from the parties	2	6	9	80	3
Election coverage on the internet	1	3	5	87	4

Source: MORI/Electoral Commission, 9–18 June 2001

Negative campaigning was rare at the local level. Wyre Forest was an exceptional example, where the incumbent MP was reviled for not defending the local hospital. The local newspaper took up the cause of the hospital, and the influence of the paper spread into the neighbouring constituency of Ludlow, where the Liberal Democrats unexpectedly won. In Romford, Andrew Rosindell, the Conservative challenger, successfully used the Labour incumbent's voting record, along with a dispute over the flying of the Union Flag in the local market, to muster the Conservatives' largest swing. He used a bull terrier called Spike, who was dressed in a Union Flag, to gain publicity for his cause. In Totnes, the wife of a former Liberal Democrat candidate publicly declared her support for the Conservative incumbent, Anthony Steen.

The elections in shire counties and some unitary authorities increased campaign activity in many areas. 'It was difficult to assess what would have happened without county council elections. My guess is that there would have been substantially less canvassing', said one Conservative MP. 'We had an extensive canvass because of the council candidates. We didn't do much by phone', reported another. In a number of seats, 'County council candidates did the traditional canvassing.' In one seat in central southern England, the local party was 'concentrating on the council elections'. For these candidates, success at Westminster was assured; performance in the county elections mattered more.

Likewise, the general election increased interest in the council elections. But securing a pledge in one election didn't mean securing a vote in the other election too. 'The crude figures suggest that 4,000 voters – around 10 per cent – split their votes by casting ballots for different parties in the local and general elections', said one Westminster candidate. Split-ticket voting, it seemed, was even higher than in 1997.

Telephone canvassing by local activists continued to increase. 'Canvassing other than by phone is practically useless', declared one veteran Labour campaigner. 'Leafleting was the only contact people had with the electorate.' The proportion of electors reporting telephone contact declined, but by less than the number of knocked-on doors. The availability of canvassers has been dwindling, and their age has been rising over successive elections. Telephone canvassing often provided a convenient alternative to door-knocking for ageing supporters. It could also facilitate access to residents of institutions and blocks of flats. It was estimated that 25 per cent of people canvassed by the Labour Party during the election would have been approached by telephone, rising to 55–60 per cent in the target seats. In one-third of constituencies, telephone canvassing was the norm, but a sixth of candidates surveyed claimed not to have canvassed by telephone at all.

However, telephone canvassing was not without its pitfalls. Up to 60 per cent of telephone numbers were unavailable or blocked. Obtaining telephone numbers had become more difficult since 1997 as more users joined the Telephone Preference System (TPS), which prohibited cold calling, and as more subscribed to telephone lines from suppliers other than BT, so that subscribers were not automatically listed in telephone directories. Others relied entirely on mobile phones, few of which were listed in the telephone book. 'We did less telephone canvassing than before because of lack of good, consistent number information', said a Labour MP. 'Many of our attempted telephone contacts were ex-directory and a significant number were TPS, and a lot of numbers were wrong', a Conservative candidate reported.

The Data Protection Act could have limited telephone canvassing, but its effects were hardly noticed in practice. Campaigners were careful to use only up-to-date telephone lists, to avoid the risk of calling someone illegally, although some candidates complained about the time that these regular updates took. Some party strategists suggested, after the election, that registered political parties should be exempted from the terms of the TPS, because people should not, in a representative democracy, be allowed to opt out of contact with democratic political parties. But such an exemption is unlikely.

Telephones had been widely used for pre-campaign survey canvassing. One Conservative in a marginal seat reported conducting an exhaustive survey canvass from November to June. Telephone knocking-up on polling day did occur, but was not as common as telephone canvassing. Some candidates were sceptical of the marginal benefit of knocking-up, whether by phone or in person.

Door-to-door canvassing remained, for many candidates, the primary form of direct contact with their electorate. Others went on walkabouts in town centres. A Yorkshire Labour MP reported spending 'one to three hours most days in the town centre'. In commuter areas, some candidates greeted their constituents at railway stations during the morning rush hour. However, some questioned the value of canvassing in the modern election campaign: 'My agent – a very Old School, retired GPO man – feels that old-style campaigning may have had its day. In particular, he is sceptical about the value of door-to-door canvassing', said a Conservative. Table 11.2 suggests that this agent was correct.

The public meeting survives – but only just. The number of people who reported having listened to a candidate speak at a political meeting has been stable at between 1 and 2 per cent over the past five elections. One Conservative had a single public meeting attended by 26 electors; 27 years earlier he had 44 meetings with never fewer than 80 electors. One rural Liberal Democrat MP remarked that he had 'totally abandoned any attempt at public meetings. We had nearly 60 last time!! Nobody noticed!!!' It was a far cry from half a century earlier, when a normal election meeting meant a couple of hundred constituents gathering in a school hall and 30 per cent of voters claimed to have attended at least one meeting.[7] Even in areas which had experienced a small revival in the public meeting, interest in 2001 was lacking: 'Meetings were very badly attended – public debates had 80 to 100 as against 400–500 in 1997', said one candidate. But in most areas, the real decline in meetings had happened over many years. The general election of 2001 merely witnessed a further dribbling away.

There were few encounters between opponents at constituency level. Where public meetings did happen, they were usually organised by interest groups, such as Churches Together, or by the media. The nature of these meetings meant that the issues which were raised tended to be specific to the host organisation rather than being representative of the concerns expressed on the doorstep. Candidates were, on the whole, cynical about the value of meetings for gaining votes: one candidate, who attended 15 multi-party meetings, positively discouraged her activists from attending such gatherings, since they could be better deployed elsewhere. Often, the audience at these meetings comprised 'only the evangelical or the unconvertible'.

There had been a marked uptake in the use of technology in 1997, especially in marginal seats, and in 2001 it spread further into safer seats. 'For the first time the Labour party in my constituency used modern campaigning techniques' said a Welsh Labour MP from a safe seat. For another safe Labour MP, 'this is the first campaign where traditional methods were abandoned'. However, modern technology was not ubiquitous: a Labour MP reported that 'in a safe constituency such as mine, we are in the early stages of IT. We used e-mail, computer lists of addresses, etc., though little else.'

Technological innovations had important impacts on practical campaigning. The effect of e-mail and the internet is discussed below, but other technologies were important. Computers were used in most constituencies to produce local literature (sometimes with templates, pictures, artwork, and stories downloaded from the party headquarters' extranets – computer networks with restricted access which made services available to activists over the internet), and to produce mailing lists for that literature.

Despite the potential for professional, home-produced literature, more was centrally written than before. Prior to the election, two-thirds of Conservative constituency parties had taken advantage of a Central Office offer to produce constituency addresses at a subsidised rate. This provided some uniformity of appearance, but it also gave Central Office the opportunity to dissuade candidates who wanted to dissent from the official line on the euro. Centrally-prepared templates accounted, on average, for 65 per cent of Labour literature, varying from under 50 per cent in safe seats to 100 per cent in key seats. Millbank offered advice on how to insert local copy into central literature. There was much more uniformity than previously amongst Liberal Democrat election addresses. This was due partly to a central printing arrangement, and partly to the artwork for this being made widely available, largely through the extranet, to people using other printing presses. The same technology that enabled the production of local literature also facilitated the slotting of small packages of local information into centrally produced templates.

The centrally produced literature was glossy and professional, but also somewhat corporate and national, lacking in feeling and local colour. Blair, Hague and Kennedy were often to be found pictured with the candidate. Many chose to slot a little local knowledge into a broadly national and generalised brochure; others trod their own path with completely local leaflets. Liberal Democrats used fewer glossy leaflets than their Labour or Conservative opponents. Several were made up to look like newspapers or newsletters, but they were not always convincing. Leaflets were often equivalent to 2–4 sides of A4 paper, although the shape and format varied widely, and most candidates delivered several different pieces of campaign material prior to and during the election campaign. The once-dominant election address had, in some places, disappeared completely. Elsewhere, it was often difficult to distinguish which of the several leaflets ought to be regarded as the key communication of a candidate's views.

The electoral register has been available on computer tape or disk since 1986, and canvass returns were often fed onto computer to produce a marked-up electronic register and knock-up cards. In a few cases the computerisation of the committee room sidelined some computer illiterate activists and reduced the camaraderie of the workers and the social aspect of running a committee room. The mobile phone revolution that took place between 1997 and 2001 – 69 per cent of the population claimed to own mobile phones by mid-2001 – meant that canvassers (and candidates) were much more easily coordinated in the field.

The parties usually sent two or three private e-mails to their candidates each day, in addition to e-mails of daily headlines, to which many candidates subscribed. This continued the trend towards e-mail which had been set in 1997, and e-mail became the primary means for disseminating information to candidates: contact with headquarters was 'almost entirely' by e-mail and through the website. 'E-mail levelled the playing field in terms of resources', said one Liberal Democrat. The pager was not dead as a campaign tool, but it was being superceded by sms (short text messages sent to mobile phones) and by e-mail.

The communications from headquarters were not to every candidate's liking. One independently minded Labour MP from a safe seat commented that 'The communications from the national party were a hindrance and I tried not to read them, let alone answer them.' 'Every message sent to my pager was negative', complained one Conservative. 'It was "don't say this", "make no comment on that".' Some candidates still resolutely hold out against the march of technology: 'I do not have e-mail, so little communication came my way – thank God!' And e-mail was not the answer to every candidate's campaigning needs: because of e-mail glitches, one Conservative 'was largely cut off from whatever the campaign was about. I don't think this affected anything.' But most candidates were at least happy, and sometimes enthusiastic, about the level of help from national and regional headquarters. The consensus amongst Conservative candidates was that they had received better support from Central Office than in 1997.

Many candidates reported having no time to watch the television news or read the national newspapers; they knew little of life beyond their constituency, save for what they read on their daily e-mail bulletins. Of those who did follow events, some criticised the content of the broadcast news, or the tone and prominence of interviewers. But others were broadly contented with the scope and content of the national coverage.

The main issues raised by voters on the doorstep concerned public services, especially health and education. Labour candidates were assailed by members of the public who wanted the changes to tuition fees in Scotland adopted in England and Wales. 'I lost students to the Liberal Democrats over fees', said a veteran Labour MP. More than one Conservative echoed the point: 'Student fees came up as a significant issue.' Some Labour candidates in Kent and Greater London faced opposition on the issue of asylum.

The Conservatives were vulnerable on pensions. However, the Conservatives had placed great emphasis on 'keep the £', and the main focus of their campaign was, at least initially, on taxation. One Conservative candidate summed up the views of a number of his colleagues: 'The Conservative campaign was technically good but was fought on completely the wrong issues. It was a bad mistake not to follow through the January poster campaign "You paid the tax, so where is ...?".'

Europe and the euro featured little on the doorstep compared with their prominence on the national stage. The lack of salience of Europe as an election issue was referred to gratefully by some Liberal Democrats, who found their voters more Eurosceptic than the national party. 'For once the national campaign was a real plus, and our usual need to distance ourselves and declare UDI did not materialise' said a Liberal Democrat.

The 'Prescott punch' was the only incident from the national scene that really became a talking point on the doorstep – 'the only un-scripted event of the campaign', as one Labour candidate put it. The punch was cited by all parties, but disproportionately by Labour candidates. Prescott seemed to have won widespread public sympathy for his actions, although there was a gender imbalance: more men than women approved of his retaliation. The 'themes of the day' from the parties' national press conferences barely registered on the doorsteps, at most providing 'mood music', although the agendas pursued by the media did have some impact on the course of local debate.

Candidates often emphasised local issues during their campaign. Usually these local issues mirrored questions of national salience – such as the state of the constituency's maintained schools, or the treatment record of the local hospital. In industrial areas, factory closures and consequent redundancies were important.

Foot and mouth appeared to be dead as an issue in the national campaign when 17 May was declared the first disease-free day since the outbreak began. However, in rural areas, rumours about the return of foot and mouth after polling day, with government slaughter lorries ready to be moved in, worried farmers. Foot and mouth restrictions remained in many constituencies, and unhappiness about the mass cull of livestock, and the wider effects on the rural economy, lived on.

The opinion polls, which made a Labour victory appear guaranteed, had mixed effects. A few Conservative candidates and their activists suffered reduced morale, but more were spurred into action by a mood of defiance in the face of the pollsters' findings. 'The older hands said that they had not seen so many helpers, or so much enthusiasm, since 1979', was a surprising report from one Conservative candidate. Labour candidates were told by their supporters that there was no necessity to turn out: 'you don't need us – it's in the bag already'. There were fears in the run-up to polling day of a so-called 'Queensland effect' – people voting Conservative to reduce the scale of Labour's landslide – but this phenomenon was not widespread. A Conservative who increased his majority in a marginal seat claimed that 'in the last week, the realisation that Blair could get a 200-plus majority swung floating voters to me. A big Blair majority scared them.' For those Liberal Democrats reading the runes closely, the opinion polls were, throughout the campaign, a source of encouragement and helped enthuse activists – particularly staff in Cowley Street – and voters.

Party leaders affected local campaigning in two ways. First, they set the tone of the national campaign: they were the figureheads that electors saw every night on television. The leader therefore helped to create the image of the party that was already in the mind of the voters before canvassers could reach them. Secondly, the party leaders and other front-benchers travelled across the country, visiting as many constituencies as possible. Visits by prominent party members have three aims: to generate publicity for the party and its message; to engage voters; and to boost the morale of local campaigners. These visits were not, however, always productive. Supporters sometimes had to be bussed in from neighbouring seats to provide an audience. Visits occupied a large amount of a local campaign team's resources, and were not always enthusiastically received by the constituency party. As had been the practice for some years, target seats received the most attention from ministers and their shadows, but even so there was a sense of irritation that when national leaders came, visits were staged to produce national, not local, impact.

The strategies of the party leaders differed: Blair visited town centres and institutions; Hague visited specific seats. John Prescott visited many constituencies on his battle bus ('although we weren't allowed to call it a "battle" bus after the Prescott punch', said a Millbank insider). Iain Duncan Smith and Ann Widdecombe carried the Conservative flag in the regions. 'Central Office', said a Conservative, 'delivered Ann Widdecombe, but shoppers seemed not to realise what she was doing here'. A minder escorting one front-bencher complained of the over-elaborate but inappropriate local briefing supplied for their travels.

The battle was widely seen as Blair versus Hague. As a Conservative put it, 'The national campaigns seemed to be a presidential run between prospective PMs.' One veteran MP thundered that 'Britain is a parliamentary democracy. It should not be lumbered with a presidential-style election.' But, after a campaign in which the parties had failed to capture the public imagination, another senior MP 'reluctantly concluded that we do need a televised debate between party leaders' in order to stimulate interest amongst the electorate.

Candidates from all parties encountered widespread dislike for William Hague amongst the electorate, although Conservative candidates were often puzzled as to why there should have been such an adverse reaction. 'Sadly, William Hague was a negative factor on the doorstep. A section of Conservative voters didn't like him', said a candidate. One Conservative MP admitted that 'Hague was seen as uninspiring, too young, and weak. Labour's allegations about bandwagons hit home.' Some conceded that he was clever, but he did not have widespread appeal. This dislike became a campaign tactic in some constituencies. 'Don't wake up to Hague' was one Labour candidate's rallying cry on polling day.

Public reaction to Tony Blair was less negative, although Conservatives reported quite a lot of hostility. 'Blair was mistrusted, but still seen as *papabile*', observed one Conservative. And there was a marked lack of gushing support from Labour candidates.

Liberal Democrats reported finding enthusiasm for Charles Kennedy: 'Kennedy came over better than anticipated', remarked one Liberal Democrat candidate; 'for once, I actually think that our leader won us some votes', said another. A third Liberal Democrat went as far as to say that 'Kennedy was far more popular than Ashdown in 1997.' Candidates from other parties were more muted in their reports of Kennedy's performance. One Conservative deemed Kennedy 'honest but uninspiring'. Another reported finding 'a good reaction to Kennedy and a poor reaction to Hague', despite the Liberal Democrats in his area running 'a vitriolic and highly targeted campaign'. Some candidates in Scotland noted the appeal of a Highlander as party leader. Some of his opponents thought, in retrospect, that Kennedy had been given something of a free ride by the media and the other parties.

Lady Thatcher's campaigning produced mixed reactions from members of her own party. She was fêted in traditional 'Essex Man' territory: in his acceptance speech Andrew Rosindell, a neo-Thatcherite, declared himself 'delighted that she chose to come to Romford to help my campaign, and, if I had not already won it before, her visit made sure of it'. But other candidates were not so impressed. 'The only thing that had an impact in the campaign was the appearance of Baroness Thatcher and that, so far as I was concerned, was entirely negative: they should have locked her up for the duration', said one Conservative MP. 'When Hague enlisted the support of She Who Used to be Obeyed, a negative impact could be felt.' The Conservatives reported a good response from core voters to Lady Thatcher's public appearances, but her appeal did not extend to the wider voting public, and Labour supporters were energised by her foray.

The 59.4 per cent of registered electors who voted did so at approximately the same time of day as voters in 1997, but slightly earlier in the day than in elections before that. Only the Liberal Democrat supporters differed markedly in their pattern of voting. If the times of voting given by the exit polls and shown in Table 11.3 are compared to the preceding elections, there has been a shift from early morning voting to late evening voting, which makes knocking-up more difficult for the parties, as they cannot focus their resources on the few remaining non-voters as voting draws to a close.

Local electioneering is uneasily poised between the 'old' media and the 'new'. Television and more centralised communication gave more scope for the party leaders and party headquarters to speak directly to the electorate. In some ways, local electioneering has undergone a revival, and studies have shown that effective local campaigning and hard-working MPs can do well. And the new technology, including the internet, may help further to revive the campaign in the constituencies.

Table 11.3   Time of voting

Time	Total	Con	Lab	LibDem
7a.m.–11a.m.	22 (22)	23 (22)	21 (24)	20 (22)
11a.m.–3p.m.	20 (20)	22 (19)	20 (20)	17 (20)
3p.m.–7p.m.	32 (33)	31 (33)	32 (32)	33 (34)
7p.m.–10p.m.	25 (25)	23 (26)	24 (24)	28 (24)

(1997 figures in parentheses)

Source: BBC/NOP Exit Poll

The e-campaign

The internet provided one of the most talked-about innovations of the 2001 campaign.[8] The 1959 campaign, 42 years earlier, had been described as the first 'television election'; many, spurred on by political activity on the internet during the 2000 elections in the United States, expected 2001 to be the first British 'internet election'.

Labour's website, started in 1994, was relaunched in March 1997 for the general election and again in 1999. The latter relaunch was more cosmetic than functional: it had a fancy front page, but no changing headline news stories, and no features with which to engage the web surfer. Whilst there was extensive information on the website, it was not well marshalled and presented. The website was relaunched again at the party conference in September 2000. Labour outsourced the design of the new site to urbanity.co.uk, a website design company, but control over the site and its content remained in-house. Labour launched *www.ruup4it.org.uk*, a site aimed at the youth vote, on 18 May 2001.

The Conservative website was very basic until October 2000 when their site, previously *www.conservative-party.org.uk*, was relaunched and rebranded as *www.conservatives.com*. The makeover was extensive and several layers of personalised content were created. The new website, designed with uevo, was engineered to exploit the internet's potential for 'narrowcasting': users had to log in and were then shown a different front page depending on whether they were a candidate, party member, journalist, or ordinary member of the public.

The Liberal Democrats had, like the other major parties, operated a website at the 1997 general election at *www.libdems.org.uk*. The website had been relaunched in spring 2000 for the party's spring conference. Their 2001 general election site, the web-design of which had been contracted out to Cix, was launched on the day that the election was announced. The website had a 'deliberately straightforward' tone, and was intended to provide information rather than entertainment.

The SNP had made great play of dropping the '.uk' suffix from its website addresses in March 1999, and Plaid Cymru followed suit. The SNP, which claims to have created the first political website in the UK, had sites at *www.snp.org* and at *www.westandforscotland.org*. Their site was rich in information and features. Plaid Cymru's site, *www.plaidcymru2001.com* was administered by a volunteer, and was limited in scope: it was not possible to join the party online. The three main parties ran separate websites in Scotland and Wales, but these were operated independently of the national sites, which were all based in London. The Welsh Labour site, *www.welshlabour.co.uk* was praised by its opponents; other regional sites did not raise comment from party managers in London. Centrally produced literature and posters often referred to the national website, rather than the regional or constituency site.

The parties had three main audiences in mind when designing their sites: party members, journalists, and the wider electorate. Each party ran a form of 'extranet' – a system which gave to party activists password-restricted access to online resources. These sites made available templates, logos, photographs and articles for use in newsletters, policy briefings for use during canvassing, and archives of news briefings. The Labour extranet included the opportunity for activists to exchange experiences and ideas. Conservatives found that the most important inclusions on their extranet were themes of the day, lines to take and press releases.

These extranets proved useful to and popular with activists, and were an inexpensive means of conveying information and campaign materials to workers in all parts of the country.

Journalists used party websites heavily during the campaign. The Conservatives launched the Media Centre section of their website on 28 March 2001, giving journalists online access to press conferences, press releases, candidate and constituency profiles, broadcast-quality audio clips, and photographs of a publishable standard. Labour and the Liberal Democrats had less extensive operations. Labour carried press releases, some press photos and live web-casts of their press conferences. The Liberal Democrats did not web-cast their press conferences, but provided the manifesto, candidate biographies, and all national press releases. However, journalists who wanted to see the press conferences from the comfort of their offices could simply watch *Sky News* or *BBC News 24*, which was easier than grappling with a web-cast. The internet took pressure off the parties' press teams: journalists could look up information for themselves, and a typical response to a telephone enquiry from a journalist was 'it's on the website'.

In 2001, the internet for the first time offered the political parties the potential for widespread, unmediated 'dialogue' with the public, with the opportunity to convey far more information than could be included in a public meeting or written election address. However, of those voters with internet access, only 18 per cent used it to find political information during the campaign. The campaign did, however, generate increased interest in the parties' websites. The number of hits on the sites during the campaign was greater than in 1997, and the number of hits during the campaign was up to four times the peacetime level. But hits are unreliable: it is impossible to distinguish between journalists, party activists, children researching school projects, and genuine floating voters, and it is not always possible to distinguish which hits are from abroad. Sites are often cached (temporarily held on alternative servers), which reduces the headline number of hits on the host server, although the Conservatives used technology provided by Red Sheriff to reduce this problem when recording page impressions. The parties were unwilling, post-election, to publish their number of hits, but one campaigner reported that web surfers stayed on the website, on average, for ten minutes – longer than many voters spent reading traditional party election material.

Parties experienced increased access to their sites on polling day and immediately thereafter. The webmasters were not clear why this should have been. Several theories were posited – voyeurism at the Conservatives' downfall, interest in the breaking news on Hague's resignation, idle web surfers staying awake and awaiting hard results – but no theory could be confirmed in the immediate aftermath of the campaign.

The manifestos were popular features of the major parties' websites. The launch of Labour's manifesto incited more than 30 unique users per second to attempt downloading the manifesto from *www.labour.org.uk*. The level of interest was so high that the site slowed almost to a standstill. The SNP said that its manifesto was downloaded 25,000 times; Labour had more copies of its manifesto downloaded than were sold in the shops; the Liberal Democrats sold more paper copies of their manifesto through their website than over the phone, despite the ability to download the manifesto for free. The Conservatives found that the manifesto and their 'My Manifesto' feature were the most visited sections of their website. 'My Manifesto', which delivered manifesto material tailored to the particular interests and socio-demographic profile of each web surfer, was a rare foray into narrowcasting in this campaign.

The parties' sites were criticised for being cyber advertising rather than attempts to engage voters in an online dialogue.[9] Of the sites, Labour's had most features with which to engage the interest of voters, including games, screensavers, and a mortgage calculator (which was advertised on a mortgage website – the only example of online banner advertising by the major parties during the campaign). 'Labour had the best freebies', admitted one opponent. Some e-campaigners repudiated suggestions that they were guilty of failing to engage with the voters: they viewed the website as an extension of the party-as-campaigning-machine; as with cross-party public meetings, it was for others to provide open discussion forums.

The three main parties' websites enabled people to join the party online. By the end of June, 1.5 per cent of the Liberal Democrats' total membership had joined through their website in the first half of 2001, and almost all of these were not previously known to the party as supporters, and therefore would not directly have been approached to join. During the campaign, Labour had as many people joining the party through the website as over the phone. Both the Liberal Democrats and the Conservatives reported a surge of web-based membership applications in the 72 hours after the polls closed. A surge in Labour's online membership applications came in the wake of the 'Prescott punch'.

In addition to the parties' national websites, 20 per cent of candidates or constituency parties had their own website. Of the 80 per cent who did not have websites, some chose this deliberately; others were hampered by a constituency party that 'knew nothing of such things'. A few candidates who had been MPs in the 1997–2001 Parliament closed down their sites because they had been created with parliamentary resources, and chose not to replace them with election sites. Most candidates who had 'MP' in their web address changed their addresses or disabled their sites for the duration of the campaign, and many sites carried an imprint, as if they had been published election literature. Nigel Evans' site had a 'campaign has started' administrative feature, which automatically took off all mention of him being Conservative MP for Ribble Valley and rebranded his site, *nigelmp.com*, as *electnigel.com*. Prior to the campaign, questions had been raised as to how election law related to candidates' sites.[10] Some e-campaigners thought that these questions proved to be over-cautious in the event, but this was previously uncharted territory, and there was prudence in caution.

The national parties' e-campaign managers had offered advice to candidates on local sites, but had no direct involvement in the development of these sites, and their style and content varied considerably.

The Conservatives offered an 'XML feed', which provided continually updated content, to candidates and others, but there was no demand. The most uniform candidate sites were those set up under Labour's 'Web in a Box' scheme. 'Web in a Box', which was run in conjunction with a private internet company, enabled Labour candidates easily to establish a basic web presence by the purchase for £180 of a pro forma website in the domain *labour.co.uk*. There was also the option of a news feed from headquarters. The scheme suited some, but was publicly criticised by an adviser of Anne Campbell, the Labour MP for Cambridge, as being worse than the £50 website used by her in 1997.[11] 'The jury's still out on "Web in a Box"', said one campaigner.

The number of 'hits' registered by candidates' websites varied markedly, as did the distribution of candidates with a website at all. Candidates' websites cited for their quality included those of Howard Dawber (Labour, Cheadle), Robert Key (Conservative, Salisbury), and Ed Davey (Liberal Democrat, Kingston and Surbiton). However, a survey of 245 candidate sites by the Hansard Society reported that web surfers were '20 per cent more likely to discover a candidate's marital status than their opinions on the European single currency, and 51 per cent more likely to find out their age than their view on hunting with hounds'.[12] Overall, candidates' websites disappointed.

Two features of the 2001 elections in the United States were the potential for cyber-squatters and the number of bogus sites. Cyber-squatters were not a major problem in the British general election. Labour and the Liberal Democrats used the same website addresses as at the 1997 general election, and visitors to the Conservatives' old address were redirected to *conservatives.com*. The Liberal Democrats had registered a number of alternative website addresses in advance of the election, which directed users to the main site, but none attracted a significant amount of traffic. The Conservatives registered *conservatives.com* well in advance of the election, and were willing, if necessary, to evict unlawful cyber-squatters. The most widely reported incidence of cyber-squatting was when the Liberal Democrats used the address *www.plaid-cymru.co.uk* to campaign for itself in Wales (Plaid Cymru's own address was *www.plaidcymru2001.com*). But the site made clear from the front page that it was a Liberal Democrat website, and neither the incident itself, nor the publicity surrounding it, altered the course of the campaign.

Bogus sites were not the problem that some foresaw. The Conservatives took legal action to close two sites in early 2001 on the grounds of copyright infringement, but no other sites were forcibly shut down. 'You don't start launching legal battles during the election campaign – it takes too long', said one campaigner. Bogus sites are only a problem if they pretend to be something that they are not and if many people know of their existence. But these two things are contradictory: if they are well known, then it will become well known that they are bogus.

The parties were always concerned about their sites' security. It was not simply a case of the security of their computer systems. In an election where the message carried by the parties' websites was, at least in part, the medium, bad publicity would be generated by a successful cyber attack. It paid to be seen as e-savvy; the worse of all worlds was to be portrayed as technologically incompetent.

None of the parties suffered from a successful attack on its website. It was reported that the Conservatives had a security scare mid-campaign, but there was no danger that their site's contents could have been altered by hackers. They learned of the problem by monitoring hackers' websites and by employing 'ethical hackers'. Labour had eschewed ethical hackers in favour of working with Oracle to make their website more secure. The Liberal Democrats had a security audit shortly before the campaign began to identify any areas where their defences needed strengthening. All parties reported some probing of their websites' defences at the margins.

All major broadcast media organisations and broadsheet newspapers ran extensive online coverage of the election campaign, but the BBC and *Guardian* sites stood out for their range and comprehensiveness. In addition to carrying extensive news coverage, these sites hosted lists of candidates, guides to the voting system and marginal constituencies, summaries of manifestos, and live results services, amongst other features. Over half of internet users accessed political information over the internet during the campaign, and the online news sites were widely viewed: the BBC Vote 2001 website recorded 2 million page views after 10 p.m. on polling day, and 15.75 million page impressions the following day.

Another feature of the campaign was political humour on the internet. *Spinon.co.uk*, a satirical site, claimed 100,000 visits from 40,000 individual users, of which 15,000 were regular users. Games available on the internet, in which users could, for example, throw an egg at John Prescott, jump on William Hague's Bandwagon, or mince their least favourite MP in a blender, were passed on by users over e-mail and viewed by an even wider audience. 'Online humour and games', said Stephen Coleman of the Hansard Society, 'successfully tapped into a popular feeling about the disconnection of politics from people – especially young people'.

Paddy Ashdown had prophesied in 1997 that 'e-mail had proven in this election incredibly useful in contacting the party machine; in the next election it could contact the voters'.[13] The 2001 election proved him correct, but the use of e-mail as an effective campaign tool was limited by legal, financial, and practical barriers.

Data Protection legislation prevented parties from contacting voters by e-mail except where the recipient had given permission to be e-mailed. Parties had to rely on subscriptions to e-mail newsletters through their websites and their membership lists to provide them with people to contact by e-mail. Parties were offered lists of e-mail addresses which had been collected by activists, but did not use these lists unless they were sure that the people on these lists had given their explicit consent to be e-mailed. 'It was important for us to be holier than thou' on the Data Protection Act and e-mail addresses, said one e-campaigner.

Good, highly profiled lists of e-mail addresses that were compliant with the Data Protection Act could be purchased, but for the lists to be of any use they cost more than any party was willing to afford. In any case, cold e-mailing was seen by many users as intrusive, and sending unsolicited e-mails could backfire. The parties, therefore, tended to restrict themselves to only those e-mailing voters who had requested information.

Many of the candidates' own websites offered constituents the opportunity to send e-mail messages to the candidate. However, few voters chose to interact. Some candidates reported receiving up to ten e-mails each day; the number of e-mails was often less. But e-mail from electors was more common than in 1997, and most candidates expected it to continue to grow in importance.

Even more marked than the internet revolution was the revolution in the ownership of mobile phones since the 1997 general election. The increase in mobile phones – fuelled by the development of the pre-pay mobiles market – meant that in June 2001 more people had mobile phones than had access to the internet; the socio-economic profile of mobile phone owners was more diverse than that of internet users. Almost half of mobile phone owners used text messaging (sms). The huge popularity of sms amongst the young offered the parties a way of reaching out to first-time voters.

Despite these facts, none of the three main parties had plans in the run-up to the election campaign to utilise mobile phones in general or sms in particular as means of contacting the public. Many people find calls to mobile phones more intrusive than calls to land line phones, and mobile phone numbers are difficult to obtain except, as with e-mail addresses, when offered by their owners. Parties were put off sms by its cost: even when purchased in bulk lots of 100,000 messages, sms messages cost 3p each to send.

Nevertheless, during the last weekend of the campaign, Labour became the first party to use mass sms. Between 10 p.m. and 10.30 p.m., in time to catch last orders in the pubs at 11 p.m., Labour sent a message 'CLDNT GVE A XXXX 4 LST ORDRS? VTE LBR ON THRSDY 4 XTRA TIME' to 6,000 mobile phones. The second message sent was aimed at young people. They sent out six different messages.

Labour strategists were happy with the impact of its deployment of sms. In addition to sending messages directly, it enabled supporters to send, via its website, selected messages to their friends. The direct effect on turnout is impossible to quantify, but the messages prompted favourable press coverage for Labour,[14] and the party deemed them a success.

Tactical voting was an area in which some hoped the internet would have an impact in 2001. The largest of the vote-swapping sites, *www.tacticalvoter.net*, which had been launched on 2 April 2001, claimed 200,000 hits during the election campaign and recorded 8,153 pledges for vote-swapping. In two constituencies – Cheadle and Dorset South – the number of vote-swap pledges on internet sites was larger than the majorities of the new victors. In the latter of these, Billy Bragg's *www.votedorset.net* had encouraged Liberal Democrat supporters to swap their votes with Labour supporters in Dorset West. However, Oliver Letwin held on comfortably in Dorset West. Bragg suggested that the publicity for the idea of tactical voting through coverage of the website in the *Dorset Echo* and beyond might have been as influential as the swapping on the website itself.

The remarkable swing to the Liberal Democrats in Kingston & Surbiton had been accompanied by the independent website *www.stophague.com*, which had encouraged support for the Labour incumbent in Wimbledon and the Liberal Democrat incumbent in Kingston & Surbiton. However, the result in Kingston was not mirrored in its eastern neighbour, and the website claimed fewer than 4,000 visitors. However, websites were not, by themselves, sufficient explanation for tactical voting in the general election.

In one of the few actions taken against websites during the campaign, the *Financial Times* reported on 11 May that the Conservatives had referred *www.stophague.com* to the Electoral Commission.[15] They questioned whether the site breached the new £500 limit for third-party election activity. The same article referred to the efforts of Ian Bruce, the Conservative candidate for Dorset South, to draw the attention of the Information Commissioner to *www.votedorset.net* on the grounds that it 'does not comply with the Data Protection Act and isn't registered with the Information Commissioner's Office'. Both complaints were turned down.

The effort that each party put into its election website in 2001 was evident, but were the resources deployed effectively? David Bowen in the *Financial Times* branded the parties' efforts an 'All-singing waste of cash'.[16] But this does not describe the reality. The websites saved the parties' money in some areas: the Conservatives, for the first time did not produce a printed copy of their *Campaign Guide*; the Liberal Democrats did not produce paper lists of candidates for distribution to the media. E-mail and the parties' extranets cut the costs of communicating between headquarters and candidates. And the lack of an online presence would have produced bad publicity in the 'offline' media. The parties' e-campaign managers were, naturally, enthusiastic about their contributions to their parties' campaigns. But the investment in the new technology was not always proportional to the returns, and the Liberal Democrats were the most enthusiastic about their ratio of costs to benefits. A senior Conservative estimated that almost one-third of the heavy investment by the Conservatives in *conservatives.com* had been recouped by savings on printing and communications costs. Nevertheless, post-election, Tim Collins MP, a vice-chairman of the Conservative Party, publicly declared that their internet operation had 'failed its cost-benefit analysis'. A party worker responded that 'it had to be done'.

This election was never likely to be an 'internet election' in the same way that 1959 was a television election, for three reasons. First, television is a 'push' technology, whereas the Web is a 'pull' technology. The effort required to search out information on the internet is much greater than with other forms of media. E-mail is a 'push' technology, but its usefulness for campaigning was hampered by a lack of addresses. Secondly, the internet has a much lower penetration of society in 2001 than television had in 1959. In 2001 33 per cent of electors had home internet access; in 1959 over 70 per cent of homes had a television set (up from under 40 per cent at the 1955 election). Thirdly, television in 1959 had few competitors. In 2001, the internet had to compete for the attention of voters with five national television channels and three 24-hour news channels, numerous radio networks, and extended coverage of the campaign in the print media. In 2001, more households had access to 24-hour television news through satellite or digital television (44 per cent) than had access to the internet. Indeed, some of the most popular sections of the internet during the election were the websites of trusted media organisations. The 1959 campaign was the first in which reporting restrictions had been lifted: before this the broadcast media did not report elections. The internet came into a market for news and information which was already saturated.

Nevertheless, it would be wrong to declare the notion of an internet election stillborn. The internet continues to revolutionise party campaign tactics and internal party communications. And the opportunities that the internet provides for personalisation of information, for its inexpensive dissemination, and for the exchange of views were all explored during the election campaign. 'The internet', as one campaigner put it, 'has significantly altered everyday life. It was no more or less important to the election than it is to everyday life.'

Notes

1. Electoral Commission, *Election 2001: The Official Results* (2001), p. 26.
2. *Ibid.*, p. 33. Due to the system of compiling postal vote statistics, it is unlikely that a more accurate figure will be calculated.
3. *Ibid.*, p. 37.
4. In February 1998, the European Court of Human Rights ruled by 14 votes to 6 that Mrs Phyllis Bowman, the Chair of the Society for the Protection of the Unborn Child, had her freedom of speech as guaranteed by the European Convention on Human Rights infringed when she was prosecuted for spending a significant sum of money during the 1992 general election campaign on the distribution of 25,000 leaflets in Halifax on the subject of the candidates' views on abortion.
5. The maximum expenditure permitted by a candidate at the constituency level was, in 2001, £5,483 per constituency plus 6.2p per elector in county constituencies and 4.6p per elector in borough constituencies.
6. Previously, the authors of the Nuffield election study have attempted to calculate the expenditure of the parties at constituency level by sampling election expense returns. However, at this election it was decided to await the Electoral Commission's comprehensive report, due by the end of 2001.
7. David Butler, *The British General Election of 1951* (London: Macmillan, 1952), p. 141.
8. A comprehensive contemporary analysis of the use of the internet in the general election campaign, which was published in July 2001, is Stephen Coleman (ed.), *2001: Cyber Space Odyssey* (2001).
9. See, for example, Ian Kearns, 'Politicians must learn to love the net', published online at <http://www.voxpolitics.com/news/voxfpub/story 229.shtml>.
10. See, for example: Phil Cain *et al.*, *Vox Politics Primer*, published online at <http://www.voxpolitics.com/primer.shtml>; Chris Ballinger and Stephen Coleman, *Electoral Law and the Internet: Some Issues Considered* (2001).
11. 'The not-quite cyber election', *Guardian*, 15 June 2001.
12. Beccy Earnshaw, 'Winning a seat in Cyber Space: candidate web sites in the 2001 general election' in Stephen Coleman (ed.), *2001: Cyber Space Odyssey* (2001).
13. David Butler and Dennis Kavanagh, *The British General Election of 1997* (Basingstoke: Macmillan, 1997), p. 215.
14. See, for example, Tom Baldwin, 'WUCIWUG – LBR is on msg for Uth', *The Times*, 5 June 2001; 'WNT 2 GT PSSD ALL NT EVRI NT? VT LBR', *Independent on Sunday*, 3 June 2001.

15. Elizabeth Rigby, 'Tories instigate probe into vote-swap websites', *Financial Times*, 11 May 2001, p. 8.
16. 1 June 2001.

12
The Campaign Reassessed

The 2001 election campaign received a poor press. Before and during the campaign there was much discussion about electoral apathy as well as about antipathy towards politicians and the political process. There was speculation over how much turnout would fall and how far this would be due to the apparent certainty of a Labour landslide, to the failure of Conservatives to address the issues which engaged voters, to the stage management of the leaders' tours, to the perceived lack of sharp ideological differences between the parties, or to the overwhelming message of the opinion polls. Supporters of electoral reform added that in safe seats many would not bother to go to the polls, knowing that their votes would be 'wasted'. But the 12 per cent drop in turnout from 1997 to a record low came as a shock to politicians and commentators alike.

For all the talk of apathy, 59 per cent claimed to be 'very' or 'fairly' interested in news about the campaign, a proportion comparable to previous elections, and audiences for television programmes even rose slightly over 1997 levels. There were also important issues at stake: the future of Britain's relations with the EU, and the level of investment in public services – and their reform. The press played its part in spreading the apathy charge. On several days, even the broadsheets failed to lead with an election story, or provide front-page coverage of the election (see Chapter 9), and, as the election advanced, the tabloids and mid-market papers cut back on coverage. Television's *Question Time*, with the party leaders open to challenge, attracted fewer than three million viewers, a figure seriously disappointing the television authorities and the party leaders. Television news programmes substantially cut back election coverage compared to 1997 and led with other stories more often than in 1997. The media seized on such unscheduled incidents as John

Prescott's punch, or Sharron Storer's berating of Tony Blair or Lady Thatcher's off-message remarks on the euro at Plymouth. The first two events reduced coverage of Labour's manifesto and the last stalled development of the Conservative attack on Labour and tax. But such incidents were few. The final report of the Loughborough University team studying the coverage of the election was headlined in the *Guardian*: 'AN ELECTION THAT MANY WATCHED BUT FEW ENJOYED'. On polling day the *Independent* welcomed the end of this 'dull, uninspiring campaign', and the *Guardian* prominently featured an article by Richard Gott, headlined 'I SHALL NOT VOTE' as well as one by Jonathan Freedland complaining about the 'cardboard characters' of the lacklustre election.

"There are cases of apathy spreading all over the country"

Pugh, *The Times*, 8 May 2001

The campaign saw no significant shifts in the importance of issues or the parties' ratings on them. The polls found that voters said health and education were the most important factors in deciding how to vote – in contrast, the media focused on Europe and tax before health (see pp. 138–68). Table 12.1 shows that, for the public at large, Europe mattered less than most other issues. Such findings led media research teams at Loughborough and Cardiff universities to conclude that public opinion did not set the agenda for media coverage of the campaign.

Tories rubbished the polls during the campaign; but, if the polls were broadly right about the huge Labour lead during the campaign, they could feel vindicated at reducing it to 9 per cent by polling day. But they were still stuck on less than a third of the vote. The sharp fall in turnout meant that all three parties lost out in terms of votes actually cast since 1997 and even more so in comparison with 1992 (see Appendix 2).

Table 12.1   Important issues

Q. At this general election, which, if any, of these issues do you think will be very important to you in helping you decide which party to vote for?

	5 June 2001 %
Health care	73
Education	62
Law & order	50
Pensions	40
Taxation	37
Managing the economy	31
Public transport	31
Unemployment	30
Asylum seekers / Immigration	27
Europe	26
Protecting the environment	26

Source: MORI

The election itself was not the cause of apathy, but it provided a stark illustration of it. For some years a growing part of the electorate has not engaged with the political process and membership of and engagement with political parties has declined (Table 12.2). The turnout for local, European and by-elections fell substantially in the 1990s, particularly after 1997. Similar trends had been observed in other countries. No doubt the style of media coverage of the political game and the voters' mixture of expectations, disappointment and cynicism shared some of the blame.

Table 12.2   Strength of party support 1992–2001

	1992 %	1997 %	2001 %
Very Strong	31	31	20
Fairly Strong	44	44	50

Source: MORI

This was also a highly self-contained election campaign. Apart from speeches on the future of the EU by the Commission President, Romano

Prodi, or by the French Prime Minister Lionel Jospin, little happening in the world outside the UK had much impact. The parties had planned press conference themes to coincide with events they knew they could exploit: Labour latched on to a supporting statement from businessmen and the Conservatives to the declaration of the result of the strike ballot among doctors.

Although the amount of public opinion polling was more limited in scale and received less media coverage than in 1997 or 1992, the indications of another landslide Labour victory hung heavily over the campaign. The poll findings imbued Labour with confidence in its own strategy and a belief that the Conservatives were alienating the majority of voters. Conservative strategists felt that their party had had the better of the first week and many commentators agreed until the opinion polls reported no diminution in the Labour lead. This in turn led many reporters to start commenting on the failure of the Conservative efforts.

Conservative aides quickly consoled themselves with the efficiency of their campaign on the ground and the way that morale at the centre was holding up. But one Central Office figure wryly offered a post-mortem: 'A first-class operation; unfortunately the diagnosis was wrong and the patient died.'

Opinion polls always create a problem for parties and leaders, especially when their ratings are trailing badly. Conservative apologists repeatedly stated that the polls were wrong, that their telephone feedback from swing voters was positive (it was not), that candidates and professionals were pleased with the responses on the doorstep (which was largely true) and that many voters had not yet made up their minds (which was true but not new). William Hague confidently stated 'The polls have been wrong before' and, 'We won the Euro-elections when the polls said we would lose.' In private, he was disappointed that his stand on the euro did not have an impact, and that the party's polls in the marginals were not more favourable. In public and private, Tony Blair worried about apathy, some of which could be reinforced by the landslide message of the polls. He wanted another big victory so that he could claim a personal mandate. In launching the campaign at St Olave's School he had called for voters to support him with their 'hearts and minds'.

As in other elections, the parties looked both backwards and forwards in their search for themes that might arouse fear or inspire hope. Blair reminded his audiences about interest rates of 15 per cent (as long ago as 1990), as well as about the spending cuts and economic recession under John Major. William Hague reminded voters of Labour's tax increases and its failures to improve public services. Looking forward, Hague warned of the abolition of the pound under another Labour government and of substantial tax increases after 2004. His use of a clock counting the hours to polling day as the hours which remained to save the pound was a play on Tony Blair's 1997 election cry that there were '24 hours to save the NHS'. Blair, in turn, warned of more privatisation and spending cuts of £8 billion (or, courtesy of Oliver Letwin, £20 billion) if the Conservatives were elected. Interestingly, both Blair and Hague, having sought to remake their parties, made few references to their parties' earlier records in government. The names and records of Harold Wilson, James Callaghan, Ted Heath and John Major had been virtually erased from their parties' history. Lady Thatcher, however, played her most prominent role in a campaign since she left the leadership.

As the parties stuck to their well-tried themes there was little meeting-ground between them. There were some differences, not least on the issues of taxation and spending and on the euro. In the 1992 general election, Conservatives had thrown Labour onto the defensive with claims that its spending plans would mean substantial income tax increases. They had also defended British membership of the ERM as a cornerstone of their economic policy and as something that would be threatened under Labour. By 2001, however, the context differed markedly on both issues. Over the previous nine years the Conservative Party had become more united around a Eurosceptic position while the case for more public spending over tax cuts seemed stronger, largely because of growing dissatisfaction with the services. In 1997, Labour sought to reassure voters that they would not increase taxes. In 2001, Blair and Brown uncompromisingly and confidently put spending on services ahead of tax cuts.

Periodically, Blair chastised journalists and interviewers about their questions on sleaze, on a referendum on the euro, on his relations with Gordon Brown, and on the style of the campaign. They should be asking him about hospitals and schools, the actual concerns of real people. He attacked reporters for concentrating on scandals, on the details of the campaign process and on the possibility of a Labour landslide.

For Labour, tax was inseparable from investment in public services. Yet over the previous four years, Labour spending on health, education and transport had increased only modestly and spending on education as a share of GDP was actually lower than under John Major. Here was a paradox. The more public dissatisfaction there was with the state of the public services, the more that Labour claims about improvements were doubted, and the higher that schools and health rose in salience, the more Labour was regarded as the party more likely to meet public concerns. Labour was running against its record in office and relying heavily on being trusted about the funding announced by Gordon Brown. The public did not believe Conservative pledges of future tax cuts – or, even more, that they would be able to make cuts and still spend more on public services. But many voters were also sceptical about Labour disavowals that it did not plan any future tax increases. MORI found that 74 per cent of voters expected taxes to rise under Labour and that a majority thought that taxes would rise under any party in government.

Behind the inflated rhetoric, however, the margins of choice were actually quite narrow. Conservative promises of £8 billion in spending cuts amounted to less than 2 per cent of total public spending. Under the plans of any party, Britain's public spending profile would remain in the middle among Western states. In the United States public spending was some 35 per cent of GDP, across Western Europe nearly 50 per cent of GDP. The Conservatives proposed to lower slightly Britain's existing 39 per cent share by the end of the Parliament, Labour to increase it by some 2 per cent and Liberal Democrats to increase it by 1 per cent. It is difficult to believe that many voters would have understood the bases of all these calculations even with the guidance of the media and the analyses of the independent Institute of Fiscal Studies. Moreover, Treasury planning totals often differ from those actually achieved in a single year.

Previous Labour leaders would have been amazed at the way in which Labour in 2001 had managed to seize so many former strong Conservative issues, notably on management of the economy. Moreover, since 1997 surveys showed that Labour had further increased its levels of support among the middle class and in south-east England, to a point where it actually ran level with the Conservative Party. Blair and Gordon Brown were confident that they had reassured that large tranche of middle-class first-time Labour voters who had feared that the party might still lapse into its bad old ways. All this provided a new context for Labour.

Few parties have entered a general election with as many advantages as Labour held over its main rival in 2001. As in 1997 it commanded majority press support, received the bulk of press campaign coverage and was headed by a charismatic figure who was quoted far more than the opposition leader. The *Echo Research* analysis of the media found that Labour politicians and spokespersons were also quoted at much greater length than Conservatives in broadcasts. According to public and private opinion polls, Labour managed throughout to maintain substantial leads on ratings of effective leadership, on economic competence, on party unity and on sense of direction. A MORI survey in the last week of May found that 34 per cent of voters rated the Conservatives' policies on national issues as 'very' or 'fairly' good (while Labour stood at 54 per cent); 27 per cent gave a similar rating to Conservative leaders (Labour, 55 per cent) and 33 per cent to the values the party stood for (Labour, 56 per cent). Labour had equally large leads on the issues which the voters considered very important in deciding how to vote, particularly on health and education (and its private polls were reassuring – see Table 12.3).

Table 12.3   Parties' key attributes during the campaign

	13 May	*5 June*
Blair doing good/excellent job	51%	56%
Hague doing good/excellent job	25%	25%
	Labour Lead	
Keeping tax right level	18%	23%
Managing the economy	34%	35%
Right approach to Europe	11% (20 May)	11%
Standing up for Britain	3%	9%
Improving standard of living	17%	21%

Source: Labour private polls

The economy, apart from tax, may not have been discussed as much as in previous elections, when inflation and unemployment were major concerns. But it was crucial as a determinant of voting choice. An analysis by ICM found that, out of a number of issues determining the vote, Labour's economic performance was most influential, followed by education, health, law and order, with Europe the least significant.

Tony Blair also approached the election as an opportunity to win a personal mandate, one that would enable him to leave his mark on history. He was aware of critics who noted how much he had to do in a second term of office if he was to be regarded as a great prime minister. While Gordon Brown minded the shop at Millbank, Blair toured the country, delivering his six major speeches and campaigning in the marginal constituencies. His determination to be photographed in schools and hospitals paid dividends in conveying his party's concern about these issues and contrasted with William Hague's conspicuous avoidance of such photo opportunities. Ronnie Duncan, of Yellow M, the Conservatives' advertising agency, pointed to a *Sun* front-page photograph of Tony Blair mingling with schoolchildren and added, 'It is difficult for a poster or a party election broadcast to compete against that and its eleven million readers.'

Rueful Conservatives acknowledged that Labour had managed to define Hague's Conservative Party in terms of past negatives, of boom and bust and cuts in public services under Thatcher and Major. Alastair Campbell's unprecedented release of the private polls on 27 May was motivated in part by a wish to show how badly the Conservatives were doing on the key issues and to drive Hague off his euro policy (which Philip Gould's groups found was working among Labour core voters). Because of worry over apathy, particularly among young working-class women Labour supporters, Blair and Brown in the last week emphasised the importance of schools and hospitals, reflected in posters, broadcasts and speeches. However, Millbank's effort to mobilise Labour's core vote supported by Blair's passionate appeal reaped little benefit. 'Could we have done better?' asked one key figure in Labour's campaign. 'Yes, our spinning and presentation may actually have undermined our ability to engage with voters.' He was one of those who thought that future campaigns would have to change drastically if they were to promote voters' interest.

The Conservative approach to the 2001 election raised interesting questions, both about strategy and contemporary conservatism. Two of its architects, Tim Collins and Andrew Lansley, offered a retrospective defence of the campaign strategy in the *Daily Telegraph* on 14 June; they argued that, if the polls had been correct over the course of the campaign, then the party had halved Labour's lead from 20 per cent in the opinion polls to 9 per cent on 7 June. This claim assumes that such large leads in the polls reflected reality throughout the campaign, something which Conservatives had ridiculed and said was contradicted by their own soundings. Collins and Lansley noted that the Conservatives gained 33 per cent of the vote which could be compared to Labour's 34 per cent in 1992; and that Labour had gone on to succeed in the 1997 general election; the Conservatives could therefore win next time round. But whereas Labour's 34 per cent in 1992 had won them 271 MPs, the Conservative 31 per cent in 2001 had gained only 166. The electoral system and tactical voting were therefore partly to blame for the Conservatives faring so poorly. These claims that 2001 was not so bad for the party require some heroic assumptions and the acceptance of questionable analogies. The bias in the electoral system and tactical voting, which also hurt the Conservatives in 1992 and 1997, are not likely to disappear in the near future. They were and they remain a fact of life for the Conservatives, at least until some fundamental changes occur in voters' perceptions of their party.

The result confirmed the Conservative Party's failure to break out of the trough into which it had fallen since September 1992; in all the following years the party's level of support remained around 30 per cent. Between 1992 and 2001 it lost an aggregate of five-and-a-half million votes and in 2001 it received its lowest percentage share since universal suffrage was introduced. Labour's hold among its middle-class and Middle England converts in 1997 was consolidated; these groups had now acquired the habit of not voting Conservative.

Labour also fared particularly well in the key Lab–Con marginal seats. One disappointed member of the Conservative strategy group commented resignedly that the campaign and the election strategy were 'a comment on what we did and failed to do over the preceding four years'. Yet the campaign themes as unveiled to the Shadow Cabinet and to Conservative MPs in December 2000 and March 2001 were largely followed. 'We delivered what we promised', said Andrew Lansley. A senior Hague adviser and architect of the core vote strategy echoed his leader when he said: 'They were the right issues and it will be seen to be a good result.' But another, who always had his doubts about the strategy said it was a 'terrible result – one extra bloody seat and 2 per cent more votes after four years'.

Although commentators criticised the thrust of the Conservative campaign, there was a high level of agreement among the 'Gang of Four', the senior shadow ministers who gathered with William Hague in Central Office at 9 p.m. every evening. After the election, however, Francis Maude and Michael Portillo called for a fundamental debate about the future of the party. In doing so they signalled in public their misgivings about the tone and content of the election themes. Portillo commented on BBC TV, moments after the declaration of his own result: 'We didn't lose because of the last few weeks, we lost because of the last four years.'

Another perspective on the party's lack of progress over the previous four years and more is seen in Table 12.4. This compares the public's ratings on the best leaders and the best parties over the last three general elections. It shows a steady and substantial decline for the Conservatives and a steady and substantial increase for Labour. Looking at the ratings for 2001, one might consider that the Conservatives did well to reach 32 per cent of the vote.

Table 12.4   Best leaders and best policies 1992–2001

Best Leaders	1992	1997	2001	Change 1992–2001
Conservative	40	21	13	−27
Labour	30	34	47	+17
Liberal Democrats	9	8	5	−4
Best Policies	1992	1997	2001	Change 1992–2001
Conservative	32	20	17	−15
Labour	34	36	42	+8
Liberal Democrats	12	13	11	−1

Source: MORI

William Hague's core vote strategy was always a risk if the party was seriously aiming for victory or even a very limited defeat. Where were the extra votes to come from? About a quarter of 1992 Conservatives had shifted to Labour or Liberal Democrat in 1997, when the Conservative Party was already the most Eurosceptic main party. Why would the 'core vote' appeal attract them back to the party? Traditionally, the Conservatives had profited from its lead over Labour on such key issues and themes as law and order, economic management, and standing up for Britain, to offset their deficits on health, education and welfare. But previous party leaders have also seen the need to be positive on the latter. Indeed, spending on health in real terms increased steadily under Margaret Thatcher and John Major. Conservatives won elections because they succeeded in retaining and looking beyond their core vote; they were a classic catch-all political party. In 2001 the party virtually conceded the battleground of economic management and public services to Labour. Hague's team hoped that many people dissatisfied with Labour on public services would vote Conservative rather than Liberal Democrat or that they would just abstain. Critics within the party, however, were saying long before polling day that the party had not done enough policy work on public services to win over those who were dissatisfied with Labour.

The architects of the core vote strategy were convinced that there was no mileage for the party in any other approach. 'We'd have done worse without the core vote strategy, we would have gone down to 27–28 per cent', said one of them. This raises the question: where else would the core have gone? The Referendum Party in 1997 had left its impact and UKIP was there to inherit the support of Eurosceptic voters. The core vote approach seemed to be directed to heading off a right-wing breakaway and achieving a 'safe' minimum; however, it risked setting a low ceiling to the maximum. The exercise in drawing 'clear blue water' between Conservative and Labour on the core issues made the party appear extreme and out of touch. Hague believed strongly in tax cuts and saving the pound. On the euro, he half jested to aides, 'If it comes, then I'm emigrating.' The hard-hitting advertisements over the three months before the campaign (on public services) had not moved public opinion, he claimed, because voters had such strong negative views about the Conservatives on these issues. Yet the advertisements had concentrated on Labour's failure to deliver rather than on Conservative plans for improving public services. The party's own research showed that the general public reaction was 'so what?' The advertisements gave reasons for not voting Labour; they did not give reasons for voting Conservative.

Conservative strategists also denied that they had gone too far in emphasising the hazards of the euro. They held three press conferences on the subject, as many as they had on education, and the first was not held until 16 days into the campaign. The perceived emphasis came in fact from media anticipation that Europe and the euro would dominate the Conservative effort (fed before the campaign by Tory spin doctors), from journalists' questions at the press conferences, from background posters, from the election broadcasts, and from interviews with leading party figures. As shown elsewhere, Europe did figure prominently in media coverage – an emphasis that did not reflect the concerns of the public. A MORI poll for *The Economist* found that voters thought that taxes, Europe and asylum *would* be important in the election, although fewer voters thought that these *should* be important. By large margins they wanted the campaign to be about health and education. The Conservatives could claim some success in agenda-setting, in so far as Europe was the most heavily covered topic of the campaign by the media, but at the cost of making the party seem obsessive about it.

Perhaps the euro theme could have been better packaged. It was late in the campaign before spokespersons gave emphasis to connecting the issue with the British government's ability to determine its own levels of taxes and spending, and therefore funding public services. Until then, the stress was on constitutional objections to joining a common currency. The claim in the last week that the election was 'the last chance to save the pound' and, later on, 'the last *fair* chance' impressed few voters. Indeed the anti-euro group, Business for Sterling, protested at the suggestion that the election was a referendum on the euro, fearing that association with an unpopular Conservative Party would undermine the anti-euro case in the referendum, if and when one was held. Certainly, Conservatives could feel disappointed that the *Sun* was not more outraged over the speeches of Prodi and Jospin.

Finally, there was the issue of the carrier of the Conservative message, William Hague. Had he, as his critics claimed, deliberately moved the Conservative Party along the policy continuum to the tough rather than the tender end? What had happened to the socially liberal Hague of 1997–98? Some colleagues commented on the complexities of Hague's personality and even of there being two Hagues – the tolerant and internationalist coexisting with the more provincial and authoritarian (see p. 47). Three years earlier the 'kitchen table' document had commented on the voters' negative perception of Hague: 'People still don't have a clear impression of William Hague, what sort of person he is, his background or what he stands for … .' 'Look', said one of the Gang of Four, 'William is not a health and education man. He is more comfortable with crime, the euro and taxes.' Another close and admiring colleague said, 'It's a myth about liberal William. We saw the real William in the election. He is a genuine right-winger.' Another Shadow Cabinet minister simply shook his head and said that William's performance in the campaign, as well as over the two to three preceding years, was a tragic waste of a brilliant man. Although disappointed with the lack of progress since 1997, Hague remained unrepentant about the campaign and, soon after the outcome, told aides that 'the forces of Conservatism are on the march'.

William Hague and many other Conservatives had put great faith in his campaign to keep Britain out of the single currency. Indeed, this was his distinctive policy achievement as party leader and it was massively endorsed by the party members. His clear stand gained the public silence of leading Tory Europhiles like Kenneth Clarke, Michael Heseltine and Chris Patten. They were determined not to incur any of the blame for the impending defeat. Although Hague's policy was supported by some 70 per cent of the public, it was not an election winner and it failed even to gain the party the electoral endorsement of the Eurosceptic *Times* and *Sun*. In 1997 Eurosceptics had argued that the determination of voters to reject the Major government was so strong that it overrode other issues including hostility to the euro. This excuse was not available in 2001. For the second successive election the most Eurosceptic party suffered a landslide defeat.

If an issue is to cause large numbers of voters to switch between political parties it has to satisfy other tests than the public being unevenly divided in its views. The euro certainly passed that first test. Voters, however, also have to see clear differences between the parties or believe that they will make a difference in government. ICM found, extraordinarily, that at the end of the campaign after heavy media coverage of the issue, a majority of Conservative voters still did not recognise the official Conservative line (Table 12.5). As many thought that the party's policy involved never joining the euro (UKIP's position) as that it merely ruled out membership for the lifetime of the next Parliament. All this Conservative discussion about something that might or might not happen and did not connect with the immediate concerns of voters simply passed over voters' heads. Labour's promise to hold a referendum before entry was a more popular and understandable position.

In addition, for voters to be moved, they also have to regard the issue as very important. All surveys on the issues which voters rated as important placed the euro and the EU near the bottom of the list. Indeed, when a *Guardian* ICM poll, published on 31 May, showed that the euro was the last in importance in a list of 11 issues, Conservatives began to backtrack and discuss other issues. By this stage, the perceived Conservative emphasis on the euro as against neglect of the public services was becoming an 'issue in itself', as Hague privately acknowledged. The softness of voters' views on the issue was also found in an NOP poll which revealed that over half of the electorate would prefer to be in the euro under a Labour government as against a third who wanted to be out of it under a Conservative government.

Table 12.5   Perceptions of the Conservative position on the euro

	All %	Cons Voters %
(a) Save the £ and never join (UKIP)	39	36
(b) Rule out joining for lifetime of next Parliament (Con)	28	37
(c) When time is right hold a referendum and recommend joining (Lab)	26	23
(d) Refuse/Don't know	9	4

Source: ICM.

Academic research has emphasised that voters rarely decide their vote on a single issue, even a salient one. Issues get merged in questions of competence and trust in a political leader or political party. A Rasmussen poll in the *Independent* found that 44 per cent of voters felt that Tony Blair was telling the truth about the euro, while only 33 per cent felt that William Hague was telling the truth. These figures call into question the strength of the views of the 70 per cent who claimed to support his opposition to the common currency. Moreover, issues are never so clearly seen as political parties wish them to be seen. The opposition and the media provide their own gloss. Tax cuts – the Conservative position – were perceived by some voters as a threat to public services. Harsh action on asylum seekers was seen by others as a form of covert racism. Rejection of the euro mattered to Conservative core voters, and to the *Daily Mail* and *Daily Telegraph*. A *Sunday Business* poll on 10 June asked Conservative supporters why they supported the party. The most popular reason, mentioned by 52 per cent, was the party's stand on the euro. But it was either a bore or xenophobic for most others.

Voting is not simply an instrumental act ('what's good for me?'). It is also often in part expressive ('how do I feel about voting for this party?'). In the latter case support for a party or candidate is a statement of the voter's values and self-characterisation: was the party's tone likely to appeal to the swing voters? Would they feel comfortable with it? Stan Greenberg, who attended a number of Labour focus groups, was impressed by the voters' expression of strong concern about the euro and asylum, both Conservative issues. But he added:

> The people who raise these issues, and presumably agree with the Conservative position, still think the Conservatives are backward-looking, negative and intolerant. There is no narrative to link these concerns, and that is required in modern elections.

The 2001 election was the nearest approximation to a party seeming to fight a single issue election, since Ted Heath's February 1974 campaign in defence of his statutory incomes policy. That was similarly unsuccessful. Although the Conservative leaders had agreed the line on the euro they had not fully anticipated the extent to which the media would emphasise it and they would be seen as relegating other issues of interest to the voters. In the middle of the campaign, one senior strategist resignedly commented 'The election result will be a verdict on the strategy.' Another senior politician, close to Hague, bluntly said after 7 June: 'a good campaign fought on the wrong issues'. Hague and those responsible for the strategy remained unapologetic, arguing that it saved them an even heavier election defeat. In private, Hague commented, correctly, that an overall image of competence, trustworthiness, and unity were more important to voters than particular issues. 'It is more important who we are than what we say.' It would be equally true to say that over time what the party said would be what the party is. A close aide admitted: 'We never looked the part in the years before the election.'

The Liberal Democrats dispensed with elaborate telephone banks and frequent private opinion polls, largely because of financial constraints. Charles Kennedy attacked the Conservatives for extremism and Labour for timidity on public spending, the euro and constitutional reform. There was more bite in his criticisms of the Conservative Party; he hoped to squeeze the Labour vote in seats where the Liberal Democrats provided the incumbent or the runner-up to the Conservatives. With the party's best share of the vote since 1987 and its highest number of seats since 1929, Liberal Democrat strategists felt pleased. Certainly Kennedy, little known at the beginning of the campaign, improved his standing more than other party leaders. A Rasmussen poll in the *Independent* on 5 June showed that 37 per cent of voters had raised their approval of Kennedy in the past month and only 16 per cent had lowered it (a net improvement of 21 per cent). The scores for the other leaders actually fell – Blair's by 8 per cent and Hague's by 12 per cent.

But with so many voters unenthusiastic about the government and even more dissatisfied with the Conservative Party, perhaps the Liberal Democrats should have fared even better. The ambitious suggestions made in the last few days that the Liberal Democrats would replace the Conservatives as the main Opposition were hardly advanced by Kennedy positioning his party nationally to the left of Labour on tax and spend, on crime, and on asylum, and being more supportive of the euro and constitutional reform than Labour, even though this brought more votes from ex-Labour supporters. Presumably, the gap was on the centre-right of the political spectrum; attacking Labour from the left hardly made sense. Given the widespread complaints about the lack of ideological differences between the main two parties and the widespread dissatisfaction with them, claims that a vote for the Liberal Democrats would be a protest against the two main parties should have been popular. Some Liberal Democrats may look back upon 2001 as a wasted opportunity.

In Scotland and Wales the nationalist parties fell back from 1999. The devolved assemblies in Edinburgh and Cardiff diminished their role at Westminster. It was plain that devolution made the national government seem less relevant. More interesting was the failure of the Greens, UKIP and the Socialist Parties to make any significant impact. The list of saved deposits by minor parties on p. 301 tells its own story.

Inevitably, the conduct of the 2001 campaign must be considered in the context of the poor turnout. Had it encouraged apathy or at least failed to foster enough interest to overcome indifference? The public was perhaps becoming bored with the ritual of modern campaigns. The morning press conferences, the set-piece media interviews with prominent politicians, the party leaders' bus trips to encounters with voters (largely staged for the benefit of cameras), instant rebuttals and the speeches before invited and largely sympathetic audiences may now be past their sell-by date. The media devoted large resources to relaying the statements and positions of politicians and parties. They selected material and provided interpretation and contextualisation for the audiences. Increasingly, in all parts of the media, this was done in an unmasking or deconstructing manner. Many voters became, as a result, more informed but also more knowing or more cynical about the political process. They certainly seemed more disillusioned (or realistic) about all the parties. Table 12.6 shows that on such key questions as keeping promises, understanding the problems facing Britain and representing all classes, the parties have been in a downward spiral between 1992 and 1997, and 1997 and 2001.

Table 12.6   **Changing party images 1992–2001**

	Con			Lab			LibDem		
	1992 %	1997 %	2001 %	1992 %	1997 %	2001 %	1992 %	1997 %	2001 %
Understands the problems facing Britain	38	20	18	40	37	28	43	23	22
Keeps its promises	20	5	5	13	9	9	11	6	6
Concerned about the people in real need in Britain	18	8	9	49	36	21	43	21	19
Represents all classes	20	10	8	28	31	24	46	27	21
Looks after the interests of people like us	21	9	11	34	30	21	23	13	11
Has sensible policies	31	14	15	30	27	27	42	25	27
Has a good team of leaders	35	10	7	29	25	25	23	12	8

Source: MORI

In 2001, as always, the politicians were determined to stick to their own agenda. The cost lay in the narrowing of issues that were discussed and in the selection of the spokespersons who appeared before the public. Foreign affairs, defence, local government, environment, Northern Ireland, constitutional changes and transport were hardly touched on. As the parties concentrated more of their campaign resources on target voters in marginal seats, so the campaign by-passed much of the electorate. Turnout fell everywhere outside Northern Ireland. Modern campaigners pride themselves on running campaigns like scientific marketing operations. Winning sufficient numbers of target voters in the hundred or so key seats, which will decide the overall result, is more important than maximising total vote across the country. Themes, media coverage, polling, canvassing, communications and allocation of the leader's time and visits, are all subject to this rule. 'We didn't want an exciting campaign', said one Labour strategist. The stage has been reached where it appears that more and more effort is precisely targeted at less and less of the electorate. The approach is encouraged by the first-past-the-post electoral system. Turnout in the 2001 election offers a fundamental indictment of modern campaigning under the present electoral arrangements and public communication system.

13
Landslide Again

Each general election has a place in history, confirming or changing the direction of politics. Because the 2001 contest produced so little alteration in the composition of the House of Commons and appeared as almost a replay of 1997, it could be classed as a mere punctuation mark in a continuing narrative. But it had a far-reaching impact on morale and thinking in each of the parties, shaping the attitudes and career prospects of leaders and of MPs. For the third successive general election, the man at the head of the losing party resigned immediately after the result was known.

Each general election campaign acquires a rhythm of its own, imprinting images and lessons in the memory both of the Westminster elites and of the mass electorate. The striking images of 2001 – the Prescott punch and the Thatcher 'Never' – may have been few but the lessons of tax and spend ('you can't have something for nothing'), and the failure of attempts to excite the British public for or against the euro, were reiterated and must leave their mark on political thinking in the years before the next election.

Labour achieved a second term of office in another landslide and the Conservatives suffered another heavy defeat. There was only a small swing (1.8 per cent) to the Conservative Party and it made a net gain of only 1 seat. Labour's majority over all other parties was cut by a mere 12 and by 7 over the Conservatives. Only 21 out of 641 seats in mainland Britain changed hands. The Liberal Democrats gained 6 seats and Labour lost 6. In Northern Ireland, however, 7 of the 18 seats changed hands, with far-reaching implications for the politics of the province.

John Curtice and Michael Steed in Appendix II emphasise the degree to which the first-past-the-post-system exaggerated Labour's victory in terms of seats. The landslides of 1945 and 1983 were won by a larger margin in vote share than Labour achieved in 2001, but they produced smaller margins of victory in seats. Their most notable findings include:

1. Conservative hostility to the euro and their less socially liberal platform played best in constituencies with large proportions of the elderly and those who are less well educated.
2. New Labour lost support most heavily in the party's traditionally safe working-class constituencies. The level of class voting in Britain appears to have reached a new low.
3. The Liberal Democrats appear to have benefited both from antipathy to the Conservative's social liberalism and from New Labour's loss of working-class support.
4. Turnout fell heavily across Great Britain but the decline was less in seats which were marginal or where there was a strong Liberal Democrat or minor party presence or where there were above average numbers of elderly or well-educated voters.
5. All parties did particularly well in seats they were defending, thereby helping to bring about a record low in the number of seats that changed hands. In Labour's case, targeted local campaigning in its most marginal seats appeared to have encouraged tactical voting by Liberal Democrats.
6. MPs of all parties continue to be able to establish a personal vote on the basis of their local reputation. In particular, this helped many Liberal Democrat MPs first elected in 1997 to turn their seats into safe ones.
7. The advent of devolution made little impact on party fortunes in Scotland and Wales. The Nationalist vote fell back sharply from the 1999 votes for the new assemblies.
8. The electoral system, already significantly biased in Labour's favour in 1997, became still more biased in 2001. Labour gained an even greater premium from the concentration of its vote in seats with declining populations and lower turnouts, while a rise in the third-party support in Labour-held constituencies further cut their vote without costing them seats effectively made them even smaller.

It will reduce the over-representation of Scotland but will not affect the bias due to the low turnouts in Labour strongholds. The review of parliamentary boundaries currently in progress can have only a modest impact on reversing this bias.

The British party system is once again highly uncompetitive in terms of parliamentary seats. A one-sided party situation in the 1980s was succeeded by a different pattern in 1997 that was confirmed in 2001. Thanks in part to the working of the electoral system, Labour has now been able to replace the Conservatives as the dominant party. And a lopsided House of Commons has consequences, largely deleterious, for the working of Parliament, for the accountability of the executive, and for political debate.

"It says The End" said William, wistfully

Ancram–Hague

John Kent, *The Times*, 9 June 2001

In the last three general elections the voting system has been significantly biased against the Conservatives. Labour was helped by the over-representation of Scotland and Wales in terms of electorate. Labour's 42 per cent of the UK vote produced over 63 per cent of seats. It gains a premium from its seats in the inner cities and industrial areas, which have declining populations and lower turnouts, and the Conservatives suffer from doing well in rural and outer suburban seats. In 1997, because of these factors, Labour seats contained some 5,200 fewer electors than Conservative seats. The gap increased in 2001 to 6,400.[1]

In Appendix 2, John Curtice and Michael Steed show that for the Conservatives and Labour to have equal numbers of seats, the Conservatives now need an 8.3 per cent lead in votes. For the Conservatives to win a clear majority they would have to be 11.5 per cent ahead. An equal number of votes for the parties would still give Labour an overall majority of 79 seats and a lead of 140 MPs over the Conservatives. This bias was exacerbated by Lib–Lab tactical voting against the Conservatives which helped Labour to retain its own marginal seats, as it did in capturing Conservative marginals in 1992 and 1997. In both cases a squeeze on LibDem support was important.

Labour also gained from an incumbency effect. It increased its percentage vote in seats which it gained in 1997 and the new Labour MPs stood again in 2001. The bias is due to be slightly reduced when in due course the Boundary Commission is expected to cut the number of Scottish seats in the House of Commons by a dozen or so.

Tony Blair declared that he regarded the election result as an 'instruction' to proceed with the reform of the public services. During the election, a skeleton staff in Number 10, following the Millbank slogan, 'The work goes on', prepared for the second term. On the day after the election a new Cabinet was announced (in which only nine of the outgoing ministers retained their old positions), as well as a restructuring of government departments, and a new set of institutions in Number 10 and the Cabinet Office, designed to help achieve better delivery of improved public services. Blair had often told critics who urged him to be more radical, 'Wait till the second term.'

There was some disagreement among Conservatives over whether the result was better or even worse than the 1997 disaster. The architects of the campaign pointed to gains, but these were minute when set against the scale of the electoral challenge. The party's landslide defeat in 1945 was followed by a narrow miss in 1950; the 1966 landslide defeat by victory in 1970. Both defeats had followed immediately or soon after long periods of Conservative electoral ascendancy; 2001 marks the first time the Conservative Party lost by landslides in consecutive general elections. The non-Labour Party alternatives were now divided between Conservative, Liberal Democrats, Nationalists and Northern Ireland Parties. Only the Ulster Unionists would be possible – if unreliable – Conservative allies. The 8.3 million total of votes was the lowest the Tory Party has achieved since 1929, when there was a much smaller electorate.

Conservative electoral successes over the twentieth century were in large part due to the party's willingness to adapt to changing circumstances – universal suffrage, the welfare state, the decline of the empire and the rise of powerful trade unions – and to embrace some of the more popular policies of other parties. In 2001 the Conservatives clearly misjudged the public mood. Their approach to Europe and the euro came across as carping and obsessive rather than constructive. On tax cuts and spending on public services, they ended up with the worst of both worlds; most voters while not believing that taxes would be reduced under Labour, equally did not believe that services would improve under the Conservative Party. Tony Blair and Gordon Brown could reflect that this was the first election for over a generation in which the tax-cutting party lost out to the party advocating greater spending on public services. Anti-Conservative tactical voting by Liberal Democrats was partly a reaction to the policy positions taken by the Conservatives on taxation, constitutional reform and the European Union.

The fragmentation of the party system, begun in the early 1970s, continued. The two main parties once again polled less than 75 per cent of the total vote; 10 parties were represented in the House of Commons and 80 MPs were drawn from parties other than Labour or Conservative, the highest number since 1923. The winding-up of the Referendum Party did little to help UKIP, which polled only 1.5 per cent of the vote. Conservatives expected to regain seats like Hastings and Harwich, which were lost in 1997 because, they thought, of Referendum intervention; in the event these seats actually swung to Labour. This was further evidence that voters did not attach the same importance to the EU as party leaders hoped. The Greens increased their vote but only from 0.4 per cent to 0.6 per cent of the total vote or 2.8 per cent per candidate. The Liberal Democrats advanced in votes and in seats, so reversing their steady decline in vote share since 1983. But their 19 per cent was still less than the 25 per cent gained by the Alliance in 1983. Although the Liberal Democrats still continued to suffer from the electoral system, they did manage to distribute their vote more efficiently in terms of gaining seats. John Curtice and Michael Steed note how many more of the LibDem seats have become less marginal: only one in four was held by a majority of less than 5 per cent. Tactical voting by Liberal Democrats remained important in punishing the Conservative Party and in helping Labour in marginal seats.

The Nationalists in Scotland made no progress in the first post-devolution general election, securing 9 per cent less of the vote than in the 1999 election for the Scottish Parliament. In Wales, Plaid Cymru added 4 per cent to its 10 per cent share in 1997 but fell back 16 per cent from its triumph in the 1999 Assembly contest and made no net gain in seats. Thanks in part to the nearly proportional electoral system, the devolution elections in 1999 produced multi-party systems in the new Scottish and Welsh legislatures, and saw Nationalists emerge as the largest opposition force to Labour. An ICM Scottish Poll conducted on 6 June showed that many Scots distinguished between votes for Westminster and for the Edinburgh Parliament. It found that SNP support in the Westminster election was 11 per cent lower than it would have been in an election for the Scottish Parliament. Scotland was no longer a Tory-free zone, following the party's capture of Galloway from the Nationalists. But the Conservatives were within striking distance of gaining only one other seat and, with just 16 per cent of the vote they became the fourth party, trailing both the Nationalists and the Liberal Democrats. The Conservative's share of the Scottish vote fell by 2 per cent, compared to a 1.5 per cent increase south of the border.

Once more, a general election in Northern Ireland took place in a world of its own. No mainland party had a serious presence there. Ian Paisley's Democratic Unionist Party strengthened its position at the expense of David Trimble's Ulster Unionist Party, and Gerry Adams' Sinn Féin did so at the expense of John Hume's SDLP. The results were widely regarded as a mark of growing polarisation in the Province and as making prospects for the peace settlement even more difficult. Strikingly, it was the only region to register an increase in turnout. Apathy was not a problem in the province because there were passionate issues at stake.

The election confirmed Labour's new appeal to the middle class and in south-east England. Both these expanding groups were crucial targets for Blair when he became Labour leader in 1994. The strategy worked in 1997, and again in 2001. Labour had nearly as much middle-class support as the Conservative Party. Now that the working class is a clear minority, class-based voting would have been a disaster for Labour. The result in 2001 showed the lowest ever gap in the traditional divide between middle-class Conservative and working-class Labour (Table 13.1). The Conservatives outscored Labour only among the home owners, middle class and over-55s, and especially among the over-65s. Across other age groups and social class groups, the voters' verdict on the party was negative (Table 13.2).

Perhaps the most notable feature of the election was the huge drop in voting. Turnout fell everywhere and the overall figure of 59.3 per cent was the lowest since 1918.[2] In every region except for Northern Ireland, the fall was between 11.6 per cent and 13.1 per cent. In Northern Ireland it actually increased by 0.6 per cent. As usual, the closeness of the constituency result affected the willingness to vote but turnout still fell 10 per cent in marginal seats, not much less than the 13 per cent in safe seats. The 71 per cent participation in 1997 was itself a record low for almost 80 years. Many people now have acquired the habit of not voting, particularly in Labour's safe seats. The electorate was not enthusiastic about endorsing Labour, but it was even more reluctant to endorse the main alternative party. The lack of support for politicians and parties and the low turnout made it something of a grudging landslide for Tony Blair. Although the second Labour term was an historic achievement, there was none of the euphoria which accompanied the party's victories in 1945 and 1997.

Table 13.1 Changes in class voting (Conservative % lead over Labour)

	Oct 74	*1983*	*1992*	*1997*	*2001*
A B C1	+37	+39	+32	+5	+4
C2	−23	+8	−1	−23	−20
D E	−35	−8	−18	−38	−31

Source: MORI

Table 13.2   Social characteristics of GB voters (%) (change from 1997)

	Conservative	*Labour*	*LibDem.*	*Turnout*
All G.B. voters	33(+2)	42(−2)	19(+2)	59
Men	32(+1)	42(−3)	18(+1)	61
Women	33(+1)	42(−2)	19(+1)	58
AB	39(−2)	30(−1)	25(+2)	68
C1	36(−1)	38(−1)	20(+2)	60
C2	29(+2)	49(−1)	15(−1)	56
DE	24(+3)	55(−4)	13 (0)	53
18–24	27 (0)	41(−8)	24(+8)	39
25–34	24(−4)	51(+2)	19(+3)	46
35–44	28 (0)	45(−3)	19(+2)	59
45–54	32(+1)	41 (0)	20.(0)	65
55–64	39(+3)	37(−2)	17 (0)	69
65+	40(+4)	39(−2)	17 (0)	70
Home-owners	43(+)	32 (0)	19(−1)	68
Council Tenants	18(+3)	60(−4)	14(+2)	52
Trade Unionists	21(+)	50(−7)	19(+1)	63

Source: MORI

There was an agonised response from politicians and the media at the turning-off of public interest. It was generally recognised that the only way for voter involvement to be seriously resuscitated would be for the contest to be more competitive; it would also help if the campaign dealt with issues to which alternative answers are being offered and that mattered to an audience that is now guided less and less by old-standing party loyalties.

Thought was also given by the Electoral Commission to technical ways of making participation easier. Their research emphasised the extent of involuntary abstention: the large number who said they would have voted had they been able to, with many claiming that the election came at an inconvenient time, or they were away on polling day or they were not registered. But there is no reason to suppose that the difficulties were any greater than in 1997 when 12 per cent more cast ballots. If this involuntary abstention has increased so suddenly when changes to election law allowed more electors to vote by post and registration for people who move homes was also speeded up, it may be due to serious imperfections in the register. But the fall from 1997 still demands explanation. Several factors can be offered for the decline.

- The result was a foregone conclusion. Every published poll gave Labour a lead by from 11 to 28 per cent. Why bother to vote?
- The election was presented by the media as boring. Was there anything to stir voters to action?
- The campaign was less active, especially in the non-targeted seats (three-quarters of the total). The numbers receiving leaflets or other partisan stimuli fell (see Table 11.1 on p. 214). Was it easy to forget that 7 June was polling day?
- The result seemed less important than before. The ICM/BBC poll found that among those 'unlikely to vote', 77 per cent did not mind who won. In 1992, 86 per cent told MORI that they saw the outcome as 'very' or 'fairly' important; in 1997 the figure was 79 per cent and in 2001 66 per cent. Did people mind who won?
- The status of politics and politicians continued to decline. MORI found Labour with a +2 rating on keeping its promises in 1997, a −23 rating in 2001. Are they all the same?
- The sense that there is a difference between the parties has fallen (poll figures). Many Labour and Conservative voters felt neither enthused nor threatened by the choice between the two main parties. Will the outcome have any impact on how life goes on?
- The attachment to political parties has declined. On the eve of the 1997 election 75 per cent told MORI that they felt strongly or fairly strongly attached to their party. In 2001 the figure was 70 per cent. How many people mind who wins?

The parties spent less nationally in 2001 than in 1997. Under the new rules, administered by the Electoral Commission, each party was permitted to spend up to £14.5 million (Chapter 11 discusses local spending). The full figures, which were due to be published by the Electoral Commission at the end of 2001, show the exact amounts spent nationally (and in each constituency). Early estimates of national expenditure suggested that Labour spent between £12 million and £13 million, the Conservatives £9 million, the Liberal Democrats £2.5 million, and the UKIP between £1 million and £1.5 million.

It is difficult to assess the significance of one striking general election result. Will it mark a new trend or be a short-lived departure from normal politics? A general election outcome may set the scene for the next Parliament but it does not determine the following general elections. Who now recalls how improbable another Labour victory looked after its third successive defeat in 1959, or its fourth in 1992? Social changes seemed to be setting Labour at a disadvantage. Today, the electoral system is significantly biased against the Conservative Party. But shocks like the winter of discontent in 1979 or like the 1992 ERM disaster, let alone the strategic judgements and misjudgements of political leaders, can still shake voters out of their established loyalties.

Critical elections are marked by an enduring realignment of the party system, in the shape of new bases of support for the parties or a significant shift in the balance between them; 1945 and 1979 are often regarded as critical elections. Over the four elections from 1979 to 1992 the Conservatives enjoyed an average 10 per cent lead over Labour in the share of the popular vote. In the 1997 and 2001 elections Labour averaged an 11 per cent lead over the Conservatives making especially big inroads among the middle class and in the South East. Because 2001 confirms so many of the realigning trends of 1997 we may also regard it as reflecting the creation of a new electoral landscape.

Note

1. J. Curtice, 'General Election 2001: repeat or revolution?' *Politics Review*, vol. 11, Sept 2001, pp. 2–5.
2. The 57.1 per cent in 1918 was much cited but in that year there was much post-war confusion. The electorate had jumped from the 8m of 1910 to 21m. Less than a third of the electorate had ever voted in a parliamentary contest. Women had the franchise for the first time. The register was compiled in a new way by unpracticed hands and there was some administrative chaos over the forces vote.

Appendix 1: The Voting Statistics

Table A1.1 Votes and seats 1945–2001 (seats in italics)

	Electorate and turnout	Total votes cast	Conservative[1]	Labour	Liberals[2]	Welsh & Scottish Nationalists	Communist	Others (mainly N. Ireland)
1945[3]	73.3% 32 836 419	100%–640 24 082 612	39.8%–213 9 577 667	48.3%–393 11 632 191	9.1%–12 2 197 191	0.2% 46 612	0.4%–2 102 760	2.1%–20 525 491
1950	84.0% 34 269 770	100%–625 28 772 671	43.5%–299 12 502 567	46.1%–315 13 266 592	9.1%–9 2 621 548	0.1% 27 288	0.3% 91 746	0.9%–2 262 930
1951	82.5% 34 645 573	100%–625 28 595 668	48.%–321 13 717 538	48.8%–295 13 948 605	2.5%–6 730 556	0.1% 18 219	0.1% 21 640	0.5%–3 159 110
1955	76.8% 34 858 263	100%–630 26 760 493	49.7%–345 13 311 936	46.4%–277 12 404 970	2.7%–6 722 405	0.2% 57 231	0.1% 33 144	0.8%–2 230 807
1959	78.7% 35 397 080	100%–630 27 859 241	49.4%–365 13 749 830	43.8%–258 12 215 538	5.9%–6 1 638 571	0.4% 99 309	0.1% 30 897	0.5%–1 145 090
1964	77.1% 35 892 572	100%–630 27 655 374	43.4%–304 12 001 396	44.1%–317 12 205 814	11.2%–9 3 092 878	0.5% 133 551	0.2% 45 932	0.6% 169 431
1966	75.8% 35 964 684	100%–630 27 263 606	41.9%–253 11 418 433	47.9%–363 13 064 951	8.5%–12 2 327 533	0.7% 189 545	0.2% 62 112	0.7%–2 201 032
1970	72.0% 39 342 013	100%–630 28 344 798	46.4%–330 13 145 123	43.%–288 12 178 295	7.5%–6 2 117 033	1.3%–1 381 819	0.1% 37 970	1.7%–5 486 557
Feb. '74	78.1% 39 770 724	100%–635 31 340 162	37.8%–297 11 872 180	37.1%–301 11 646 391	19.3%–14 6 058 744	2.6%–9 804 554	0.1% 32 743	3.1%–14 958 293
Oct. '74	72.8% 40 072 971	100%–635 29 189 178	35.8%–277 10 464 817	39.2%–319 11 457 079	18.3%–13 5 346 754	3.5%–14 1 005 938	0.1% 17 426	3.1%–12 897 164

	Electorate and turnout	Total votes cast	Conservative[1]	Labour	Liberals[2]	Welsh & Scottish Nationalists	Greens	Others (mainly N. Ireland)
1979	76.0% / 41 093 264	100%–635 / 31 221 361	43.9%–339 / 13 697 923	37.%–269 / 11 532 218	13.8%–11 / 4 313 804	2.%–4 / 636 890	0.1% / 38 116	3.2%–12 / 1 001 447
1983	72.7% / 42 197 344	100%–650 / 30 671 136	42.4%–397 / 13 012 315	27.6%–209 / 8 456 934	25.4%–23 / 7 780 949	1.5%–4 / 457 676	0.2% / 53 848	2.9%–17 / 90. 875
1987	75.3% / 43 181 321	100%–650 / 32 536 137	42.3%–376 / 13 763 066	30.8%–229 / 10 029 778	22.6%–22 / 7 341 290	1.7%–6 / 543 559	0.3% / 89 753	2.3%–17 / 762 615
1992	77.7% / 43 249 721	100%–651 / 33 612 693	41.9%–336 / 14 092 891	34.4%–271 / 11 559 735	17.8%–20 / 5 999 384	2.3%–7 / 783 991	0.5% / 171 927	3.%–17 / 1 004 765
1997	71.5% / 43 757 478	100%–659 / 31 286 597	30.7%–165 / 9 602 857	43.2%–418 / 13 516 632	16.8%–46 / 5 242 894	2.5%–10 / 782 570	0.2% / 63 991	6.6%–20 / 2 077 653
2001	59.4% / 44 403 238	100%–659 / 26 368 798	31.7%–166 / 8 357 622	40.7%–412 / 10 724 895	18.3%–52 / 4 812 833	2.5%–9 / 660 197	0.6% / 166 487	6.2%–20 / 1 646 764[4]

Notes:

1. Includes Ulster Unionists 1945–70.
2. Liberals 1945–79; Liberal–SDP Alliance 1983–87; Liberal Democrats 1992–
3. The 1945 figures exclude university seats and are adjusted for double counting in the 15 two-member seats.
4. Other results for 2001 include:

Party	Votes	% Share	Av vote %	Candidates	Lost Deposits	Party	Votes	% Share	Av vote %	Candidates	Lost Deposits
UK Independence	390 575	1.5%	2.1	428	422	British National	47 129	0.2%	3.9	33	28
Greens	166 487	0.6%	2.8	145	135	Liberal	10 920	0.0%	3.2	9	8
Scottish Socialist	72 279	0.3%	3.3	72	62	ProLife Alliance	9 453	0.0%	0.7	37	37
Socialist Alliance	60 496	0.2%	1.8	98	95						
Socialist Labour	57 536	0.2%	1.4	114	113	Independent	127 590	0.5%	2.2	139	128

Table A1.2   Regional results 2001

UNITED KINGDOM

	Seats won in 2001 (change since 1997)				Share of votes cast 2001 (percent change since 1997)					
	Conservative	Labour	LibDem	Nat & Other	Turnout	Conservative	Labour	LibDem	Nationalists	Other
England	165	323 (-6)	40 (+6)	1	59.1 (-12.1)	35.2 (+1.5)	41.4 (-2.2)	19.4 (+1.5)	–	3.9 (-0.8)
South	106	106 (-2)	30 (+2)	–	60.3 (-11.6)	38.4 (+0.9)	34.6 (-0.9)	22.8 (+1.0)	–	4.2 (-1.0)
Midlands	42	78 (-4)	4 (+3)	1 (+1)	60.3 (-12.0)	37.1 (+2.0)	43.2 (-2.9)	15.8 (+1.3)	–	3.9 (-0.5)
North	17	139	6 (+1)	– (-1)	56.3 (-13.0)	28.2 (+1.9)	51.5 (-3.4)	16.9 (+2.2)	–	3.4 (-0.7)
Wales	–	34	2	4	61.6 (-11.9)	21.0 (+1.5)	48.6 (-6.1)	13.8 (+1.4)	14.3 (+4.3)	2.3 (-1.1)
Scotland	1 (+1)	56	10	5 (-1)	58.2 (-13.1)	15.6 (-1.9)	43.9 (-1.6)	16.4 (+3.4)	20.1 (-2.0)	4.0 (+2.1)
Great Britain	166 (+1)	413 (-6)	52 (+6)	10 (-1)	59.2 (-12.2)	32.7 (+1.2)	42.0 (-2.4)	18.8 (+1.7)	2.6	3.9 (-0.5)
Northern Ireland*	–	–	–	18	67.8 (+0.6)	0.3 (-0.9)	–	–	–	99.7 (+0.9)
United Kingdom	166 (+1)	413 (-6)	52 (+6)	28 (-1)	59.4 (-12.1)	31.7 (+1.0)	40.7 (-2.5)	18.3 (+1.5)	2.5	6.8

REGIONS

	Seats won in 2001 (change since 1997)				Share of votes cast 2001 (percent change since 1997)					
	Conservative	Labour	LibDem	Nat & Other	Turnout	Conservative	Labour	LibDem	Nationalist	Other
South East	86 (+2)	90 (-3)	15 (+1)	–	59.1 (-12.1)	38.4 (+0.6)	37.1 (-1.0)	20.2 (+1.2)	–	4.3 (-0.8)
Greater London*	13 (+2)	55 (-2)	6	–	55.2 (-11.7)	30.5 (-0.7)	47.3 (-2.1)	17.5 (+2.9)	–	4.7
Inner London	2	23	1	–	50.3 (-10.6)	22.8 (-1.4)	53.5 (-3.6)	17.2 (+4.4)	–	6.4 (+0.6)
Outer London	11 (+2)	32 (-2)	5	–	57.9 (-12.2)	34.1 (-0.3)	44.4 (-1.5)	17.6 (+2.2)	–	3.8 (-0.4)
Rest of S.E.	73	35 (-1)	9 (+1)	–	61.3 (-12.3)	42.6 (+1.2)	31.7 (-0.2)	21.6 (+0.2)	–	4.1 (-1.2)
Outer Met. Area	42	19 (-1)	1 (+1)	–	60.8 (-12.9)	43.6 (+1.1)	33.0 (-0.2)	19.4 (+0.3)	–	4.0 (-1.2)
Outer S.E.	31	16	8	–	61.8 (-11.7)	41.5 (+1.4)	30.2 (-0.2)	24.0 (+0.1)	–	4.3 (-1.3)
South West*	20 (-2)	16 (+1)	15 (+1)	–	64.9 (-10.0)	38.5 (+1.8)	26.3 (-1.5)	31.2 (-0.1)	–	4.0 (-1.5)
Devon & Cornwall	4 (-1)	4	8 (+1)	–	65.5 (-9.5)	37.0 (+2.2)	21.6 (-1.5)	36.0 (+0.7)	–	5.4 (-1.4)
Rest of S.W.	16 (-1)	12 (+1)	7	–	64.6 (-10.2)	39.3 (+1.6)	28.5 (+0.5)	28.9 (-0.5)	–	3.3 (-1.6)
East Anglia	14	7 (-1)	1 (+1)	–	63.7 (-10.6)	41.7 (+3.0)	35.8 (-2.5)	19.0 (+1.1)	–	3.5 (-1.6)
East Midlands*	15 (+1)	28 (-2)	1 (+1)	–	60.9 (-12.3)	37.3 (+2.4)	45.1 (-2.8)	15.4 (+1.8)	–	2.2 (-1.5)
West Midlands*	13 (-1)	43 (-1)	2 (+1)	1 (+1)	58.5 (-12.4)	35.0 (+1.2)	44.8 (-3.0)	14.7 (+0.9)	–	5.5 (+0.8)
W. Mids. Met. Co.	4	25	–	–	54.6 (-12.8)	30.6 (+0.8)	51.3 (-2.0)	13.1 (+1.7)	–	5.1 (-0.5)
Rest of W. Mids.	9 (-1)	18	2 (+1)	–	61.8 (-12.2)	39.3 (+2.1)	40.3 (-2.5)	16.6 (+0.5)	–	3.7 (-0.1)
Yorks & the Humber*	7	47	2	–	56.7 (-11.6)	30.2 (+2.3)	48.6 (-3.3)	17.1 (+1.1)	–	4.0 (-0.1)
S. Yorks Met. Co.	–	14	1	–	52.4 (-11.7)	18.8 (+2.1)	58.9 (-3.3)	18.0 (+1.4)	–	4.2 (-0.2)
W. Yorks Met. Co.	–	23	–	–	56.6 (-12.5)	30.0 (+1.2)	51.5 (-2.5)	14.0 (+1.0)	–	4.5 (+0.3)
Rest of Yorks & Humb	7	10	1	–	60.0 (-10.4)	38.2 (+3.1)	38.1 (-3.8)	20.3 (+1.0)	–	3.4 (-0.4)

	Seats				Votes %					
	Con	Lab	LibDem	Nat	Turnout	Con	Lab	LibDem	Nat	Other
North West	7	60	3	—	55.3 (−14.6)	28.3 (+1.2)	51.8 (−2.4)	16.5 (+2.2)	—	3.4 (−1.0)
Gtr. Manchr. Met. Co.	1 (−1)	25	2 (+1)	—	52.9 (−15.0)	24.3 (+0.2)	53.7 (−2.7)	18.3 (+2.2)	—	3.7 (+0.3)
Merseyside Met. Co.	—	15	1	—	51.8 (−15.8)	20.1 (+0.3)	58.7 (−3.1)	17.8 (+3.3)	—	3.4 (−0.5)
Rest of N.W.	6 (+1)	20 (−1)	—	—	60.1 (−13.3)	35.3 (+1.4)	45.5 (−2.6)	13.6 (+1.3)	—	5.5 (−0.1)
Northern	3	32	3	—	57.6 (−11.8)	24.6 (+2.5)	55.7 (−5.2)	17.1 (+3.9)	—	2.5 (−1.2)
Tyne & Wear Met. Co.	—	13	1	—	53.3 (−12.2)	17.7 (+0.4)	62.9 (−4.2)	16.6 (+4.8)	—	2.8 (−1.0)
Rest of Northern	3	19	2	—	60.0 (−11.6)	28.1 (+3.4)	52.1 (−5.5)	17.4 (+3.4)	—	2.4 (−1.2)
Wales*	—	34	2	4	61.6 (−11.9)	21.0 (+1.5)	48.6 (−6.1)	13.8 (+1.4)	14.3 (+4.3)	2.3 (−1.1)
Industrial S. Wales	—	24	2	—	60.1 (−12.2)	18.1 (+0.8)	55.5 (−7.3)	12.4 (+1.8)	11.4 (+5.7)	2.6 (−0.9)
Rural Wales	—	10	—	4	64.1 (−11.4)	25.6 (+2.4)	37.7 (−4.0)	16.0 (+0.8)	18.9 (+2.1)	1.8 (−1.3)
Scotland*	1 (+1)	56	10	5 (−1)	58.2 (−13.1)	15.6 (−1.9)	43.9 (−1.6)	16.4 (+3.4)	20.1 (−2.0)	4.0 (+2.1)
Central Clydeside	—	23	—	—	54.7 (−13.9)	10.4 (−1.4)	55.5 (−2.5)	10.3 (+2.9)	18.1 (−2.0)	5.7 (+2.9)
Rest of Ind. Belt	—	25	1	—	59.3 (−13.7)	15.3 (−2.2)	48.7 (−2.4)	13.4 (+3.6)	18.7 (−1.6)	3.8 (+2.6)
Highlands	—	2	4	—	60.9 (−9.7)	14.2 (+0.3)	27.5 (−1.1)	33.3 (+1.7)	21.4 (−2.2)	3.7 (+1.3)
Rest of Scotland	1 (+1)	6	5	5 (−1)	60.1 (−12.1)	22.4 (−2.8)	27.6 (+0.9)	23.5 (+3.9)	24.0 (−2.8)	2.4 (+0.7)

Notes: The English Regions are the eight *Standard Regions* as they were defined by the Office of Population Censuses and Surveys (OPCS, now Office for National Statistics).

The *Outer Metropolitan Area* comprises those seats wholly or mostly in the Outer Metropolitan Area as defined by the ONS. It includes: the whole of Surrey and Hertfordshire; the whole of Berkshire except Newbury; and the constituencies of Arundel & South Downs; Crawley; Horsham; Mid-Sussex (West Sussex); Aldershot; Hampshire North–East (Hampshire); Chatham & Aylesford; Dartford; Faversham & Mid Kent; Gillingham; Gravesham; Maidstone & The Weald; Medway; Sevenoaks; Tonbridge and Malling; Tunbridge Wells (Kent); Beaconsfield; Chesham & Amersham; Wycombe (Buckinghamshire); Bedfordshire South–West; Luton North; Luton South (Bedfordshire); Basildon; Billericay; Brentwood & Ongar; Castle Point; Chelmsford West; Epping Forest; Harlow; Rayleigh; Rochford & Southend East; Southend West; Thurrock (Essex).

Industrial Wales includes Gwent, the whole of Glamorgan, and the Llanelli constituency in Dyfed.

The *Central Clydeside Conurbation* includes those seats wholly or mostly in the Central Clydeside Conurbation as defined by the Registrar-General (Scotland). It comprises the whole of the Strathclyde region except the following constituencies: Argyll & Bute; Ayr; Carrick; Clydesdale; Cunninghame South; Greenock & Inverclyde.

The *Rest of Industrial Belt* comprises the regions of Central; Fife (except Fife North–East); and Lothian.

The *Highlands* comprises the following constituencies: Argyll & Bute; Caithness, Sutherland & Easter Ross; Inverness East, Nairn & Lochaber; Orkney & Shetland; Ross, Skye & Inverness West; the Western Isles.

In all but four cases the European Parliament constituencies are covered in the table above. These constituencies are indicated with an asterisk(*). The results for the four other European Parliament constituencies are:

Constituency	Seats			Votes %			
	Con	Lab	LibDem	Con	Lab	LibDem	Other
South East	53	22	8	42.9	29.4	23.7	4.1
Eastern	34	20	2	41.8	36.8	17.5	3.9
North West	9	64	3	29.3	50.7	16.7	3.3
North East	1	28	1	21.3	59.4	16.7	2.6

Table A1.3   Constituency results, Great Britain 2001

This table lists the votes in each constituency in percentage terms.

The constituencies are listed alphabetically within counties (except that in Greater London the constituencies are listed alphabetically within each borough).

The figure in the 'Other' column is the total percentage received by all the 'Other' candidates – except the UKIP, the Green Party, Socialist Labour, and the Socialist Alliance, which are listed separately for seats in England and Wales. In Scotland the Scottish Socialist Party's result is given in place of those of the Socialist Alliance.

† denotes a seat won by different parties in 1997 and 2001

‡ denotes a seat that changed hands at a by-election between 1997 and 2001

* denotes seat held by the Speaker in either 1997 or 2001

Swing is given in the conventional (or 'Butler') form – the average of the Conservative % gain and the Labour % loss (measured as % of the total poll). It is only reported for those seats where those parties occupied the top two places in 1997 and 2001. This is the practice followed by all the Nuffield studies since 1955.

ENGLAND	% Voting	Change in voting 1997–2001	% Con	Con change 1997–2001	% Lab	Lab change 1997–2001	% LibDem	LibDem change 1997–2001	% Green	% UKIP	% Socialist Labour	% Socialist Alliance	% Other	Swing
Avon, Bath	64.9	−10.7	29.1	−2.1	15.7	−0.7	50.5	+2.0	3.2	1.5	–	–	–	–
Bristol East	57.4	−12.3	21.8	−1.6	55.0	−1.9	17.1	+2.4	2.8	1.4	1.1	0.8	–	+0.2
North-West	60.6	−12.7	28.7	−0.6	52.1	+2.2	15.9	+2.7	–	2.5	0.8	–	–	−1.4
South	56.5	−12.2	22.3	+1.1	56.9	−3.1	14.8	+1.4	3.0	1.2	0.6	1.2	–	+2.1
West	65.6	−7.1	28.8	−4.0	36.8	+1.6	28.9	+0.9	3.5	0.9	1.1	–	–	–
Kingswood	65.4	−12.3	28.4	−1.6	54.9	+1.1	14.7	+1.9	–	2.1	–	–	–	−1.4
Northavon	70.7	−8.3	34.7	−4.3	11.6	−4.1	52.4	+10.0	–	1.3	–	–	–	–
Wansdyke	70.1	−9.1	35.5	+0.2	46.8	+2.8	14.4	−2.4	1.9	1.3	–	–	–	−1.3
Weston-Super-Mare	62.8	−10.9	38.7	+1.0	19.8	+1.9	39.5	−0.6	–	1.4	–	–	0.6 (3)	–
Woodspring	68.7	−9.9	43.7	−0.8	25.6	+4.9	24.2	−6.1	2.6	0.9	–	–	2.9 (2)	–
Bedfordshire, Bedford	59.9	−13.6	32.8	−0.9	47.9	−2.7	15.8	+3.5	–	1.1	–	–	2.4 (2)	+0.9
Bedfordshire Mid	66.1	−12.2	47.4	+1.4	30.1	−2.4	19.7	+2.9	–	2.7	–	–	–	+1.9
North-East	65.1	−12.4	49.9	+5.6	31.0	−1.6	16.4	+2.1	–	2.7	–	–	–	+3.6
South-West	60.8	−14.4	42.1	+1.4	40.4	−0.1	14.8	+0.5	–	2.7	–	–	–	+0.8
Luton North	59.3	−14.0	31.2	−3.1	56.7	+2.1	9.7	+0.6	–	2.4	–	–	–	−2.6
South	57.0	−13.4	29.4	−1.9	55.2	+0.3	10.9	+1.3	2.0	1.5	–	0.7	0.3	−1.1
Berkshire, Bracknell	60.7	−13.8	46.6	−0.7	33.0	+3.2	17.1	+1.7	–	2.6	–	–	0.7	−2.0
Maidenhead	62.0	−13.6	45.0	−4.8	15.2	−2.9	37.4	+11.2	–	1.7	–	–	0.6	–
Newbury	67.3	−9.3	43.5	+5.6	6.9	+1.4	48.2	−4.7	–	1.3	–	–	–	–
Reading East	58.4	−11.7	32.0	−3.2	44.8	+2.1	18.5	+0.0	2.4	1.2	–	0.9	0.2 (2)	−2.6
West	58.6	−11.5	32.0	−6.9	53.1	+8.0	12.8	+0.1	–	2.0	–	–	–	−7.4

	% Voting	Change in voting 1997–2001	% Con	Con change 1997–2001	% Lab	Lab change 1997–2001	% LibDem	LibDem change 1997–2001	% Green	% UKIP	% Socialist Labour	% Socialist Alliance	% Other		Swing
ENGLAND															
Slough	53.8	–14.1	26.2	–3.1	58.3	+1.6	10.5	+3.2	–	1.9	–	–	3.1	(3)	–2.3
Windsor	57.0	–16.4	47.3	–0.9	24.1	+5.8	26.1	–2.5	–	2.5	–	–	–		–
Wokingham	64.1	–11.0	46.1	–4.0	17.4	+0.6	32.4	+1.1	–	2.0	–	–	2.0		–
Buckinghamshire, Aylesbury	61.4	–11.5	47.3	+3.1	23.2	+1.0	26.9	–2.6	–	2.5	–	–	–		–
Beaconsfield	61.6	–9.2	52.8	+3.5	21.8	+1.7	21.6	+0.3	–	3.9	–	–	–		–
Buckingham	69.4	–9.1	53.7	+3.9	24.2	–0.5	20.0	–4.7	–	2.1	–	–	–		+2.2
Chesham & Amersham	64.7	–9.0	50.5	+0.1	18.8	–0.9	24.3	+0.4	–	3.0	–	–	1.0		–
Milton Keynes North-East	62.4	–10.4	38.1	–0.9	42.0	+2.5	17.8	+0.4	2.5	2.2	–	–	–		–1.7
South-West	59.2	–12.2	34.2	+0.7	49.5	–4.2	10.6	–1.3	–	1.9	–	0.6	1.1		+2.5
Wycombe	60.2	–10.8	42.4	+2.5	35.3	–0.1	17.0	–1.5	2.1	2.4	–	–	0.5	(2)	+1.3
Cambridgeshire, Cambridge	60.6	–8.6	22.9	–3.0	45.1	–8.3	25.1	+8.9	2.4	1.2	–	1.7	0.7	(2)	–
Cambridgeshire North-East	60.1	–12.7	48.1	+5.1	34.9	+1.0	14.0	–2.4	3.3	2.5	–	–	0.5		+2.0
North-West	62.3	–11.9	49.8	+1.7	31.4	–0.8	15.8	+0.7	–	2.0	–	–	1.0		+1.3
South	67.1	–9.0	44.2	+2.2	24.3	–0.8	26.9	+1.0	2.4	1.8	–	–	0.4	(2)	–
South-East	63.5	–11.3	44.2	+1.2	26.4	–0.1	26.9	+1.8	–	2.5	–	–	–		–
Huntingdon	62.5	–12.4	49.9	–5.4	22.8	–0.6	23.9	+9.1	–	3.4	–	–	–		–
Peterborough	61.3	–11.5	38.0	+2.8	45.1	–5.2	14.5	+3.8	–	2.4	–	–	–		+4.0
Cheshire, City of Chester	63.8	–14.3	33.1	–1.1	48.5	–4.5	14.7	+5.2	–	2.0	–	–	1.7	(2)	+1.7
Congleton	62.7	–14.7	46.3	+5.1	30.5	+2.9	21.6	–8.2	–	1.7	–	–	–		–
Crewe & Nantwich	60.2	–13.3	30.4	+3.5	54.3	–3.9	13.5	+1.7	–	1.8	–	–	–		+3.7
Eddisbury	64.2	–11.5	46.3	+3.8	36.0	–4.1	15.7	+2.5	–	2.0	–	–	–		+3.9
Ellesmere Port & Neston	60.9	–16.7	29.1	+0.1	55.3	–4.3	11.6	+2.7	1.9	2.0	–	–	–		+2.2

ENGLAND	% Voting	Change in voting 1997-2001	% Con	Con change 1997-2001	% Lab	Lab change 1997-2001	% LibDem	LibDem change 1997-2001	% Green	% UKIP	% Socialist Labour	% Socialist Alliance	% Other	Swing
Halton	54.1	−14.2	18.6	+0.9	69.2	−1.7	12.2	+4.9	–	–	–	–	–	+1.3
Macclesfield	62.3	−12.6	48.9	−0.7	33.1	−0.6	18.0	+1.3	–	–	–	–	–	−0.1
Tatton†	63.5	−12.9	48.1	+10.7	27.3	–	18.6	–	–	1.9	–	–	4.2 (5)	–
Warrington North	53.7	−16.8	22.8	−1.2	61.7	−0.4	13.4	+3.1	–	2.0	–	–	–	−0.4
South	61.2	−15.0	33.0	+0.5	49.3	−2.9	16.3	+3.2	–	1.4	–	–	–	+1.7
Weaver Vale	57.6	−15.5	27.9	−0.6	52.5	−3.9	14.4	+2.1	–	1.4	–	–	3.8 (2)	+1.7
Cleveland, Hartlepool	56.2	−9.4	20.9	−0.5	59.1	−1.6	15.0	+1.0	–	–	2.4	–	2.6 (3)	+0.5
Middlesbrough	49.8	−15.0	19.1	+2.0	67.6	−3.9	10.4	+1.9	–	–	1.2	1.7	–	+2.9
South & Cleveland East	61.5	−14.4	34.0	−0.9	55.3	+0.6	10.7	+3.2	–	–	–	–	–	−0.7
Redcar	57.7	−13.2	25.1	+2.0	60.3	−7.1	12.6	+3.1	–	–	2.0	–	–	+4.5
Stockton North	54.3	−14.7	22.1	+3.3	63.4	−3.4	11.9	+1.0	–	–	–	–	–	+3.3
South	62.2	−13.8	32.4	−0.6	53.0	−2.3	13.6	+4.5	2.6	–	–	1.0	–	+0.8
Cornwall, North	63.8	−9.1	33.8	+4.3	9.7	+0.3	52.0	−1.1	–	4.4	–	–	–	–
South-East	65.4	−10.1	35.5	−0.3	12.4	−0.4	45.9	−1.2	–	3.8	–	–	2.3	–
Falmouth & Camborne	64.3	−10.8	29.9	+1.1	39.6	+5.7	24.5	−0.7	–	2.8	–	–	3.2 (2)	−2.3
St Ives	66.3	−8.7	31.2	+0.0	13.3	−1.9	51.6	+7.1	–	3.9	–	–	–	–
Truro & St Austell	63.5	−10.4	32.3	+5.8	13.7	−1.6	48.3	−0.2	–	3.3	–	–	2.4 (3)	–
Cumbria, Barrow & Furness	60.3	−11.8	30.3	+3.1	55.7	−1.6	12.2	+3.3	–	1.8	–	–	–	+2.4
Carlisle	59.4	−13.3	34.8	+5.8	51.2	−6.3	11.7	+1.2	–	–	–	0.8	1.6	+6.0
Copeland	64.9	−11.3	37.5	+8.3	51.8	−6.4	10.7	+1.5	–	–	–	–	–	+7.3
Penrith & The Border	65.3	−8.3	54.9	+7.3	18.5	−3.1	21.8	−4.9	–	2.1	–	–	2.7 (3)	–
Westmorland & Lonsdale	67.8	−6.4	46.9	+4.7	10.9	−9.7	40.4	+7.0	–	1.2	–	–	0.6 (2)	–

	% Voting	Change in voting 1997-2001	% Con	Con change 1997-2001	% Lab	Lab change 1997-2001	% LibDem	LibDem change 1997-2001	% Green	% UKIP	% Socialist Labour	% Socialist Alliance	% Other	Swing
ENGLAND														
Workington	63.4	−11.7	29.6	+5.1	55.5	−8.7	12.5	+4.4	–	–	–	–	2.5	+6.9
Derbyshire, Amber Valley	60.3	−15.6	35.7	+2.2	51.9	−2.8	12.4	+4.7	–	–	–	–	–	+2.5
Bolsover	56.9	−14.4	19.5	+2.8	68.6	−5.4	11.9	+2.6	–	–	–	–	–	+4.1
Chesterfield†	60.7	−10.2	8.1	−1.1	42.0	−8.8	47.8	+8.3	–	–	0.7	1.0	0.4 (2)	–
Derby North	57.6	−15.9	35.0	+0.8	50.9	−2.3	14.1	+5.1	–	–	–	–	–	+1.5
South	55.7	−12.0	24.3	−0.9	56.4	+0.2	19.3	+4.9	–	–	–	–	–	−0.5
Derbyshire North-East	58.9	−13.7	26.5	+1.3	55.6	−4.8	17.8	+3.5	–	–	–	–	–	+3.1
South	64.1	−14.1	35.6	+4.3	50.7	−3.8	10.1	+1.1	–	2.1	1.1	–	0.5 (2)	+4.1
West	67.4	−10.7	48.0	+5.9	33.4	−0.1	15.7	−1.8	–	1.3	–	–	1.6 (3)	+3.0
Erewash	61.9	−15.9	34.9	−1.6	49.2	−2.5	11.5	+2.9	–	1.4	0.8	–	2.1 (2)	+0.4
High Peak	65.2	−13.7	37.3	+1.8	46.6	−4.2	16.1	+4.9	–	–	–	–	–	+3.0
Devon, East	68.1	−7.8	47.4	+4.0	16.7	−1.0	30.3	+1.2	–	5.6	–	–	–	–
North	68.3	−9.6	38.2	−1.3	10.1	+0.4	44.2	−6.5	2.4	5.0	–	–	–	–
South-West	66.1	−9.9	46.8	+3.9	31.6	+2.7	18.4	−5.4	–	3.2	–	–	–	+0.6
West & Torridge	70.5	−7.2	40.0	+1.5	10.7	−1.7	42.2	+0.3	2.3	4.8	–	–	–	–
Exeter	64.2	−13.3	27.4	−1.2	49.8	+2.3	12.4	−5.6	2.4	2.1	–	1.0	4.9	−1.7
Plymouth Devonport	56.6	−13.0	27.1	+2.9	58.3	−2.6	10.8	+0.1	–	2.3	0.7	0.8	–	+2.7
Sutton	57.1	−9.9	31.5	+1.2	50.7	+0.6	14.3	+0.5	–	2.5	0.9	–	–	+0.3
Teignbridge†	69.3	−7.6	39.3	+0.1	12.4	−5.6	44.4	+5.7	–	3.8	–	–	–	–
Tiverton & Honiton	69.2	−8.7	47.1	+5.7	11.9	−0.9	35.8	−2.7	1.8	2.3	–	–	1.1	–
Torbay	65.7	−8.1	36.4	−3.2	9.4	−5.4	50.5	+10.9	–	3.2	–	–	0.5 (2)	–
Totnes	67.9	−8.1	44.5	+8.0	12.2	−4.2	37.2	+2.3	–	6.1	–	–	–	–

ENGLAND	% Voting	Change in voting 1997-2001	% Con	Con change 1997-2001	% Lab	Lab change 1997-2001	% LibDem	LibDem change 1997-2001	% Green	% UKIP	% Socialist Labour	% Socialist Alliance	% Other	Swing
Dorset, Bournemouth East	59.2	-11.0	43.3	+1.9	19.9	-1.3	33.7	+2.3	–	3.1	–	–	–	–
West†	54.2	-12.0	42.8	+1.2	28.8	+4.3	25.2	-2.6	–	3.2	–	–	–	–
Christchurch	67.4	-11.2	55.1	+8.7	15.1	+8.2	27.8	-14.8	–	2.0	–	–	–	–
Dorset Mid & Poole North†	65.6	-10.1	41.1	+0.4	15.5	-0.3	42.0	+2.7	–	1.4	–	–	–	–
North	66.3	-10.0	46.7	+2.4	11.2	+0.9	38.7	-0.4	–	2.1	–	–	1.3 (3)	–
South†	65.5	-8.5	41.6	+5.5	42.0	+6.0	14.4	-5.8	–	2.0	–	–	–	-0.2
West	67.0	-9.0	44.6	+3.5	13.6	-4.1	41.8	+4.1	–	–	–	–	–	–
Poole	60.7	-10.1	45.1	+3.0	26.9	+5.3	25.5	-5.3	–	2.5	–	–	–	–
Durham, Bishop Auckland	57.2	-11.8	22.7	+2.5	58.8	-7.1	15.7	+6.4	2.7	–	–	–	–	+4.8
Darlington	62.0	-11.9	30.3	+2.0	56.3	-5.2	10.9	+3.7	–	–	0.6	–	0.7 (2)	+3.6
Durham North	57.0	-12.4	18.8	+4.3	67.2	-3.1	14.0	+3.0	–	–	–	–	–	+3.7
North-West	58.5	-10.5	20.9	+5.6	62.5	-6.2	14.9	+4.1	–	–	1.7	–	–	+5.9
Durham, City of	59.6	-11.3	17.3	-0.2	56.1	-7.2	23.7	+8.4	–	3.0	–	–	–	–
Easington	53.6	-13.4	10.3	+1.8	76.8	-3.4	10.3	+3.1	–	–	2.5	–	–	+2.6
Sedgefield	62.0	-10.6	20.9	+3.1	64.9	-6.3	9.0	+2.5	–	2.4	1.3	–	1.6 (3)	+4.7
East Sussex, Bexhill & Battle	64.9	-9.4	48.1	+0.0	19.4	+1.3	24.7	-0.8	–	7.8	–	–	–	–
Brighton Kemptown	58.0	-12.8	35.3	-3.6	47.8	+1.3	10.4	+0.7	3.3	1.4	0.9	–	1.0 (2)	-2.4
Pavilion	58.8	-14.8	25.1	-2.6	48.7	-5.9	13.1	+3.6	9.3	0.9	1.4	–	1.4 (2)	+1.6
Eastbourne	60.7	-12.1	44.1	+2.0	13.3	+0.8	39.3	+0.9	–	2.0	–	–	1.3	–
Hastings & Rye	58.4	-11.3	36.6	+7.5	47.1	+12.7	10.3	-17.6	1.7	2.2	–	–	2.0 (4)	-2.6
Hove	59.2	-9.8	38.3	+1.9	45.9	+1.3	9.1	-0.5	3.3	0.9	–	1.3	1.4 (4)	+0.3
Lewes	68.5	-7.9	34.9	-5.6	7.3	-3.3	56.3	+13.1	–	1.4	–	–	–	–
Wealden	63.5	-10.8	49.8	+0.0	20.3	+3.1	23.7	-2.0	2.4	2.9	–	–	0.9	–

ENGLAND	% Voting	Change in voting 1997–2001	% Con	Con change 1997–2001	% Lab	Lab change 1997–2001	% LibDem	LibDem change 1997–2001	% Green	% UKIP	% Socialist Labour	% Socialist Alliance	% Other	Swing
Essex, Basildon	55.1	−16.5	33.8	+3.0	52.7	−3.1	9.0	+0.3	–	3.4	–	1.0	–	+3.0
Billericay	58.1	−14.1	47.4	+7.6	36.4	−0.9	13.9	−1.9	–	2.4	–	–	–	+4.3
Braintree	63.6	−12.5	41.3	+1.2	42.0	−0.7	11.3	−0.3	2.5	1.5	–	–	1.5	+0.9
Brentwood & Ongar	67.3	−9.5	38.0	−7.4	12.6	−9.5	15.6	−10.7	–	1.4	–	–	32.4 (5)	–
Castle Point†	58.4	−13.9	44.6	+4.5	42.1	−0.3	7.8	−1.4	–	3.2	–	–	2.2 (3)	+2.4
Chelmsford West	61.5	−15.4	42.5	+1.9	29.5	+3.1	23.3	−5.9	1.7	1.6	–	–	1.4	–
Colchester	55.4	−14.2	29.9	−1.5	25.0	−5.6	42.6	+8.2	–	1.4	–	–	1.1	–
Epping Forest	58.4	−14.4	49.1	+3.6	29.3	−6.3	18.6	+5.2	–	3.0	–	–	–	+5.0
Essex North	62.7	−12.6	47.4	+3.5	31.5	−1.7	17.5	−2.1	–	3.6	–	–	–	+2.6
Harlow	59.8	−14.6	34.8	+2.7	47.8	−6.3	13.4	+4.0	–	3.0	–	1.0	–	+4.5
Harwich	62.1	−8.4	40.2	+3.7	45.6	+6.9	8.5	−4.6	–	5.1	–	–	0.5 (2)	−1.6
Maldon & Chelmsford East	63.7	−12.2	49.2	+0.6	30.1	+1.3	15.9	−3.5	2.2	2.6	–	–	–	−0.4
Rayleigh	61.0	−13.6	50.1	+0.4	30.7	+1.8	15.5	−4.3	–	3.7	–	–	–	−0.7
Rochford & Southend East	53.5	−10.1	53.6	+4.8	34.8	−4.9	7.4	−2.0	2.6	–	–	–	1.6	+4.9
Saffron Walden	65.2	−11.4	48.9	+3.6	22.6	+1.1	24.9	−1.9	–	3.5	–	–	–	–
Southend West	58.3	−11.5	46.3	+7.6	25.1	+2.3	24.9	−8.2	–	3.7	–	–	–	–
Thurrock	48.8	−17.0	29.8	+3.0	56.5	−6.8	10.3	+2.2	–	3.4	–	–	–	+4.9
Gloucestershire, Cheltenham	61.9	−12.1	35.2	−1.1	12.0	+1.9	47.7	−1.7	1.8	1.2	–	–	2.1 (4)	–
Cotswold	67.5	−8.5	50.3	+4.0	22.6	−0.1	24.2	+1.3	–	2.9	–	–	–	–
Forest of Dean	67.3	−11.7	38.8	+3.2	43.4	−4.8	12.9	+0.6	2.8	1.5	–	–	0.6 (2)	+4.0
Gloucester	59.4	−14.2	37.7	+2.0	45.8	−4.2	14.3	+3.8	–	1.7	–	0.6	–	+3.1
Stroud	69.9	−8.8	37.4	−0.5	46.6	+3.9	10.9	−4.5	3.5	1.6	–	–	–	−2.2
Tewkesbury	64.3	−12.1	46.1	+0.3	26.9	+0.7	26.2	−1.8	–	–	–	–	0.7 (2)	–

	% Voting	Change in voting 1997–2001	% Con	Con change 1997–2001	% Lab	Lab change 1997–2001	% LibDem	LibDem change 1997–2001	% Green	% UKIP	% Socialist Labour	% Socialist Alliance	% Other	Swing
ENGLAND														
Greater London														
Barking & Dagenham, Barking	45.5	−15.9	23.0	+5.4	60.9	−4.9	9.8	+0.3	–	–	–	–	6.4	+5.1
Dagenham	46.5	−15.3	25.7	+7.2	57.2	−8.5	10.2	+2.7	–	–	0.9	0.9	5.0	+7.8
Barnet, Chipping Barnet	60.5	−10.4	46.4	+3.4	40.0	−0.9	13.6	+1.2	–	–	–	–	–	+2.1
Finchley & Golders Green	57.3	−10.8	37.8	−2.0	46.3	+0.2	12.1	+0.8	3.2	0.8	–	–	–	−1.1
Hendon	52.2	−12.4	34.3	−2.7	52.5	+3.1	11.6	+0.7	–	1.0	–	–	0.7 (2)	−2.9
Bexley, Bexleyheath & Crayford	63.5	−12.6	39.9	+1.5	43.6	−1.9	11.1	−0.1	–	1.9	–	–	3.5	+1.7
Erith & Thamesmead	50.2	−15.7	25.8	+5.6	59.3	−2.8	11.4	−0.6	–	–	3.5	–	–	+4.2
Old Bexley & Sidcup	62.1	−13.4	45.4	+3.4	37.5	+2.4	13.7	−2.4	–	3.4	–	–	–	+0.5
Brent, East"	49.9	−16.0	18.2	−4.1	63.2	−4.1	10.6	+2.8	4.7	0.6	1.3	–	1.4	+0.0
North	57.7	−12.8	29.3	−10.8	59.4	+8.7	11.3	+3.2	–	–	–	1.7	1.6	−9.8
South	51.2	−13.2	12.6	−3.3	73.3	+0.3	10.8	+3.1	2.1	–	–	–	–	−1.8
Bromley, Beckenham	63.1	−10.9	45.3	+2.8	34.4	+1.0	16.0	−2.1	–	1.7	–	–	0.5	+0.9
Bromley & Chislehurst	62.9	−10.7	49.5	+3.2	28.6	+3.4	18.9	−4.8	–	2.9	–	–	–	−0.1
Orpington	68.4	−8.0	43.9	+3.3	10.8	−7.0	43.3	+7.7	–	2.0	–	–	–	–
Camden, Hampstead & Highgate	54.2	−10.5	24.6	−2.6	46.9	−10.5	20.5	+8.1	4.7	0.9	–	1.6	0.8 (4)	+4.0
Holburn & St Pancras	49.6	−7.6	16.9	−1.0	53.9	−11.1	18.0	+5.5	6.0	1.0	1.2	3.1	–	–
Croydon, Central	59.1	−10.5	38.5	−0.1	47.2	+1.6	11.2	+0.4	–	1.2	–	–	1.9 (2)	−0.9
North	54.7	−13.5	23.3	−3.9	63.5	+1.4	10.4	+2.7	–	1.4	–	1.3	–	−2.6
South	61.4	−12.1	49.2	+1.9	29.9	+4.6	18.3	−2.9	–	2.2	–	–	0.4 (2)	−1.4
Ealing, Acton & Shepherd's Bush	52.6	−11.4	25.1	−0.7	54.1	−4.2	16.6	+5.8	–	1.3	0.8	1.4	0.6	+1.8
North	58.0	−12.0	29.3	−7.9	55.7	+2.0	11.2	+4.2	2.3	1.5	–	–	–	−4.9
Southall	56.8	−8.9	18.3	−2.5	47.5	−12.5	10.0	−0.4	4.5	–	2.0	–	17.8 (5)	+5.0

ENGLAND	% Voting	Change in voting 1997-2001	% Con	Con change 1997-2001	% Lab	Lab change 1997-2001	% LibDem	LibDem change 1997-2001	% Green	% UKIP	% Socialist Labour	% Socialist Alliance	% Other	Swing
Enfield, Edmonton	55.8	−14.5	30.8	+0.6	58.9	−1.4	7.0	+0.7	–	1.2	–	0.9	1.3 (3)	+1.0
North	56.6	−13.9	40.7	+4.4	46.7	−4.0	8.8	−0.2	–	1.1	–	–	2.8 (4)	+4.2
Southgate	63.1	−7.6	38.6	−2.5	51.8	+7.6	7.0	−3.7	1.6	0.7	–	–	0.3 (2)	−5.1
Greenwich, Eltham	58.7	−16.4	32.1	+1.0	52.8	−1.8	12.2	+3.7	–	2.1	–	–	0.7 (2)	+1.4
Erith & Thamesmead, (See Bexley)														
Greenwich & Woolwich	52.0	−12.9	19.2	+0.7	60.5	−2.9	15.6	+3.1	–	–	1.1	1.5	–	+1.8
Hackney														
North & Stoke Newington	49.0	−2.2	15.0	−2.0	61.0	−4.1	14.1	+3.9	7.4	–	2.6	–	–	+1.1
South & Shoreditch	47.4	−6.6	13.8	+0.5	64.2	+4.8	14.6	−0.4	–	–	–	4.6	2.9 (3)	–
Hammersmith														
Ealing Acton & S.B., (See Ealing)														
Hammersmith & Fulham	56.4	−12.3	39.8	+0.1	44.3	−2.5	11.8	+3.1	3.2	0.8	–	–	–	+1.3
Haringey														
Hornsey & Wood Green	58.0	−8.9	15.7	−6.2	49.9	−11.9	25.8	+14.5	5.1	–	0.7	2.5	0.4	–
Tottenham	48.2	−6.8	13.9	−1.8	67.5	−1.8	9.5	−1.3	4.6	–	–	3.7	0.9	+0.0
Harrow, East	58.9	−11.8	32.2	−3.3	55.3	+2.8	12.5	+4.3	–	–	–	–	–	−3.0
West	63.5	−8.7	36.4	−2.8	49.6	+8.1	12.9	−2.6	–	1.1	–	–	–	−5.4
Havering, Hornchurch	58.3	−13.9	42.3	+5.0	46.4	−3.8	8.2	+0.4	–	2.5	–	–	0.5	+4.4
Romford†	59.6	−10.9	53.0	+11.4	36.3	−6.9	8.0	+0.1	–	1.5	–	–	1.2	+9.1
Upminster†	59.6	−12.6	45.5	+6.0	41.9	−4.3	9.4	−0.1	–	3.2	–	–	–	+5.2
Hillingdon, Hayes & Harlington	56.3	−16.0	24.1	−3.1	65.7	+3.7	6.0	−1.4	–	–	–	–	4.2 (2)	−3.4
Ruislip-Northwood	61.1	−13.1	48.8	−1.5	28.5	−4.4	19.3	+3.1	1.9	–	–	–	1.5	+1.5

ENGLAND	% Voting	Change in voting 1997-2001	% Con	Con change 1997-2001	% Lab	Lab change 1997-2001	% LibDem	LibDem change 1997-2001	% Green	% UKIP	% Socialist Labour	% Socialist Alliance	% Other	Swing
Uxbridge	57.6	−14.7	47.1	+3.6	40.9	−1.0	10.3	−0.6	–	1.8	–	–	–	+2.3
Hounslow, Brentford & Isleworth	53.0	−16.6	29.1	−2.6	52.3	−5.2	13.5	+5.2	3.0	0.9	–	0.9	0.3 (2)	+1.3
Feltham & Heston	49.4	−15.5	24.2	−2.8	59.2	−0.5	13.8	+4.7	–	–	1.8	–	1.0 (3)	−1.1
Islington, North	48.8	−12.7	10.8	−2.2	61.9	−7.4	19.0	+5.4	6.2	–	1.7	–	0.5	–
South & Finsbury	47.4	−12.7	13.7	+0.7	53.9	−8.6	28.1	+6.9	–	–	–	2.9	1.3 (3)	–
Kensington & Chelsea	45.2	−4.4	54.4	+0.8	23.2	−4.8	15.7	+0.5	4.2	1.5	–	–	1.0 (2)	+2.8
Regent's P. & Ken. N., (See Westminster)														
Kingston-upon-Thames														
Kingston & Surbiton	67.5	−6.8	28.2	−8.3	8.8	−14.3	60.2	+23.5	1.2	0.9	0.6	–	0.1	–
Richmond Park, (See Richmond)														
Lambeth, Dulwich & W. N., (See Southwark)														
Streatham	48.7	−10.4	17.9	−3.8	56.9	−5.9	18.3	+4.8	4.4	–	–	2.4	–	–
Vauxhall	44.8	−8.7	13.4	−1.8	59.1	−4.7	20.1	+4.1	4.4	–	–	2.6	0.3 (2)	–
Lewisham, Deptford	46.3	−11.6	12.4	−2.3	65.0	−5.8	11.7	+2.8	6.5	–	–	4.3	–	+1.8
East	51.6	−14.8	23.8	−2.1	53.7	−4.6	16.4	+5.2	–	1.2	–	1.5	3.3	+1.2
West	50.6	−13.5	22.4	−1.5	61.1	−0.9	13.5	+3.7	–	1.6	–	–	1.5 (2)	−0.3
Merton, Mitcham & Morden	57.8	−14.6	24.1	−5.6	60.4	+2.1	10.1	+2.5	2.4	1.3	–	–	1.7	−3.8
Wimbledon	64.3	−9.0	36.6	+0.1	45.7	+3.0	13.0	−3.6	2.4	1.0	–	–	1.2	−1.5
Newham, East Ham	52.3	−8.0	16.7	+0.6	73.1	+8.5	7.0	+0.5	–	1.2	2.1	–	–	−3.9
Poplar & Canning Town, (See Tower H.)														
West Ham	48.9	−9.5	16.4	+1.4	69.9	−3.0	7.4	+0.0	4.1	2.2	–	–	–	+2.2
Redbridge, Chingf'd & W. G., (See Waltham F.)														

ENGLAND	% Voting	Change in voting 1997-2001	% Con	Con change 1997-2001	% Lab	Lab change 1997-2001	% LibDem	LibDem change 1997-2001	% Green	% UKIP	% Socialist Labour	% Socialist Alliance	% Other	Swing
Ilford North	58.4	-13.2	40.5	-0.2	45.8	-1.6	11.7	+1.4	–	1.9	–	–	–	+0.7
South	54.3	-15.1	25.7	-4.4	59.6	+1.1	11.3	+5.0	–	3.4	–	–	–	-2.8
Leyton & Wansted, (See Waltham Forest)														
Richmond, Richmond Park	67.6	-9.7	37.6	-1.9	11.3	-1.3	47.7	+3.0	2.5	0.7	–	–	0.2 (2)	–
Twickenham	67.4	-10.7	33.4	-4.3	13.8	-1.8	48.7	+3.6	2.8	1.2	–	–	–	–
Southwark, Camberwell & Peckham	46.8	-8.9	10.9	-0.7	69.6	+0.1	13.3	+2.1	3.2	–	–	1.9	0.3	–
Dulwich & West Norwood	54.3	-10.3	22.7	-1.5	54.9	-6.1	15.2	+4.4	5.0	–	0.7	2.2	–	+2.3
Southwark North & Bermondsey	50.1	-10.8	7.6	+0.6	30.8	-9.5	56.9	+8.3	2.0	0.7	–	–	1.9 (3)	–
Sutton, Carshalton & Wallington	60.3	-13.0	33.8	+0.3	18.4	-5.5	45.0	+6.8	1.5	1.2	–	–	–	–
Sutton & Cheam	62.4	-12.7	38.0	+0.1	13.2	-2.2	48.8	+6.5	–	–	–	–	–	–
Tower Hamlets, Bethnal Green & Bow	48.5	-12.7	24.3	+3.2	50.5	+4.1	15.5	+3.5	4.3	–	–	–	5.5 (2)	-0.5
Poplar & Canning Town	45.4	-13.1	19.8	+4.8	61.2	-2.0	11.1	+0.8	–	–	–	2.8	5.1	+3.4
Waltham Forest														
Chingford & Woodford Green	58.5	-12.2	48.2	+0.7	33.4	-1.2	15.5	+0.0	–	–	–	–	2.9	+1.0
Leyton & Wansted	54.8	-8.5	19.7	-2.5	58.0	-2.8	16.0	+0.9	3.1	1.1	–	2.1	–	+0.2
Walthamstow	53.5	-9.3	18.1	-2.2	62.2	-1.0	14.6	+0.9	–	0.9	–	–	4.3 (3)	-0.6
Wandsworth, Battersea	54.5	-14.4	36.5	-2.9	50.3	-0.5	12.1	+4.7	–	–	–	–	1.1 (2)	-1.2
Putney	56.5	-14.9	38.4	-0.5	46.5	+0.8	13.6	+2.9	–	1.0	–	–	0.5	-0.7
Tooting	54.9	-12.9	26.4	-0.7	54.1	-5.6	14.9	+5.5	4.6	–	–	–	–	+2.4
Westminster														
Cities of London & Westminster	47.2	-10.9	46.3	-0.9	33.1	-2.0	15.4	+3.1	3.9	1.4	–	–	–	+0.5
Regent's Park and Kensington North	48.8	-15.4	26.9	-2.0	54.6	-5.3	12.6	+4.1	3.4	1.0	–	1.2	0.2 (2)	+1.6

ENGLAND

Greater Manchester

	% Voting	Change in Voting 1997–2001	% Con	Con change 1997–2001	% Lab	Lab change 1997–2001	% LibDem	LibDem change 1997–2001	% Green	% UKIP	% Socialist Labour	% Socialist Alliance	% Other	Swing
Altrincham & Sale West	60.7	−12.6	46.2	+3.0	39.4	−0.8	14.4	+1.8	–	–	–	–	–	+1.9
Ashton-under-Lyne	49.1	−16.3	19.1	+0.1	62.5	−5.0	11.8	+2.1	2.1	–	–	–	4.5	+2.6
Bolton North-East	56.0	−16.4	32.7	+2.3	54.3	−1.8	10.3	+0.4	1.6	–	1.0	–	–	+2.1
South-East	50.1	−15.1	24.2	+4.5	61.9	−7.0	11.5	+2.8	–	–	2.4	–	–	+5.7
West	62.4	−15.0	33.6	−1.5	47.0	−2.5	18.4	+7.6	–	–	–	1.0	–	+0.5
Bury North	63.0	−15.1	36.6	−0.9	51.2	−0.6	12.1	+3.9	–	–	–	–	–	−0.1
South	58.8	−16.9	26.9	−5.4	59.2	+2.3	13.9	+5.5	–	–	–	–	–	−3.9
Cheadle†	63.2	−14.1	42.3	−1.4	14.0	−1.8	42.4	+4.7	–	–	–	–	–	–
Denton & Reddish	48.5	−18.3	19.6	−1.7	65.2	−0.2	12.4	−0.9	–	1.4	–	–	–	−0.8
Eccles	48.3	−17.3	20.7	+2.0	64.5	−2.2	14.8	+4.1	–	2.8	–	–	–	+2.1
Hazel Grove	59.1	−18.2	30.1	−0.4	16.2	+4.3	52.0	−2.5	–	1.7	–	–	–	–
Heywood & Middleton	53.1	−15.2	27.6	+4.6	57.7	+0.0	11.2	−4.5	–	–	–	–	3.5 (2)	+2.3
Leigh	49.7	−16.0	18.2	+2.6	64.5	−4.4	12.8	+1.6	–	2.1	2.3	–	–	+3.5
Makerfield	50.9	−15.9	17.6	+2.2	68.5	−5.1	11.4	+3.1	–	–	–	2.5	–	+3.6
Manchester Blackley	44.9	−12.5	14.4	−0.8	68.9	−1.1	11.4	+0.4	–	–	1.8	1.7	–	+0.1
Central	39.1	−12.9	9.0	−2.8	68.7	−2.3	15.7	+3.4	3.9	–	1.9	–	1.7	–
Gorton	42.7	−13.2	9.9	−1.8	62.8	−2.5	21.3	+3.8	3.1	–	1.2	–	0.8	–
Withington	51.9	−14.1	15.3	−4.1	54.9	−6.7	22.0	+8.4	4.4	1.7	–	3.4	–	–
Oldham East & Saddleworth	61.0	−12.9	16.1	−3.6	38.6	−3.1	32.6	−2.8	–	1.5	–	–	11.2	–
West & Royton	57.6	−8.5	17.7	−5.7	51.2	−7.6	12.4	+0.6	2.3	–	–	–	16.4	+1.0
Rochdale	56.7	−13.3	13.4	+4.6	49.2	−0.2	34.9	−5.1	1.8	–	–	–	0.6 (2)	–
Salford	41.6	−14.7	15.3	−2.1	65.1	−3.9	16.2	+5.9	–	–	–	1.8	1.6 (3)	–

	% Voting	Change in voting 1997-2001	% Con	Con change 1997-2001	% Lab	Lab change 1997-2001	% LibDem	LibDem change 1997-2001	% Green	% UKIP	% Socialist Labour	% Socialist Alliance	% Other	Swing
ENGLAND														
Stalybridge & Hyde	48.4	−17.3	27.8	+3.3	55.5	−3.4	13.5	+1.5	–	3.2	–	–	–	+3.4
Stockport	53.3	−18.0	25.9	+3.6	58.6	−4.3	15.5	+4.9	–	–	–	–	–	+3.9
Stretford & Urmston	55.0	−14.7	27.1	−3.4	61.1	+2.6	10.0	+1.8	–	–	–	–	1.8 (2)	−3.0
Wigan	52.5	−15.3	20.8	+3.9	61.7	−6.8	14.8	+4.8	–	–	–	2.6	–	+5.4
Worsley	51.0	−16.8	23.8	−0.5	57.1	−5.1	17.5	+3.9	–	–	1.6	–	–	+2.3
Wythenshawe & Sale East	48.6	−14.6	24.0	−1.1	60.0	+1.9	12.3	−0.1	2.5	–	1.2	–	–	−1.5
Hampshire, Aldershot	57.9	−13.2	42.2	−0.5	25.2	+1.0	27.6	−2.8	1.4	1.8	–	–	1.9 (3)	–
Basingstoke	60.7	−13.1	42.7	−0.6	40.9	+1.7	13.9	−3.1	–	2.5	–	–	–	−1.2
Eastleigh	63.8	−12.9	34.3	+0.6	21.9	−4.9	40.7	+5.6	1.3	1.8	–	–	–	–
Fareham	62.5	−13.3	47.1	+0.2	31.6	+4.7	18.7	−0.9	–	2.6	–	–	–	−2.2
Gosport	57.1	−13.1	43.6	+0.0	37.1	+6.4	15.1	−4.5	–	2.9	1.3	–	–	−3.2
Hampshire East	63.8	−12.0	47.6	−0.4	19.6	+2.5	29.9	+1.8	–	2.8	–	–	–	–
North-East	61.6	−12.0	53.2	+2.3	19.9	+3.8	23.0	+0.3	–	3.9	–	–	–	–
North-West	63.7	−10.7	50.1	+4.9	25.4	+1.8	21.2	−2.9	–	3.2	–	–	–	–
Havant	57.6	−12.9	43.9	+4.2	33.5	+1.5	18.6	−3.8	2.0	1.4	–	–	0.6 (2)	+1.3
New Forest East	63.2	−11.3	42.4	−0.5	21.7	−3.1	33.4	+1.1	–	2.5	–	–	–	–
West	65.0	−9.5	55.7	+5.2	14.7	+0.4	25.8	−2.0	–	3.7	–	–	–	–
Portsmouth North	57.4	−12.7	36.7	−0.9	50.7	+3.5	10.3	−0.3	–	1.5	–	–	0.8 (2)	−2.2
South	50.9	−12.9	29.1	−2.1	23.9	−1.4	44.6	+5.1	–	0.8	–	1.6	–	–
Romsey†‡	68.7	−7.8	42.1	−3.9	8.2	−10.3	47.0	+17.5	–	1.5	–	–	1.2	–
Southampton Itchen	54.0	−15.6	27.4	−1.0	54.5	−0.3	15.0	+3.3	–	2.0	0.5	0.6	–	−0.3
Test	56.3	−15.0	25.5	−2.5	52.5	−1.7	18.1	+4.4	–	1.9	0.9	1.1	–	−0.4
Winchester	72.3	−6.0	38.3	−3.8	5.9	−4.6	54.6	+12.5	–	1.1	–	–	0.1	–

	% Voting	Change in voting 1997–2001	% Con	Con change 1997–2001	% Lab	Lab change 1997–2001	% LibDem	LibDem change 1997–2001	% Green	% UKIP	% Socialist Labour	% Socialist Alliance	% Other	Swing
ENGLAND														
Hereford & Worcester														
Bromsgrove	67.1	–10.1	51.7	+4.6	33.9	–3.9	11.9	+0.0	–	2.4	–	–	–	+4.3
Hereford	63.5	–11.8	38.7	+3.4	15.1	+2.6	40.9	–7.1	2.6	2.7	–	–	–	–
Leominster	68.0	–8.6	49.0	+3.7	16.8	–0.6	26.8	–1.0	3.6	3.4	–	–	0.4 (2)	–
Redditch	59.2	–14.3	38.9	+2.8	45.6	–4.2	10.3	–0.7	1.8	3.4	–	–	–	+3.5
Worcester	62.0	–12.5	35.5	–0.2	48.6	–1.5	12.6	+0.1	–	3.3	–	–	–	+0.7
Worcestershire Mid	62.4	–11.9	51.1	+3.7	27.4	–1.5	18.8	+0.1	–	2.7	–	–	–	+2.6
West	67.1	–9.1	46.0	+0.9	14.0	–1.7	34.0	–3.3	2.5	3.5	–	–	–	–
Wyre Forest†	68.0	–7.4	19.1	–17.1	22.1	–26.6	–	–	–	0.8	–	–	58.1	–
Hertfordshire, Broxbourne	54.9	–15.5	54.1	+5.3	30.4	–4.3	11.0	–0.3	–	2.3	–	–	2.2	+4.8
Hemel Hempstead	63.7	–13.1	38.5	–0.6	46.6	+0.9	12.8	+0.5	–	2.1	–	–	–	–0.8
Hertford & Stortford	62.8	–12.8	44.7	+0.6	32.8	+1.4	19.9	+2.2	–	2.6	–	–	–	–0.4
Hertfordshire North-East	64.9	–12.5	44.1	+2.4	36.4	+0.6	17.2	–1.0	–	2.3	–	–	–	+0.9
South-West	64.4	–12.4	44.3	–1.7	27.0	–0.9	26.3	+4.0	–	1.8	–	–	0.6	–0.4
Hertsmere	60.3	–13.0	47.8	+3.5	36.0	–2.2	15.2	+2.3	–	–	1.0	–	–	+2.9
Hitchin & Harpenden	66.9	–11.1	47.3	+1.5	32.5	–0.6	18.0	–2.1	–	1.3	–	–	0.8 (2)	+1.1
St Albans	66.3	–11.2	35.2	+2.0	45.4	+3.4	17.9	–3.1	–	1.4	–	–	–	–0.7
Stevenage	61.3	–15.5	31.7	–1.1	51.9	–3.5	14.2	+5.3	–	–	–	1.1	1.2 (3)	+1.2
Watford	61.2	–13.4	33.3	–1.5	45.3	+0.0	17.4	+0.7	1.9	1.2	–	0.9	–	–0.7
Welwyn Hatfield	63.9	–14.7	40.4	+3.9	43.2	–3.9	14.1	+0.5	–	1.9	–	–	0.5	+3.9
Humberside														
Beverley & Holderness	61.7	–11.2	41.3	+0.2	39.6	+0.8	15.9	–2.6	–	3.2	–	–	–	–0.3

	% Voting	Change in voting 1997-2001	% Con	Con change 1997-2001	% Lab	Lab change 1997-2001	% LibDem	LibDem change 1997-2001	% Green	% UKIP	% Socialist Labour	% Socialist Alliance	% Other	Swing
ENGLAND														
Brigg & Goole	64.6	−8.9	39.2	+2.7	48.9	−1.3	9.2	−0.8	–	1.7	1.0	–	–	+2.0
Cleethorpes	62.0	−11.4	36.3	+2.9	49.6	−2.0	12.0	+0.6	–	2.1	–	–	–	+2.5
Great Grimsby	52.3	−13.8	23.1	+1.0	57.9	−1.9	19.0	+0.9	–	–	–	–	–	+1.5
Haltemprice & Howden	65.5	−9.9	43.2	−0.8	15.7	−7.9	38.9	+10.1	–	2.2	–	–	–	–
Hull East	46.4	−12.5	13.8	+0.1	64.6	−6.7	14.9	+5.1	–	3.9	2.7	–	–	–
North	45.4	−11.5	17.1	+2.1	57.2	−8.7	19.7	+5.1	–	2.3	–	1.7	2.0 (3)	–
West & Hessle	45.8	−12.4	20.5	+2.4	58.4	−0.3	15.1	−3.1	–	3.0	1.2	–	1.8 (2)	–
Scunthorpe	56.3	−12.5	28.9	+2.6	59.8	−0.6	9.4	−1.0	–	–	–	–	1.9 (3)	+1.6
Yorkshire East	59.9	−10.6	45.9	+3.2	35.9	−0.8	14.5	−4.0	–	3.8	–	–	0.7 (2)	+2.0
Isle of Wight†	59.7	−12.0	39.7	+5.7	15.2	+2.1	35.3	−7.5	2.0	3.3	0.3	–	4.1 (3)	–
Kent, Ashford	62.5	−11.7	47.4	+6.0	32.1	+0.4	15.1	−4.6	2.8	2.6	–	–	–	+2.8
Canterbury	60.9	−11.7	41.5	+2.8	36.9	+5.6	17.8	−5.9	2.0	1.8	–	–	–	−1.4
Chatham & Aylesford	57.0	−13.9	37.3	−0.1	48.3	+5.2	11.8	−3.2	–	2.5	–	–	–	−2.6
Dartford	61.9	−12.7	40.6	+0.3	48.0	−0.6	8.5	−0.9	–	2.2	–	–	0.8	+0.5
Dover	65.1	−13.5	37.2	+4.4	48.8	−5.7	11.4	+3.5	–	2.5	–	–	–	+5.0
Faversham & Kent Mid	60.4	−12.9	45.6	+1.3	35.5	−0.5	13.5	+1.1	1.9	2.0	–	–	1.5	+0.9
Folkestone & Hythe	64.1	−8.6	45.0	+6.0	20.2	−4.7	32.1	+5.3	–	2.6	–	–	–	–
Gillingham	59.5	−12.5	39.1	+3.2	44.5	+4.7	13.6	−5.4	–	2.2	–	0.5	–	−0.7
Gravesham	62.7	−14.0	38.8	−0.1	49.9	+0.2	9.2	+1.5	–	2.1	–	–	–	−0.1
Maidstone & The Weald	61.6	−12.1	49.6	+5.5	27.0	+0.8	19.9	−2.5	–	2.1	–	–	1.3 (2)	+2.4
Medway	59.5	−12.8	39.2	+2.3	49.0	+0.1	9.3	−0.8	–	2.5	–	–	–	+1.1
Sevenoaks	63.9	−11.5	49.4	+4.0	25.6	+1.0	21.6	−2.5	–	2.7	–	–	0.7	+1.5

	% Voting	Change in Voting 1997–2001	% Con	Con change 1997–2001	% Lab	Lab change 1997–2001	% LibDem	LibDem change 1997–2001	% Green	% UKIP	% Socialist Labour	% Socialist Alliance	% Other	Swing
ENGLAND														
Sittingbourne & Sheppey	57.5	–14.8	36.5	+0.2	45.8	+5.2	14.1	–4.2	–	1.7	–	–	1.8	–2.5
Thanet North	59.3	–9.5	50.3	+6.2	34.4	–4.0	11.0	–0.4	–	2.3	–	–	2.0 (3)	+5.1
South	64.2	–7.5	41.1	+1.3	45.7	–0.5	9.4	–2.3	–	1.3	–	–	2.6 (3)	+0.9
Tonbridge & Malling	64.4	–11.2	49.4	+1.4	29.9	+2.7	17.9	–1.3	–	2.8	–	–	–	–0.7
Tunbridge Wells	62.3	–11.8	48.9	+3.7	23.2	+2.8	24.7	–5.0	–	3.3	–	–	–	–
Lancashire, Blackburn	55.5	–9.5	31.2	+6.6	54.1	–0.9	8.1	–2.4	–	2.9	1.4	1.3	0.9 (2)	+3.7
Blackpool North & Fleetwood	57.2	–14.4	37.3	+1.8	50.8	–1.4	9.7	+1.1	–	2.2	–	–	–	+1.6
South	52.2	–15.5	33.0	–1.4	54.3	–2.7	10.6	+2.1	–	2.1	–	–	–	+0.7
Burnley	55.6	–11.3	20.9	+0.6	49.3	–8.6	16.2	–1.2	–	2.3	–	–	11.3	+4.6
Chorley	62.2	–15.3	34.7	–1.2	52.3	–0.7	11.2	+2.7	–	1.8	–	–	–	–0.3
Fylde	62.0	–10.9	52.3	+3.4	30.8	–0.9	14.8	+0.1	–	2.2	–	–	–	+2.1
Hyndburn	57.6	–14.7	33.2	+1.3	54.7	–0.9	9.6	+1.0	–	2.6	–	–	–	+1.1
Lancashire West	59.0	–15.8	32.0	+3.0	54.5	–5.9	11.6	+4.4	3.0	–	–	–	2.0 (3)	+4.4
Lancaster & Wyre	66.3	–8.6	42.2	+1.6	43.1	+0.3	10.3	–1.3	1.7	1.4	–	–	–	+0.6
Morecambe & Lunesdale	60.7	–11.6	37.3	+0.6	49.6	+0.7	9.2	–2.2	–	2.2	–	–	–	–0.1
Pendle	63.2	–11.3	33.9	+3.6	44.6	–8.7	13.8	+2.2	–	2.8	–	–	5.0	+6.1
Ribble Valley	66.2	–12.4	51.5	+4.8	19.9	+4.2	28.6	–6.4	–	–	–	–	–	–
Preston	50.0	–15.7	23.0	+1.0	57.0	–3.8	13.2	–1.5	2.8	–	–	–	4.1 (3)	+2.4
Rossendale & Darwen	58.8	–14.6	36.3	+4.1	49.0	–4.7	14.7	+4.1	–	–	–	–	–	+4.4
South Ribble	62.5	–14.6	38.1	+0.5	46.4	–0.4	15.5	+4.9	–	–	–	–	–	+0.5
Leicestershire, Blaby	64.5	–11.5	46.4	+0.6	33.4	–0.4	17.4	+2.5	–	–	–	–	2.8	+0.5
Bosworth	64.4	–12.1	44.4	+3.8	39.4	+0.7	16.2	–1.6	–	–	–	–	–	+1.5

	% Voting	Change in voting 1997–2001	% Con	Con change 1997–2001	% Lab	Lab change 1997–2001	% LibDem	LibDem change 1997–2001	% Green	% UKIP	% Socialist Labour	% Socialist Alliance	% Other	Swing
ENGLAND														
Charnwood	64.5	–12.7	48.2	+1.8	32.2	–3.8	16.2	+3.4	–	3.3	–	–	–	+2.8
Harborough	63.3	–11.9	44.7	+2.9	20.0	–5.2	33.4	+3.9	–	2.0	–	–	–	–
Leicester East	62.1	–7.1	24.5	+0.5	57.6	–7.9	12.3	+5.3	–	–	2.1	–	3.6 (3)	+4.2
South	58.0	–8.3	23.1	–0.7	54.5	–3.5	17.2	+3.4	2.9	0.8	1.6	–	–	+1.4
West	50.9	–12.2	25.2	+1.5	54.2	–1.0	15.3	+1.1	3.2	–	1.1	1.0	–	+1.2
Leicestershire North-West	65.8	–14.0	33.9	+3.0	52.1	–4.3	10.3	+1.7	–	2.3	–	–	–	+3.6
Loughborough	63.2	–12.4	35.3	–2.4	49.7	+1.2	12.8	+1.0	–	2.1	–	–	1.4 (2)	–1.8
Rutland & Melton	65.0	–10.0	48.1	+2.3	29.8	+0.8	17.8	–1.4	1.7	2.6	–	–	–	+0.8
Lincolnshire														
Boston & Skegness	58.4	–10.5	42.9	+0.5	41.6	+0.6	12.4	–4.2	1.3	1.8	–	–	–	–0.1
Gainsborough	64.2	–10.3	46.2	+3.1	27.1	–1.7	26.7	–1.5	–	–	–	–	–	+2.4
Grantham & Stamford	62.2	–11.1	46.1	+3.3	36.3	–1.4	14.4	+1.9	–	3.2	–	–	–	+2.3
Lincoln	56.0	–14.9	31.2	+0.2	53.9	–1.0	12.7	+1.8	–	2.3	–	–	–	+0.6
Louth & Horncastle	62.1	–10.3	48.5	+5.0	31.5	+1.8	20.1	–4.4	–	–	–	–	–	+1.6
Sleaford & North Hykeham	65.3	–8.9	49.7	+5.7	32.0	–2.3	16.2	+1.0	–	2.2	–	–	–	+4.0
South Holland & The Deepings	62.5	–9.2	55.4	+6.2	31.4	–1.9	10.3	–5.3	–	2.9	–	–	–	+4.0
Merseyside, Birkenhead	47.7	–18.1	16.7	+1.5	70.5	–0.3	12.8	+3.8	–	–	–	–	–	+0.9
Bootle	49.0	–17.7	8.0	–0.5	77.6	–5.3	8.5	+2.8	–	–	3.5	2.4	–	–
Crosby	64.3	–12.9	32.5	–2.3	55.1	+4.1	11.1	–0.4	–	–	1.3	–	–	–3.2
Knowsley North & Sefton East	53.0	–17.1	16.3	–1.0	66.7	–3.2	13.8	+2.7	–	–	1.5	–	1.7 (3)	+1.1
South	51.8	–15.7	11.6	–1.0	71.3	–5.9	13.0	+4.7	–	–	2.9	–	1.2 (2)	–
Liverpool Garston	50.2	–14.9	15.5	–0.2	61.4	+0.1	23.1	+4.1	–	–	–	–	–	–
Riverside	34.1	–17.5	8.4	–1.1	71.4	+0.9	16.7	+3.4	–	–	–	3.6	–	–

	% Voting	Change in voting 1997–2001	% Con	Con change 1997–2001	% Lab	Lab change 1997–2001	% LibDem	LibDem change 1997–2001	% Green	% UKIP	% Socialist Labour	% Socialist Alliance	% Other	Swing
ENGLAND														
Walton	43.0	−16.5	6.1	−0.3	77.8	−0.6	14.6	+3.4	–	1.6	–	–	–	–
Wavertree	44.3	−18.4	9.6	−1.1	62.7	−1.7	24.4	+2.8	–	1.1	1.1	1.1	–	–
West Derby	45.5	−15.8	8.0	−0.6	66.2	−5.0	10.9	+1.9	–	–	2.5	–	14.9	–
St Helens North	53.3	−15.7	18.8	+1.5	61.1	−3.8	17.6	+4.8	–	1.0	–	–	–	+2.6
South	51.9	−14.6	13.8	−1.1	49.7	−18.9	23.1	+9.7	–	–	4.4	6.9	1.0 (3)	–
Southport	58.1	−13.9	36.5	+0.5	16.6	+4.4	43.8	−4.3	–	1.3	–	–	1.9	–
Wallasey	57.6	−16.0	28.0	+4.1	60.8	−3.8	11.2	+2.9	–	–	–	–	–	+3.9
Wirral South	65.6	−15.4	34.8	−1.6	47.4	−3.5	17.8	+7.4	–	–	–	–	–	+0.9
West	65.0	−12.0	37.2	−1.8	47.2	+2.3	15.6	+2.9	–	–	–	–	–	−2.1
Norfolk, Great Yarmouth	58.4	−12.7	39.1	+3.5	50.4	−3.0	8.4	−2.6	–	2.1	–	–	–	+3.2
Norfolk Mid	70.1	−6.0	44.8	+5.2	36.1	−1.2	14.5	−0.5	2.1	2.5	–	–	–	+3.2
North†	70.2	−5.9	41.8	+5.3	13.3	−11.7	42.7	+8.4	1.2	1.1	–	–	–	–
North-West†	66.2	−8.4	48.5	+7.0	41.7	−2.1	8.4	−1.2	–	1.4	–	–	–	+4.6
South	67.6	−10.7	42.2	+2.0	24.5	−1.5	29.9	+1.6	1.9	1.5	–	–	–	–
South-West	63.1	−10.0	52.2	+10.2	34.5	−3.3	10.7	−3.2	–	2.6	–	–	–	+6.7
Norwich North	60.9	−14.8	34.6	+2.1	47.4	−2.3	14.8	+2.2	1.7	1.0	–	–	0.5 (2)	+2.2
South	64.7	−7.8	24.8	+1.1	45.5	−6.2	22.6	+4.0	3.4	1.1	–	1.2	1.5	+3.7
Northamptonshire, Corby	65.3	−12.4	37.2	+3.8	49.3	−6.1	10.1	+2.6	–	1.8	1.6	–	–	+5.0
Daventry	65.5	−11.3	49.2	+2.9	32.2	−2.2	16.1	+1.2	–	2.4	–	–	–	+2.5
Kettering	67.4	−8.1	43.5	+0.5	44.7	+1.4	10.2	−0.5	–	1.6	–	–	–	−0.5
Northampton North	56.0	−14.0	30.4	−3.0	49.4	−3.3	17.7	+5.0	–	1.4	–	1.0	–	+0.2
South	59.8	−11.9	41.1	+0.0	42.9	+0.5	12.5	+1.4	–	2.4	–	–	1.1 (2)	−0.2
Wellingborough	65.9	−8.9	42.2	−1.6	46.8	+2.6	9.3	+0.0	–	1.7	–	–	–	−2.1

ENGLAND	% Voting	Change in voting 1997–2001	% Con	Con change 1997–2001	% Lab	Lab change 1997–2001	% LibDem	LibDem change 1997–2001	% Green	% UKIP	% Socialist Labour	% Socialist Alliance	% Other	Swing
Northumberland														
Berwick-upon-Tweed	63.8	–10.2	28.1	+4.0	17.7	–8.5	51.4	+5.9	–	2.8	–	–	–	–
Blyth Valley	54.6	–14.1	15.9	+2.5	59.7	–4.5	24.4	+2.0	–	–	–	–	–	–
Hexham	70.9	–6.6	44.6	+5.8	38.6	+0.4	15.0	–2.4	–	1.7	–	–	–	+2.7
Wansbeck	59.4	–12.3	12.8	–1.2	57.8	–7.7	22.8	+6.8	2.5	1.3	–	–	2.9 (2)	–
North Yorkshire														
Harrogate & Knaresborough	64.7	–8.2	34.6	–3.8	7.4	–1.4	55.6	+4.0	–	1.8	–	–	0.6	–
Richmond (Yorks)	67.4	–6.0	58.9	+10.1	21.9	–5.9	17.9	–0.5	–	–	–	–	1.3	+8.0
Ryedale	66.0	–8.7	47.2	+3.4	14.7	–3.2	36.1	+2.7	–	2.0	–	–	–	+0.9
Scarborough & Whitby	63.2	–8.4	39.6	+3.4	47.2	+1.6	8.4	–5.8	2.2	2.0	–	–	0.5	+0.9
Selby	64.5	–10.4	40.8	+1.7	45.1	–0.8	11.1	–1.0	1.8	1.3	–	–	–	+1.3
Skipton & Ripon	65.3	–10.1	52.4	+5.8	17.4	–5.0	26.1	+0.9	–	4.2	–	–	–	–
Vale of York	66.1	–9.8	51.6	+6.9	25.8	–0.6	20.2	–3.6	–	2.4	–	–	–	+3.8
York, City of	59.0	–14.2	23.5	–1.2	52.3	–7.7	17.8	+6.6	3.1	1.2	–	1.4	0.8	+3.2
Nottinghamshire, Ashfield	53.6	–16.4	24.4	+4.2	58.1	–7.0	11.3	+1.6	–	–	1.0	1.5	3.7 (2)	+5.6
Bassetlaw	56.9	–13.5	30.2	+5.3	55.3	–5.7	12.7	+2.5	–	–	1.8	–	–	+5.5
Broxtowe	66.5	–11.9	36.7	–0.8	48.6	+1.6	14.7	+2.8	–	–	–	–	–	–1.2
Gedling	63.9	–11.6	38.3	–1.2	51.1	+4.3	10.6	+0.7	–	–	–	–	–	–2.7
Mansfield	55.2	–15.4	27.2	+6.0	57.1	–7.3	15.7	+4.7	–	–	–	–	–	+6.7
Newark[†]	63.5	–10.9	46.5	+7.1	37.5	–7.8	13.2	+1.8	–	–	–	1.0	1.8 (2)	+7.4
Nottingham East	45.5	–14.7	24.3	+0.8	59.0	–3.3	13.0	+2.9	–	–	–	3.8	–	+2.0
North	46.7	–16.2	23.8	+3.5	64.5	–1.2	10.6	+2.6	–	–	–	–	–	+2.3
South	50.1	–16.4	27.2	–0.5	54.5	–0.8	16.6	+3.7	–	1.7	1.1	–	–	+0.1

	% Voting	Change in voting 1997–2001	% Con	Con change 1997–2001	% Lab	Lab change 1997–2001	% LibDem	LibDem change 1997–2001	% Green	% UKIP	% Socialist Labour	% Socialist Alliance	% Other	Swing
ENGLAND														
Rushcliffe	66.5	−12.4	47.5	+3.1	34.0	−2.2	13.6	−0.7	2.3	2.6	–	–	–	+2.7
Sherwood	60.7	−14.9	33.8	+5.1	54.2	−4.3	11.9	+3.3	2.5	1.3	–	–	–	+4.7
Oxfordshire, Banbury	61.8	−13.4	45.2	+2.3	35.0	+0.2	15.9	−0.8	2.6	3.2	–	–	–	+1.0
Henley	64.3	−13.3	46.1	−0.3	21.1	−1.6	27.0	+2.3	3.8	1.4	–	–	–	–
Oxford East	53.5	−15.5	18.7	−3.3	49.4	−7.4	23.4	+8.7	2.8	0.9	0.7	1.8	0.8 (3)	–
West & Abingdon	64.5	−12.6	30.0	−2.6	17.7	−2.5	47.8	+4.9	2.2	1.9	–	–	0.8 (3)	+0.3
Wantage	64.5	−13.7	39.6	−0.2	28.2	−0.7	28.0	+1.5	2.2	1.6	–	–	–	–
Witney	65.9	−10.8	45.0	+2.0	28.8	−1.8	20.3	+0.5	2.0	2.0	–	–	2.0 (2)	+1.9
Shropshire, Ludlow†	68.4	−7.2	39.4	−3.0	13.4	−12.0	43.2	+13.5	2.0	2.0	–	–	0.5 (2)	−2.1
Shrewsbury & Atcham	66.6	−8.7	37.4	+3.4	44.6	+7.6	12.4	−12.6	1.9	3.2	–	–	0.8 (2)	+4.6
Shropshire North	63.1	−9.6	48.6	+8.4	35.2	−0.7	12.8	−7.6	–	2.5	–	–	–	+1.6
Telford	51.9	−13.7	27.4	+0.0	54.6	−3.2	12.9	+1.1	–	3.6	–	1.5	–	+1.6
Wrekin, The	63.0	−13.5	38.4	−1.8	47.1	+0.1	11.4	−1.1	–	3.1	–	–	–	−1.0
Somerset, Bridgwater	64.6	−10.0	40.4	+3.5	26.8	+2.0	30.0	−3.6	–	2.8	–	–	–	–
Somerton & Frome	70.3	−7.1	42.4	+3.1	11.6	−4.7	43.6	+4.1	–	1.7	–	–	0.7	–
Taunton†	67.6	−8.8	41.7	+3.0	14.9	+1.4	41.3	−1.4	–	2.1	–	–	–	–
Wells	69.2	−8.7	43.8	+4.4	15.4	−2.7	38.3	−0.1	–	2.2	–	–	0.3	–
Yeovil	63.4	−9.4	36.0	+8.4	14.7	−0.2	44.2	−4.6	1.6	2.3	–	–	1.1	–
South Yorkshire														
Barnsley Central	45.8	−13.8	13.1	+3.3	69.6	−7.4	14.7	+5.2	–	–	–	2.6	–	–
East & Mexborough	49.5	−14.4	12.4	+1.0	67.5	−5.6	15.9	+5.5	–	2.0	2.2	–	–	–
West & Penistone	52.9	−12.1	22.8	+4.5	58.6	−0.7	18.6	+0.6	–	–	–	–	–	+2.6
Don Valley	55.3	−11.0	28.6	+4.0	54.6	−3.6	11.2	+1.4	–	2.1	1.3	–	2.2 (2)	+3.8

ENGLAND	% Voting	Change in voting 1997-2001	% Con	Con change 1997-2001	% Lab	Lab change 1997-2001	% LibDem	LibDem change 1997-2001	% Green	% UKIP	% Socialist Labour	% Socialist Alliance	% Other	Swing
Doncaster Central	52.1	−11.7	23.7	+2.7	59.1	−3.0	12.9	+3.5	–	2.7	–	1.5	–	+2.9
North	50.5	−12.8	14.7	−0.1	63.1	−6.7	10.6	+2.1	–	2.3	–	–	9.3 (2)	+3.3
Rother Valley	53.2	−14.0	21.7	+5.0	62.1	−5.5	12.5	+0.9	–	3.7	–	–	–	+5.2
Rotherham	50.7	−12.1	19.4	+5.1	63.9	−7.4	10.6	+0.2	2.0	2.5	–	1.2	0.5	+6.2
Sheffield Attercliffe	52.4	−12.3	15.2	−0.9	67.8	+2.5	14.2	−1.5	–	2.8	–	–	–	−1.7
Brightside	46.7	−10.8	10.2	+1.8	76.9	+3.4	8.8	−5.8	–	1.4	1.4	1.4	–	–
Central	48.5	−4.6	10.9	−1.0	61.4	−2.2	19.7	+2.5	3.4	0.9	1.0	2.5	0.2	–
Hallam	63.4	−8.9	31.0	−2.1	12.4	−1.1	55.4	+4.1	–	1.1	–	–	–	–
Heeley	54.4	−10.6	14.2	−1.4	57.0	−3.7	22.7	+1.4	–	1.9	2.0	–	–	–
Hillsborough	56.6	−14.4	18.3	+3.8	56.8	+0.0	22.6	−3.3	2.3	2.3	–	–	–	–
Wentworth	52.8	−12.6	18.8	+3.8	67.5	−4.8	10.8	+1.6	–	2.9	–	–	–	+4.3
Staffordshire, Burton	61.8	−13.3	38.6	−0.8	49.0	−2.0	9.6	+1.1	–	2.1	–	–	0.6	+0.6
Cannock Chase	55.9	−16.4	30.1	+2.9	56.1	+1.3	13.8	+5.1	–	–	–	–	–	+0.8
Lichfield	65.3	−12.1	49.1	+6.2	38.5	−3.9	10.7	−0.6	–	1.6	–	–	–	+5.1
Newcastle-under-Lyme	58.8	−14.8	27.6	+6.1	53.4	−3.1	15.5	+1.5	–	1.5	–	–	2.0 (2)	+4.6
Stafford	65.3	−11.3	36.6	−2.6	48.0	+0.4	9.5	−1.1	–	5.2	–	–	0.7	−1.5
Staffordshire Moorlands	63.9	−13.4	35.3	+2.8	49.0	−3.2	13.9	+1.8	–	1.8	–	–	–	+3.0
South	60.3	−13.9	50.5	+0.5	34.2	−0.5	11.6	+0.3	–	3.7	–	–	–	+0.5
Stoke-on-Trent Central	47.4	−15.1	18.8	+2.1	60.7	−5.6	14.7	+2.7	–	–	–	–	5.9 (2)	+3.8
North	51.9	−13.4	18.8	−1.3	58.0	−7.2	11.9	+1.2	–	–	–	–	11.3 (2)	+2.9
South	51.4	−14.5	24.6	+2.3	53.8	−8.2	13.1	+2.9	–	–	–	–	8.5 (3)	+5.2
Stone	66.3	−11.5	49.1	+2.2	35.8	−3.8	15.1	+3.0	–	–	–	–	–	+3.0
Tamworth	57.8	−16.3	37.6	+0.8	49.0	−2.8	11.7	+3.7	–	1.7	–	–	–	+1.8

ENGLAND	% Voting	Change in Voting 1997-2001	% Con	Con change 1997-2001	% Lab	Lab change 1997-2001	% LibDem	LibDem change 1997-2001	% Green	% UKIP	% Socialist Labour	% Socialist Alliance	% Other		Swing
Suffolk, Bury St. Edmunds	66.0	-9.0	43.5	+5.1	38.5	+0.8	13.9	-4.3	–	1.7	1.2	–	1.3	(2)	+2.2
Ipswich	57.0	-14.9	30.5	-0.6	51.3	-1.4	15.2	+3.0	–	1.6	0.6	0.8	–		+0.4
Suffolk Central & Ipswich North	63.5	-11.7	44.4	+1.8	37.1	+1.2	16.1	-4.5	–	2.4	–	–	–		+0.3
Coastal	66.4	-9.4	43.3	+4.8	34.8	+2.0	18.2	-3.2	–	3.7	–	–	–		+1.4
South	66.2	-11.0	41.4	+4.1	30.2	+0.9	24.9	-2.8	–	3.5	–	–	–		+1.6
West	59.6	-11.9	47.6	+6.7	37.5	+0.4	11.8	-2.2	–	3.1	–	0.9	–		+3.2
Waveney	61.5	-13.1	32.6	-1.9	50.7	-5.3	11.4	+2.4	2.1	2.3	–	–	–		+1.7
Surrey, Epsom & Ewell	62.8	-11.2	48.1	+2.5	26.5	+2.1	22.1	-0.7	–	3.3	–	–	–		+0.2
Esher & Walton	61.9	-12.4	49.0	-0.9	23.6	+0.9	22.5	+2.1	–	4.9	–	–	–		-0.9
Guildford†	62.9	-12.5	41.4	-1.1	13.7	-3.8	42.6	+8.4	–	1.5	–	–	0.8		–
Mole Valley	69.5	-9.4	50.5	+2.5	16.6	+1.9	29.0	-0.3	–	2.8	–	–	1.0		–
Reigate	60.7	-13.1	47.8	+4.0	27.5	-0.3	21.1	+1.1	2.9	2.7	–	–	0.9		+2.1
Runnymede & Weybridge	56.1	-15.3	48.7	+0.1	29.0	-0.5	16.3	+0.0	–	3.1	–	–	–		+0.3
Spelthorne	60.8	-12.8	45.1	+0.2	37.3	-0.9	14.7	+1.6	–	2.9	–	–	–		+0.6
Surrey East	62.7	-11.9	52.5	+2.4	19.1	-2.1	24.4	+2.0	–	3.9	–	–	–		–
Heath	59.5	-14.7	49.7	-1.9	21.4	+0.3	25.7	+3.9	–	3.3	–	–	–		–
South-West	66.9	-11.1	45.3	+0.7	8.7	-0.7	43.6	+3.8	–	2.4	–	–	–		–
Woking	60.3	-12.4	46.0	+7.6	20.3	-0.7	30.3	+3.0	–	3.4	–	–	–		–
Tyne & Wear, Blaydon	57.4	-13.6	11.4	-1.8	54.8	-5.1	33.8	+10.0	–	–	–	–	–		–
Gateshead E & Washington W	52.5	-14.7	14.8	+0.6	68.1	-3.9	14.9	+4.1	–	2.2	–	–	–		+2.3
Houghton & Washington E	49.5	-12.6	14.3	+1.4	73.2	-3.2	12.5	+4.8	–	–	–	–	–		–
Jarrow	54.6	-14.2	14.7	-0.3	66.1	+1.2	15.0	+4.0	–	2.1	–	–	2.2	(3)	–

	% Voting	Change in voting 1997–2001	% Con	Con change 1997–2001	% Lab	Lab change 1997–2001	% LibDem	LibDem change 1997–2001	% Green	% UKIP	% Socialist Labour	% Socialist Alliance	% Other	Swing
ENGLAND														
Newcastle-upon-Tyne Central	51.3	–14.0	21.3	–2.2	55.0	–4.2	21.7	+6.7	2.0	–	2.1	–	–	–
East & Wallsend	53.2	–12.4	11.8	–2.1	63.1	–8.1	19.6	+9.0	–	–	1.3	–	2.1 (3)	–
North	57.5	–11.5	20.4	+1.0	60.1	–2.0	19.4	+4.9	–	–	–	–	–	+1.5
South Shields	49.3	–13.3	16.9	+2.3	63.2	–8.3	16.8	+8.0	–	2.3	–	–	0.9 (2)	+5.3
Sunderland North	49.0	–10.0	17.9	+1.2	62.7	–5.6	12.1	+1.7	–	–	–	–	7.4 (3)	+3.4
South	48.3	–10.5	20.1	+1.2	63.9	–4.2	11.8	+0.2	–	1.5	–	–	2.8 (2)	+2.7
Tyne Bridge	44.2	–12.9	13.3	+2.2	70.5	–6.3	12.3	+4.4	–	–	2.0	–	–	+4.3
Tynemouth	67.4	–9.6	33.5	+0.1	53.2	–2.1	11.6	+2.8	–	–	–	1.9	–	+1.1
Tyneside North	57.7	–10.1	14.6	+0.9	69.5	–3.3	12.4	+1.9	–	–	0.6	–	–	+2.1
Warwickshire, Nuneaton	60.1	–14.1	34.7	+3.8	52.1	–4.1	11.1	+2.3	–	1.7	–	0.9	–	+4.0
Rugby & Kenilworth	67.4	–9.7	39.7	–2.6	45.0	+2.0	13.8	–0.4	–	2.1	–	–	–	–2.3
Stratford-on-Avon	64.4	–11.8	50.3	+2.0	16.7	–3.9	28.8	+3.2	–	2.0	–	–	–	–
Warwick & Leamington	65.8	–9.4	37.6	–1.2	48.8	+4.3	11.1	–0.7	2.1	1.5	–	1.2	–	–2.7
Warwickshire North	60.2	–14.5	32.4	+1.2	54.1	–4.3	11.4	+3.9	–	2.1	–	–	–	+2.8
West Midlands														
Aldridge-Brownhills	60.6	–13.7	50.2	+3.0	40.2	–1.5	8.6	–2.6	–	–	–	1.0	–	+2.3
Birmingham Edgbaston	56.0	–13.0	36.6	–2.0	49.1	+0.5	12.0	+2.3	–	–	1.1	–	1.2	–1.2
Erdington	46.6	–14.3	24.2	–3.3	56.8	–2.0	11.8	+1.6	–	1.7	1.1	2.2	2.2	–0.6
Hall Green	57.5	–13.7	34.5	+1.1	54.6	+1.1	8.8	–0.8	–	2.1	–	–	–	+0.0
Hodge Hill	47.9	–13.0	20.0	–4.0	63.9	–1.7	8.1	–0.4	–	1.0	1.1	–	6.0 (3)	–1.2
Ladywood	44.3	–10.0	11.3	–2.0	68.9	–5.2	8.2	+0.3	–	0.9	1.4	–	9.3 (3)	+1.6
Northfield	52.8	–15.5	29.6	+1.6	56.0	–1.5	11.2	+0.8	–	1.9	0.5	0.7	0.2	+1.5

ENGLAND

	% Voting	Change in voting 1997–2001	% Con	Con change 1997–2001	% Lab	Lab change 1997–2001	% LibDem	LibDem change 1997–2001	% Green	% UKIP	% Socialist Labour	% Socialist Alliance	% Other	Swing
Perry Barr	52.6	–12.0	23.1	+1.4	46.5	–16.5	22.9	+13.0	–	0.9	4.1	1.2	1.1 (2)	+9.0
Selly Oak	56.3	–13.9	26.6	–1.1	52.4	–3.2	16.3	+4.2	3.3	1.4	–	–	15.9 (4)	+1.0
Sparkbrook & Small Heath	49.3	–7.8	10.8	–6.7	57.5	–6.7	13.2	+3.9	–	1.7	0.5	0.8	–	–
Yardley	57.2	–14.0	13.1	–4.7	46.9	–0.1	38.3	+5.4	–	1.1	–	–	–	–
Coventry North-East	50.4	–14.0	18.8	–0.6	61.0	–5.2	11.2	+3.1	–	–	–	7.1	2.0 (2)	+2.3
North-West	55.5	–15.2	25.9	–0.4	51.4	–5.4	13.7	+3.2	–	1.5	–	–	7.4	+2.5
South	55.3	–13.4	29.5	+0.5	50.2	–0.7	14.1	+4.9	–	–	1.0	3.7	1.4 (2)	+0.6
Dudley North	55.9	–13.4	34.5	+3.1	52.1	+0.9	8.7	+0.5	–	–	–	–	4.7	+1.1
South	55.4	–16.3	31.1	+1.6	49.8	–6.8	14.9	+4.0	–	2.4	–	1.8	–	+4.2
Halesowen & Rowley Regis	59.8	–13.8	34.2	+1.4	53.0	–1.1	10.4	+1.9	–	2.4	–	–	–	+1.2
Meriden	59.9	–11.7	47.7	+5.7	39.2	–1.8	11.1	–1.9	–	2.0	–	–	–	+3.7
Solihull	62.6	–11.8	45.4	+0.8	25.6	+1.3	26.0	+0.7	–	2.2	–	–	0.8	–
Stourbridge	61.8	–14.6	37.6	+1.8	47.1	+0.0	12.1	–2.2	–	1.9	1.2	–	–	+0.9
Sutton Coldfield	60.5	–12.4	50.4	–1.8	27.2	+3.3	19.0	–0.3	–	2.7	–	–	0.7 (2)	–2.6
Walsall North	48.9	–15.1	29.1	+1.5	58.1	+1.5	9.0	–0.3	–	2.5	–	1.3	–	+0.0
South	55.7	–11.6	30.5	–1.2	59.0	+1.1	6.8	+0.5	–	2.8	–	1.0	–	–1.1
Warley	54.1	–10.8	22.8	–1.3	60.5	–3.3	10.6	+0.8	–	–	6.2	–	–	+1.0
West Bromwich East	53.4	–12.0	26.0	+1.6	55.9	–1.3	13.8	–1.1	–	2.6	1.8	–	–	+1.4
West*	47.7	–6.6	25.1	–	60.8	–4.5	6.8	–	–	1.6	1.2	–	4.5	–
Wolverhampton North-East	52.1	–14.9	28.6	+0.7	60.3	+1.0	7.9	+2.6	–	3.2	–	–	–	–0.1
South-East	50.6	–13.4	21.8	+1.6	67.4	+3.7	8.8	–0.7	–	–	–	–	2.0	–1.0
South-West	60.9	–11.2	39.7	–0.2	48.3	–2.1	8.4	+0.2	2.0	1.7	–	–	–	+1.0

	% Voting	Change in voting 1997–2001	% Con	Con change 1997–2001	% Lab	Lab change 1997–2001	% LibDem	LibDem change 1997–2001	% Green	% UKIP	% Socialist Labour	% Socialist Alliance	% Other	Swing
ENGLAND														
West Sussex														
Arundel & South Downs	64.7	–11.2	52.2	–0.9	20.7	+2.4	22.4	–3.4	–	4.7	–	–	–	–
Bognor Regis & Littlehampton	58.2	–11.3	45.2	+1.0	30.7	+2.2	17.6	–6.4	2.0	4.6	–	–	–	–0.6
Chichester	63.8	–10.7	47.0	+0.6	21.4	+4.2	24.1	–4.8	2.6	4.8	–	–	–	–
Crawley	55.2	–17.4	32.2	+0.4	49.3	–5.7	12.7	+4.5	–	2.9	0.7	0.6	–	+3.0
Horsham	63.8	–12.0	51.5	+0.7	20.2	+1.5	24.6	–0.2	–	2.9	–	–	1.7 (2)	–
Sussex Mid	64.9	–12.9	46.2	+2.7	19.0	+0.3	31.1	–0.5	–	2.5	–	–	0.8 (2)	–
Worthing East & Shoreham	59.9	–13.0	43.2	+2.7	29.0	+5.0	22.9	–7.6	–	2.8	–	–	1.3	–
West	59.7	–12.1	47.5	+1.3	21.5	+5.2	26.5	–4.6	–	4.5	–	–	2.1	–
West Yorkshire, Batley & Spen	60.5	–12.5	36.7	+0.4	49.9	+0.5	10.3	+1.5	1.5	1.5	–	–	–	+0.0
Bradford North	52.7	–10.4	24.1	–1.5	49.7	–6.3	19.8	+5.3	1.7	–	–	–	–	+2.4
South	51.3	–14.4	28.3	+0.3	55.8	–0.9	10.6	–0.7	–	2.2	1.6	0.9	4.6	+0.6
West	53.3	–9.6	37.3	+4.3	48.2	+6.7	6.4	–8.4	7.0	1.1	–	–	0.6	–1.2
Calder Valley	63.0	–12.4	36.2	+1.1	42.7	–3.4	16.0	+1.3	2.2	1.5	–	–	1.4	+2.3
Colne Valley	63.3	–13.5	30.5	–2.2	40.4	–0.9	24.9	+2.3	2.3	2.0	–	–	–	–0.6
Dewsbury	58.8	–11.2	30.2	+0.1	50.5	+1.1	12.0	+1.7	1.5	1.3	–	–	–	–0.5
Elmet	65.6	–11.1	38.9	+2.7	48.0	–4.4	10.9	+2.2	–	2.2	–	–	4.5	+3.6
Halifax	57.8	–12.7	33.8	+1.7	49.0	–5.3	14.6	+2.6	–	2.6	–	–	–	+3.5
Hemsworth	51.8	–16.1	21.0	+3.2	65.4	–5.2	11.3	+2.5	–	–	2.3	–	–	+4.2
Huddersfield	55.0	–12.5	24.9	+3.9	53.2	–3.2	15.0	–2.2	3.5	1.7	0.6	1.1	–	+3.6
Keighley	63.4	–12.9	39.0	+2.2	48.2	–2.4	10.9	+1.1	–	1.9	–	–	–	+2.3
Leeds Central	41.7	–12.5	14.3	+0.5	66.9	–2.7	13.2	+2.0	–	2.8	–	2.8	–	+1.6

ENGLAND	% Voting	Change in voting 1997–2001	% Con	Con change 1997–2001	% Lab	Lab change 1997–2001	% LibDem	LibDem change 1997–2001	% Green	% UKIP	% Socialist Labour	% Socialist Alliance	% Other	Swing
East	51.5	–11.3	19.4	+0.8	62.9	–4.5	13.5	+3.2	–	2.2	1.4	–	0.5 (2)	+2.6
North-East	62.0	–9.8	31.3	–2.6	49.1	+0.0	15.9	+2.0	–	1.0	0.4	–	2.3 (3)	–1.3
North-West	58.2	–11.5	29.6	–2.5	41.9	+2.0	26.9	+3.3	–	1.6	–	–	–	–2.3
West	50.0	–12.7	15.6	–1.9	62.1	–4.5	10.4	+1.4	8.0	2.4	–	–	1.4	+1.3
Morley & Rothwell	53.5	–13.5	25.6	–0.8	57.0	–1.5	14.2	+3.1	–	3.2	–	–	–	+0.3
Normanton	52.2	–16.1	27.0	+3.4	56.1	–4.5	14.6	+2.2	–	–	2.3	1.1	–	+3.9
Pontefract & Castleford	49.7	–16.7	17.6	+4.0	69.7	–6.0	7.4	+0.0	–	2.4	1.9	–	–	+5.0
Pudsey	63.3	–11.0	35.6	–0.7	48.1	+0.0	14.2	+0.2	–	2.1	–	–	–	–0.3
Shipley	66.1	–10.0	40.9	+3.1	44.0	+0.6	10.9	–4.2	3.0	1.3	–	–	–	+1.3
Wakefield	54.5	–14.5	30.6	+2.2	49.9	–7.5	12.4	+1.2	2.6	1.6	1.5	1.3	–	+4.8
Wiltshire, Devizes	63.7	–10.7	47.2	+4.4	24.9	+0.7	22.1	–4.5	–	2.9	–	–	2.9 (3)	–
Salisbury	65.3	–8.4	46.6	+3.7	17.5	–0.1	30.1	–2.1	2.1	3.7	–	–	–	–
Swindon North	61.0	–12.6	33.7	–0.1	52.9	+3.1	11.6	–1.4	–	1.9	–	–	–	–1.6
South	61.0	–11.8	34.4	–1.4	51.3	+4.5	11.9	–2.5	–	1.6	–	–	0.8	–2.9
Westbury	66.7	–9.5	42.1	+1.5	21.4	+0.3	31.6	+1.7	2.4	2.5	–	–	–	–
Wiltshire North	66.6	–8.0	45.5	+1.7	14.3	+0.0	38.2	+0.4	–	2.1	–	–	–	–

WALES	% Voting	Change in voting 1997-2001	% Con	Con change 1997-2001	% Lab	Lab change 1997-2001	% LibDem	LibDem change 1997-2001	% Plaid Cymru	Plaid Cymru change 1997-2001	% Green	% UKIP	% Socialist Labour	% Socialist Alliance	% Other	Swing
Clwyd, Alyn & Deeside	58.6	–13.5	26.3	+3.5	52.3	–9.6	12.9	+3.2	3.3	+1.5	2.5	1.4	–	–	1.3 (3)	+6.5
Clwyd South	62.4	–11.2	24.8	+1.8	51.4	–6.7	10.2	+0.9	11.8	+5.5	–	1.6	–	–	–	+4.3
West	64.1	–11.0	35.6	+3.1	38.8	+1.7	11.4	–1.4	12.8	–0.5	–	1.4	–	–	–	+0.7
Delyn	63.3	–12.5	26.6	+0.6	51.5	–5.7	15.4	+5.2	6.5	+2.7	–	–	–	–	–	+3.2
Vale of Clwyd	63.1	–11.5	32.2	+2.4	50.0	–2.7	9.5	+0.7	7.1	+1.2	–	1.2	–	–	–	+2.5
Wrexham	59.5	–12.2	22.5	–1.4	53.0	–3.1	17.1	+3.9	5.9	+2.7	–	1.4	–	–	–	+0.9
Dyfed, Carmarthen E & Dinefwr†	70.4	–8.2	12.9	+0.9	35.6	–7.3	7.4	–0.2	42.3	+7.7	–	1.7	–	–	–	–
West & Pembrokeshire S	65.3	–11.1	29.3	+2.7	41.6	–7.6	8.8	+0.6	18.6	+6.0	–	1.5	–	–	0.2	+5.1
Ceredigion	61.7	–12.1	19.4	+4.6	15.4	–8.9	26.9	+10.4	38.2	–3.3	–	–	–	–	–	–
Llanelli	62.3	–8.4	9.5	–2.6	48.6	–9.3	8.5	–0.7	30.8	+11.9	1.4	–	1.1	–	–	–
Preseli Pembrokeshire	67.8	–10.5	33.3	+5.6	41.3	–6.9	10.6	–2.5	12.6	+6.3	–	0.9	1.2	–	–	+6.3
Gwent, Blaenau Gwent	59.5	–12.8	7.5	+0.9	72.0	–7.4	9.3	+0.6	11.1	+5.9	–	–	–	–	–	–
Islwyn	61.9	–10.1	8.0	+0.2	61.5	–12.6	13.2	+4.8	11.8	+5.6	–	–	1.3	–	4.0 (2)	–
Monmouth	71.5	–9.3	41.9	+2.7	42.8	–5.0	11.4	+1.9	2.4	+1.3	–	1.5	–	–	–	+3.8
Newport East	55.7	–17.3	23.2	+1.8	54.7	–2.9	14.0	+3.6	4.8	+2.9	–	1.3	1.3	–	0.6	+2.4
West	58.7	–15.9	26.2	+1.8	52.7	–7.8	11.7	+2.0	7.1	+5.5	–	1.4	–	–	0.8	+4.8
Torfaen	57.7	–14.0	15.9	+3.6	62.1	–7.0	11.2	–1.0	7.7	+5.3	–	1.9	–	1.3	–	+5.3
Gwynedd, Caernarfon	61.4	–12.4	15.2	+2.9	32.3	+2.8	6.3	+1.4	44.3	–6.6	–	1.9	–	–	–	–
Conwy	62.8	–12.5	23.7	–0.6	41.8	+6.8	16.9	–14.3	16.4	+9.6	–	1.1	–	–	–	–
Meirionnydd Nant Conwy	63.5	–12.5	18.8	+2.8	22.7	–0.4	8.9	+1.9	49.6	–1.0	–	–	–	–	–	–
Ynys Mon†	64.0	–11.4	22.5	+1.0	35.0	+1.8	8.1	+4.3	32.6	–6.8	–	1.1	–	–	0.7 (2)	–
Mid Glamorgan, Bridgend	60.1	–12.2	25.3	+2.5	52.5	–5.5	14.4	+2.9	7.1	+3.3	–	–	–	–	0.6	+4.0
Caerphilly	57.2	–12.8	11.4	+0.7	58.5	–9.3	9.0	+0.7	21.1	+11.4	–	–	–	–	–	–

WALES	% Voting	Change in voting 1997–2001	% Con	Con change 1997–2001	% Lab	Lab change 1997–2001	% LibDem	LibDem change 1997–2001	% Plaid Cymru	Plaid Cymru change 1997–2001	% Green	% UKIP	% Socialist Labour	% Socialist Alliance	% Other	Swing
Cynon Valley	55.5	–13.7	7.6	+0.8	65.6	–4.1	9.4	–0.9	17.3	+6.7	–	–	–	–	–	–
Merthyr Tydfil & Rhymney	57.4	–11.8	7.2	+0.8	61.8	–14.9	7.5	+0.1	14.6	+8.6	–	–	2.2	–	6.7 (3)	–
Ogmore	58.2	–14.9	11.1	+1.4	62.0	–11.9	12.8	+3.6	14.0	+6.9	–	–	–	–	–	–
Pontypridd	58.0	–13.5	13.3	+0.4	59.9	–3.9	10.8	–2.6	13.7	+7.2	–	1.6	–	–	0.6	–
Rhondda	60.7	–10.8	4.6	+0.8	68.3	–6.1	4.5	–1.2	21.1	+7.7	–	–	–	–	–	–
Powys, Brecon & Radnorshire	71.8	–10.4	34.8	+5.9	21.4	–5.3	36.8	–4.0	3.4	+2.0	–	1.2	–	–	1.5 (2)	–
Montgomeryshire	65.5	–9.4	27.9	+1.8	11.9	–7.3	49.4	+3.5	6.7	+1.7	–	2.7	–	–	2.2 (3)	–
South Glamorgan, Cardiff Central	58.3	–10.7	15.9	–4.2	38.6	–5.1	36.7	+11.8	4.8	+1.2	1.9	0.6	–	0.8	1.3 (3)	–
North	69.0	–10.7	31.6	–2.0	45.9	–4.6	15.3	+4.4	5.7	+3.2	–	1.4	–	–	0.6	+1.3
South & Penarth	57.5	–10.8	21.8	+1.1	56.2	+2.8	12.8	+3.4	5.5	+2.3	–	1.4	–	1.2	1.0	–0.8
West	58.4	–10.5	21.3	–0.2	54.6	–5.8	13.1	+2.2	9.6	+4.8	–	1.4	–	–	–	+2.8
Vale of Glamorgan	67.4	–12.6	35.0	+0.7	45.4	–8.5	12.2	+3.0	6.3	+3.7	–	1.0	–	–	–	+4.6
West Glamorgan, Aberavon	60.8	–11.1	7.6	–0.3	63.1	–8.2	9.7	–1.6	9.7	+3.9	1.6	–	–	0.8	8.9 (3)	–
Gower	63.4	–11.6	27.5	+3.7	47.3	–6.5	12.1	–0.9	10.3	+5.2	–	–	1.1	–	–	+5.1
Neath	62.4	–11.9	9.5	+0.8	60.7	–12.8	9.5	+3.2	18.3	+10.2	–	–	–	1.4	0.6	–
Swansea East	52.5	–14.7	10.1	+0.8	65.2	–10.2	10.2	+1.3	11.5	+8.1	1.5	1.5	–	–	–	–
West	56.2	–12.0	19.0	–1.5	48.7	–7.5	16.6	+2.0	10.6	+3.9	2.0	2.0	–	1.1	–	+3.0

SCOTLAND	% Voting	Change in voting 1997-2001	% Con	Con change 1997-2001	% Lab	Lab change 1997-2001	% LibDem	LibDem change 1997-2001	% SNP	SNP change 1997-2001	% Green	% UKIP	% Socialist Labour	% Scottish Socialist	% Other	Swing
Borders, Roxburgh & Berwickshire	61.2	−12.6	22.7	−1.2	15.6	+0.7	48.8	+2.3	9.7	−1.5	–	1.6	–	1.6	–	–
Tweeddale, Ettrick & Lauderdale	63.9	−12.5	15.4	−6.7	26.7	−0.7	42.3	+11.0	12.3	−4.7	–	–	–	2.1	1.2	–
Central, Falkirk East	58.5	−14.8	9.6	−4.3	55.0	−1.1	8.9	+3.7	23.2	−0.7	–	–	–	2.2	–	–
West	57.7	−15.0	7.5	−4.6	51.9	−7.5	7.1	+2.0	24.2	+0.8	–	–	1.1	2.3	6.3 (3)	–
Ochil	61.3	−15.6	12.0	−2.6	45.3	+0.3	9.2	+4.0	30.1	−4.2	–	–	0.6	2.1	1.1	–
Stirling	67.7	−14.2	24.8	−7.7	42.2	−5.2	11.7	+5.5	16.3	+2.9	–	–	–	2.8	–	−1.3
Dumfries & Galloway, Dumfries	67.7	−11.2	28.2	+0.1	48.9	+1.4	11.6	+0.6	9.6	−2.4	–	–	–	1.6	–	−0.6
Galloway & Upper Nithsdale†	68.1	−11.6	34.0	+3.5	20.2	+3.9	10.3	+3.9	33.8	−10.0	–	–	–	1.6	–	–
Fife, Dunfermline East	57.0	−13.2	9.4	−0.6	64.8	−2.0	7.6	+1.7	14.7	−0.8	–	1.0	–	2.6	–	–
West	57.1	−12.3	10.2	−2.4	52.8	−0.2	15.6	+2.0	17.4	−1.7	–	1.5	–	2.4	–	–
Fife Central	54.6	−15.3	7.2	−1.8	56.3	−2.3	8.5	+2.1	25.3	+0.3	–	–	–	2.6	–	–
North-East	56.0	−14.6	23.6	−2.9	11.4	+1.1	51.7	+0.4	10.3	−0.4	–	–	–	1.8	1.2	–
Kirkcaldy	54.6	−12.3	10.7	−3.0	54.1	+0.5	10.1	+1.5	22.2	−0.6	–	–	–	2.9	–	–
Grampian, Aberdeen Central	52.8	−12.9	14.2	−5.3	45.5	−4.3	17.2	+4.0	20.3	+4.1	–	–	–	2.7	–	–
North	57.6	−13.2	10.0	−5.0	43.3	−4.5	16.4	+2.3	28.6	+6.8	–	–	–	1.5	–	–
South	62.6	−10.2	19.2	−7.1	39.8	+4.6	27.9	+0.3	11.6	+1.8	–	–	–	1.3	–	–
Aberdeenshire W & Kincardine	62.0	−11.1	30.8	−4.1	12.3	+3.2	43.5	+2.5	12.2	−0.8	–	–	–	1.1	–	–
Banff & Buchan	54.5	−14.2	20.1	−3.7	14.2	+2.3	9.0	+3.0	54.2	−1.5	–	1.0	–	1.5	–	–
Gordon	61.7	−10.2	21.8	−4.3	12.8	+2.5	48.5	+5.8	15.5	−4.3	–	–	–	1.4	–	–
Moray	57.3	−10.7	23.1	−4.5	25.1	+5.2	15.7	+6.8	30.3	−11.2	–	0.9	–	2.5	2.4 (2)	–
Highlands																
Caithness, Sutherland & Easter Ross	60.3	−9.7	14.1	+3.3	25.3	−2.5	36.4	+0.8	21.2	−1.7	–	–	–	2.2	0.8 (2)	–

SCOTLAND	% Voting	Change in voting 1997–2001	% Con	Con change 1997–2001	% Lab	Lab change 1997–2001	% LibDem	LibDem change 1997–2001	% SNP	SNP change 1997–2001	% Green	% UKIP	% Socialist Labour	% Scottish Socialist	% Other	Swing
Inverness East, Nairn & Lochaber	63.2	−9.3	13.3	−4.2	36.8	+2.9	22.2	+4.7	25.6	−3.3	–	–	–	2.1	–	–
Ross, Skye & Inverness West	61.6	−10.0	8.9	−2.0	16.9	−11.8	54.1	+15.4	14.0	−5.4	2.0	1.3	–	2.0	0.8	–
Lothian, East Lothian	62.5	−13.1	17.8	−2.1	47.2	−5.5	17.6	+7.1	14.5	−1.1	–	–	1.0	1.7	–	+1.7
Edinburgh Central	52.0	−15.1	16.4	−4.8	42.1	−4.9	18.5	+5.4	14.0	−1.7	5.3	–	–	3.7	–	–
East & Musselburgh	58.2	−12.5	11.3	−4.1	52.6	−1.0	14.5	+3.7	17.2	−1.7	–	–	–	4.3	–	–
North & Leith	53.2	−13.3	13.9	−3.9	45.9	−1.0	19.4	+6.4	15.9	−4.1	–	–	0.8	4.0	–	–
Pentlands	65.1	−11.6	36.1	+3.7	40.6	−2.4	10.8	+0.8	10.8	−2.1	–	0.3	–	1.4	–	+3.1
South	58.1	−13.7	16.6	−4.7	42.2	−4.7	27.4	+9.7	9.9	−3.0	–	–	–	2.5	1.4	–
West	63.8	−14.1	22.5	−5.4	23.1	+4.3	42.4	−0.9	10.2	+1.4	–	–	–	1.7	–	–
Linlithgow	58.0	−15.8	9.0	−3.6	54.4	+0.2	8.3	+2.4	25.5	−1.2	–	–	–	2.2	0.7	–
Livingston	55.6	−15.4	8.3	−1.1	53.0	−1.9	11.0	+4.3	23.5	−3.8	–	1.0	–	3.1	–	–
Midlothian	59.1	−15.0	9.6	−1.3	52.7	−0.8	12.8	+3.7	21.3	−4.1	–	–	–	2.9	0.6	–
Tweeddale, Ettrick & L., (See Borders)																
Orkney & Shetland	52.4	−11.4	18.7	+6.4	20.6	+2.3	41.3	−10.6	14.7	+2.0	–	–	–	4.6	–	–
Strathclyde, Airdrie & Shotts	54.4	−17.0	6.2	−2.7	58.2	−3.6	7.5	+3.3	19.3	−5.0	–	–	0.5	3.7	4.5	–
Argyll & Bute	63.0	−9.1	20.8	+1.8	24.5	+8.9	29.9	−10.3	20.7	−2.3	–	–	–	4.0	–	–
Ayr	69.3	−10.9	37.0	+3.2	43.6	−4.9	5.4	+0.7	11.9	−0.5	–	0.3	–	1.8	–	+4.0
Carrick, Cumnock & Doon Valley	61.8	−13.2	18.2	+1.3	55.3	−4.5	7.3	+2.0	15.6	−1.0	–	–	0.9	2.6	–	+2.9
Clydebank & Milngavie	61.8	−13.1	10.8	−1.7	53.1	−2.1	12.0	+1.6	20.0	−1.0	–	–	–	4.0	–	–
Clydesdale	59.3	−12.3	13.2	−3.1	46.6	−5.9	10.8	+2.4	26.2	+4.1	–	0.7	–	2.5	–	–

SCOTLAND	% Voting	Change in voting 1997–2001	% Con	Con change 1997–2001	% Lab	Lab change 1997–2001	% LibDem	LibDem change 1997–2001	% SNP	SNP change 1997–2001	% Green	% UKIP	% Socialist Labour	% Scottish Socialist	% Other	Swing
Coatbridge & Chryston	58.1	−14.2	7.2	−1.4	65.3	−3.0	7.6	+2.1	14.8	−2.1	—	—	—	5.1	—	—
Cumbernauld & Kilsyth	59.7	−15.3	4.9	−1.9	54.4	−4.3	6.5	+2.7	29.0	+1.2	—	—	—	4.3	0.8	—
Cunninghame North	61.5	−12.6	19.7	−3.7	46.0	−4.2	9.0	+3.5	21.2	+2.7	—	—	1.1	2.9	—	—
South	56.2	−15.3	9.9	−0.2	58.4	−4.3	7.4	+2.9	18.4	−2.2	—	—	1.4	4.4	—	—
Dumbarton	60.4	−13.0	13.7	−4.0	47.5	−2.1	15.5	+7.9	19.3	−3.8	—	—	—	4.0	—	—
East Kilbride	62.6	−12.2	10.2	−1.8	53.3	−3.3	10.3	+3.0	22.6	+1.7	—	—	—	3.6	—	—
Eastwood	70.7	−7.5	28.7	−4.8	47.6	+7.9	12.9	+1.2	8.5	−4.5	—	—	—	1.7	0.5 (2)	−6.4
Glasgow Anniesland	50.1	−13.6	9.9	−1.5	56.5	−5.3	12.1	+4.9	15.1	−1.9	—	—	0.7	5.6	—	—
Baillieston	47.2	−15.0	6.8	−1.0	61.0	−4.6	6.7	+2.8	18.7	−0.3	—	—	—	6.7	—	—
Cathcart	52.6	−15.0	13.4	+0.6	54.4	−3.0	11.0	+4.1	14.9	−3.6	—	—	—	6.3	—	—
Govan	46.8	−17.8	8.6	−0.2	49.3	+5.2	11.1	+5.2	23.9	−11.0	—	—	—	6.1	1.0 (3)	—
Kelvin	43.6	−12.6	8.9	−1.9	44.8	−6.1	17.7	+3.6	16.8	−4.5	4.8	—	—	6.9	—	—
Maryhill	40.1	−16.3	5.2	−0.7	60.4	−4.6	10.7	+3.5	15.8	−1.0	—	—	—	7.8	—	—
Pollok	51.4	−15.1	5.6	−0.4	61.3	+1.4	6.4	+2.9	16.7	−1.1	—	—	—	10.0	—	—
Rutherglen	56.3	−13.8	11.3	+2.0	57.4	−0.1	12.6	−1.9	14.1	−1.1	—	—	1.1	4.5	—	—
Shettleston	39.7	−14.9	5.3	−0.2	64.7	−8.5	5.4	+1.4	16.6	+2.7	—	—	—	6.8	—	—
Springburn*	43.7	−15.3	—	—	66.6	−4.8	—	—	19.3	+2.9	—	—	—	7.8	6.2 (3)	—
Greenock & Inverclyde	59.3	−11.7	10.6	−0.9	52.5	−3.6	17.7	+3.9	14.9	−3.6	—	—	—	4.2	—	—
Hamilton North & Bellshill	56.8	−14.1	8.7	−1.7	61.8	−2.2	7.8	+2.7	17.1	−1.9	—	—	0.6	3.9	—	—
South	57.3	−13.7	7.0	−1.6	59.7	−5.9	8.9	+3.8	19.3	+1.7	—	0.6	—	4.4	—	—
Kilmarnock & Loudoun	61.7	−15.5	10.5	−0.3	52.9	+3.1	8.4	+4.4	25.4	−9.0	—	—	—	2.7	—	—
Motherwell & Wishaw	56.6	−13.5	10.6	−0.4	56.2	−1.2	9.4	+3.0	19.2	−3.1	—	—	0.2	4.2	—	—

SCOTLAND	% Voting	Change in voting 1997-2001	% Con	Con change 1997-2001	% Lab	Lab change 1997-2001	% LibDem	LibDem change 1997-2001	% SNP	SNP change 1997-2001	% Green	% UKIP	% Socialist Labour	% Scottish Socialist	% Other	Swing
Paisley North	56.6	-12.0	8.9	-0.7	55.5	-4.0	10.0	+3.0	21.1	-0.7	–	–	–	3.6	1.0	–
South	57.2	-12.3	7.5	-1.1	58.4	+0.9	10.4	+1.0	19.3	-3.9	–	–	–	2.7	1.5 (3)	–
Renfrewshire West	63.3	-12.5	16.5	-2.1	46.9	+0.4	12.5	+4.8	21.3	-5.1	–	–	–	2.8	–	–
Strathkelvin & Bearsden	66.1	-12.7	16.0	-4.1	46.4	-6.5	18.2	+8.4	16.0	-0.2	–	–	–	3.4	–	–
Tayside, Angus	59.3	-12.8	25.0	+0.3	23.4	+7.7	14.3	+4.9	35.2	-13.0	–	–	–	2.1	–	–
Dundee East	57.3	-12.2	12.0	-3.7	45.2	-5.9	8.6	+4.5	31.4	+4.8	–	–	–	2.7	–	–
West	54.4	-13.3	9.1	-4.1	50.6	-3.2	9.0	+1.3	27.3	+4.0	–	–	–	4.1	–	–
Ochil, (See Central)																
Perth	61.5	-12.4	29.6	+0.3	25.5	+0.7	12.8	+4.8	29.7	-6.6	–	–	–	2.4	–	–
Tayside North	62.5	-11.8	31.6	-4.2	14.8	+3.6	11.3	+3.2	40.0	-4.7	–	–	–	1.6	0.6 (2)	–
Western Isles	60.3	-9.7	9.5	+2.8	45.0	-10.6	6.5	+3.4	36.8	+3.4	–	–	–	2.2	–	–

Table A1.4   Constituency results, Northern Ireland 2001

	% Voting	Change in voting 1997–2001	% UUP	% DUP	% Other Unionist	Unionist Change 1997–2001	% APNI	APNI change 1997–2001	% Con	Con change 1997–2001	NIWC	% SDLP	SDLP change 1997–2001	% SF	SF change 1997–2001	% WP	Republican change 1997–2001	% Other
Antrim East	59.1	+0.9	36.4	36.0	3.0	+12.1	12.5	–7.7	2.2	–4.6	–	7.3	+2.7	2.5	+0.9	–	+3.7	–
Antrim North	66.1	+2.3	21.0	49.9	–	+0.6	2.6	–3.6	–	–	–	16.8	+1.0	9.8	+3.5	–	+4.5	–
Antrim South‡	62.5	+4.6	37.1	34.8	2.2	+7.9	4.5	–7.2	–	–	–	12.1	–4.1	9.4	+3.9	–	–0.2	–
Belfast East	62.8	–0.4	23.3	42.7	10.0	+8.0	15.9	–7.9	2.2	–0.2	–	2.4	+0.8	3.4	+1.3	0.3	+1.8	0.2
Belfast North†	66.8	+2.6	12.1	41.1	–	+1.3	–	–	–	–	–	21.1	+0.7	25.4	+5.2	0.6	+5.8	0.3
Belfast South	63.5	+1.3	45.1	–	2.9	–2.4	5.4	–7.5	–	–	–	30.8	+6.4	7.7	+2.6	0.5	+8.8	0.3
Belfast West	67.5	–6.8	6.3	6.6	–	+9.5	–	–	–	–	7.9	19.3	–19.4	67.3	+11.4	1.8	–7.8	0.5
Down North†	58.8	+0.8	56.0	–	36.3	+26.2	–	–	2.2	–2.8	–	3.4	–1.0	0.8	–	–	–0.1	1.2
Down South	70.8	+0.0	17.6	15.0	–	–0.2	1.3	–2.1	–	–	–	46.3	–6.6	19.7	+9.4	–	+2.8	–
Fermanagh & S Tyrone†	78.0	+3.2	34.0	–	13.2	–4.3	–	–	–	–	–	18.7	–4.2	34.1	+11.0	–	+6.8	–
Foyle	68.9	–1.8	6.9	15.2	–	+0.5	1.2	–0.5	–	–	–	50.2	–2.3	26.6	+2.6	–	+0.3	–
Lagan Valley	63.2	+1.0	56.5	13.4	–	+1.0	16.6	–0.6	–	–	–	7.5	–0.2	5.9	+3.4	–	+2.7	–
Londonderry East†	66.1	+1.4	27.4	32.1	–	–1.7	4.1	–2.3	–	–	–	20.8	–0.9	15.6	+6.5	–	+5.6	–
Newry and Armagh	76.8	+1.3	12.3	19.4	–	–2.1	–	–	–	–	–	37.4	–5.6	30.9	+9.9	–	+4.3	–
Strangford†	59.9	+0.4	40.3	42.8	1.9	+10.5	6.7	–6.4	–	–	–	6.1	–0.6	2.2	+0.9	–	–0.4	–
Tyrone West†	79.9	+0.3	30.4	–	–	–4.1	–	–	–	–	–	28.7	–3.3	40.8	+10.0	–	+6.1	–
Ulster Mid	80.5	–5.6	–	31.5	–	–4.9	–	–	–	–	–	16.9	–5.2	51.6	+11.5	1.0	+6.9	–
Upper Bann	69.6	+1.7	33.8	29.8	–	+8.5	–	–	–	–	–	15.1	–9.2	21.3	+9.2	1.0	–0.1	–
Total	67.8	+0.6	26.8	22.5	3.9	+2.2	3.6	–4.4	0.3	–0.9	0.4	21.0	–3.2	21.7	+5.7	0.3	+2.4	0.2

Notes:
APNI: Alliance Party of Northern Ireland
DUP: Democratic Unionist Party
NIWC: Northern Ireland Women's Coalition
SDLP: Social Democratic & Labour Party
SF: Sinn Féin
UUP: (Official) Ulster Unionist Party
WP: Workers' Party
Other U: Other Unionist, viz. Progressive Unionist Party (Antrim South, Belfast South), United Kingdom Unionist (Down North), NI Unionist (Antrim South, Strangford), Independent Unionist (Fermanagh & South Tyrone)
'Unionist Change' is the change in the total vote for Official Unionists, Democratic Unionists and other Unionists.
'Republican Change' is the change in the total vote for the SDLP, Sinn Féin, and the Workers' Party.

Table A1.5   Outstanding results 2001

Seats changing hands at the 2001 General Election (1997 victors in parentheses)

Conservative gains (9)
Castle Point *(Labour)*
Galloway & Upper Nithsdale *(SNP)*
Isle of Wight *(LibDem)*
Newark *(Labour)*
N W Norfolk *(Labour)*
Romford *(Labour)*
Tatton *(Independent)*
Taunton *(LibDem)*
Upminster *(Labour)*

Labour gains (3)
South Dorset *(Conservative)*
West Bromwich West *(Speaker)*
Ynys-Mon *(Plaid Cymru)*

Liberal Democrat gains (8)
Cheadle *(Conservative)*
Chesterfield *(Labour)*
Guildford *(Conservative)*
Ludlow *(Conservative)*
Mid Dorset & North Poole *(Conservative)*
North Norfolk *(Conservative)*
Romsey *(Conservative)*
Teignbridge *(Conservative)*

Plaid Cymru gain
Carmarthen East & Dinefwr *(Labour)*

Independent gain
Wyre Forest *(Labour)*

Speaker gain
Glasgow Springburn *(Labour)*

DUP gains (3)
Belfast North *(UUP)*
East Londonderry *(UUP)*
Strangford *(UUP)*

Sinn Féin gains (2)
Fermanagh & South Tyrone *(UUP)*
West Tyrone *(UUP)*

Ulster Unionist gain
North Down *(UKUP)*

Source: House of Commons Research Paper 01–054

10 Highest Turnouts (GB)
%
72.3	Winchester
71.8	Brecon & Radnorshire
71.5	Monmouth
70.9	Hexham
70.7	Eastwood
70.7	Northavon
70.5	Devon W & Torridge
70.4	Carmarthen E & Din.
70.3	Somerton & Frome
70.2	North Norfolk

10 Lowest Decreases in Turnout (GB)
%
-2.2	Hackney N & Stoke N'ton
-4.4	Kensington & Chelsea
-4.6	Sheffield Central
-5.9	Norfolk North
-6.0	Norfolk Mid
-6.0	Richmond (Yorks)
-6.0	Winchester
-6.4	Westmorland & Lon.
-6.6	Hackney S & Shoreditch
-6.6	West Bromwich W

10 Biggest Increases in Turnout (NI)
%
4.6	Antrim South
3.2	Fermanagh & S Tyr.
3.0	Belfast North
2.3	Antrim North
1.7	Upper Bann
1.4	Londonderry East
1.3	Newry and Armagh
1.3	Belfast South
1.0	Lagan Valley
0.9	Antrim East

10 Lowest Turnouts (GB)
%
34.1	Liverpool Riverside
39.1	Manchester Central
39.7	Glasgow Shettleston
40.1	Glasgow Maryhill
41.6	Salford
41.7	Leeds Central
42.7	Manchester Gorton
43.0	Liverpool Walton
43.6	Glasgow Kelvin
43.7	Glasgow Springburn

10 Smallest Majorities
%	Votes	
0.1	33	Cheadle (LD)
0.1	53	Fermanagh & S Tyr. (SF)
0.1	48	Perth (SNP)
0.2	74	Galloway & U. Nith. (Con)
0.3	153	South Dorset (Lab)
0.4	128	East Antrim (UUP)
0.4	235	Taunton (Con)
0.5	269	Orpington (Con)
0.7	358	Braintree (Lab)
0.7	338	Weston-S-Mare (LD)

5 Highest Turnouts (NI)
%
80.5	Ulster Mid
79.9	Tyrone West
78.0	Fermanagh & S Tyr.
76.8	Newry and Armagh
70.8	Down South

10 Best Results

Conservative	% change	Labour	% change	Liberal Democrat	% change
Romford	+11.4	Hastings & Rye	+12.7	Kingston & Surb	+23.5
Tatton	+10.7	Argyll & Bute	+8.9	Romsey	+17.5
Norfolk SW	+10.2	Brent North	+8.7	Ross, Skye & IW	+15.4
Richmond (Yorks)	+10.1	East Ham	+8.5	Hornsey & WG	+14.5
Christchurch	+8.7	Christchurch	+8.2	Ludlow	+13.5
Shropshire N	+8.4	Harrow West	+8.1	Lewes	+13.1
Yeovil	+8.4	Reading West	+8.0	B'ham Perry Barr	+13.0
Copeland	+8.4	Eastwood	+7.9	Winchester	+12.5
Totnes	+8.0	Angus	+7.7	Cardiff Central	+11.8
Billericay	+7.6	Enfield Southgate	+7.6	Maidenhead	+11.2

10 Worst Results

Conservative	% change	Labour	% change	Liberal Democrat	% change
Wyre Forest	−17.1	Wyre Forest	−22.1	Hastings & Rye	−17.6
Brent North	−10.8	St Helen's South	−18.9	Christchurch	−14.8
Kingston & Surb	−8.3	B'ham Perry Barr	−16.5	Conway	−14.3
Ealing North	−7.9	Merthyr Tydfil	−14.9	Shrewsbury & Atch	−12.6
Stirling	−7.7	Kingston & Surb	−14.3	Brentwood & Ong	−10.7
Brentwood & Ong	−7.4	Neath	−12.8	Orkney & Shetland	−10.6
Aberdeen South	−7.1	Islwyn	−12.6	Argyll & Bute	−10.4
Reading West	−6.9	Ealing South	−12.5	Bradford West	−8.4
B'ham Spark & SH	−6.7	Ludlow	−12.0	Southend West	−8.2
Tweeddale etc.	−6.7	Ogmore	−11.9	Congleton	−8.2

10 Largest SNP Votes

%	
54.2	Banff & Buchan
40.1	North Tayside
36.9	Western Isles
35.3	Angus
33.8	Galloway & U.N.
31.4	Dundee East
30.3	Moray
30.2	Ochil
29.7	Perth
29.0	Cumbernauld & Kilsyth

10 Highest Plaid Cymru Votes

%	
49.6	Meirionnydd-N-Cn
44.4	Caernarfon
42.4	Carmarthen E & Din.
38.3	Ceredigion
32.6	Ynys Mon
30.9	Llanelli
21.1	Caerphilly
21.1	Rhondda
18.7	Carmarthen W & P.
18.4	Neath

Green Party Saved Deposits

%

9.3 Brighton Pavilion
8.0 Leeds W
7.4 Hackney N & Stoke New.
7.0 Bradford W
6.5 Lewisham Deptford
6.2 Islington North
6.0 Holborn & St Pancras
5.3 Edinburgh Central
5.1 Hornsey & Wood Green
5.0 Dulwich & W Norwood

UKIP Saved Deposits

%

7.8 Bexhill & Battle
6.1 Totnes
5.6 Devon East
5.2 Stafford
5.1 Harwich
5.0 Devon North

Scottish Socialist Party Saved Deposits

%

10.0 Glasgow Pollok
7.8 Glasgow Maryhill
7.8 Glasgow Springburn
6.9 Glasgow Kelvin
6.8 Glasgow Shettleston
6.7 Glasgow Baillieston
6.1 Glasgow Govan
6.3 Glasgow Cathcart
5.6 Glasgow Anniesland
5.1 Coatbridge & Chry.

BNP Saved Deposits

%

16.4 Oldham W & Royton
11.3 Burnley
11.2 Oldham E & Sadd.
6.4 Barking
5.1 Poplar & Canning

Other Minor Parties Saved Deposits (Great Britain)

%

58.1 Wyre Forest (Ind)
31.5 Brentwood & Ongar (Ind)
14.9 L'pool W.Derby (Liberal)
13.0 B'ham Spark and SH (People's Justice Party)
12.3 Ealing Southall (Ind)
11.3 Stoke North (Ind)
9.3 Doncaster North (Ind)
7.4 Coventry NW (Ind)
7.1 Coventry NE (Soc All)
6.9 St Helens South (Soc All)
6.7 B'ham Ladywood (People's Justice Party)
6.5 Aberavon (Ind)
6.2 Warley (Soc Lab)
6.1 Merthyr Tydfil (Ind)
5.1 Sunderland North (Ind)

Major Parties' Lost Deposits

%

4.9 Cumbern. & K. (Con)
4.6 Rhondda (Con)
4.5 Rhondda (LD)

A1.6 By-election results, 1997–2001

Constituency	Date	Turnout (%)	Con (%)	Lab (%)	LibDem (%)	Nat (%)	UKIP (%)	Green (%)	Soc. Lab (%)	Soc. Al/ SSP (%)	Others (%)
Uxbridge	1997	72.4	43.6	41.8	10.9	–	–	–	–	–	3.7 (2)
	31.7.97	55.5	51.1	39.3	5.6	–	0.1	–	–	–	3.9 (7)
	2001	57.6	47.1	40.9	10.3	–	1.8	–	–	–	0.7
Paisley South	1997	69.1	8.7	57.5	9.4	23.3	–	–	–	0.4	3.4 (3)
	6.11.97	43.1	7.0	44.1	11.0	32.5	–	–	0.7	1.3	1.6 (2)
	2001	57.2	7.5	58.4	10.4	19.4	–	–	–	2.7	5.1 (3)
Beckenham	1997	74.3	42.5	33.4	18.1	–	–	–	–	–	3.0 (5)
	20.11.97	43.6	41.2	37.4	18.4	–	–	–	–	–	0.5
	2001	63.1	45.3	34.4	16.0	–	0.9	–	–	–	4.6 (4)
Winchester (a)	1997	78.3	42.0	10.5	42.1	–	1.7	–	–	–	0.9 (4)
	20.11.97	68.7	28.4	1.7	68.0	–	0.8	2.1	–	–	0.1
	2001	72.3	38.3	5.9	54.6	–	1.0	–	–	–	–
Leeds Central	1997	54.2	13.7	69.6	11.3	–	1.1	–	–	–	3.6 (2)
	10.6.99	19.6	12.3	48.2	30.8	–	2.7	3.6	1.8	–	2.4 (2)
	2001	41.7	14.3	66.9	13.2	–	2.8	–	–	–	–
Eddisbury	1997	75.6	42.5	40.1	13.2	–	–	–	–	–	4.1
	22.7.99	51.4	44.8	40.2	13.8	–	–	–	–	2.8	1.2 (3)
	2001	64.2	46.3	36.0	15.7	–	2.0	–	–	–	–
Hamilton South	1997	71.1	8.6	65.6	5.1	17.6	–	–	–	–	3.1 (2)
	23.9.99	41.3	7.2	36.9	3.6	34.0	0.3	–	1.2	9.5	7.6 (5)
	2001	57.3	7.0	59.7	8.9	19.4	0.6	–	–	4.4	–
Wigan	1997	67.7	16.9	68.6	10.0	–	–	–	–	–	3.5 (2)
	23.9.99	25.0	18.0	59.6	13.3	–	5.2	–	1.5	–	2.6 (4)
	2001	52.5	20.8	61.7	14.8	–	–	1.0	–	2.6	–
Kensington and Chelsea	1997	54.7	53.6	28.0	15.3	–	1.5	–	–	–	1.7 (5)
	25.11.99	29.7	56.4	22.0	9.4	–	2.3	–	–	–	7.6 (13)
	2001	45.2	54.4	23.2	15.7	–	1.5	–	–	–	1.0 (2)
Ceredigion	1997	73.9	14.9	24.3	16.5	41.6	–	–	–	–	2.7
	3.2.00	45.6	16.5	14.4	23.0	42.8	1.9	2.3	–	–	1.4 (2)
	2001	61.7	19.4	15.4	26.9	38.3	–	4.2	–	–	–

Constituency	Year	Turnout (%)									
Romsey	1997	76.4	46.0	18.6	29.4	–	3.5	–	–	–	2.5
LibDem gain	4.5.00	55.5	42.0	3.7	50.6	–	2.3	–	–	–	1.4 (2)
	2001	68.7	42.1	8.2	47.0	–	1.5	–	–	–	1.2
Tottenham	1997	56.9	15.7	69.3	10.8	–	–	2.8	–	5.4	1.4 (3)
	22.6.00	25.4	16.0	53.5	19.1	–	0.8	3.7	–	3.7	1.4 (2)
	2001	48.2	13.9	67.5	9.5	–	–	4.6	–	1.4 (3)	0.9
Glasgow, Anniesland	1997	63.8	11.5	61.8	7.2	17.1	0.3	–	–0.7	7.1	1.0
	23.11.00	38.4	10.8	52.1	8.1	20.8	–	–	–	5.6	–
	2001	50.1	9.9	56.5	12.1	15.1	–	–	0.7	–	–
Preston	1997	65.8	21.9	60.8	14.7	–	–	–	–	5.7	2.6 (2)
	23.11.00	29.6	25.0	45.7	16.2	–	2.1	2.1	–	–	3.2 (3)
	2001	50.0	23.0	57.0	13.2	–	–	2.8	–	–	4.0 (2)
West Bromwich West (b)	1997	54.4	–	–	–	–	–	–	–	–	100 (3)
Labour gain	23.11.00	27.6	33.9	51.1	9.5	–	1.3	–	1.2	–	4.2
	2001	47.7	25.1	60.8	6.8	–	1.6	–	–	–	4.5
Falkirk West	1997	72.6	12.1	59.3	5.1	23.4	–	–	–	5.1	–
	21.12.00	36.2	8.3	43.5	3.2	39.9	–	–	–	2.3	6.3 (2)
	2001	57.7	7.5	51.9	7.1	24.2	–	–	0.6	–	

(a) General election result challenged and election re-run.
(b) Constituency was won in 1997 by the Speaker. The major parties did not contest the constituency at that election.

Northern Ireland by-election

Constituency	Date	Turnout (%)	Sinn Féin (%)	SDLP (%)	UUP (%)	DUP (%)	Alliance (%)	Other (%)
South Antrim	1997	57.9	5.5	16.2	57.5	–	11.6	9.2 (2)
DUP gain	21.9.00	43.0	8.5	11.4	35.3	38.8	6.6	0.2
UUP recovery	2001	62.5	9.4	12.1	37.1	34.8	4.5	2.2

Appendix 2:
An Analysis of the Results

John Curtice and Michael Steed

At first glance, the outcome of the 2001 election would not appear to raise many questions worthy of extensive analysis. The result appeared to be little more than a repeat of the outcome in 1997. Labour emerged with just six fewer seats, the Liberal Democrats six more and the Conservatives just one extra. Fewer seats changed hands in total than at any previous comparable election.[1]

Yet a slightly closer glance at the result reveals a lot more of interest. First, Labour may not have lost many seats, but it did lose votes. The party's share of the vote in Great Britain[2] fell by 2.4 per cent. This is a far bigger drop than that suffered by any of the Conservative governments re-elected between 1983 and 1992 and it is also no better than the 2 per cent drop suffered by the first full-term Labour government in 1950. It even matches the drop suffered by Jim Callaghan's Labour government when it was thrown out of office in 1979. At 42.0 per cent Labour's share of the British vote was less than that secured by any other post-war government bar the two administrations formed by Labour in 1974.

Second, turnout fell precipitately. At 59.4 per cent across the UK as a whole, it was nearly 12 points lower than in 1997 – the lowest turnout officially recorded at any election since 1918. However, in 1918 the recorded turnout (57.2 per cent) was affected by the circumstances of war and the electorate had been trebled. Given that turnout never fell below 70 per cent at any point between 1922 and 1997, it is safe to conclude that voluntary abstention was at a higher level in 2001 than at any previous general election since the advent of the mass franchise.

Third, the 1997 result was in many respects exceptional. Labour won more seats than ever before. The Conservatives won their lowest share of the vote since 1832. And the Liberal Democrats emerged with more MPs than at any election since 1929. The repetition of an apparently exceptional result may well be a signal that the pattern of British electoral politics has in fact undergone a fundamental change.

These observations provide the framework for the analysis in this appendix. We examine how and why turnout fell. We consider the pattern of Labour's performance and of the other parties. And we ask why Labour did so well in terms of seats despite the fact that it did not do particularly well in terms of votes. As in previous appendices in this series, our principal source of evidence comprises the election results themselves, and in particular measures of the change in party support since 1997.

Table A2.1   **Measures of change since 1997**

	Overall	Mean	Median	Standard Deviation
Change in Con vote	+1.2	+0.8	+0.7	3.1
Change in Lab vote	–2.4	–1.9	–1.7	4.1
Change in LibDem vote	+1.7	+1.5	+1.7	4.0
Total-vote swing	+1.8	+1.4	+1.3	2.6
Two-party swing	+2.2	+1.1	+1.0	3.7
Change in turnout	–12.2	–12.3	–12.4	2.5

The following seats have been excluded from the calculation of the mean, median and standard deviation of all except change in turnout: Brentwood & Ongar (Independent vote above 30% in 2001), Glasgow Springburn (no Conservative or Liberal Democrat candidates in 2001); Tatton (no Labour or Liberal Democrat candidates in 1997); West Bromwich West (no Conservative or Liberal Democrat candidates in 2001); Wyre Forest (no Liberal Democrat candidate, 2001).

Total-vote swing is the average of the change in the Conservative share of the vote and the Labour share of the vote. Two-party swing is the change in the Conservative share of the vote cast for Conservative and Labour only (that is, the two-party vote). In both cases a plus sign indicates a swing to the Conservatives, a minus sign a swing to Labour.

A summary of how the 2001 result did in fact differ from that in 1997 is provided in Table A2.1, which shows the overall, mean, median and standard deviation of a number of key measures of change. Three points stand out. First, as in all other recent elections there was considerable variation in the pattern of change from one constituency to another. For example, while the standard deviation of two-party swing is a little lower than it was at the last three elections to be fought on unchanged constituency boundaries, it was still higher than at any previous such post-war election.[3] This election did not mark any return to uniformity of movement across the country. Instead Britain once again exhibited a highly variable electoral geography.

The second point to note is that there was more variation in Labour and Liberal Democrat performance than there was in that of the Conservatives. This is also in line with other recent elections. Another feature of recent elections, again repeated in Table A2.2, is that there is a stronger correlation between the performance of Labour and the Liberal Democrats than there is between either of those and Conservative performance. This might indicate, as it did in 1997, that switching between Labour and the Liberal Democrats came more easily to their voters than it did between either of those two parties and the Conservatives. However, this time the correlation between Liberal Democrat and Conservative performance was also relatively high, so clearly we can anticipate a more complex pattern when we seek to explain an unusually good Liberal Democrat performance.

In any event there is virtually no correlation at all between the change in Conservative and the change in Labour shares of the vote. This is in stark contrast to the pattern that has been typical in British elections since they have been dominated by the Conservative and Labour parties. This raises the prospect that movements to and from these parties over the last four years have been the product of very different influences. Certainly it would appear to be wise to analyse those two parties' performances separately rather than simply focus on the swing between them, however measured.

Table A2.2   Correlations between changes in party performance (1997 correlations in brackets)

Conservative and Labour	−0.04	(−0.41)
Conservative and Liberal Democrat	−0.45	(−0.19)
Liberal Democrat and Labour	−0.59	(−0.63)

The third and final point to note from Table A2.1 is that the overall change in the Conservative share of the vote, calculated by adding up the votes across Great Britain as a whole, is significantly higher than the mean change, calculated by averaging the swings in each of the individual 636 comparable constituencies. At the same time the drop in Labour's mean share of the vote was lower than the drop in its overall share of the vote. Inevitably these differences are also reflected in the two measures of swing, most notably in respect of two-party swing where the mean swing to the Conservatives was only half the overall swing. Such a difference can have a significant impact on the operation of the electoral system and is thus something for which we have to account.

There is however one other significant feature of the 2001 election that is not captured by either of the two tables presented so far. This is the performance of the nationalists and other parties. Between them they won 6.5 per cent of the vote in Great Britain. While this was less than the 7.0 per cent they secured in 1997, it is well above the level recorded at any other previous election. Moreover, whereas in 1997 most of the increase in support for other parties could be accounted for by a 3 per cent vote cast for anti-European candidates from the Referendum Party and the UK Independence Party, in 2001 there were also significant levels of support for Socialist and Green candidates. It appears that the grip of Britain's three largest political parties on the affections of the electorate has weakened significantly. Why this might have happened and what its consequences might have been for the larger parties is evidently a question we need to consider.[4]

We begin our analysis by looking at turnout. We then examine the performances of the three main British parties. In particular we examine in which kind of constituency a party did particularly well or badly, and we also analyse the impact of local political circumstances on how people voted. We then turn to the performance of the nationalists and of smaller parties not currently represented at Westminster before finally analysing how the electoral system translated votes into seats in the House of Commons. In presenting the results of our analysis we will largely make use of relatively straightforward tabular presentations, but more technically minded readers may wish to note that most of these are underpinned by the results of the more formal multivariate modelling.

Turnout

The low turnout was far from unexpected. Not only had turnout been lower in 1997 than at any election since 1929, but local and European elections held between 1998 and 2000 had also seen new record low levels of turnout. Even the level of participation in the first Scottish, Welsh and London elections was rather less than many advocates of devolution had anticipated.

At least three key explanations have been offered as to why turnout has been falling at recent elections in this country.[5] Some suggest long-term changes in the electorate, such as declining party identification, which have produced an electorate less motivated to participate in the electoral process and perhaps one more disillusioned and distrustful of politicians. Others suggest that it simply reflects more immediate political circumstances, such as the large and continuous lead for Labour in the opinion polls and a perceived lack of difference between the parties. Yet others argue that much of the decline in turnout is occasioned by more traditional left-wing voters staying at home because they are dissatisfied with Labour's move towards the ideological centre.[6]

The pattern of the variation in the drop in turnout provides some evidence for all three explanations. Older people are least likely to be influenced by any growing disinclination to participate in elections.[7] Disillusion and distrust of politics and politicians tends to be highest amongst the less well educated.[8] So if the first explanation is correct we might expect to find that turnout fell least in those constituencies with a relatively old age profile and a relatively well-educated population. And as Table A2.3 illustrates, both patterns are present to some degree.

Table A2.3   Patterns of change in turnout

	Well Educated	Older People	% LibDem 1997	% Others 2001	% Lab 1997
Very Low	−13.4	−12.2	−13.4	−12.5	−10.8
Low	−12.6	−13.3	−12.7	−12.3	−11.2
High	−11.6	−12.5	−11.6	−12.4	−13.1
Very High	−11.3	−10.7	−10.8	−11.7	−13.2

Well Educated. % of adults aged 18+ with a degree as measured by the 1991 Census. Very Low, less than 9% (141 seats); Low 9–13% (203); High, 13–17% (158); Very High, over 13% (139).

Older People. % adults aged 65+ as estimated by Experian. Very Low; less than 17.5% (117 seats); Low 17.5–10% (193); High, 20–22.5% (188); Very High, over 22.5% (143).

% LibDem 1997. % vote won by Liberal Democrats 1997. Very Low; less than 10% (196 seats); Low, 10–14% (180); High, 14–22% (116); Very High, over 22% (149).

% Others 2001. % vote won by parties other than Con, Lab, LibDem and Nat 2001. Very Low, less than 2% (128 seats); Low 2–3% (152); High, 3–6% (257); Very High, over 6% (104).

% Lab 1997. % vote won by Labour 1997. Very Low, less than 30% (155 seats); Low 30–45% (108); High, 45–60% (229); Very High, over 60% (148).

But equally there are signs that politics mattered. If voters were demotivated by a perceived lack of difference between the Conservatives and Labour we might expect to find that turnout fell less where the local choice was less obviously just between the Conservatives or Labour. And, as Table A2.3 also shows, turnout did fall less where the Liberal Democrats were strongest in 1997, while there are signs too that turnout fell less where candidates other than from the three main British parties or the two nationalist parties mounted a relatively strong challenge locally.

At the same time if voters felt there was little point in voting because the outcome of the elections was clear, we would expect to find that turnout would fall less in those seats which the 1997 election had rendered newly marginal. And indeed turnout fell on average by 10.9 per cent in such seats (where the winners' majority was less than 10 per cent in 1997 but had previously been greater), nearly a couple of points less than elsewhere. Of course this finding also supports the claims of those who believe that the preponderance of safe seats under the British electoral system depresses interest among electors. Certainly the list of highest turnouts in Table A1.5 mainly comprises constituencies which have either changed hands or been won by narrow margins at recent elections. It also includes some of the most rural of all constituencies, nicely illustrating that it is not only access to polling stations that matters.

But perhaps the most important evidence that voters' perceptions of the choices confronting them made a difference comes from Northern

Ireland. Here, in an election which became a referendum amongst unionist voters on the future of the Good Friday agreement, turnout actually rose slightly, by 0.6 per cent. Evidently the very different election campaign in the province persuaded voters that their election at least mattered.

Meanwhile if more traditional and perhaps more left-wing voters were inclined to stay at home then we might expect to find that turnout would fall most in those seats where Labour were previously strongest. Certainly that is what happened when Labour tumbled to its unexpected defeat in the 1999 European elections.[9] And as we can see from the final column of Table A2.3, that pattern was repeated in 2001. This result is even more striking given that the difference between the level of turnout in the average Conservative seat and that in the average Labour one had already widened to a record level at both the 1992 and 1997 elections.[10]

Beyond these three key patterns, there are two other points of note. First, turnout fell less in the most rural constituencies, dropping by 9.8 per cent in those seats which are substantially rural and by 10.6 per cent in those which are moderately so.[11] Concerns that the outbreak of foot and mouth disease would depress the turnout in many rural areas were apparently wide of the mark.

Second, there was some limited regional variation. As Appendix 1 shows, turnout fell most heavily in the North-West, something that cannot simply be accounted for by any of the patterns we have described so far. But concerns that the advent of devolution in Scotland and Wales would depress interest in UK general elections in those parts of the UK were largely not realised. Turnout fell no more in Wales than it did in England, although in Scotland it did fall by 1 per cent more.

Indeed, for all the apparently systematic variation identified, what is most striking is the relative uniformity of the drop in turnout. All of the differences in Table A2.3 are small relative to the nationwide drop in participation. Turnout was below its 1997 level in every single constituency in Great Britain. Even in Wyre Forest, where a local campaign mobilised voters to elect an Independent MP with a record vote, turnout still dropped by 7.4 per cent.

It should not thus be surprising that there is relatively little association between how much turnout fell in a constituency and how well the parties performed. There is but a hint that the Conservatives may occasionally have done a little better in seats where turnout fell less, as the correlation coefficient between the Conservative performance and turnout change is +0.10. In Labour's case the hint is even weaker with a correlation coefficient at +0.05. In contrast the Liberal Democrats appear occasionally to have done a little better where turnout fell most (correlation co-efficient, –0.12). We thus need to be aware that while a little of the variation in party performance that we analyse below might be the product of variation in the propensity of different parties' supporters to stay at home, it does not appear to be a major component.

Social and regional variation in party performance

One of the striking features about the Labour Party under Tony Blair has been its attempt to reinvent itself. In part this has involved a shift to a more centrist position in terms of policy. But it has also been marked by an attempt to change the party's image. Instead of being a party associated with the working class, trade unions or the unemployed, it has attempted to make itself one that is equally attractive to less traditional Labour sources of support such as the middle class, big business and the south of England.[12] Moreover, the party maintained this new ideological and sociological tone throughout Tony Blair's first term in office.

Meanwhile, under William Hague the Conservatives also adopted a somewhat different strategy from the past. During the course of his leadership the party came increasingly to focus on opposition to the single currency together with a conservative stance on moral and social issues, ranging from asylum seekers to tax incentives for people to marry rather than live together. In contrast to the socio-economic issues, such as nationalisation, that have traditionally divided the Conservative and Labour parties in post-war Britain, attitudes towards such moral and social issues are more strongly related to educational attainment and age than to social class. Those with less education and those who are older are more likely to adopt a sceptical position on the single European currency and a conservative position on moral and social issues such as the role of marriage.[13]

Meanwhile the Liberal Democrats took up policy positions at the election that to a considerable degree put themselves at odds with both Labour and the Conservatives. In contrast to Labour they indicated a willingness to increase taxes in order to spend more on education and health while they also suggested renationalising the railway industry. Meanwhile the party was not only willing to indicate its belief that Britain should ideally join the single currency, but its leader Charles Kennedy was also strongly critical of the Conservatives' stance on such issues as asylum seekers.

Of course voters may not have taken any notice of these policy stances. But if they did we might anticipate that Labour would have lost support more heavily in constituencies with a relatively large working-class population than in more middle-class ones. We might also expect that the Conservatives would have gained ground most heavily in those seats with an older age profile and where the highly educated are relatively thin on the ground. And if both of these prove to be the case, we might also anticipate that the Liberal Democrats would perform best in working-class seats, those with a younger age profile, and those with a relatively large number of graduates.

Table A2.4   Social correlates of party performance

| | Mean Change in % vote since 1997 | | | |
	Con	*Lab*	*LibDem*	*(Seats)*
Employers and managers				
Very Low	+0.1	–3.6	+2.5	(150)
Low	+0.7	–2.4	+2.1	(176)
High	+1.4	–1.4	+0.5	(152)
Very High	+0.9	–0.3	+0.8	(158)
Education				
% with degree				
Very Low	+1.2	–3.5	+1.6	(139)
Low	+1.3	–2.0	+1.2	(202)
High	+1.0	–1.0	+1.0	(157)
Very High	–0.6	–1.4	+2.5	(138)
Age Profile				
% older people				
Very Low	–1.1	–1.8	+2.5	(117)
Low	+0.4	–2.2	+2.1	(191)
High	+1.2	–2.2	+1.5	(186)
Very High	+2.3	–1.2	–0.2	(142)

Definitions: Employers and Managers: % economically active heads of households in socio-economic groups 1, 2 and 3 as measured by the 1991 Census. Very Low; less than 15%; Low 15%–19%; High, 19%–23%; Very High, over 23%.
Education and Age Profile: see Table A2.3

Table A2.4 indicates that there is some evidence to support all of these expectations. We measure the class composition of a constituency by the percentage of employers and managers it contains, a measure that Miller has previously shown to be the strongest correlate of Labour and Conservative support in a constituency.[14] And we can see that Labour clearly did worse the lower the proportion of employers and managers (and thus the more working class) a constituency was. Meanwhile, the opposite is largely true for the Liberal Democrats, while the Conservative performance fails to exhibit any consistent relationship with the class composition of a constituency at all.

We can also see that the Conservatives actually lost ground where the proportion of graduates was well above average, while the Liberal Democrats performed particularly well in such seats. However, it would appear from this table that, in most seats, Labour's performance was even more strongly related to the proportion of graduates in a constituency. We must, of course, bear in mind that relatively working-class constituencies also tend to be those with fewer graduates, potentially making it difficult to distinguish between the impact of class and education. Therefore, in Table A2.5 we show what happens if we classify constituencies according to both whether they have an above or below average number of graduates *and* whether they have an above or below average number of employers and managers. This shows that the proportion of graduates makes relatively little difference to Labour's performance, while the effect of higher education on Conservative or Liberal Democrat performance becomes even clearer.

Table A2.5   Party performance by class and educational composition

	Change in % vote since 1997			
(a) seats with below average proportion of employers and managers				
% with degree	*Con*	*Lab*	*LibDem*	
Below Average	+0.8	−2.9	+1.9	(265)
Above Average	−1.3	−3.1	+3.8	(61)
(b) seats with above-average proportion of employers and managers				
% with degree	*Con*	*Lab*	*LibDem*	
Below Average	+2.8	−1.3	−0.6	(76)
Above Average	+0.6	−0.7	+1.1	(234)

Definitions: below average proportion of employers and managers: very low and low groups as defined at Table A2.4; above average, high and very high groups.
Below average with degree: very low and low groups as defined at Table A2.3; above average, high and very high groups.

Meanwhile, returning to Table A2.4 we can see that the age profile of a constituency also made a difference along the lines that we anticipated. The Conservatives were more successful at increasing their share of the vote where there were more older people, while the opposite was true so far as the Liberal Democrats are concerned. In contrast, the age profile of a constituency appears to have made relatively little difference to Labour's performance.

So in many respects the variation in party performance was consistent with what we might expect if voters were responding to the rather distinctive appeals being made by the parties at the 2001 election.[15] The rebranding of Labour seems to have weakened even further the party's historic link with working-class voters and communities, a link that had already reached a record low in 1997.[16] The Conservatives' focus on Europe and social issues appears to have had more resonance amongst older and less well-educated voters rather than with its traditional core vote, the middle class. These rather divergent patterns of Labour and Conservative performance help to explain why we saw earlier that they were uncorrelated with each other. Meanwhile the Liberal Democrats appear to have performed their traditional role in British politics of acting as a party of protest for both Labour and Conservative voters who are currently unhappy with their party's stance, thereby ensuring that their performance was correlated both with Labour's and with that of the Conservatives.

But to say simply that about the Liberal Democrats would be to miss a vital point. While the party has long been relatively successful at winning support amongst well-educated middle-class professionals,[17] it has not traditionally been particularly strong amongst more left-wing working-class voters. Indeed the Liberal Democrats remain a party whose support is distinctly stronger in middle-class than in working-class constituencies. But in 2001 the gap narrowed somewhat. It may well be that if New Labour continues to remain in the centre of British politics, the Liberal Democrats will have an opportunity to make further advances in what has previously been rather barren territory for the party.[18]

However, it would be wrong to imply that Labour always performed better where it has traditionally been strong and less well where it has not. True, one other notable feature of its performance was that it did relatively well in the southern third of England (that is, the areas defined by the South East and South West government regions) even after allowing for the more middle-class nature of that part of the country. Even so, Labour suffered unusually heavy losses in one part of the home of 'Essex man', that is the eastern fringes of London and the south of Essex where the party lost ground particularly heavily when it was first defeated by Mrs Thatcher in 1979.[19] That pattern in 1979 gave rise to the myth that Labour had lost contact with the kinds of upwardly mobile skilled working-class voters who were allegedly relatively common in that corner of England. Concern at the apparent loss of this group was certainly one of the motivations behind the rebranding of the party as New Labour. Yet, in 11 seats across this area Labour's vote fell on average by no less than 3.8 per cent while the Conservative made a highly unusual 5.9 per cent advance.[20] However, as this performance cannot be accounted for by the class, educational or age profile of these constituencies, it may be unwise to consider what happened in South Essex in 2001 to be typical of the wider story of this election.

Throughout the last Parliament, one area of traditional Labour weakness that appeared rather impervious to New Labour's attempts to appeal to all sections of society was the countryside. One source of friction was an attempt by a Labour MP to ban hunting with dogs. Farmers, already hit by the impact of BSE in the early 1990s, suffered further from the high value of the pound under Labour. Then in September 2000 the fuel tax protestors mobilised broader rural support, reflecting higher car usage in less densely populated areas. Finally, the outbreak of foot and mouth gave Conservative MPs another opportunity to claim that the Labour government was insensitive to the needs of rural areas. Between them, these developments seemed to suggest the rise of a new political self-consciousness amongst countryside dwellers before the 2001 election.

Table A2.6   The countryside effect

Proportion of constituency rural	Mean Change in % vote since 1997							
	All Seats				Conservative-held seats 1997			
	Con	Lab	LibDem		Con	Lab	LibDem	
Effectively none	−0.1	−2.3	+2.3	(259)	+1.7	+1.1	−1.1	(19)
Tiny fringe	+0.5	−2.4	+1.6	(171)	+2.0	−0.1	−0.4	(37)
Small element	+1.7	−1.0	+0.6	(92)	+1.9	−0.1	+0.3	(47)
Moderate	+2.3	−0.6	+0.2	(55)	+3.3	−0.3	−0.7	(29)
Substantial	+3.0	−2.1	+0.3	(59)	+4.1	−2.0	−0.7	(32)

Definitions: Effectively none: % living in postcode areas classified as Mosaic Group 'country dwellers' as measured by Experian. Effectively less than 0.5%; Tiny fringe: 0.5%–5%; Small element, 5–15%; moderate 15–25%; substantial, above 25%.

Table A2.6 reveals that the countryside did indeed behave rather differently from the rest of Britain. Most distinctive was the performance of the Conservatives whose vote rose on average by about two points more than the national average in the one-fifth or so most rural seats in the country. Less immediately obvious from the table is Labour's relatively weak performance in such seats, where the average drop in Labour's vote is no higher than it was in much of urban Britain. However, given that most of these rural seats are also relatively middle-class constituencies, such a performance by Labour is rather less than might be expected. One way of seeing this is to confine our analysis to the 165 seats that the Conservatives were defending, as we do in the three right-hand columns of Table A2.6. Here we can see quite clearly that Labour in particular did relatively badly in rural Britain.[21]

In contrast Labour performed fairly well, and the Conservatives very badly, in one area of relative Labour strength: Scotland. This UK general election was the first in both Scotland and Wales since the advent of devolution. Some inside the Labour Party in Scotland had been concerned that allegedly more left-wing voters in Scotland would react particularly badly to the UK Labour government's centrist stance, while others were concerned that Scots might use the UK general election to cast a negative judgement on the performance of the Labour-led Scottish Executive. In the event, neither fear was realised. Labour's share of the vote fell by just 1.6 per cent, lower than any of labour's traditional English heartlands.

Even more dramatically different was the Conservative performance in Scotland. Rather than matching the modest recovery that the party achieved in the rest of Britain, Scottish Conservatives saw their support fall away yet further. Indeed, for the first time since 1922 the party secured fewer votes than the Liberal Democrats (who clearly did not suffer from their involvement as junior partner in the Scottish Executive coalition) and thus ended up in fourth place in the Scottish popular vote for the first time ever. Apparently the party's attempts to regain its credibility amongst Scots through its acceptance of devolution and its involvement in the Scottish Parliament (including the adoption of different policies from English Conservatives on tuition fees and the long-term care of the elderly) have yet to bear fruit.

In Wales, however, the politics of devolution clearly had some impact on the result. Labour suffered serious and unexpected losses at the hands of Plaid Cymru in the first Assembly election in 1999, and again performed relatively badly in 2001. The party's share of the vote fell more than it did in other parts of Britain. At 7.2 per cent the difference between Labour's share of the vote in Wales and that in England was lower than at any previous general election since 1935. It would appear that some Labour voters have still not forgiven the UK Labour leadership for its attempts to ensure that Alun Michael became the First Secretary of the new assembly rather than the more popular Rhodri Morgan.

A repeated theme of behaviour at elections from 1959 onwards has been the North/South divide, which had opened up so strongly in British electoral politics up to 1987, but which Labour was able to narrow in 1992 and 1997. The broad regional pattern of Labour performance in 2001 does appear to have continued this more recent success; its sole gain from the

Tories in Dorset duly extended the party's geographical spread. So we might have expected that for the Conservatives, too, there would be some reversal of the 1955/87 geographical divergence. This does not prove to be so. Indeed, the party's poor performance in Scotland, an above average performance in some parts of eastern England, and the South Essex phenomenon, were all echoes of what happened during the 1980s. The areas that responded best to Thatcherism (or perhaps benefited most from the Lawson boom) turned out to be a little more willing to vote Tory in 2001 than in 1997. In all previous general elections since the present two-party system was established, regional variations in the swing have been mirror performances between Conservative and Labour. That this pattern was broken in 2001, with Labour's socio-geographic appeal broadening a little while that of the Tories tended to narrow[22] could be another indicator of how British electoral politics are now changing.

Local political circumstances

So far we have primarily focused on how the national strategies and appeals of the parties appear to have been reflected in where parties did relatively well or badly. Now we examine how local constituency circumstances might have influenced voters and hence affected the outcome. For these certainly appear to have played a key role at this election.

Table A2.7 indicates why this is so. It analyses the performance of the three main parties according to who shared first and second place in 1997 together with the size of the majority. One point immediately stands out. All three parties did relatively well in seats that they were defending by small majorities. For example, the Conservatives' share of the vote rose by no less than 4.4 per cent in the most marginal seats that they were defending against Labour, and by 3.8 per cent where they faced a Liberal Democrat challenge. Meanwhile, Labour managed to reverse the national tide by increasing its share of the vote (by 2.5 per cent) in those seats where it was most vulnerable to the Conservatives, and the Liberal Democrats advanced by no less than 7.7 per cent in those seats where they had less than a 5 per cent lead over the Conservatives.

None of these patterns can just be accounted for by the social character or regional location of each party's most marginal seats. Rather, they are an indication that the outcome in these seats was influenced by the local political circumstances of the constituency. How might this be so? There would appear to be three possibilities.

First, in the case of Labour and the Liberal Democrats, virtually all of the seats where they were defending a small 1997 majority were seats that the party gained at the last election. As a result most were being defended by the current incumbent MP for the first time. The intervening four years will have given those MPs the opportunity to develop a personal vote on the basis of how well they are thought to have promoted the needs of the constituency and looked after the interests of their constituents. Meanwhile any personal vote that might have been obtained by the previous (usually Conservative) MP is likely to have been lost. Certainly such personal voting has been evident at recent elections, and so could well account for some or all of the pattern in Table A2.7.[23]

Table A2.7   **Party competition and party performance**

1st/2nd 1997	% majority	Mean change in % vote since 1997			
		Con	Lab	LibDem	
Con/Lab	0–5	+4.4	−0.4	−1.9	(20)
	5–10	+3.6	−0.7	−1.1	(25)
	10 +	+1.9	−0.1	−0.4	(47)
Lab/Con	0–5	+1.3	+2.5	−2.2	(19)
	5–10	+0.2	+1.5	−0.6	(38)
	10+	+0.5	−3.5	+2.6	(282)
Con/LibDem	0–5	+3.8	−2.2	+1.2	(12)
	5–10	+2.1	−1.1	+0.4	(9)
	10+	+1.8	−0.0	+0.2	(51)
LibDem/Con	0–5	−1.3	−4.1	+7.7	(13)
	5–10	−1.3	+0.1	+1.4	(5)
	10+	+0.4	−0.1	−0.2	(21)
Lab/LibDem	All	−0.7	−3.2	+1.7	(30)
LibDem/Lab	All	+0.9	−5.1	+5.1	(6)

Seats where a nationalist was in first or second place in 1997 are excluded.

However, this potential explanation might not be thought to have much relevance to the position of most Conservative MPs in marginal seats. After all, most of them had been MPs prior to 1997, and thus any personal vote that they may have developed over the years should already be reflected in the vote that they obtained in 1997. However, MPs have most incentive to develop a reputation as a good local MP in marginal constituencies. And while most MPs in Conservative-held marginal seats may have been in Parliament for some time, most would not previously have considered themselves to have been in a marginal seat. So after the scale of the swing against them in 1997 turned previously safe seats into marginal ones, some Conservative MPs may have decided that they had more reason to develop a reputation as a good local MP than might have previously been the case.

A second possible explanation is that each of the parties may have deployed more campaigning resources in their marginal constituencies, which may have enabled them to garner more votes. Certainly, a number of studies have argued that the strength of a party's local organisation can make a significant difference to its share of the vote, and this might be particularly the case in a low-turnout election.[24] All parties now attempt to 'target' constituencies: so-called 'priority', 'key' or 'battleground' seats are given additional resources from the centre, not just during the campaign itself but also over an extended period beforehand. At the same time, party activists may be encouraged to campaign in these seats rather than in their own local constituency. After the 1997 election, we concluded that while the Liberal Democrats' targeting exercise at that election had apparently made a difference to their performance, Labour's efforts had not. However, if local organisation can make a difference and if targeting is effective then in theory parties ought to do better in those seats that they target.[25]

Finally, our third possible explanation is that the pattern in Table A2.7 is the result of tactical voting, that is voters who believe that their own preferred party has no chance of winning, backing another party in order to secure the defeat of the party they least like. Such voting occurred on an unprecedented scale in 1997, especially with Liberal Democrat and Labour supporters switching between these two parties in order to unseat the Conservatives.[26] But many of the seats that were marginal after 1997 had not previously appeared to be so marginal, and in some seats where the two anti-Conservative candidates had then argued strenuously over which was better placed to win, the 1997 outcome had clarified the pattern. So, perhaps some voters in such seats were encouraged to vote tactically this time around, when they had not done so in 1997, and it could thus be that in each case this tended to work to the benefit of the party currently defending the seat.

Although these possible explanations are logically distinct, identifying which has actually occurred is not necessarily straightforward. After all, the MP who has been newly elected to a marginal seat has good reason not only to seek to develop a reputation as a good local MP but also to try and strengthen his local party organisation, while the constituency is likely to be a prime candidate for a targeting exercise in which one of the aims may be to try and encourage voters to vote tactically. Equally the direction of causation is not always clear. A party may decide which constituencies to target on the basis of which have already shown signs of making progress locally. If so any above-average performance amongst target seats may be as much a reflection of progress that was made before any central help was received rather than reflecting the impact of that help.

Even so, we can come to some reasonably clear conclusions about the impact of these three processes at this election and how far they can account for the relative success of all three parties in their most marginal seats. So far as personal voting is concerned, this clearly had most impact on the Liberal Democrats' performance. This can be seen by comparing what happened in two very different situations. On the one hand the Liberal Democrat vote fell on average by 4.9 per cent in those seats where the incumbent Liberal Democrat MP was not defending the seat.[27] On the other hand, the party's vote rose on average by 6.3 per cent in those seats which the party captured for the first time in 1997 and where the incumbent MP was restanding.

Table A2.8   Labour performance and incumbency

	Mean Change in Labour % Share of the Vote since 1997	
Seat gained by Labour 1997, new MP standing, Previous Con MP not standing	–0.1	(80)
Seat gained by Labour 1997, new MP standing, Previous Con MP standing	–0.5	(16)
Incumbent Lab MP stood down 1997, new MP standing	–1.5	(39)
Same Labour MP defending seat 1997 and 2001	–4.1	(190)
Incumbent Labour MP stood down 2001	–5.7	(38)

There also seems to be little doubt that Labour benefited from the ability of many of those who were newly elected in 1997 to develop a personal vote. This can be seen in Table A2.8, which shows how the presence or absence of an incumbent MP affected Labour's performance in those seats it was defending in 2001. Labour consistently did better where a Labour MP who was elected for the first time in 1997 was attempting to defend the seat in 2001. This was particularly true of those seats that Labour did not hold prior to 1997. Meanwhile Labour lost ground most in those seats where the incumbent Labour MP stood down and where the party may thus have lost the benefit of their personal vote.[28]

The Conservatives too did less well in those seats they were defending where the incumbent MP was not standing again. On average the Conservative vote only increased by 1.1 per cent in those seats where the MP who had successfully defended the seat in 1997 stood down at this election. In contrast, the party's vote increased by 2.7 per cent where the incumbent MP was standing again.

So there seems to be little doubt that personal voting played a role in the performance of all three parties (and, even more strikingly, the SNP and Plaid Cymru; see below p. 324). In contrast, the evidence about the impact of targeting is more mixed. Only one of the parties, Labour, officially targeted seats that it was defending and thus only its exercise can possibly help account for its relative success in its most marginal seats. Both the Conservatives and the Liberal Democrats in contrast focused their exercises on those seats that they hoped to gain rather than seats they were defending, although we should bear in mind that all of the parties appear to have made changes to their list of target seats as circumstances and expectations changed.

Labour divided its target seats into two categories.[29] Most attention was given to its so-called 'battleground seats'. And in these Labour indeed did relatively well, increasing its share of the vote on average by 1.5 per cent. However, in its second tier of target seats, called 'priority seats', the party's share of the vote fell on average by 2.4 per cent, exactly the same as it did in all those seats that were not targeted at all. So at most Labour's targeting exercise was a mixed success.

In practice many of the seats on Labour's target list were also on that of the Conservatives. But there is little evidence that the Conservatives' exercise had much success in neutralising Labour's efforts. Amongst those seats where the party was challenging Labour, the Conservatives' share of the vote rose just as much in the seats that they did not target (+0.5 per cent) as it did in those that they did. The same is true in those seats where the party was challenging the Liberal Democrats. One possibility is that as the party with the longest list of target seats, the Conservatives simply spread their target-seat resources too thinly.

Table A2.9   Party performance in Liberal Democrat targets

	Mean change in % share of the vote since 1997			
(a) Con/LibDem seats	*Con*	*Lab*	*LibDem*	
Targeted	+2.5	–3.5	–0.9	(19)
Not Targeted	+1.9	+0.4	+3.4	(54)
(b) Lab/LibDem seats				
Targeted	–2.7	–2.1	+3.0	(6)
Not Targeted	–0.2	–3.4	+1.4	(24)

The party with the shortest list of target seats was the Liberal Democrats. And as Table A2.9 shows, the evidence is consistent with their efforts having had some impact. Amongst those seats where the Liberal Democrats started off second to the Conservatives, the party performed on average four points better in those seats that it targeted than it did in those that it did not. However, amongst those seats where it was challenging Labour, the difference is a more modest one-and-a-half points.

However, one other feature of Table A2.9 should also be noticed. The Liberal Democrats' relative success in those Conservative-held seats that it targeted came at the expense of Labour rather than the Conservatives. Indeed the Conservatives actually performed slightly better in those seats than they did in other seats that they were defending against the Liberal Democrats. This of course should not surprise us given that we have already established that the Conservatives did relatively well in marginal seats that they were defending. So if Liberal Democrat targeting did make a difference, then in Conservative/Liberal Democrat seats it did so primarily by encouraging some voters who might otherwise have voted Labour to make a tactical switch to the Liberal Democrats. Some of these seats were ones where the Liberal Democrats had not previously been close challengers to the Conservatives and thus were constituencies where Labour voters would not previously have had as much incentive to vote tactically. Whether they would have made that switch anyway in the absence of any targeting exercise by the Liberal Democrats must however remain a moot point.

Certainly there is little evidence that further tactical voting played much of a role in enabling the Liberal Democrats to perform relatively well in the most marginal seats they were defending. As we saw in Table A2.7, while on average Labour performed relatively badly in such seats, so also did the Conservatives. So while the Liberal Democrats may have retained much of the support they had obtained in these seats through a tactical squeeze on Labour at previous elections, there is no clear evidence that there was a significant increase in tactical voting in these seats this time around.[30]

On the other hand, despite the apparent evidence that both targeting and personal voting appear to be part of the explanation for Labour's relative success in the most marginal seats it was defending, it appears that tactical voting by Liberal Democrats may well have been the decisive factor. Note that even if we confine our attention to those seats that Labour targeted as battleground seats and where the incumbent Labour MP was standing again, Labour still performed better in the most marginal seats that it was defending than elsewhere.[31] Of course this could reflect the fact that Labour MPs in highly marginal seats would have had a particularly strong incentive to raise their profile and develop their local organisation within their constituency over the previous four years. However, we can also observe from Table A2.7 that the Conservatives did not perform particularly badly in Labour's most marginal seats, and that this was especially so in those constituencies where Labour's majority was less than 5 per cent. Rather, it is the Liberal Democrats who appear to have been squeezed. If organisation and the local popularity of the incumbent Labour MP did play a decisive role in these seats, they only appear to because they encouraged Liberal Democrats to vote tactically in the very particular highly competitive circumstances created locally by the outcome of the 1997 election.

But if some further tactical switching from the Liberal Democrats to Labour occurred in Labour's most marginal seats, what happened in the most marginal seats that the Conservatives were defending? Certainly Labour did not perform particularly badly in these seats. The 0.4 per cent drop in its share of the vote in those seats where the Conservatives had a 1997 majority of less than 5 per cent is well in line with its performance generally in those seats it did not win in 1997.[32] Rather, once again it appears to have been the Liberal Democrats who were squeezed, their vote falling in much the same way as it did in Labour's marginals. It would seem that we might have to conclude that while Liberal Democrat voters switched tactically to Labour in Labour's most marginal seats, they did so to the Conservatives' advantage in the Conservatives' most marginal constituencies.

This seems unlikely.[33] Certainly if it were the case we would expect to find that the Conservatives did best in these marginal seats where the Liberal Democrats did worst while Labour's performance was largely unaffected by how well or badly the Liberal Democrats did. However, this proves not to be the case.[34] It is more likely that what happened in these seats is that the Conservatives gained additional votes from those who might have voted Labour or Liberal Democrat or abstained, thanks perhaps to the local MP being more visible locally over the last four years, but that this was counterbalanced to some degree by tactical switching by Liberal Democrats in Labour's favour.

So, it looks as though we can best account for the relative success of each of the parties in their most marginal seats as follows. So far as Labour is concerned, targeting and personal voting may have played some role, but it seems unlikely that the party would have done as well as it did in its most marginal seats without some tactical squeezing of the Liberal Democrat vote. But in the case of the Conservatives and the Liberal Democrats, personal voting appears the most credible explanation, though this is undoubtedly easier to demonstrate in the case of the latter than the former. At the same time, however, the advantages that accrued to the incumbent party from these factors were sometimes counterbalanced by other forces. In particular the Conservatives' ability to defend their seats was sometimes threatened by tactical voting, voting that was perhaps encouraged by efforts at targeting. This seems to be particularly the case in those seats the party was defending against the Liberal Democrats.

The pattern of local party competition thus now appears to play a key role in influencing how some voters behave in British elections. Less important, however, appears to be the particular ideological position adopted by the local MP. In particular we can find little evidence that the stance taken by the local Conservative candidate on British membership of the single European currency made much difference to their performance. Of the Conservative candidates who were standing in seats that the party was defending, 22 could be classified as at least potentially in favour of Britain's membership of the euro while 46 were 'sceptical' about joining and as many as 96, 'ultrasceptical'.[35] However, at 2.6 per cent, the average increase in the share of the vote recorded by the ultrasceptics was little different from the 2.9 per cent recorded by those who were potentially in favour.

Nationalists and smaller parties

As we noted at the beginning, a relatively high proportion of the vote was again won by parties other than the Conservatives, Labour or Liberal Democrats. The most signficant performances were of course those of the nationalist parties in Scotland and Wales. In Wales, Plaid Cymru advanced to its highest share of the vote yet in a UK general election. Its 14.3 per cent of the vote was nearly three points higher than its previous high of 11.5 per cent recorded as long ago as 1970. In contrast the SNP suffered an unexpected fall of two points to 20.1 per cent. However neither party came anywhere close to its performance in the first devolution election when Plaid Cymru made a dramatic breakthrough to 28.4 per cent in the constituency vote and the SNP scored 28.7 per cent. This contrast between the results of the devolved and the UK general election supports the contention that the advent of devolved elections has created a far more favourable arena for the nationalist parties than UK general elections.[36]

Plaid Cymru's performance in the 1999 devolved elections had been notable not only for the size of the party's vote across the principality as a whole but also for the particularly strong advance it made in many South Wales valleys seats, enabling it to capture such Labour strongholds as Islwyn and Rhondda. It appeared as though the party was extending its appeal beyond the Welsh-speaking community in which it has hitherto prospered. But for the most part the party found it relatively difficult to maintain this advance in the predominantly English-speaking valleys. Three of the four biggest increases in the party's share of the vote since 1997 were in fact in constituencies where over 20 per cent of the adult population speaks Welsh, and the only seat that it gained, Carmarthen East & Dinefwr, was the one seat that the party did not previously hold where over half the population speaks Welsh. Meanwhile the three biggest falls in party support compared with the 1999 devolved elections were in South Wales valley seats.[37]

The party did, however, lose ground in all four of the heavily Welsh-speaking seats that it was defending. In part this reflects the fact that in all but one case, the MP that won the seat in 1997 was not standing again, having opted instead to pursue a career in the Welsh Assembly. This meant that the party lost any personal vote that had been established by the incumbent MP. Thus in both Ynys Mon and Caernarfon, the party's share of the vote fell by nearly seven points, costing it the former. In Ceredigion, however, where the 1997 victor resigned after being elected to the Welsh Assembly, giving an opportunity for a new incumbent MP to begin to establish a personal vote after his by-election victory in February 2000, the drop in Plaid support was only half as big. In contrast in Merionnydd Nant Conwy where the 1997 incumbent did stand again, the drop in support was just 1.1 per cent.

As in the case of Plaid, only one of the SNP's existing MPs opted to defend their Westminster seat, the remainder choosing to focus on the new Scottish Parliament in Edinburgh. And as in the case of Plaid the loss of personal votes for the incumbent MP affected the SNP's performance too. In the two constituencies where the incumbent MP stood down after having won the seat at the last three general elections, SNP support fell on average by no less than 12.1 per cent. Meanwhile in the three seats that the party had first won more recently (in one case in a 1995 by-election, in the other two in 1997), and where the party had thus had little or no opportunity in 1997 to benefit from an accumulated personal vote, the average drop was a more modest 7.2 per cent. In contrast in the one seat still being defended by the incumbent, Banff & Buchan, the fall in support was, at 1.5 per cent, little different from across Scotland as a whole. Apart from these instances, however, there was little systematic variation in the SNP performance. Most importantly the party's vote remained very evenly spread and despite retaining second place in votes across Scotland as a whole, the SNP was left with just one seat where it held second place and was no more than 10 per cent behind Labour.

Of the remaining smaller parties, by far the biggest challenge was posed by the United Kingdom Independence Party which, following the demise of the Referendum Party, became the sole vehicle for the anti-European cause. Even so, it failed to make the impact that the Referendum Party had done four years earlier. On average in those seats that were fought by UKIP this time around and by either the Referendum Party and/or UKIP in 1997, the share of the vote cast for the anti-European standard bearer was 1.6 per cent lower, with the heaviest falls typically occurring in those seats where the anti-European vote was highest in 1997. Even so, the party still tended to do best in constituencies whose social profile is most commonly associated with Euroscepticism (that is those with an older age profile) and least well in those with a relatively young population. It also tended to do rather better in seats with a low proportion of people with degrees, away from the most urban constituencies, and in the southern half of England outside of London.

The most successful of the small parties was the Scottish Socialist Party which fought all 72 seats in Scotland for the first time, following the election of its charismatic leader Tommy Sheridan to the Scottish Parliament in 1999. It won no less than 3.1 per cent of the vote in Scotland, the biggest incursion by a small party in any of the territories of Great Britain since the rise of the nationalists in Scotland and Wales in 1970. South of the border, the far left advanced less strongly, but even so Socialist candidates from the Socialist Alliance and the Socialist Labour Party in combination secured an average vote of 2.0 per cent in seats in England fought by at least one of them, up from 1.7 per cent in 1997 – despite more than doubling the number of seats they fought. As a result more votes were cast for far-left candidates across Britain as a whole than at any election since 1945. As one might anticipate all of the candidates of the far left tended to do best in working-class and more urban constituencies, in short in those places which commonly give Labour its largest majorities.

Meanwhile the Greens recorded their best ever performance in a UK general election with an average vote of 2.8 per cent in the 145 seats they fought. In seats which they fought both this time and in 1997, their share of the vote rose on average by 1.6 per cent. Their vote rose less the higher the level of car ownership in a constituency, suggesting that the party's rise in support was at least in part shaped by its distinctive environmentalist message. Meanwhile the British National Party was the only party not currently represented in Parliament to win over 10 per cent of the vote in a constituency, achieving this in both Oldham constituencies and in Burnley. Oldham at least was experiencing a high level of racial tension at the time of the election (albeit tension that may have been heightened by the activities of the BNP) and this appears to given the party an unusually fertile environment in which to secure votes. Across Britain as a whole the party's share of the vote rose by just 0.3 per cent on average in the 13 seats which the party fought both this time and in 1997.

Britain's first-past-the-post system was arguably less successful, then, at dissuading voters from voting for small parties not currently represented at Westminster than at any time since 1945. It may be that these parties simply profited from the lower turnout because their small but committed bands of followers were more likely to go to the polls. But if that is so it is somewhat surprising that there is no relationship between the change in the vote cast for small parties and turnout. More likely, perhaps, it may be that these parties have been able to gain credibility from their ability to secure representation in the European Parliament, the Scottish Parliament, and the Greater London Assembly where elections are fought under some variety of proportional representation. Certainly these parties were usually least likely to make progress in marginal seats where the disincentive to cast a vote for a smaller party was at its strongest.

But we would suggest that the most plausible explanation of the success of these parties is that they profited from a perception amongst some voters that none of the main parties currently adequately encompasses their views. For each of the small parties was usually fishing in rather different waters for its votes. Success for both Green candidates and the far left appears to have come primarily at Labour's expense while the success or otherwise of UKIP appears to have had most impact on the Conservatives' performance.

It was widely suggested that one of the motivations behind William Hague's decision to move his party in a more Eurosceptic direction was to repair the damage that was thought had been inflicted on his party by the Referendum Party's success in 1997. True, analysis of the 1997 result had cast doubt on the degree to which the anti-European vote had been procured in 1997 at the particular expense of the Conservatives.[38] While those who had cast an anti-European vote in 1997 were indeed disproportionately people who had voted Conservative in 1992, many had already defected from the Conservatives prior to the creation of the Referendum Party in 1995 and, in the absence of an anti-European candidate in 1997, would probably still not have voted Conservative. In short, while the Conservatives might well have good reason to hope to recapture many of these lost votes, it was less clear that they would do so simply by expressing a more avowedly anti-European message.

In the event, however, it appears that the Conservatives were the principal beneficiaries of the decline in the anti-European vote in 2001, recapturing some of the voters that they lost in 1997. As Table A2.10 shows, the Conservatives were the only party that consistently did better, the more the anti-European vote fell. Thus, for example, its share of the vote rose by 3.3 per cent in those seats where the anti-European vote was four points or more less than it had been in 1997 while it rose by 0.2 per cent where there was a drop in the anti-European vote of less than two points. Overall there is a clear negative correlation of –0.28 between the change in the anti-European vote and the change in the Conservative vote, whereas there is little or no correlation between the change in the anti-European vote and either the Labour (0.00) or Liberal Democrat (–0.07) performance. Meanwhile multivariate analysis indicates that this relationship between Conservative and UKIP performance is not simply an artefact of the various other features of the Conservative performance we have already discussed.

Table A2.10   **The impact of the anti-European vote**

	Mean change in % vote since 1997			
Change in anti-European vote 1997–2001	*Con*	*Lab*	*LibDem*	
Down 4% or more	+3.3	–1.5	+1.7	(28)
Down 2%–4%	+1.8	–2.0	+1.5	(203)
Down 0%–2%	+0.2	–1.9	+1.8	(310)
Up	–0.2	–1.4	–0.1	(66)

Table based on those constituencies where an anti-European candidate (that is a candidate from the Referendum party or UKIP) stood in 1997 or in 2001 or on both occasions.

There is though one caveat to this picture. While the Conservatives appear to have profited where the anti-European vote fell, it seems to have been the Liberal Democrats who lost out most in the minority of seats where there was a higher anti-European vote this time around (particularly in those seats where there had not been an anti-European candidate in 1997). The Liberal Democrats' vote fell back a little on average in these seats, sharply against the trend elsewhere, while the Conservatives hardly did any worse than they did in seats where the anti-European vote fell only slightly. So we again have some evidence to suggest that Britain's most pro-European party is also vulnerable to a strong anti-European performance.

Meanwhile, we can also identify a similar relationship between the performance of the far left and that of Labour. Labour did worst where the combined vote for Socialist candidates rose most or where such a candidate stood for the first time in 1997. Its vote fell least in those seats where a Socialist candidate withdrew. In contrast, neither the Conservative nor the Liberal Democrat performance (or indeed that of the SNP in Scotland) showed any systematic relationship with that of the Socialists.[39] In short, it appears that one of the reasons for the relative success of far-left Socialist candidates was dissatisfaction amongst some Labour voters with their party's move to the centre. Similar analysis for the Greens also suggests that their votes came disproportionately at the expense of both Labour and the Liberal Democrats rather than the Conservatives.

The electoral system

It is widely argued that the single member plurality electoral system commonly provides the party with most votes – a bonus in terms of seats. This would suggest that perhaps we should not be surprised that Labour should have secured 63 per cent of Commons seats with 42 per cent of the vote in Great Britain and a 9.3 per cent lead over the Conservatives. Such an outcome would appear to be no more than the electoral system performing in the way that it is meant to.

However, a closer look raises some doubts about whether this is so. For example, Labour won 20 more seats than would have been expected even if the so-called 'cube law', which aims to model the size of the winners' bonus, had been in operation.[40] Meanwhile, Labour's 9.3 per cent lead over the Conservatives in Great Britain was less than that enjoyed by Clement Attlee in 1945 and Margaret Thatcher in both 1983 and 1987. Yet its overall majority of 167 was substantially greater than the majorities of 144 and 102 secured by Mrs Thatcher. Perhaps most strikingly of all, it is a far larger majority than that of 21 obtained by John Major in 1992 even though Mr Major's lead in votes (7.6 per cent) was not that far short of Mr Blair's.

To some degree we should perhaps not be surprised at these apparent discrepancies. Both our own work and that of others demonstrated that the electoral system was exhibiting a stronger bias in Labour's favour at the last election than at any previous post-war election.[41] For example, if the geography of party support remained as it was in 1997, Labour would have won 80 more seats than the Conservatives in the event that the two parties won the same share of the overall vote. But in fact the outcome in seats was even more to Labour's advantage than might have been expected given how the electoral system was operating in 1997. If the change in each party's share of the overall vote had been replicated in every constituency then Labour would have won 402 seats (11 fewer than they actually obtained), the Liberal Democrats, 48 (4 fewer), while the Conservatives would have secured 180 – no fewer than 14 more.[42]

So why was the electoral system apparently even more favourable to Labour at this election than it was in 1997? There are two possibilities.

It is well established that there are two main reasons why the single member plurality system can treat one party more favourably than another for any given division of the vote between them.[43] The first is that one party wins more votes in smaller constituencies. The second is that one party's vote is more efficiently distributed than the other's. So the electoral system could have become even more biased in Labour's favour either if the party's vote became even more strongly concentrated in smaller seats or if its votes became more efficiently distributed.

Both in fact happened to some degree, though the former process was more important than the latter. We have already noted when we discussed Table A2.1 above that the mean drop in Labour's share of the vote was 0.5 per cent less than the overall fall. This is an indication that Labour's vote became more heavily concentrated in smaller constituencies.[44] Meanwhile the median drop was also yet a little lower than the mean, though only by 0.1 per cent. This is an indication of Labour's vote having become slightly more efficiently distributed. At the same time the mean increase in the Conservatives' share of the vote was lower than the overall increase while the median increase was yet lower still.

There were three main reasons why Labour's vote became increasingly concentrated in smaller constituencies. First, as we saw in Table A2.3, turnout fell most in those constituencies where Labour was strongest in 1997. This pattern reduced Labour's share of the overall vote without doing any damage to its ability to win seats. Second, the pattern of migration since 1997 meant that, as has become the norm, the electorate in Labour-held seats grew less rapidly than that in Conservative-held seats. On average the electorate increased between 1997 and 2001 by 1,514 voters in those seats that the Conservatives were defending while it rose by just 361 in the average Labour seat. This simply served to exacerbate the existing under-representation of Conservative voters.

The third reason for the increased bias is a little more subtle. What in fact matters in determining whether there is bias in favour of the Conservatives or Labour is not so much whether there is a difference in the total number of votes cast in the constituencies each party wins, but rather whether there is a difference in the total number of votes cast for those two parties alone. Votes cast for the Liberal Democrats and other parties are irrelevant to the relationship between votes and seats for the two main parties, as long as they do not actually win a constituency. All that such votes do is effectively to reduce the number of votes that the Conservatives or Labour need to win the constituency themselves.

As we have already noted, for the most part the Liberal Democrats have tended to do better in constituencies where the Conservatives are relatively strong than in those where Labour is. But we also noted that at this election, the Liberal Democrats advanced more strongly in the latter kind of constituency. At the same time, we have also noted an increase in votes for Socialist candidates, who generally did best in Labour seats, and a decline in the anti-European vote, which was stronger in Conservative ones in 1997. Overall the percentage of the vote given to Liberal Democrats and others increased from 18.5 per cent to 21.0 per cent in seats won by Labour in 1997 while it fell from 28.3 per cent to 25.3 per cent in those being defended by the Conservatives. In short, while the Conservatives still benefit somewhat from this source of bias, their advantage was much reduced in 1997.

The only measure in Table A2.1 that is sensitive to changes in the size of the vote cast for the two main parties rather than just changes in the total number of votes cast is in fact the two-party swing. And as we noted, this is the measure that shows the biggest difference between its mean and overall figure in that table. In short, changes in the size of the electorate, in the turnout, and in votes cast for third parties halved the effective swing to the Conservatives at this election.

In fact Labour's final tally of 413 seats is exactly in line with what would have happened if the mean two-party swing of 1.1 per cent had occurred in each and every constituency. By that yardstick, therefore, any changes in the relative efficiency of the two main parties' votes had no significant impact on the size of Labour's majority. In practice, however, Labour did manage to win votes where it would most count by securing a swing to themselves in the most marginal seats that they were defending, thanks primarily to tactical voting by Liberal Democrats. However, such tactical switching helped Labour to save no more than a handful of seats that they might otherwise have lost, while it helped the party to secure just one seat from the Conservatives, Dorset South.[45] Still, the Conservatives only captured some seats from Labour at all because some Labour marginals swung to the Conservatives against the national trend. Decisive in this respect was the Conservative upsurge in South Essex, where the party made three of its five gains from Labour (Castle Point, Romford and Upminster), and its relatively strong performance in rural Britain, where it recaptured two of the most rural seats Labour had gained in 1997 (North-West Norfolk and Newark).

But the Conservatives not only lost out to Labour, they also lost a net total of four more seats than they might have anticipated to the Liberal Democrats if the mean change in each party's share of the vote had been replicated everywhere. This is despite their performing rather better than average in those seats that were most vulnerable to a Liberal Democrat challenge. In three seats the Conservatives clearly lost out as a result of tactical switching by Labour voters to the benefit of the Liberal Democrats.[46] However two other Liberal Democrat gains are better accounted for simply by a relatively poor local Conservative performance.[47]

So, changes in the efficiency of the distribution of party support, including that induced by tactical voting, played only a relatively small role in accounting for the Conservatives' difficulties in winning seats at this election. However, we should bear in mind that we might have anticipated that the level of anti-Conservative tactical voting might have declined at this election now that there was no longer a Conservative administration to be removed from office. This certainly appeared to be what was happening in local elections during the course of the last Parliament.[48] But for the most part this did not occur. At most, a decline in anti-Conservative voting was evident in the two seats that the Liberal Democrats lost to the Conservatives, though it may only have been decisive in one of them.[49] So while additional anti-Conservative tactical voting appears to have had relatively little impact at this election, in stark contrast to 1997, the Conservatives largely continued to suffer from the increase in tactical voting that was registered in 1997.

Table A2.11   The relationship between seats and votes

| | % Votes | | Seats | | | |
Swing to Con	Con	Lab	Con	Lab	LibDem	Others
0%	32.7	42.0	166	413	52	28
1%	33.7	41.0	177	407	48	27
2%	34.7	40.0	184	401	47	27
3%	35.7	39.0	199	388	44	28
4%	36.7	38.0	208	380	43	28
4.7%	37.4	37.4	224	364	43	28
5%	37.7	37.0	232	358	41	28
6%	38.7	36.0	249	342	40	28
6.5%	39.2	35.5	263	329	39	28
7%	39.7	35.0	274	318	39	28
8%	40.7	34.0	287	307	38	27
8.8%	41.5	33.2	297	297	38	27
9%	41.7	33.0	300	294	38	27
9.3%	42.0	32.7	305	290	37	27
10%	42.7	32.0	315	280	37	27
10.4%	43.1	31.6	330	269	35	25
11%	43.7	31.0	337	263	34	25
12%	44.7	30.0	351	249	33	26

Others include 18 seats in N. Ireland.

332 The British General Election of 2001

The overall bias that now exists in the electoral system can be seen in Table A2.11. As in previous such tables in this series, it shows the number of seats that would be won by each party for any given uniform total-vote swing. In so doing it shows the impact on the parties' ability to win seats of the current distribution of party support across constituencies. Two key findings in the table illustrate the difficulties that face the Conservatives. First, if the Conservatives were to win the same share of the vote as Labour, they would win no fewer than 140 seats less than Labour – 60 more than the disadvantage they suffered in 1997. Second, in order to win an overall majority of one the Conservatives would have to be no less than 11.5 per cent ahead of Labour in votes, whereas Labour could be as much as 3.7 per cent *behind* the Conservatives and still retain their overall majority.[50] In 1997 in contrast, the respective figures were 10.1 per cent and 1.5 per cent.

Some of this bias is likely to be removed by the time of the next election. The Boundary Commissioners have already initiated a review of constituency boundaries that could well be implemented before the country goes to the polls again. Not only should the review equalise constituency electorates within each of England, Scotland and Wales, but it will also eliminate, for the time being at least, Scotland's over-representation at Westminster.[51] But although both of these moves will help to reduce the bias that arises from differences in electorate size, it will not remove them entirely, not least because the review will already be five years out of date in England by the likely earliest date for the next election, 2005. And of course it will do nothing to eliminate the other sources of bias that we have seen working against the Conservatives at this election. Those will only disappear if the geography of party support changes.

Conclusion

In many respects the outcome of the 2001 election appears to vindicate New Labour's electoral strategy. For the most part, the party was relatively successful at retaining its support in those constituencies where the party had traditionally found it relatively more difficult to win votes. At the same time New Labour appears to have been more successful in deploying its local organisational resources than the Conservatives while it maintained the informal coalition of tactical support from those who might otherwise vote Liberal Democrat, thereby helping it further to defend its most vulnerable marginal seats.

Yet there was evidently also a price to pay. Voters were particularly likely to stay at home in Labour's safer seats where the party also lost ground to the Liberal Democrats and candidates of the far left. The party may be unwise to assume that its more left-wing supporters will always feel that they have nowhere else to go. But in the meantime, thanks to the operation of the first-past-the-post electoral system, these movements cost Labour votes without losing it seats. As a result Britain's electoral system produced a more biased result than ever before. That may be good news for New Labour but whether it is good for the health of Britain's democracy is a far more debatable point.

Acknowledgements

We are deeply indebted to Martin Range of Oxford University for his highly skilled and efficient computing support and to Louisa Welby-Everard of the BBC for her tireless efforts in ensuring the effective and accurate collection of the results of the 2001 election. We are also very grateful to Richard Webber of Experian for so generously supplying us with data compiled by his company on the current social and economic composition of parliamentary constituencies.

Notes

1. Twenty-one constituencies in Great Britain (excluding those affected by the Speaker) changed hands as between 1997 and 2001, of which only six were between the two largest parties. In 1955, after allowing for boundary change, the equivalent figure lies between 21 and 23, all exchanged between Conservative and Labour. See calculations in D. E. Butler, *The British General Election of 1955* (London: Macmillan 1955), p. 157.
2. Our analysis is also confined to Great Britain.
3. The standard deviation of two-party swing in comparable seats was 4.1 in each of October 1974–79, 1983–87 and 1987–92. It was previously never higher than 3.1 at an election fought on unchanged boundaries. (When an election is fought on changed boundaries estimates of the variance in party support are inflated by errors in the estimate of what the outcome of the last election would have been on the new boundaries.)
4. We should also note that at 74.7 per cent the combined share of the vote cast for the Conservative and Labour parties was lower than at any post-war election apart from 1983.
5. Falling turnout is also a trend across Western Europe; in that wider context some broader explanations, focusing more on long-term societal change, may be more relevant. We restrict our analysis here to one country's change between 1997 and 2001, but it may be noted that our finding of a smaller drop in turnout in constituencies with more older voters and in more rural areas is consistent with the view that living in more stable communities tends to encourage interest in public affairs, including a willingness to vote.
6. C. Bromley, J. Curtice and B. Seyd, in A. Park et al., *British Social Attitudes: the 18th Report* (London: Sage, 2001); M. Wattenberg, 'The Decline of Party Mobilization', in R. Dalton and M. Wattenberg (eds), *Parties without Partisans: Political Change in Advanced Industrial Democracies* (Oxford: Oxford University

Press, 2000); A. Heath, 'Were Traditional Labour Voters Disillusioned with New Labour? Abstention at the 1997 General Election', in P. Cowley et al. (eds), *British Elections and Parties Review*, vol. 10 (2000); A. Heath and B. Taylor, 'New Sources of Abstention', in G. Evans and P. Norris (eds), *Critical Elections: British Parties and Voters in Long-Term Perspective* (1999).

7. A. Park, 'Young People and Apathy', in R. Jowell et al. (eds), *British Social Attitudes; the 16th Report: Who Shares New Labour Values?* (Aldershot: Ashgate, 1999).

8. J. Curtice and R. Jowell, 'The Sceptical Electorate', in R. Jowell et al. (eds), *British Social Attitudes; the 12th Report* (Aldershot: Dartmouth, 1995).

9. J. Curtice and M. Steed, 'An Analysis of the Result', in D. Butler and M. Westlake, *British Politics and European Elections 1999* (1999).

10. In 1997 the turnout in seats won by Labour averaged 69.7 per cent and that in seats won by the Conservatives, 74.4 per cent. In 2001 the equivalent figures were 56.8 per cent and 63.2 per cent.

11. Substantially rural seats are those in which 25 per cent or more are living in postcode areas classified by Mosaic Group as 'country dwellers'. Moderately rural seats are those where between 15 and 25 per cent fall into that category.

12. I. Budge, 'Party Policy and Ideology: Reversing the 1950s?', in G. Evans and P. Norris (eds), *Critical Elections: British Parties and Voters in Long-Term Perspective* (1999); A. Heath, R. Jowell and J. Curtice, *The Rise of New Labour: Party Policies and Voter Choices* (2001).

13. See, for example, C. Bromley and J. Curtice, 'Is there a Third way?', in R. Jowell et al. (eds), *British Social Attitudes: the 16th Report* (1999).

14. W. Miller, 'Social Class and Party Choice in England: A New Analysis', *British Journal of Political Science*, 8 (1978), 257–74.

15. We may also note that those living in seats with a high ethnic minority population also appeared to react relatively unfavourably to the Conservatives' campaign, which in respect of asylum seekers at least was claimed by some to be racist. The Conservative vote fell by 0.7 per cent in seats with a high ethnic minority population whereas it rose elsewhere by 1.3 per cent. Meanwhile Labour's vote appears to have fallen rather less in those constituencies with a very low proportion of employers and managers which also had a relatively high ethnic minority population. (Ethnic minority seats are classified as those where 5 per cent or more of adults aged 16+ identified themselves as other than 'white' in the 1991 Census.)

16. G. Evans, A. Heath and C. Payne, 'Class: Labour as a Catch-All Party?', in G. Evans and P. Norris (eds), *Critical Elections: British Parties and Voters in Long-Term Perspective* (1999).

17. J. Curtice, 'Who Votes for the Centre Now?', in D. MacIver (ed.), *The Liberal Democrats* (London: Prentice Hall/Harvester Wheatsheaf, 1996).

18. See also J. Curtice, '2001: Repeat or Revolution', *Politics Review* 11 (2001), 1, 2–5.

19. J. Curtice and M. Steed, 'An Analysis of the Voting', in D. Butler and D. Kavanagh, *The British General Election of 1979* (London: Macmillan 1980).

20. These 11 seats are all those seats in the London Boroughs of Barking & Dagenham and Havering together with Basildon, Billericay, Castle Point, Rochford & Southend East, Southend West and Thurrock.

21. There is however no evidence that Labour did consistently badly in those seats where there had been a high incidence of foot and mouth. For example, while Labour did do particularly badly (and the Conservatives well) in Cumbria and some adjacent Pennine constituencies, one of the areas most badly affected by foot and mouth, the same was not true of Devon, which was similarly badly affected.

22. As a political consequence, by gaining seats such as North West Norfolk and Taunton, the Conservatives have become an even more rural party in Parliament. Their one Scottish gain (Galloway & Upper Nithsdale) was in the most rural constituency on the Scottish mainland and still leaves them without representation from urban central Scotland. Meanwhile, by losing Cheadle they are left with only one MP from the five major Northern conurbations in place of two in 1997. Only in South Essex did they gain urban seats.

23. J. Curtice and M. Steed, 'The Results Analysed', in D. Butler and D. Kavanagh, *The British General Election of 1997* (London: Macmillan, now Palgrave, 1997), p. 312; J. Curtice and M. Steed, 'The Results Analysed', in D. Butler and D. Kavanagh, *The British General Election of 1992* (London: Macmillan, 1992); B. Cain, J. Ferejohn and M. Fiorina, *The Personal Vote: Constituency Service and Electoral Independence* (Cambridge, Mass.: Harvard University Press, 1987); P. Norton and B. Wood, 'Do Candidates Matter? Constituency-Specific Vote Changes for Incumbent MPs 1983–87', *Political Studies*, 42 (1994), 227–38.

24. See, for example, D. Denver and G. Hands, *Modern Constituency Electioneering* (1997); P. Whiteley and P. Seyd, 'Labour's Vote and Local Activism', *Parliamentary Affairs*, 45 (1992), 582–95; C. Pattie, P. Whiteley, R. Johnston and P. Seyd, 'Measuring Local Campaign Effects: Labour Party Constituency Campaigning at the 1987 General Election', *Political Studies*, 42 (1994), 469–79; C. Pattie, R. Johnston and E. Fieldhouse, 'Winning the Local Vote: The Effectiveness of Constituency Campaign Spending in Great Britain, 1983–92', *American Political Science Review*, 89 (1995), 969–83.

25. J. Curtice and M. Steed, 'The Results Analysed', in D. Butler and D. Kavanagh, *The British General Election of 1992* (1992), pp. 311–12.

26. J. Curtice and M. Steed, 'The Results Analysed', in D. Butler and D. Kavanagh, *The British General Election of 1997* (1997); G. Evans, J. Curtice and P. Norris, 'New Labour, New Tactical Voting?', in D. Denver et al. (eds), *British Elections and Parties Review*, Vol. 8 (1998).

27. Three of these seats were ones captured by the Liberal Democrats in 1997 and where the incumbent Liberal Democrat MP may not have had the opportunity to develop a personal vote. However in two of these cases (Brecon & Radnorshire and Southport), the Liberal Democrat MP had been MP for the constituency prior to the 1992 election and had thus had the opportunity to develop a personal vote. Still, as we might expect, if we ignore those three cases, the average drop was as high as 6.2 per cent.

28. This includes two cases where the retiring incumbent Labour MP had gained the seat from a Conservative incumbent in 1997. Here Labour's vote fell on average by 3.2 per cent, well below the performance in other seats that the party gained in 1997.

29. For further details see P. Seyd, 'The Labour Campaign', in P. Norris (ed.), *Britain Votes 2001* (Oxford: Oxford University Press, 2001).

30. Note also that both the Conservatives and Labour performed better where incumbent Liberal Democrat MPs did not defend their seat than where they did. The Conservative vote rose on average by 1.7 per cent in seats where the incumbent Liberal Democrat MP stood down while it fell by 2.7 per cent where a new incumbent was defending the seat for the first time. The equivalent figures for Labour are an increase of 3.0 per cent and a decline of 2.1 per cent respectively. So the personal voting for Liberal Democrat MPs that we identified above does not appear to be a by-product of rises and falls in the incidence of tactical voting.

31. Amongst these seats, Labour's vote rose on average by 2.4 per cent where its 1997 majority was less than 5 per cent, by 1.6 per cent where it was between 5 and 10 per cent, while it rose by just 0.3 per cent where the 1997 majority was more than 10 per cent.

32. The one exception to this rule appears to have been the Conservatives' most marginal seat, Dorset South, where Labour recorded the second largest increase in its vote in any seat where it started off second to the Conservatives, thereby enabling it to take the seat.

33. After all, according to an ICM poll conducted for the BBC poll over the weekend before polling day, 52 per cent of those who intended to vote Liberal Democrat said that Labour were their second-choice party whereas only 19 per cent said the Conservatives were.

34. The correlation between the Labour and the Liberal Democrat performance in Con–Lab marginals is –0.65 while that between the Conservatives and the Liberal Democrats is only –0.25. In contrast, our interpretation that Labour benefited from a tactical squeeze on the Liberal Democrats in Labour/Conservative marginals is supported by the pattern of correlations in those seats. The correlation between the Labour and the Liberal Democrat performance is –0.60 while that between the Conservatives and the Liberal Democrats is only –0.40.

35. Our classification of the stance of Conservative candidates is based on the information posted on the web by pro-European Conservatives at http://www.proeuro.co.uk/europhobes/CAT2.htm.

36. L.Paterson et al., *New Scotland, New Politics?* (Edinburgh: Edinburgh University Press, 2001); J. Curtice, 'Is Devolution Succouring Nationalism?', *Contemporary Wales* 14 (2001), 80–103.

37. These were Islwyn (–30.1), Rohondda (–27.6) and Cynon Valley (–25.1). Overall the correlation between the percentage of Welsh speakers and the percentage voting Plaid Cymru was, at 0.87, only slightly down on the 0.90 that pertained in 1997 and was well up on the 0.76 figure for the 1999 devolved elections.

38. J. Curtice and M. Steed, 'The Results Analysed', in D. Butler and D. Kavanagh, *The British General Election of 1997* (1997), pp. 305–8; A. Heath, R. Jowell and K. Thomson, 'Euroscepticism and the Referendum Party', in D. Denver et al. (eds), *British Elections and Parties Review*, vol. 8 (1998).

39. Labour's share of the vote fell on average by 3.5 per cent in those seats where the socialist vote rose by more than 1 per cent, and by 3.2 per cent in those

where a socialist candidate stood for the first time. In contrast, Labour's vote fell by 2.5 per cent on average where the socialist vote rose by less than 1 per cent and fell by just 0.9 per cent where a socialist stood in 1997 but not in 2001. Again multivariate analysis suggests this relationship is not simply a spurious one.

40. M. Kendall and A. Stuart, 'The Law of Cubic Proportion in Election Results', *British Journal of Sociology*, 1 (1950), 183–96.

41. J. Curtice and M. Steed, 'Neither Representative nor Accountable: First-Past-the-Post in Britain' (paper presented at the Annual Workshops of the European Consortium for Political Research, 1998); D. Rossiter et al., 'Changing Biases in the Operation of the UK's Electoral System, 1950–97, *British Journal of Politics and International Relations,* 2 (1999), 133–64; R. Johnston et al., *From Votes to Seats (*2001).

42. The Conservative figure becomes 181 if one also takes into account Martin Bell's decision not to defend his seat in Tatton which he captured from the Conservatives in 1997.

43. R. Johnston, *Political, Electoral and Spatial Systems* (Oxford: Clarendon Press, 1979).

44. C. Soper and J. Rydon. 'Under-representation and Electoral Prediction', *Australian Journal of Politics and History*, 4 (1958), 94–106.

45. There is just one seat, Kettering, which Labour should have lost on a 1.1 per cent two-party swing but did not and where an apparent squeeze on the Liberal Democrat vote could have been decisive. Even if we look at the rather larger number of seats vulnerable to a 1.4 per cent total vote swing, only two or three other seats (Lancaster, Harwich and perhaps Braintree) can be added to this list.

46. These are Ludlow, Norfolk North and Romsey, in all of which there were double-digit drops in Labour's vote. In the case of Romsey this tactical squeeze had first been induced by the by-election held in May 2000. To these we can probably add one further seat, Guildford, where although Labour's vote fell by only a couple more points than might otherwise have been expected, this was probably decisive in giving the Liberal Democrats their 1.2 per cent majority.

47. In both Cheadle and Dorset Mid & Poole North, which the Liberal Democrats captured from the Conservatives, Labour's vote fell only slightly while the Conservative vote either fell or barely rose.

48. J. Curtice, *Lessons from the Local Elections: How FPP Could Fail to Deliver Labour a Second Term* (London: Make Votes Count, 2000).

49. The clear case appears to be Taunton. In the Isle of Wight, however, the Liberal Democrats may not have lost the seat but for an above-average performance by the Conservatives as well.

50. Blau has argued that such calculations should be made using two-party rather than total-vote swing as only the former keeps the frequency distribution of the two-party vote across constituencies unchanged. Moreover, we have seen that two-party swing gives a more reliable guide to the actual operation of the electoral system at this election. This alternative method, however, shows largely the same story, giving Labour 131 more seats than the Conservatives when the two parties have the same share of the vote, up from 62 in 1997.

See A. Blau, 'Seats–Votes Relationships in British General Elections, 1955–1997' (D.Phil. thesis, University of Oxford, 2001).
51. J. Curtice, 'Reinventing the Yo-Yo: A Comment on the Electoral Provisions of the Scotland Bill', *Scottish Affairs*, 23 (Spring 1998), 41–53.

Select Bibliography

Anderson, P. and Mann, N. (1997) *Safety First: The Making of New Labour* (London: Granta).

Ashdown, P. (2000) *The Ashdown Diaries volume I: 1988–1997* (London: Allen Lane).

Ashdown, P. (2001) *The Ashdown Diaries volume II: 1997–1999* (London: Allen Lane).

Ballinger, C. and Coleman, S. (2001) *Electoral Law and the Internet* (London: Hansard Society).

Berrington, H. (2001) 'After the Ball was Over: The British General Election of 2001' *West European Politics* (forthcoming).

Blackburn, R. and Plant, R. (1999) *Constitutional Reform: The Labour Government's Constitutional Reform Agenda* (London: Longman Higher Education).

Blumler, J. and Coleman, S. (2001) *Realising Democracy Online* (London: IPPR).

Bogdanor, V. (2001) *Devolution in the United Kingdom* (Oxford: Oxford University Press).

Brazier, R. (1999) *Constitutional Practice: The Foundations of British Government* (Oxford: Oxford University Press).

Brown, A. et al. (1998) *The Scottish Electorate* (London: Macmillan, now Palgrave).

Brown, C. (1997) *Fighting Talk: The Biography of John Prescott* (Simon & Schuster).

Butler, D. and Westlake, M. (2000) *British Politics and European Elections 1999* (Basingstoke: Macmillan, now Palgrave).

Clarke, H. et al. (1998) 'New Models for New Labour: the Political Economy of Labour Party Support, January 1992 – April 1997' *American Political Science Review* 92, 559–75.

Coleman, S. (ed.) (2001) *Elections in the Age of the Internet* (London: Hansard Society).

Coleman, S. (ed.) (2001) *2001: Cyber Space Odyssey* (London: Hansard Society).

Cowley, P. et al. (eds) (2000) *British Election and Parties Review*, Vol. 10 (London: Frank Cass).

Crewe, I. et al. (1998) *Political Communications: Why Labour Won the General Election of 1997* (London: Frank Cass).

Crewe, I. (2001) 'Elections and Public Opinion', in Seldon A. (ed.).

Crewe, I. and Fox, A. (1999) *British Parliamentary Constituencies on CD-ROM* (Gloucester: Polemic Books).

Dale, I. (ed.) (2000) *British Political Party Manifestos, 1900–1997* (London: Routledge).

Denver, D. and Hands, G. (1997) *Modern Constituency Electioneering* (London: Frank Cass).

Denver, D. et al. (1997) *Scotland Decides* (London: Frank Cass).

Denver, D. et al. (eds) (1998) *British Elections and Parties Review*, Vol. 8 (London: Frank Cass).

Electoral Commission (2001) *Election 2001: The Official Results* (London, Politico's).

Evans, G. (1998) 'Euroscepticism and Conservative Electoral Support: How an Asset Became a Liability', *British Journal of Political Science,* 28: 573–90.

Evans, G. (ed.) (1999) *The End of Class Politics? Class Voting in Comparative Context* (Oxford: Oxford University Press).

Evans, G. and Norris, P. (eds) (1999) *Critical Elections: British Parties and Voters in Long-Term Perspective* (London: Sage).

Fairclough, N. (2000) *New Labour, New Language* (London: Routledge).

Flynn, P. (1999) *Dragons Led by Poodles: The Inside Story of a New Labour Stitch-Up* (London: Politico's).

Franklin, B. (1998) *Tough on Soundbites, Tough on the Causes of Soundbites* (London: Catalyst Trust).

Geddes, A. and Tonge, J. (eds) (1997) *Labour's Landslide* (Manchester: Manchester University Press).

Gibbons, V. (ed.) (2001) *The People Have Spoken: Who Votes and Who Doesn't* (London: Hansard Society).

Giddens, A. (1999) *The Third Way: Renewal of Social Democracy* (Cambridge University Press).

Giddens, A. (2000) *The Third Way and its Enemies* (Oxford: Polity).

Gould, P. (1998) *The Unfinished Revolution* (London: Little, Brown).

Hames, T. and Sparrow, N. (1997) *Left Home: The Myth of Tory Abstentions* (London: CPS).

Hay, C. (1999) *The Political Economy of New Labour* (Manchester: Manchester University Press).

Heath, A. et al. (2001) *The Rise of New Labour: Party Politics and Voter Choices* (Oxford: Oxford University Press).

Heffernan, R. (1998) 'Labour's Transformation: A Staged Process with No Single Point of Origin', *Politics* 18, 101–6.

Henig, S. and Baston, L. (2000) *Guide to the General Election* (London: Politico's).

Johnston, R. et al. (2001) *From Votes to Seats: The Operation of the UK Electoral System since 1945* (Manchester: Manchester University Press).

Jones, N. (1999) *Sultans of Spin* (London: Victor Gollancz).

Jones, N. (1999) *The Control Freaks* (London: Politico's).

Jones, N. (2001) *Campaign 2001: An Election Diary* (London: Politico's).

Kampfer, J. (1999) *Robin Cook* (London: Phoenix).

Kilfoyle, P. (2000) *Left Behind: Lessons from Labour's Heartlands* (London: Politico's).

King, A. (ed.) (2001) *British Political Opinion 1937–2000* (London: Politico's)

King, A. (ed.) (2001) *Leaders, Personalities, and the Outcome of Democratic Elections* (Oxford University Press).

King, A. et al. (1998) *New Labour Triumphs: Britain at the Polls* (Chatham NJ: Chatham House) 177–207.

Kocham, A. (2000) *Ann Widdecombe* (London: Politico's).

Lees-Marchment, J. (2000) *Political Marketing and British Political Parties* (Manchester University Press).

Leonard, D. and Mortimore, R. (2001) *Elections in Britain* (Basingstoke: Palgrave, 4th edn).

Ludlam, S. and Smith, M. (eds) (2001) *New Labour in Government* (Basingstoke: Palgrave).

McIntyre, D. (2000) *Peter Mandelson* (London: HarperCollins).

McLean, I. et al. (1999) 'Between First and Second Order: A Comparison of Voting Behaviour in European and Local Elections in Britain' *European Journal of Political Research* 35, 389–414.

Marquand, D. (1999) *The Progressive Dilemma* (London: Phoenix Giant, 2nd edn).

Moon, N. (1999) *Opinion Polls: History, Theory and Practice* (Manchester University Press).

Nadler, J.-A. (2000) *William Hague: In His Own Right* (London: Politico's).

Newton, K. and Brynin, M. (2001) 'The National Press and Party Voting in the UK' *Political Studies* 49, 265–85.

Norris, P. and Gavin, N. (eds) (1997) *Britain Votes 1997* (Oxford University Press).

Norris, P. et al. (1999) *On Message: Communicating the Campaign* (London: Sage).

Oborne, P. (1999) *Alastair Campbell: New Labour and the Rise of the Media Class* (London: Aurum).

Pattie, C. and Johnson, R. (1998) 'Voter Turnout at the British General Election of 1992: Rational Choice, Social Standing or Political Efficacy?' *European Journal of Political Research* 33, 263–83.

Pattie, C. and Johnson, R. (1999) 'Context, Conversation and Conviction: Social Networks and Voting at the 1992 British General Election' *Political Studies* 47, 877–89.

Pattie, C. and Johnson, R. (2001) 'A Low Turnout Landslide: Abstention at the British General Election of 1997' *Political Studies* 49, 286–305.

Pym, H and Kochan, N. (1998) *Gordon Brown: The First Year in Power* (London: Bloomsbury).

Rallings, C. and Thrasher, M. (1999) *British Parliamentary Results 1983–1998* (Aldershot: Ashgate).

Rallings, C. and Thrasher, M. (1999) *New Britain: New Elections* (London: Vacher Dod).

Rallings, C. and Thrasher, M. (eds) (1999) *Media Guide to the New Parliamentary Constituencies* (Local Government Chronicle Elections Centre / BBC, ITN, PA News and Sky).

Rallings, C. and Thrasher, M. *Local Election Handbooks 1995–1999* (Plymouth: Local Government Chronicle Elections Centre, University of Plymouth).

Rallings, C. and Thrasher, M. (2001) 'Elections and Public Opinion: The End of the Honeymoon?' *Parliamentary Affairs* 54, 322–36.

Rallings, C. and Thrasher, M. (2001) 'Measuring the Level and Diversities of Split-Ticket Voting at the 1979 and 1997 British General and Local Elections' *Political Studies* 49, 323–30.

Rawnsley, A. (2000) *Servants of the People* (London: Hamish Hamilton).

Rentoul, J. (2001) *Tony Blair* (London: Little, Brown).

Riddell, P. (2000) *Parliament Under Blair* (London: Politico's).

Rose, R. (2001) *The Prime Minster in a Shrinking World* (London: Little, Brown).

Routledge, P (1998) *Gordon Brown: The Biography* (London: Simon and Schuster).

Routledge, P. (1999) *Mandy: The Unauthorised Biography of Peter Mandelson* (London: Simon and Schuster).

Scammell, M. (1999) 'Political Marketing Lessons for Political Science', *Political Studies* 47, 718–39.

Seldon, A. (ed.) (2001) *The Blair Effect* (London: Little, Brown).

Seyd, P. (1999) 'New Parties / New Politics?' A Case Study of the British Labour Party, *Party Politics* 383–405.

Shaw, E. (2001) 'New Labour: New Pathways to Parliament' *Parliamentary Affairs* 54, 35–53.

Taylor, B. and Thomsom, K. (eds) (1999) *Scotland and Wales: Nations Again?* (Cardiff: University of Wales Press) pp. 95–117.

Taylor, G. (1999) *The Impact of New Labour* (Basingstoke: Macmillan, now Palgrave).

Toynbee, P. and Walker, D. (2001) *Did Things Get Better?* (London: Penguin).

Waller, R. and Criddle, B. (1999) *The Almanac of British Politics* (6th edn) (London: Routledge).

Walters, S. (2001) *Tory Wars: The Conservatives in Crisis* (London: Politico's).

Webb, P. (2000) *The Modern British Party System* (London: Sage).

Webb, P. (2001) 'Parties and Party Systems: Modernisation, Regulation and Diversity' *Parliamentary Affairs* 54, 308–21.

White, C. et al. (1999) *Voter Volatility: Voting Behaviour and the 1997 General Election* (London: National Centre for Social Policy Research).

Whiteley, P. and Seyd, P. (1998) 'The Dynamics of Party Activism in Britain: A Spiral of Demobilisation?' *British Journal of Political Science* 28, 113–37.

Willetts, D. and Forsdyke, R. (1999) *After the Landslide* (London: Centre for Policy Studies).

Worcester, R. and Mortimore, R. (1999) *Explaining Labour's Landslide* (London: Politico's).

Worcester, R. and Mortimore, R. (2001) *Explaining Labour's Second Landslide* (London: Politico's).

Young, H. (1998) *This Blessed Plot* (London: Macmillan).

Index

Cardiff, 72, 211, 236, 249
Cardiff South, 192
Cardiff University, 126
Carmarthen East & Dinefwr, 324
Carr, S., 172
Carrington, M., 206
Carville, J., 33, 127
Castle Point, 330, 335
Channel 4 News, 134, 135
Cheadle, 197, 228, 231, 335, 337
Chisholm, M., 24
Chronology 1997–2000, 9–14; Jan.-
    May 2001, 79; May-June 2001,
    96
Church, Judith, 184
Churches Together, 218
Churchill, Sir W., 45, 184
churning, 122
Citizen, 191
Clark, D., 184
Clarke, E., 183
Clarke, K., 5, 38, 44, 48, 56, 85, 141,
    185, 194, 200, 246
Clarke, T., 191
class and voting, 4, 23, 240, 256–7,
    311
Clause IV, 43
Clifton-Brown, G., 200, 201, 207
Clinton, W., 22, 23, 26, 27, 33, 127
coal-miners, 202
Coe, Lord, 44, 45, 97, 131
Coffman, Hilary, 94
Coleman, S., 233
Collins, T., 55, 56, 61, 86, 151, 232,
    242
Commission for Racial Equality
    (CRE), 84
Common Sense Revolution, 41, 50, 52
computers, 218
Concerned Parents, 211
Congdon, D., 206
Connery, S., 118
Conservatives in 1997–2001, 5, 25,
    37, 65; guarantees, 50; in
    campaign, 91–110; private polls,
    128–30; broadcasts, 151; in con-
    stituencies, 211–24; and e-mail,
    224ff; assessed, 235–45
Consignia, 211

constitutional reform, 24
Conway, D., 205
Cook, G., 30, 33, 127
Cook, R., 8, 102, 146, 148, 200
Coombs, S., 205
Cooper, A., 40, 43, 44, 59, 121
Cooper, Yvette, 147
Corbett, R., 183
core vote strategy, 53–4, 61, 244
Costain, F., 70
council tenants, 257
Countryside Alliance, 18
country vote, 314
Courier & Advertiser, 117, 120
Cowley, P., 334
Cox, T., 198
Cranborne, Viscount, 17, 46
Crewe, I., 35, 36
Crime, 26, 33, 151
Cruddas, J., 195
Cryer, Ann, 200, 207
Cryer, J., 200
Cumbria, 80
Cunliffe, L., 183
Cunningham, J., 6, 200
Curtice, J., 120, 122, 251–5, 333, 334,
    337
Cyber Space Odyssey 2001, 233
cyber-squatters, 228

Dacre, N., 148
Dacre, P., 57
Dagenham 195, 335
Daily Express, 90, 91, 156, 157, 160,
    161, 164, 174
Daily Mail, 3, 24, 27, 57, 80, 99, 108,
    117, 147, 151, 156, 157, 160,
    161, 162, 163, 166, 172, 173,
    174, 180, 247
Daily Record, 117, 119
Daily Star, 157, 164, 165, 172
Daily Telegraph, 3, 27, 48, 57, 80, 97,
    107, 108, 120, 121, 122, 151,
    156, 165, 166, 168, 172, 173,
    174, 175, 242, 247
Daisley, P., 192
Dalton, R., 333
Dalyell, T., 200, 201, 207
Damazer, M., 148

Guardian, 100, 120, 121, 122, 123,
   129, 131, 155, 166–7, 161, 165,
   173, 174, 229, 236
Guildford, 197, 337
Gummer, J.S., 85, 185

hackers, 229
Hague, Ffion, 97
Hague, W., as leader 4–5, 17, 18; Lab
   and, 25–6; and Cons, 37–63; in
   campaign, 91–110; on air, 127,
   129; in press 150, 154, 164;
   candidates and, 215, 222;
   assessed, 222, 248–50
Halliwell, Geri, 149
Hamblin, M., 131
Hames, T., 63
Hamilton, D., 202
Hamilton, N., 7, 60
Hamlyn, Lord, 33
Hammond, Sir A., 75
Hans, G., 335
Hansard Society, 228
Hare, D., 166
Harman, Harriet, 3
Harmsworth family, 157
Harris poll, 121
Harris, E., 66
Harris, M. 50
Harrogate, 52, 54, 65
Hartlepool, 72, 103
Harwich, 255, 337
Hassan, G., 114
Hastings, 255
Hatfield, 19
Hattersley, R., 155
Havard, D., 192
Havering, 335
headlines (television news), 136–7
Heal, Sylvia, 200
health, 4, 23, 26, 51, 86, 92, 94, 112,
   113, 119, 172, 181
Heath, A., 23, 36, 44, 126, 131, 334,
   337
Heath, Sir E., 48, 49, 82, 104, 189,
   198, 239
Heathcoat Amory, D., 207
Heffer, S., 63

Hendrick, M., 197
Hendry, C., 206
Herald, 117, 120
Heseltine, M., 5, 44, 48, 56, 185, 246
Heyes, D., 192
Hinduja family, 7, 66, 75, 163
Hitchens, P., 157
Hogg, D., 200, 201, 207
Hole, Shana, 97
Hollick, Lord, 157
Holmes, M., 68
home-owners, 257
Horam, J., 104
hospitals, 74, 104
House of Lords, 17; 46
*How to Select and Reselect Your
   Candidate,* 187
Howard, M., 38, 41
Howarth, A., 183
Hoyle, Lindsay, 200
Huggett, R., 210
Hughes, S., 16, 67, 72, 102
Human Rights Act 1998, 18
Hume, J., 256
Humphrys, J., 101, 147
Hunter, Anji, 82, 94
hunting, 18–19, 66, 220
Hyman, P., 29, 35, 96, 128

ICM, 56, 59, 100, 104, 120, 121ff,
   128–30, 246, 256, 336
IG Index, 55
In Europe, Not Run By Europe, 47
incumbency, 254, 318–19
Independent, 120, 121–2, 122, 147,
   157, 173, 102, 167, 172, 175,
   247, 248
Independent on Sunday, 120
independents, 210, 301
industrial relations, 16
inflation, 2
Institute for Fiscal Studies, 4, 142, 240
Institute for Public Policy Research
   (IPPR), 28
Irvine, Lord, 33
Israel, 137
issues, surveys on, 33–4, 138, 221,
   236–7, 245, 250